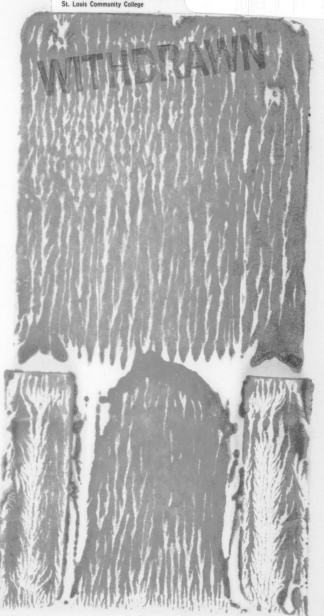

AN ECONOMIC
HISTORY OF ROME

AN ECONOMIC
HISTORY OF ROME

by

TENNEY FRANK

Second Edition Revised

New York
COOPER SQUARE PUBLISHERS, INC.
1962

PRINTED IN THE U.S.A.   BY NOBLE OFFSET PRINTERS, INC.,   NEW YORK 3, N. Y.

PREFACE

In the first edition of this book, issued seven years ago, an attempt was made to sketch Roman economic history through the republican period and to describe the methods of production and distribution in the industry of the Augustan era. The material for a second volume which was to carry the story through the Empire was then largely in hand, but before the text could be completed Professor Rostovtzeff's brilliant book, *The Social and Economic History of the Roman Empire*, appeared. That book supplies so well the long-felt want of a good reference list of source materials for the Empire that there no longer appears to be a need for my projected volume. However, since my history has been out of print for several years and a new edition has been requested, it has seemed advisable to issue a revision and at the same time to extend the sketch into the fourth century of the Empire.

This extension will not of course be taken as an attempt to invite students away from the indispensable volume with which Professor Rostovtzeff has so generously enriched our studies and for which there can be no substitute. Since, however, the materials are exceedingly difficult to interpret and there still exists a wide difference of opinion especially regarding the causes of the economic decline, I venture to hope that an independent treatment of the problem will not be without value. The new chapters are IX, X, XVIII-XXII.

T. F.

November 1, 1926.

CONTENTS

xi

CHAPTER I

AGRICULTURE IN EARLY LATIUM

ITALY's wealth in ancient times as in modern lay in her food-producing soil. Gold was never found in the peninsula, and but little silver. Iron and copper were mined only in a narrow strip of Etruria, too circumscribed to entice many Romans into industries. The commerce of the seas was developed and held by people less well endowed with productive land, races compelled to trade if they were to survive. Agriculture was therefore Italy's industry, in particular the cultivation of the Western littoral composed of the ejecta of the many volcanoes between central Etruria and Naples, and of the deep alluvial deposits of the Po valley. The hardy farmers of the Roman Campagna it was who organized the irresistible legions that united Italy and through the united strength of Italy the Mediterranean world, and it was the submersion of this stock of farmers that hastened the end of ancient civilization.

The ancestors of the Latin peoples who shaped the Roman republic can now be traced from beyond the Alps.[1] About two thousand years before our era scattered groups of them were coming over the central and

[1] Von Duhn, *Italische Gräberkunde;* Randall-MacIver, *The Villanovans.*

1

eastern Alps from the Danube into the Po valley, settling at first in lake dwellings, then throughout the
central part of the Po valley in villages well protected
by moats and artificial water channels.   They were
far more civilized than the neolithic savage tribes that
were then somewhat thinly scattered over Italy.   Cultivators of the soil, these Italici made use of domestic animals and good bronze farm implements, and they
probably partitioned as private property the land
which they took.   It is not likely that the savages who
were there before contested possession with any vigor.
Peoples who use land chiefly as hunting ground do not
risk enslavement or death in the defense of their lands.
These early invasions spread over a long period, but
they were uniform and thorough-going in their results.
The villages and cemeteries of the Italici usually show
a consistent culture and little evidence of having absorbed foreign elements.[2]   These tribes took most of
the fertile land of the Po valley during the second millennium (an age of bronze in Italy), and in the early
iron age (1600-800 B.C.) most of Tuscany and Latium
was similarly settled.   The progress of these people can
readily be traced by their compact cemeteries of ciner-
ary urns, for they practiced the custom of burning

[2] The highly inflected Italic dialects would probably have suffered as Latin did in 6th century France, Spain and Italy, if
there had been a similar race-mixture in prehistoric times.   North
America provides a good example of how hunting tribes give way
before landseeking farmers.   The South American Indians, who
were cultivators of the soil, remained to defend it and were consequently submerged.

their dead, not till then known in Italy. Other tribes closely related to these, who had however not adopted the custom of cremation, entered Italy somewhat later and settled in the less desirable Apennine region, all the way from Bologna to Lucania. These were later known as the Sabellic tribes. Their language and religion prove that they were probably cousins of the cremating group who had parted company from them not long before the first invasion. In the eighth century the Sabellic folk came down into the Tuscan and Latin plains and mingled freely with the cremating folk. At Rome, in fact, on the Alban hills, and even on the coast of Antium inhumation is found to be more customary than cremation for a brief period during the seventh and sixth centuries.[3] By the eighth century, when these invasions had reached their culmination, almost the whole of Italy had been settled by Indo-European farm folk.

Just what value such details may have in an economic history we cannot estimate until we can determine what racial inheritance meant in the days when the compact Indo-European tribes were slowly shaping well-defined and distinct languages and cultural types in central Europe. That the invaders came from the interior with the arts of agriculture well developed proved to be a long enduring factor in their economic

[3] Antonielli, *Bull. Palet. Ital.*, 1924, 154; Bryan, *Hut Urns;* L. A. Holland, *The Faliscans*. The Ligurians who held the northern Apennines and the Alps west of Turin seem to have been an earlier group of invading Indo-Europeans, see Conway, in *Cambridge Anc. Hist.* IV, p. 383 ff.

history; that all were related in language and in civil and religious custom must have made Rome's task of unifying Italy relatively easy; and it may prove a reliable conjecture that a noticeable capacity for self-government, a distrust of impulsive action, and a preference for social co-operation were traits which could be counted upon so long as these peoples predominated in the peninsula.

The Latin plain in its present conformation is very recent, so recent that the last masses of volcanic ash probably post-date the pyramids of Egypt. The process of formation continued from long before the glacial periods and all through them.[4] More than fifty craters, from which the ash and lava poured, can still be found within twenty-five miles of the imperial city. Long periods of tranquillity intervened when jungles grew up over the temporary surface, only to be buried under a new mass of ashes. The deep cuttings of the railways that run out of the eastern gates of Rome expose repeated layers of black and yellow soil lying between thick strata of tufa and ash; they mark the jungles of former intervals of rest. The present surface is not old. The mouth of the Tiber has apparently silted in as much alluvium since Ostia lay upon the seashore in Sulla's day as the river carried down between the last great eruption and Ostia's foundation. Though the Sabine hills immediately behind this plain show numerous sites of habitation several millennia old—some being the homes of savages of the palaeolithic age—

[4] A. Verri, *Origine e Trasformazione della Campagna, 1911.*

and though there are traces throughout the peninsula of the earliest peoples of the Terramara civilization, the oldest graves of the Forum, the Palatine, and of Grottaferrata cannot with certainty be placed earlier than the iron age, perhaps not more than a thousand years before Cicero.

The Latin plain is then of very recent date, and human cultivation of it of still more recent. It is well known that the volcanic ash that falls from Vesuvius is rich in phosphates and potash and that a moderate admixture of it in the soil acts as an excellent fertilizer. In fact, the Campanian farmer living in the shadow of Vesuvius is not averse to an occasional eruption if only the volcano behaves with moderation. The later ash-strata of the Alban volcanoes had an abundance of these same ingredients, though a large percentage of the original elements has leached out with time. However, the ash alone did not lend itself to cultivation at once, since grain needs an abundance of nitrogenous matter, and a solider soil than the ash at first provided. Before men could inhabit the Latin plain we must posit a period of wild growth and the invasion of jungle plants and forests which could create a sufficiently thick humus for agricultural purposes. Such forests did invade the plain. Not only do all the authors preserve the traditions of forests and sacred groves that are mentioned in the tales of early kings, but Theophrastus[5] still knew of Latium as a source of timber

[5] Theophrastus, *Hist. Plant.* V, 8; cf. Pais, *Storia Critica di Roma*, I, 627.

as late as the third century: "The land of the Latins is well watered, and the plains bear the laurel and myrtle and remarkable beech trees. Trunks are found that singly suffice for the keel beams of the great Tyrrhenian ships. Fir and pine grow upon the hills. The Circaean promontory is thickly overgrown with oaks, laurels, and myrtle." It is interesting to find that the beech then grew in the Latin plains, for now that the Campagna is parched and treeless it has withdrawn to the hills.

With this growth of timber from a subsoil which had many excellent qualities, a very rich soil was being formed for farming when once the Alban volcanoes should cease pouring out the flames that kept the hill-peoples back in fear. There can be little doubt that the region was far from being semi-arid then as it is now. To-day the grass parches brown in June, not to revive again till near October, and the wheat is hurried to a premature harvest in the middle of June. But Varro sets July down as the month of harvest in his day, and summer rains are frequently mentioned in the classical authors. It would be hazardous to assume a theory of "climatic pulses" by way of explanation of this difference, and it is doubtful whether a mere two thousand years in the long recession of the glacial area could cause a perceptible change in temperature. The explanation of the change is perhaps to be found in the almost complete deforestation of Latium and the mountains behind. There can be little doubt that when the Sabine ridge from Praeneste to Monte Gennaro and the whole Volscian range were a thick forest instead of the parched white rocks that now stand out, they retained the rain-water and afforded a lasting subsoil supply and an abundance of nightly dewfalls which do not now exist when the last rains of spring leap off the bare rocks and flow away at once in torrents.

When, therefore, the early settlers pushed down into the Campagna and burned out "clearings" for farming (indeed the Terramara folk had then practiced systematic agriculture in the Po valley for many centuries), they found a soil remarkably fertile, though not yet very deep, and a warmth and humidity that make the harvest rich. As was to be expected from such conditions, the population in time grew dense. There is nothing improbable in the tradition of the fifty villages that Pliny has preserved. The treasures now being gathered into the museum of the Villa Giulia from the ruins of sixth century Ardea, Satricum, Lanuvium, Gabii, Praeneste, Nemi, Velitrae, Norba, and Signia, speak of an era of prosperity that no one dared imagine a few decades ago. The ancient lords of these cities, which became malarial wastes before Cicero's day, decked themselves and their homes in the gold and precious stones of all the lands from the Baltic Sea to the Mesopotamian valley. Yet the wealth which made possible all this display did not spring from Latin industry or from commerce directed by Latins, if we may trust the archaeological evidence available. It was the produce of a rich soil cultivated with unusual intensity which paid for it, and kept alive a thick popu-

lation such as would probably compare with the
swarming tenantry of the Po valley of to-day.

There are numerous relics from that remarkable
agricultural period still to be found in Latium, traces
of drains, tunnels, and dams that are all too little
known. The modern Italian farmer who hardly finds
his land worth the merest labor of planting and har-
vesting fails to see how in a former day the owners
could have secured returns for such enormous expendi-
ture of labor. A convenient place to study the intricate draining system of that time is the district below
Velitrae. Here as De La Blanchère[6] discovered more
than forty years ago the ground is honeycombed with
an elaborate system of tunnels running down the slopes
of the hills toward the Pontine marshes, *cuniculi* as he
calls them, about 3 by 1½ feet, cut in the tufa a few
feet below the surface and usually along the sides of
the numerous ravines. De La Blanchère was unfortunately misled by the then prevailing "miasmatic" theory
of malaria into believing that these tunnels were cut to
drain the soil of pest waters. But they occur only on

[6] De La Blanchère, in *Mél. d'archeol. et d'hist.* 1882, also art.
Cuniculus, in *Daremberg-Saglio*. He has probably over empha-
sized the use of these canals in draining marshes and subsoil
moisture, and seems also to have included in his discussions some
tunnels that are apparently house drains, service tunnels and
horizontal cisterns. The *cuniculi* of the city are sometimes
erroneously brought into the discussion of drains. Many of these
were doubtless secret passage-ways dug to afford avenues of
escape or retreat during the proscriptions of the civil wars and
during slave uprisings. *Cuniculi* have been found as far north
as Bieda, see *Röm. Mitt.* 1915, 185.

the slopes where the land drains all too readily without aid; they do not touch the stagnant Pontine marshes below. However, he also suggested as a possible theory what seems indeed to be the true explanation. They were apparently cut at a time of such overpopulation that every foot of arable ground must be saved for cultivation. By diverting the rain waters from the eroding mountain gullies into underground channels the farmers not only checked a large part of the ordinary erosion of the hillside farms but also saved the space usually sacrificed to the torrent-bed. It would be difficult to find another place where labor has been so lavishly expended to preserve the arable soil from erosion. The ground must have been very valuable, and the population in great need to justify such heroic measures for the insurance of the annual harvest. Similar systems are found in the valleys north of Veii and were probably built under similar conditions. Indeed, the remarkable cutting seventy-five yards long at Ponte Sodo[7] near the citadel rock of Veii through which the Fosso di Formello has ever since flowed seems to have been undertaken to save a few acres of the circling

[7] Since Roman Veii stood near this Ponte Sodo (Solidum), it is probably this tunnel that later tradition assigned to the sappers and miners of Camillus' army. The stories of mining operations at the siege of Veii may account for the strange tales that connected the emissarium of Lake Albanus with the Veian siege (Livy, V, 15). The Romans do not mention the tunnel that drains Lake Nemi, though it is twice as long as the Alban one. It apparently was cut before the temple of Diana became very important. The Valle Aricciana and the crater lake on the via Praenestina were also drained at an early date.

river bed for cultivation. Similarly the emissarium of the Alban lake, 1,300 yards long and 7 to 10 feet high, was cut through solid rock to save a few hundred acres of arable soil on the sloping edge within the crater. Even with the tools of modern engineers, that task would not now be considered a paying investment. Finally let the student of intensive tillage take a morning walk from Marcellina up Monte Gennaro through the steep ravine of Scarpellata. It is usually dry, but after a heavy rain the water pours down in torrents, carrying off what little soil may tend to accumulate. To save alluvial patches in the course of this ravine the ancient farmers built elaborate dams of finely trimmed polygonal masonry that still withstand the torrents. The masonry is largely made of huge blocks weighing half a ton each and is in no wise inferior to the magnificent polygonal masonry of Segni's town walls. And yet one of these dams could hardly save more than an acre of arable soil.

It is impossible after surveying such elaborate undertakings to avoid the conclusion that Latium in the sixth century was cultivated with an intensity that has seldom been equalled anywhere. When, furthermore, we consider that the tools of that period were the spade and the mattock, we may be sure that each man's allotment was very small, doubtless no more than the two jugera that Varro assures us sufficed for the support of the ancient Latin family. It follows that Latium supported a very densely settled population. With these facts in view the historian can understand whence came

the armies that overran the limits of Latium and overwhelmed all obstruction when once they were set in
motion, why Veii fell, why the burning of Rome was
so quickly repaired, and why Campania called all the
way to Rome for aid when threatened by the Samnites.
It is very probable that when the soil began to show
signs of over-cropping under this severe strain and an
incapacity to feed the population which is proved by
the desperate methods mentioned above, the growing
generations found it necessary to seek more room, and
that the expansion of the Latin tribe dates from this
condition.

Of the social organization of these early Latins of
the sixth century we have of course no contemporaneous description; the inconsistent conjectures of Roman
writers who lived many centuries later, based as they
generally were upon institutions that had come into
being through the intervening revolutions, provide but
uncertain material for history. The safest course is
to rely as far as possible upon archaeology, upon the
fragments of the twelve tables that were written down
in the middle of the fifth century, and upon whatever
inferences can be drawn from the earliest political institutions and social practices that are vouched for by
trustworthy writers.

Some deductions for instance may be made from the
presence of the extensive agricultural undertakings already mentioned. These could not have been organized
and carried through by small land holders, for the tunnels ran beneath hundreds of individual plots; nor

could the primitive democratic communities which we sometimes posit for Latium have provided the initiative and sustained efforts that they imply. It is highly probable that these drainage tunnels and dams were undertaken by landlords who owned extensive tracts and who could command and direct the labor of numerous tenants. In brief they suggest that a villa system not unlike the manorial system of England of the twelfth century pervaded Latium at the time. And this inference accords with the evidence available from other sources.

Such a system would explain the Roman institution of clientship as a survival of the personal relationship which in time established itself between the lord and his tenant or serf. The client of those early days had some duties that remind us strikingly of services imposed upon the medieval villein. He was, for instance, bound to make contributions for the dowry of his lord's daughter[8] and toward the ransom of his lord if the latter was captured in war, and also to go to battle with his lord. It would also explain the miserable political and social condition of the plebeians at the beginning of historical times. To be sure the earliest republican laws and the twelve tables represent the plebeian as a citizen capable of owning property. But he had little else and occupied the civil position of one who had but recently emerged from a lower status. He had, for instance, no right to hold a magistracy in the state, he had lost the privilege of consulting the gods officially,

[8] Dion. Halic. *Antiq.* II, 10, 1.

a plebeian could not marry anyone of patrician blood for fear that children of such a union might inherit patrician rights, and since the patrician group in the Senate had the power of veto, his vote had less than full value.

The villa furthermore was recognized in the earliest law, which indeed calls it the *hortus,* or the enclosure, while a manorial system with very small freeholds for the peasants seems to be recognized when the garden plot of two jugera (one and one-half acres) is called an inheritance, *heredium.*[9] Perhaps also we may find a survival of the open field system in the "strips,"[10] in which the land was assigned in Rome's two earliest citizen colonies, Ostia and Antium.

Whether the peasant of the Latin village of the sixth century had actually fallen into real bondage[11] as had the helots of Sparta, Thessaly, and Crete we cannot now determine, but it seems clear at least that his condition was in no way superior to that of the villein of

[9] *Leges XII Tabularum,* VII, 3 (Bruns, *Fontes*); Varro, 1, 10, 2. This is supported by the fact that the surveyors in plotting out the land for colonies conserved a two-acre measure in the "centuriation," and that early colonies granted freeholds of very small plots. At Tarracina (327 B.C.) only two jugera were given; later colonists were given somewhat larger allotments (2½, 3, 4 jugera) and finally in the Gracchan days thirty jugera.

[10] *Lacineis adsignatus, Liber colon.* (Ed. Rud.) 229, 18, for Antium; 236, 7, for Ostia.

[11] This is the view of Neumann, *Bauernbefreiung;* cf. E. Meyer, art. *Plebs, Conrads Handwörterbuch;* Botsford, *Roman Assemblies,* pp. 16-65.

the better class of manors before the time of the Black Death. The numerous villages of such peasants clustering about the lord's villas and the community temple must in many respects have resembled in form and in social organization the medieval manorial villas. An idea of the social contrast between the classes may be gathered by comparing the elaborate jewelry of the princely tombs at Satricum with the meager furniture of the peasant dugout found near by.[12]

It would be useless to raise once more the old questions regarding a possible anterior "community ownership" and the beginnings of property rights at Rome; nor is there any reason to expect conclusive evidence on these points. The supposed traces of communism[13] at Rome are few. The community pastures and wastes near the Latin cities may or may not be survivals of more extended communism: a study of medieval institutions has revealed that township-meadows have frequently been acquired in a late day. Mommsen indeed found it significant that according to the oldest code a man's property reverted to his fellow clansmen if he died intestate and without heirs,[14] but this again may be a relatively late invention of the lawmakers. However that may be, the laws of private property had developed long and far before the fifth century when the

[12] See *Monumenti Antichi*, XV, p. 83, and Della Seta, *Museo di Villa Giulia*, I., p. 235.

[13] Mommsen, *Röm. Staatsr.* III, p. 23; Pöhlmann, *Gesch. des antik. Kommunismus*, II, 443; Vinogradoff, *Growth of the Manor.*

[14] *Leges XII Tab.* V, 3.

twelve tables[15] were drawn up.   Since the Terremare[16] settlements of the Po valley reveal that the ancestors of the Romans were orderly agriculturists more than a millennium before these laws were written, it is highly probable that the Latin people respected property rights before they settled the plains about Rome.

[15] *Ibid.* V, 3, *Uti legassit super pecunia tutelave suae rei, ita jus esto.*

[16] Peet, *The Stone and Bronze Ages in Italy.*

CHAPTER II

The Early Trade of Latium and Etruria

More than a millennium before Rome's foundation, as the Egyptian records show,[1] men traded and thieved on the high-seas of the Mediterranean. Later the Amarna tablets reveal Lycian pirates preying upon Egyptian and Cypriote merchants; and Phoenician traders resorted to Spain for British tin before the days of Hiram. It was probably in the eighth century that the Tyrsenian immigrants — who mingling with the Umbrians of Italy fathered the great Etruscan race[2]— came overseas from the Asia Minor coast. North of the Tiber the adventurers seized several towns from Caere to Vulci. The old cemetery at Tarquinii with its almost complete change from Villanovan urn-burial[3] to a new type of trench grave is a striking proof of how sudden was the invasion in southern Etruria. In the eighth and seventh centuries the new people,

[1] Köster, *Schiffart in 3 und 2 Jahrtausend v. Chr.* 1924; Cary, *The Greeks and Ancient Trade,* Jour. Hell. St. 1924; L. E. W. Adams, *A Study in the Commerce of Latium..*

[2] Körte, *art. Etrusker*, Pauly-Wissowa. Schulze, *Lat. Eigennamen* has called attention to the great number of Etruscan names that consist of Italic roots and Etruscan suffixes. The explanation lies of course in a thoroughgoing race-mixture.

[3] Von Duhn, *Italische Gräberkunde,* 310; Randall-MacIver, *The Villanovans.*

now generously mingled with Italian subjects, as their personal names and the religious cults show, spread quickly, first over the iron and copper-bearing region of northern Tuscany, then beyond to the Po valley and also south through the Trerus valley into Campania. Latium indeed escaped for a long time—too thickly settled, it would seem, for easy conquest—but Praeneste, the Latin fort-town on the Sabine slope, was seized to guard the land route between Etruria and the Campanian outposts of the south.

Not long after the arrival of these first Orientals, began the westward flow of Greek[4] colonists. From Epirus and the western Peloponnese came numberless shiploads of landseekers who established the prosperous cities of South Italy. Sparta followed with a colony at Tarentum. About the middle of the eighth century Chalcis of Euboea settled far off Cumae on the bay of Naples, a city that soon became the schoolmistress of central Italy, and then both sides of the Sicilian straits, founding cities at Naxos, Zancle, and Rhegium. Chalcis, herself situated on a narrow strait, had naturally acquired an instinctive appreciation of the commercial value of such a position. Further north the Greeks discovered that the Latin and Etruscan tribes were already in complete possession, as the Etruscans in their turn encountered the Greeks blocking their progress coastwards when they presently ar-

[4] Beloch, *Griechische Gesch*[2]. I, 1, 237 ff.; A. Reinach, *L'hellénisation du monde antique.*

rived in Campania. Then Corinth, already a trading and manufacturing town that had planted trading posts on the Adriatic islands, sent, about 735 B. C., a flourishing colony to Syracuse.

Although the Ionian Greeks of Asia Minor, and especially the progressive city of Miletus, had reaped large profits in Thracian and Pontic trade, the Rhodians turned to the southern coast of Sicily—Gela and Acragas—a century later, and about 600 B. C. the Phocaeans founded Marseilles near the Rhone to which their hardy ships had long resorted. Even though the Latins did not for a long time come into direct contact with these various Greek colonies, their civilization soon felt the influences of the Aegean arts and crafts which these colonists brought westward from their former homes.

The Etruscan neighbors of Latium failed at first to keep in touch with the Asiatic coast from which they had come. Perhaps the whole nation had migrated, leaving no kinsfolk behind with whom to communicate. To be sure, Mesopotamian ideas are plentiful in the religious cults and astrological lore of the Etruscans, but material proofs of an Eastern commerce, except in such meager trifles as the Phoenicians had brought to the West even before the Etruscan migration, are rare for the earliest period. It was not long, however, before some of the Etruscan princes grew wealthy on the serf-tilled plantations of a soil still very productive, and then the Eastern sea-farers sought them out. The

Phoenician[5] merchants in particular who were losing to the Ionian Greeks the profitable Aegean markets held since Homeric days now sought compensation in the west, in Spain, Tuscany, and Libya. The tombs of Caere and Praeneste—only twenty miles from Rome—that have disclosed the richest products of this Phoenician trade are now generally dated somewhat after 700 B. C. For the story of early commerce the most significant objects discovered in them are the silver and gilded bowls wrought apparently by Phoenician craftsmen with designs drawn from Hittite, Egyptian, and Mesopotamian patterns; the carved ivory plates such as Tyrian artisans are said to have made for the intarsia work of Solomon's temple; the painted ostrich eggs that appear wherever Phoenician traders resorted, and the ubiquitous Egyptian glass beads and scarab-amulets, with plentiful Phoenician imitations of both.

That moreover Greek traders also came up the coast before the end of the eighth century is shown by the presence of proto-Corinthian vases in these same tombs.[6] The first example of this Greek ware may have come by way of Cumae from Chalcis, but before long the importations were augmented by Corinthian

[5] Poulsen, *Der Orient und die Frühgriechische Kunst*, 116 ff.; Kahrstedt, *Phoenikischer Handel*, Klio, 1912, 461 ff.; Curtis *Memoirs of the American Academy in Rome*, vols. III and V.

[6] Lorimer, *The Fabrics called Proto-Corinthian*, Jour. Hell. Stud. 1912, 326 ff.; Perrot and Chipiez, IX, 574 ff.; Gabrici, *Cuma*, Monumenti Antichi, XXII, 343 ff.; Von Duhn, *Ital. Gräberkunde*, index; Prinz, *Klio*, Beiheft VII.

sea-farers who carried the wares of their own city to their colony of Syracuse, whence they quickly found their way northward. Corinth indeed, borrowing ideas and apparently also artisans from Tyre, and taking advantage of the disfavor into which Phoenician traders were falling in Greek lands, now undertook to capture the Greek market in Tyrian fabrics, perfumes and ointments, and made as containers for the latter those delicate earthenware bottles that have become the archaeologists' criteria of seventh century chronology. Corinth's position on the gulf gave her a great advantage in the new western trade, and excavations on the sites of Syracuse, Cumae and the Etruscan cities of Caere and Tarquinii prove that she knew how to profit by it.

During all this time Rome remained a group of farm villages. The Latin soil was indeed rich and breeding a dense population, a tribe so strong that the Etruscans could not make their way across the Tiber southward except by a road that hugged the rocky slopes of the Sabine mountains. The busy farmers of the plain seem all the while to have cut themselves off from contact with the Phoenician traders who so constantly bartered with the neighboring cities of Etruria. The very name "Poeni" the Romans got from Syracusan traders who succeeded the Phoenicians, and the Latin words for things of commerce and parts of ships they learned from sea-farers of Syracuse and Cumae. Even the earliest Cumaean trade, so well attested by the imported ware of Corneto, seems to have found no favor whatever in Latium.[7] On the site of Rome nothing has yet been discovered corresponding to the rich stores of gold, silver, amber and ivory, so abundant in neighboring sites above the river. A few fragments of early proto-Corinthian ware have indeed been unearthed, but this pottery was far from costly, and such trifles may well have been bought by the villagers of the seven hills from traders who used the directest road from Caere to Praeneste and Campania.

With the passing of the seventh century many important events changed the course of Italian commerce. Phoenician[8] trade diminished rapidly, partly because of Assyrian pressure in Syria, partly because of the growth of Greek trade stimulated and supported by the widely scattered colonies, partly, it may be, because Syracuse, now engaged in commerce, could use her commanding position below the Sicilian straits to hinder her rivals—and the enmity between the Syracusans and the Phoenicians had deep roots. At any rate the Latin language shows clearly the influence of contact with the Syracusans between the periods of Phoenician

[7] Gabrici, op. cit., points out that Cumaean ware went to the Etruscan cities north of the Tiber in great quantities for a long time without entering Latium. It would, therefore, seem that Latian culture did not keep pace with Etruria in the seventh century. Satricum, however, seems to have been touched by the Greek traders, probably because Satricum was the port of entry for goods consigned to Praeneste, already in Etruscan hands. Absence of black-figured ware in Latium is perhaps due to the simplicity of funeral furniture and the rite of cremation.

[8] Beloch, *Griech. Gesch*[2]. I, ii, 249.

and Etruscan ascendency, that is, apparently, near the close of the seventh century; and the excavations of Cumae have revealed the existence of close communications between that city and Syracuse at this same period.

It was also about the end of the seventh century that the Etruscan armies succeeded at last in overwhelming Latium and thus decisively connecting Campania with Etruria. Here and there princes took possession of the villages and, it would seem, assumed ownership of the land. At Rome the separate villages of the Palatine, Esquiline, and Quirinal hills were organized into one city about which a strong stone wall was built.[9] The city came in time to be the seat of an Etruscan sovereign who ruled over all the lords of Latium. Palaces were built for the kings, and temples to the vague spirits that were now identified with gods which the Etruscans had shaped out of Italic, Greek, and Oriental syncretisms. Labor was imported to adorn the rapidly growing city, and a harbor[10] was built at the mouth of the Tiber in order to invite Etruscan and Greek seafarers.

Still it is doubtful whether even then Rome actually became an important center for maritime trade. The sea-going craft of that day[11] relied largely upon sails and were too poorly manned to pull cargoes against a

[9] *Notes on the Servian Wall.* Am. Jour. Arch. 1918, 175 ff., and *Roman Buildings of the Republic*, p. 112.

[10] *Rome's First Coinage*, Class. Phil. 1919, 314.

[11] Huvelin, *Mercatura*, Daremberg-Saglio.

stiff river current such as the Tiber carried; the skippers moreover needed to beach their ships and carry their wares to the market place, and bargain in person. Far more desirable for that kind of trade was a convenient sand-bar such as lay below Caere and Tarquinii or a small and peaceful river-mouth such as Satricum[12] possessed in the Astura river or Ardea in the Incastro and the Numicus. Rome's early growth probably owed less to her position with reference to sea-trade than to her command of the Tiber barrier at the point where Etruscan land-roads from Tarquinii, Caere and Veii most conveniently crossed for Tibur, Praeneste, the Campanian road of the Trerus valley, and for the Latin cities of Tusculum, Lanuvium, Velitrae, Norba, Ardea, Satricum and Tarracina.

Nevertheless Rome and the whole of Latium were kept in close touch with Mediterranean commerce throughout the century of Etruscan occupation. Although the Latins succeeded in preserving their language and the essentials of their democratic ideals against the day of liberation, this period was one of profound cultural significance. Everywhere farm villages were transformed into cities where Punic and Sicilian and Massiliot traders hawked their wares in the market-places and where Phocaean and Corinthian artists and craftsmen found employment in the adornment of temples, palaces, and tombs.[13]

[12] Strabo, V, 2, somewhat to our surprise calls the mouth of the Astura a useful roadstead even in his day.

[13] Della Seta, *Museo di Villa Giulia*, 1918. Mrs. Arthur Strong, *Jour. Rom. Stud.* 1914, 160 ff. The immigration of Ionians was

It was also about 600 B. C. that the Phocaeans of Asia Minor, outclassed in the Pontic trade by Milesians, settled Marseilles in order to profit from trade with the western Celts and Iberians. This was an event of prime importance for Italy since it assured in the passing Phocaean commerce a steady communication with the progressive and art-loving Ionians of Asia. It was doubtless the tales that these skippers brought home regarding opportunities in the luxurious cities of the West that induced artists and craftsmen in large numbers to try their fortunes in Italy. But this colony brought new resources to Italy. Entering into competition with the Phoenician sea-traders the Massiliots opened up a new route through Gaul for the acquisition of British tin which the bronze industry of the Italian cities must have. They also brought down iron from German and Spanish mines, and raw products, like wool and hides, for the industrial cities. Finally, the increased use of amber ornaments in Etruscan cities at this time is a proof of how extensively the new colony quickened the trade of the West as far off as the Baltic sea.

There is also noticeable toward the beginning of the sixth century a striking increase at Etruscan sites in the amount of Corinthian ware and of native ware made on Corinthian models.[14] It has been plausibly suggested that the reason for this lay in the political

doubtless strongest in the middle of the sixth century when the Persians subdued the Ionian cities; Herod. I, 164.

[14] Perrot, IX, 628.

upheavals at Corinth which (about 583) drove many prominent men with their clients into exile. Some of these exiles seem to have found a refuge in Tuscany, where they engaged in their former pursuits or taught others the arts they knew. The Roman legend of Demaratus, the Corinthian whose son by an Etruscan mother became the powerful King Tarquin of Rome, is by no means improbable. The Emperor Claudius who later referred to the story vouched for its existence in very old Etruscan records.[15]

Finally, the student of early Italian commerce will find in Naucratis[16] near the Nile-mouth an interesting indicator of the trade passing between the East and the West. This "ancient Shanghai," as it has aptly been called, was an industrial and trading post which the usually exclusive Egyptian permitted the Ionian trading cities to found in their land. Here there grew up vigorous factories that sent out not only wares made in the latest Ionian fashions but also articles of Egyptian cults and personal adornment. The products of this peculiar art, found in abundance in Italy, are therefore proof of communication with such cities as Rhodes, Miletus, Clazomenae, and Phocaea which shared in the industries of Naukratis, especially since they are found in conjunction with artistic objects that closely resemble the works of art discovered near these very cities of Asia.

[15] Körte, *Jahrb. Arch. Inst.* 1897, 57.

[16] Prinz, *Funde aus Naukratis*, Klio, Beiheft VII; Herodotus, II, 178.

There is then abundant evidence of the extensive foreign influence which reached western Italy. To determine however who in each case carried the trade and what part the Etruscans and Latins took in the industry and commerce of the period is more difficult.

During the sixth century when Latium was in their power, the Etruscans were at the height of their successes, controlling western Italy from the Alps to Campania and commanding the trade of the Tyrrhenian sea if they so chose. Their wealth doubtless depended largely upon the exploitation of the natives who as serfs were made to till the soil for them. Large and rich cities like Caere, Tarquinii, and Vulci did not lie in the metalliferous zone nor did they hold peculiarly advantageous positions for commerce though they doubtless profited by bringing goods of the interior to sea-farers. As a race, however, the Etruscans seem everywhere to have taken a keen interest in industry. Their peculiarly Oriental fondness for color, ornament, and luxurious dress and their deep religious sense that demanded the precise use of articles of cults and of the tomb gave rise to extensive native industries. Thus even towns like Praeneste[17] which had no raw materials became industrial centers from which we have recovered finely wrought jewelry in gold and precious stones, an abundance of engraved bronze mirrors and many elaborate articles of household use. In all this work, despite an apparent lack of originality of design, the technique was so skillfully developed that it

[17] Matthies, *Praenest. Spiegel*, 34.

often becomes impossible to say whether a given piece of work was of native or imported craftsmanship. And so, many of the products of the period are classed by archaeologists, according to design, as Phoenician-Etruscan, Ionic-Etruscan or Corinthian-Etruscan. At this time, too, vast quantities of vases were made in the Ionian and Corinthian styles and presently in the famous Attic black-figure which betray, if at all, their western origin only in an Etruscan legend or in some slight aberration in the interpretation of the myths which they undertook to represent. In the architecture of their temples the Etruscans generally adopted Ionic and Sicilian designs. It would seem in fact that Greek architects were usually imported to build them. Since, moreover, Etruria lacked good building stone they adopted from Ionia and Sicily a free use of timber. The beam ends, architraves, and pediments of wood, were accordingly adorned with terracotta relief-slabs. The moulds for the requisite processions of charioteers, hunters, maenads and satyrs and all the rest may at first have been imported from Ionia, or Ionian artists themselves may have been called in to design them, but native craftsmen continued to design others with such meticulous precision that it is difficult to say where native work begins. The ruins of Veii and Falerii, Satricum and Velitrae, and even of Rome have supplied cult-statues and temple figures in terracotta that can hardly be matched in beauty by the contemporary work in Greece or Asia Minor.[18]

[18] Della Seta, *Cat. Villa Giulia Museum;* E. D. Van Buren,

On the sea also the Etruscans apparently played a part during the sixth century. The Greeks—who doubtless lost some of their profits because of this new competition—were wont to call the Etruscan seafarers pirates. To what extent the name was deserved cannot be established. The methods of a business rival, especially if he be of a different race and successful, are usually impugned, whatever they may be. The objects of art found in sixth-century Etruscan tombs would indicate in any case that Ionian, Attic, Corinthian, Chalcidian, Syracusan, Cumaean and Carthaginian ware all reached Etruria with little hindrance. Nor is it probable that Etruscan traders carried the Aegean ware all the way, since Greek writers show little explicit knowledge of the Etruscans. Accordingly it would seem that the Etruscan piracy or competition did not extend to the point of closing the Tyrrhenian sea to foreign merchants.

The Etruscan policy on the sea was doubtless influenced by Carthaginian precedents. Early in the sixth century Carthage had been much strengthened by the accretion of powerful Phoenician families that the Assyrian invaders had driven from Tyre.[19] Carthage henceforth began to close the African and Spanish waters to Greek traders[20] and accordingly made a

---

Terra-Cotta Revetments in Latium; Giglioli, *Notizie. Scavi,* 1919; Frank, *Castor Temple,Mem. Am. Acad. V.*

[19] Myers, *Handbook of the Cesnola Collection,* p. xxxiv.

[20] The Rhodians attempted to plant colonies in western Sicily about 580 but were prevented by the Carthaginians. See also the

treaty of close co-operation with the Etruscans. About 537 the two combined to destroy the Phocaean colony in Corsica and later made an attempt to take Cumae, a raid that failed only because of the interference of Syracuse. We may suppose, therefore, that a line was being drawn between the Greeks on the one hand and Carthage and the Etruscans on the other, and that both sides made difficulties for their opponents whenever possible. Greek skippers probably abstained from going singly into the Tyrrhenian sea as Etruscans and Carthaginians seem not to have ventured frequently into Greek waters. Perhaps that is why Greek trade increased at Adriatic ports whence the wares of Greece spread through Italy,[21] why in the same century a land-route up from Apulia to Cumae[22] was well travelled, and again why Cumaean products tended to take the land-route from Capua to Falerii. There is even some evidence that sharp rivalry existed between the various Greek trading cities themselves, for Croton's destruction of Sybaris[23] in 510 seems in part to have been due to the fact that Sybaris commanded the valuable portage over the lower ridge of Italy whereby she had escaped from whatever restrictions the Syracusans, Zancleans, or Etruscans imposed

Romano-Punic treaty of 509 B.C., Pol. III, 22, and Arist. *Pol.* III, 5, 10.

[21] Dall' Osso, *Guida illustrata del Museo di Ancona.*

[22] Gabrici, *Cuma,* 420.

[23] Herodotus, VI, 21.

below or above the Sicilian straits. It is at least significant that the great trading city of Miletus, which had
long been on unfriendly terms with Chalcis and therefore with the colonies of the straits, showed particular
distress at the fall of Sybaris. Apparently the Milesians had needed the portage road for their wares
destined for the northwest.

However, we have no right to assume that absolute
trade restrictions had as yet been anywhere imposed
except by Carthage. Lack of friendly relations might
result in raids upon unwelcome traders venturing
abroad unescorted, but the fact remains that the importations of the sixth century into Etruscan territory
were so varied and extensive that a relatively free
trade must have existed.[24] Obviously the whole of
Etruria could not be made to accept any theory of
mare clausum for the benefit of a few coast towns that
participated in the carrying-trade when such a policy
would greatly reduce the commerce of cities not on the
coast. Furthermore any attempt to close the seas on a
long and open coast like Italy's when the towns of the
interior held the advantage of numerous land-routes
would be quite futile.

Judging from the objects of foreign trade found in
Etruria on sixth century sites we may tentatively picture the commercial situation as follows. Carthaginian

[24] Caere had the reputation later of having pursued a liberal
trade policy. After Rome became independent Caere was of
course compelled to keep an open port if she wished to retain
her trade.

shippers probably had free access to Etruscan ports in accordance with treaties resembling the first Punic-Roman treaty quoted by Polybius III, 22. This trade, however, connected Italy only with Africa, Spain, Britain (chiefly through Spain) and to some slight extent with Syria and Egypt. The Etruscans themselves carried on a vigorous coast-wise trade, resorting, it would seem, to Marseilles, to Cumae, and to the Sicilian straits. Since they seem not to have passed frequently into Greek waters[25] they must have procured their cargoes of Greek wares at the western end of portage routes, for instance, at Laos, Temesa and Medma, and to some extent from Sicilian ports and Cumae. The Greek traders, in turn, from Corinth and Ionia could therefore unload cargoes at south-Italian and Sicilian ports for further transshipment, though there can be little doubt that Phocaeans on the way to Marseilles stopped at Etruscan ports and that Syracuse carried an important part of the coastal trade throughout the century. Her powers on the sea and her position near the straits were such that she could not read-

[25] The lack of Athenian coins in Etruscan hoards and of intimate references to the Etruscans in Athenian records seem to prove that Etruscan shippers did not often reach the Piraeus during the sixth century. The exchange of such wares doubtless took place near the Sicilian straits. Cf. De Sanctis, *Storia dei Rom.* I, 442; Pais, *Storia Critica*, I, 357; Helbig, Rendiconti Lincei, 1889; Gött. Gel. Anz. 1912. Hackl, *Merkantile Inschriften*, p. 94, has pointed out that on the early Athenian vases the trademarks are generally in the Ionic lettering. From this he infers that the ware was ordered and distributed by Ionic merchants.

ily be thwarted. It was doubtless Syracuse[26] that spread the rapidly increasing products of Athens northward during the century before Athens became a carrying nation.

Latium was, of course, though not an aggressive participant, a sharer in all this activity during the sixth century. Rome had grown so populous that sea-farers must have resorted to her market-place whenever possible, and the land-routes from Etruria, Campania, Latium and the Sabine interior crossed at Rome's bridge. Furthermore ships put in below Ardea, some twenty miles south of Rome, to trade with the Rutuli and the towns of the Alban hills, and especially at the mouth of the Astura river to trade at Satricum, the terminal of the important roads that led inland between Velitrae and Norba to Praeneste on the North-South road and to the Italic tribes in the Hernican, Volscian, and Aequian hills.

Since bartering required a fair balance of trade Latium must have paid for the foreign wares with products in her possession, but we have some difficulty in ascertaining what these could have been.[27] Rome may have had some share in the metal industry which is so well attested for Praeneste. Plutarch, who may have had access to reliable information on the point, mentions gilds of gold- and copper-smiths as existing

[26] Syracuse was one of the earliest cities in the West to adopt the Attic standard in her coinage, Gardner, *History of Ancient Coinage*, 214.

[27] On early Roman industry see Pinza, *Bull. Com.* 1912, 50.

in the regal period, and the Vicus Tuscus of Rome may have derived its name from a colony of Etruscan artisans. Indeed the famous Capitoline wolf,[28] treasured by modern Rome as one of its most precious relics, seems to be a sixth century masterpiece of Ionian-Etruscan art which, if made at Rome, would be a product of that industry. There could have been little exportation of grain, Latium's chief product, in the light ships of that day, but the Latins could supply the mountain tribes of the interior with grain in exchange for wool and hides which might then be conveniently exported. Furthermore their grain may also have been used in procuring copper from the industrial cities beyond the Tiber which in turn could serve as payment for imports. At any rate Latium must have exported copper since the Latin word *nummus* came to be current in Sicily for money. Similarly the Sicilian word for pork, which seems to come from Latin *arvina*, indicates that the early Latins raised swine enough for purposes of exchange.

From the very end of the period, immediately after the expulsion of the Etruscan tyrants and the establishment of the Republic, we have a commercial treaty between Carthage and Rome—fortunately preserved by Polybius—which throws more light on the commercial methods of that day than do the confused heaps of

[28] Petersen, *Klio*, 1909, 34; Carcopino, *La Louve du Capitole*, 1925.

broken ware. This document, one of the most valuable records of ancient history reads as follows:[29]

"There shall be friendship between the Romans and their allies, and the Carthaginians and their allies, on these conditions:

(a) "Neither the Romans nor their allies are to sail beyond (west of)[30] the Fair Promontory, unless driven by stress of weather or the fear of enemies. If any one of them be driven ashore there he shall not buy or take

[29] Polybius, III, 22. Polybius places this treaty "in the first consulship of the republic, the year in which the Capitoline temple was dedicated, twenty-eight years before Xerxes' invasion of Greece," that is, in 509-8 B.C. Despite this explicit dating of a treaty then still available in the Capitoline temple, Mommsen, Täubler (*Imperium Romanum*, p. 269) and many others have dated it in 348 B.C. However, a careful study of Rome's territorial growth leads to the conclusion that the political provisions of this treaty accord with the date given by Polybius and no other. Carthage assumes in the third clause that Rome was sovereign over all the coast towns as far as Tarracina. Immediately after the revolution, Rome supposed that she would inherit and exercise the sovereignty over Latium as the Etruscan king had done. A few years after the revolution when hard pressed by the Etruscans she had to win the good will and support of the Latins by surrendering this claim and acknowledging the autonomy of the sister cities of Latium in a league. Never again till after 341 could the Latin cities be called "subjects" of Rome, and no one would claim that this treaty is later than 341. We must, therefore, admit that Polybius is approximately correct in his date.

[30] In commenting upon this treaty in III, 23, Polybius apparently thought *epekeina* meant South, that is the region generally called Libya in his day. However, the next treaty quoted by Polybius (III, 24) which is more explicit proves that the north coast of Africa west of the promontory is meant.

anything for himself save what is needful for the repair of his ship and the service of the gods, and he shall depart within five days.

(*b*) "Men landing for traffic in Libya or Sardinia shall strike no bargain save in the presence of a herald or town-clerk. Whatever is sold in the presence of these, let the price be secured to the seller on the credit of the state.

(*c*) "If any Roman comes to the Carthaginian province in Sicily he shall enjoy all rights enjoyed by others.

(*a'*) "The Carthaginians shall do no injury to the people of Ardea, Antium, Laurentum, Circeii, Tarracina, nor any other people of the Latins that are subject to Rome.

(*b'*) "From those townships of Latium which are not subject to Rome they shall hold their hands; and if they take one shall deliver it unharmed to the Romans.

(*c'*) "They shall build no fort in Latium; and if they enter the district in arms, they shall not stay a night therein."

This, our earliest existing commercial treaty of the West, is so precise and carefully constructed that it permits us to posit a long development of international diplomacy in the Tyrrhenian sea before the close of the sixth century. It is apparent that the day had long passed when, as in Homer's day, men generally assumed that all sea-farers were on occasion sea-rovers.

It also reveals Carthage as a far more important commercial and political state than Rome,[31] for Carth-

[31] Frank, *Mercantilism and Rome's foreign policy*, Am. Hist.

age obviously composed and imposed this treaty. The numerous restrictions mentioned first are all in favor of Carthage. Indeed it is difficult to see how any state that had the least interest in commerce and the power to protect it would acquiesce in such terms. Nor must it be inferred that the clause excluding Roman ships from Numidia implies an extensive Roman commerce. These prohibitions which accord with customary Punic policy were probably inserted in view of a possible future development of Roman trade, or in memory of what Etruscan Rome had done before the revolution. The treaty does not prove anything for the trade of Rome after the expulsion of the kings, an event that must have involved a marked emigration of the commercial and industrial classes. Certain it is that the liberated Latin people, true to old instincts, presently turned landward and that in the fifth century Latium was less frequently visited by foreign traders. In fact we shall find that Carthage did not consider it worth while to offer a new commercial treaty until the democracy of the fourth century showed some interest in foreign trade by colonizing Ostia, and even that treaty[32]

Rev. 1913, 234. Täubler, *Imperium Romanum* (1913), 264, has demonstrated that the clauses concerning the surrender of the site of a captured city and the submission of trade-disputes to public settlement follow Punic and not Roman ideas. Kahrstedt, *Klio*, loc. cit., has quite missed the political significance of this treaty.

[32] Polybius, III, 24. The date is 348 B.C. The political situation implied in it accords with the conditions in Latium just before the Latin war.

shows that Rome was incapable of asking for equitable terms.

The document also shows that Carthage had already advanced far in the enforcement of a practice of *mare clausum*. She reserved the Numidian and Moorish coast, and probably therefore the straits of Gibraltar, completely for her own traders. This was, of course, practicable since the desert protected her from competition from the rear. Sardinia and Libya are not yet wholly closed, as by the next treaty, since the Punic fleet was still too small to enforce such restrictions, but their market-places are supervised by state officials who protect the Punic interests. Only western Sicily, whose back gates could not be closed, was open to all comers. As for Rome, on the other hand, the treaty simply assumes the open door at her port. Obviously we are to conclude that this was the traditional policy of Italian cities and that it had been so in Etruscan Rome. Indeed the very fact that Carthage, the long-standing ally of Etruria, could make a commercial treaty with Rome immediately after the revolt from Etruria is good evidence that the Etruscan-Punic alliance did not and had not reserved the Tyrrhenian sea to the two signatories. We have seen above why, with the numerous land routes of Italy, an attempt to close this sea would have been futile.

The treaty then on the one hand reveals Carthage as a powerful commercial nation which is eager to monopolize trade routes and to gain as many new ports of entry as possible; on the other hand it implies that while Rome may in the past have taken some part in shipping she was now more concerned about the territorial integrity of Latium than about commerce and was willing to keep her ports open to all law-abiding sea-farers.[33]

[33] Since opinions have varied widely regarding the reliability of early Roman historians, it is only fair that every historian of Rome should inform the reader of his attitude on this basic question. In the present volume, Polybius, Diodorus, and even Livy have been freely used in the belief that they provide an account of the Republican period which may, with some caution, be trusted. The Romans, respectors of law and legal forms to an unusual degree, preserved copies of their treaties, laws, and senatorial decrees, and also the high priests' brief record of events. The pontifical annals purported, to be sure, to record only events of religious significance, but since only men of political dignity became priests, their annals were apt to contain many items of political import.

The common assumption that most records were destroyed by the Gauls in 390 B.C. is far from probable. Archaeologists believe that most of the temples escaped destruction and with them the records they contained. Apparently the Celts, as is often the case with primitive peoples, respected the holy places. At any rate, the treaties, which were kept on the Capitol, survived. (See Frank, *Roman Buildings*, pp. 78 and 83.)

The earlier historians of Rome, like Fabius Pictor, were statesmen trained to acquire an accurate knowledge of laws and treaties. It is incorrect to ascribe to such men the loose historical methods that were followed by the rhetorical romancers who wrote for entertainment in Sulla's day. The care and knowledge they employed in affairs of state they doubtless used in their composition of history.

In using later historians who have filled in the Fabian skeleton with legendary material, we may in general assume that the main structure of the chronology is reliable—allowing of course for a discrepancy of three or four years for the early period—that the consular lists are equally safe, and that in large part the laws, treaties, senatus consulta, colonial dates, and dates of important wars are acceptable. It must, however, be remembered that bills proposed but not passed and senatorial debates were not recorded, and that the pontifical records had no space for such things as military movements. Hence when such things occur in the accounts of the period before 300 B.C. they must be considered as mere oral tradition which it is safest to reject wholly. After such purgation the account afforded by our literary sources seems to be in reasonable accord with the latest conclusions of archaeology. (See Frank, in *Am. Hist. Rev.*, vol. 32.)

CHAPTER III

The Rise of the Peasantry

The sixth century ended with a revolution[1] that drove the Etruscan tyrants out of Rome. That this was not entirely a nationalistic movement we may infer from the fact that many of the nobles prominent in the new government bore Etruscan names.[2] Nor does it bear the marks of being a democratic stroke: the succeeding government was in every respect oligarchic in form. But it inaugurated a bitter struggle of two centuries between the patricians who controlled the state, and the plebeians who bore many of its burdens although enjoying few of a citizen's privileges. This new revolution shows in its endless checks and counter checks, its intricate compromises and juristic fencing, the patient legal-mindedness of the Roman race. No nation in history except the English has under like pressure produced a similar drama of bloodless revolu-

[1] The story of the revolution is of course full of legendary elements. However, in view of the persisting hatred of "kings" in historical times, and the definite provisions in early laws against the crime of *adfectare regnum* it is safest to assume that the political consciousness had actually been deeply affected by a revolution which stirred the city to its foundations. Acts of very deep significance are not likely to be wholly distorted by legend.

[2] See Schulze, *Röm. Eigennamen.*

tion. Recent criticism[3] has been prone to call the
struggle wholly political, pointing out that the traditional narrative of it was produced after the Gracchan
days and was therefore probably colored by ideas that
emerged in a later day. However, even if there be
over-much economic interpretation of the early revolution in Livy, the laws which the struggle produced are
abiding testimony that the battle was fought largely on
economic grounds; and early Roman society reveals a
caste system largely based upon economic premises.
The story of the struggle, therefore, has a place in a
Roman economic history.

Before the revolution the great bulk of the peasants
was in the position of more or less free villeins. We
do not know that there was actual serfdom, and we
are never told of a definite "freeing of the serfs,"
though recent historians[4] have suggested that the crea-
tion of "tribunes of the plebs" in 495 may imply such
an act. If some or many of the peasants had fallen
into serfdom the liberation may of course have been a
gradual movement which therefore left no trace in the
laws that survived. So, for instance, it is possible that
the Etruscan autocrats of Rome had pursued a policy
of weakening the powerful landlords and of protecting
the peasants for the sake of bolstering up their own
power; or again the lords during the revolution may

[3] See Niese, *Hermes*, 1888, p. 410. De Sanctis, *Storia dei Romani*, II. 213.

[4] Neumann, *Bauernbefreiung*, 1900, in part accepted by E.
Meyer, article *Plebs*, in Conrads *Handwörterbuch*.[3]

have resigned their rights to many customary services in order to assure the loyalty of their villeins in the struggle with the king's troops. Such things occurred everywhere in the breaking up of the medieval feudal system.[5] At any rate no sure trace of serfdom is found in the early republic, for the so-called Servian constitution, while based mainly upon an economic division in the electorate and in the army, giving the predominance of power to rich landholders, constitutes a large part of the army from peasants whom it assumes to be freeholders. Whether the peasants were serfs or free in the sixth century, however, they were in a miserable economic condition.

In the first place their lots were small and of decreasing value. The very works of reclamation which we have noticed are proof that the land was being driven to the capacity of its production in order to feed an overcrowded population. That the soil was being overworked and refused to respond to all the requirements is also shown by the frequent notes in Livy[6] recording famines and food commissions in the fifth century. If

[5] Cf. Lipson, *The Economic History of England*, p. 77. Since various types of serfdom were to be found in early Sparta, Crete, Thessaly, in the Hellenistic kingdoms of Asia and Egypt, and probably in Gaul and Spain, its absence in Italy would be remarkable.

[6] Cf. Livy, II, 9; 34; 52; III, 32; IV, 12; 25; 52. Some of these passages are doubtless based upon conjecture, but it must be remembered that the priestly *annales* made a point of recording things of religious import like *quotiens annona cara, quotiens lunae aut solis lumine caligo aut quid obstiterit,* Cato, *Orig. frag.* 77.

furthermore the peasants had recently received their allotments, as seems probable, they must have had all the problems of economic independence to face on their own responsibility and with little experience. This occurred too at a time when the penalties of an extremely severe property law permitted debtors to be reduced to a state of peonage or to be sold into foreign lands as slaves. If under such conditions the peasants called for material relief as Livy so insistently contends, is his story not reasonable? And if they also asked for a better standing in court and equal political rights, this was due in no small measure to the fact that they knew that the most direct road to a more comfortable existence led by way of civil and political equality.

Certain urban classes possessing inferior rights also shared in the contest. The aggressive policy of the kings who had brought Rome into the currents of Etruscan commerce and industry had invited many workmen to Rome. Doubtless Rome had some share in the production of such things as we can attribute to most of the neighboring cities,[7] gold jewelry, engraved and chased work in silver for ornaments and toilet articles, all kinds of utensils in copper and iron, pottery and architectural ornaments of terracotta, clothing, armour, and much besides. Commerce required serv-

[7] Pinza, *Bull. Com.* 1912, p. 53. Rome later spread so rapidly over the regions where the early habitations and graves had been that very little has survived from which to judge the state of her earliest industry. The best records naturally come from the neighboring cities which dwindled away because of Rome's increase.

ice at the docks,[8] in transportation and in shops. Much labor was employed in the building of temples, public works and palaces. But many of those who had been invited to the city by these industries were left in difficulties on the expulsion of the kings, for Rome was not only then severed from Etruria, the home of these industries, but also apparently from the currents of commerce. Very few articles dating from the fifth century have been found at Rome which indicate contact with Greece or the East, and the seaport at Ostia seems to have fallen into neglect. An idle proletariat quite ripe for revolution resulted. Was the *lex Icilia de Aventino publicando*[9] of 456, an effort to pacify this class with small plots of land, and were the first four tribunes intended as official patrons for these city poor to take the place of the king whose expulsion had left them without protection?

Livy[10] connects the first "secession" of the plebeians with the Latin wars that followed the expulsion of the kings. He had of course no contemporaneous source that provided an explanation of causes and effects, but his conjecture is wholly reasonable. This was a period

[8] There are no traces of a sixth-century village at Ostia, but there was a strong tradition that one existed. About the middle of the fourth century a small colony was planted there and the village fortified by a wall which seems to have enclosed six acres of ground: Calza, *Notizie Scavi*, 1923, 178.

[9] Rosenberg, *Hermes*, 1913, 371, thinks the *lex* a proof that the plebeians of the city were still non-citizens who could be kept within a "pale," but a "pale" is not an Italic institution.

[10] Livy, II, 32.

of liberation for the Latins as well as for the Roman plebeians, and the one movement may well have induced the other. The first Carthaginian treaty, as we have seen, implied that the kings of Rome had made their city master of Latium as far as Tarracina and the new Republic in this treaty assumed that it would continue the same hegemony. This of course could not last, for the new government, having incurred the hostility of the Etruscans, was too weak for such a task. The Latins naturally claimed their former position of freedom in a tribal union;[11] when refused they

[11] The tribal union later called the "Latin league" went through constant changes, some phases of which we seem able to define.

(a) Before the Etruscans entered Latium, there must have been some common tribal cult which made for unity of action even in political matters, especially in times of danger.

(b) The Etruscan princes gaining possession of various hill-towns shattered this union. The leadership throughout Latium established by the Roman king was based upon the king's power not upon racial unity, for it extended over Volscian towns like Tarracina and Antium.

(c) The attempt of the Roman Republic to continue this hegemony after 509 failed, the Latin cities forming an independent Latin league from which even Rome was excluded—if, as is usually assumed, the ancient inscription cited by Cato (*Hist. Rom. Frag.* Cato, 58) gives a complete list of the members. The northern line of cities was made up of Tibur, Tusculum, Aricia, Lanuvium, Lavinium, the southern line by Ardea, Pometia, and Cora. The league therefore had slightly more territory than Rome, but failed to gain the adhesion of the Latin town of Praeneste (perhaps still under Etruscan rule) and the Volscian territory from Antium to Tarracina which Etruscan Rome had commanded. The date of this league can be fixed at about 500+ by the fact that the Latin colonies of Signia and Norba had apparently not yet been founded, while Cora is included, Rosenberg, *Hermes*, 1919, p. 159.

fought for it, and in time gained their point so that a Latin league was founded in which they formed an element of equal standing with Rome. It was in this struggle, according to Livy, that the hard pressed government called the peasantry into army service, and thus gave the plebeians an opportunity to bargain for representatives, called tribunes, who were to protect their interests.

(*d*) After a few years of separation Rome made a treaty with the league, not as one of nine members but as an equal half of the league. This *foedus Cassianum*, plausibly dated by Livy (II, 33, 4) in 493, is given by Dion. Hal. VI, 95. During the rest of the century this Latin league worked in fair harmony in defending Rome's border against the Etruscans and the south Latin border against the Aequi and Volsci.

(*e*) In the fourth century Rome began to assume leadership because of her ability to act as a unit among cities of diverse interests. After several disagreements on this score, especially after Rome was weakened by the Gallic invasion, it became necessary to renew the league by a new agreement in 358.

In 343 there was a general revolt of the Latins against Rome's assumption of superiority, and the Roman victory in the Latin war enabled her to form the federation into which she fitted the old league members at will. The Latin cult was continued in a perfunctory way on Rome's responsibility, and all Latin communities (50 or 60, Pliny, III, 69) were admitted to the festival on equal terms including many towns that had belonged to Rome (e.g., Gabii, Bovillae, etc.) or to the other former members of the league (e.g., Bola, Corioli, etc.).

Since after 493 there was *commercium* and *conubium* between all Latins of the league, and residence secured citizenship in any city, we may assume that economic changes whether at Rome or in any part of Latium quickly made themselves felt throughout the territory of the league.

The institution of tribunes[12] was in many respects peculiar, and implies in its very form something about the nature of the grievances that were to be corrected. The tribunes, at first apparently four, were *sacrosanct*, which implies that the plebeians had formed a separate body in the state and had compelled the government to take an oath to respect the persons of their representatives under penalty of divine vengeance. This fact proves that tradition was correct in attributing the plebeian victory to a strike. Moreover the fact that the tribune's power at first was not magisterial, but personal, applicable in the aid of individuals and that only within the city walls, justifies the inference that his services were those of an advocate to be exercised in cases of alleged injustice of the court and its agents. It was the tribune's business therefore to protect the personal liberty of the poor man who was in danger of falling under the debtor's sale, and at least to see that he had his days of grace and an opportunity to summon his friends to his relief. The whole institution in short points to economic grievances as the starting point of the revolution.

Once organized however, the tribunes readily extended their powers. The meetings of the plebeians for elections enabled them to discuss and formulate further measures, to instruct their representatives, and

[12] Livy, II, 33; Diod. XI, 68. The early number and the date (495 or 471) were matters of dispute among the Romans. See especially Mommsen, Staatsr. II, 272, E. Meyer, Art. *Plebs* in Conrads *Handwörterbuch*, and Rosenberg on *sacrosanctus* in *Hermes*, 1913, 359.

when they had grown into a compact body to use pressure upon the government through threats of tribunal interference. Thus in 452 they forced the government to promise a codification and publication of customary law whereby arbitrary rulings might be checked and a basis laid for intelligent reforms. A few years[13] later they compelled the legislative assembly to recognize a plebiscite as a bill which the assembly must consider, and presently social distinctions were removed by the permission of intermarriage between plebeians and patricians. In 393 an old custom of the Latin league was resurrected and some of the territory recently taken from Veii was distributed to all citizens, each receiving seven jugera. To the great significance of this act we must recur; suffice it here to say that, as the distribution was a proof of democratic power and set a precedent for the party's policy, it also in turn strengthened the party by lifting a large number of the proletariat into the class of property owners, thus giving them better standing in the legislative assembly and doubtless starting many on the road to economic success. Their increased strength enabled them finally by means of the Licinian-Sextian law of 366 to gain entrance into the consulship,[14] the highest magistracy

[13] The traditional dates are: twelve tables, 451; the laws of Horatius and Valerius recognizing in some measure the plebiscite, 449; lex Canuleia permitting *conubium*, 445.

[14] The Licinian-Sextian laws contained, according to Livy, a clause restricting the rental of public lands. Recent critics have with Niese, *Hermes*, 23, 410, placed this restriction in the second century. However, in two subsequent passages, Livy indicates

in the state, and to strengthen their opportunities of sharing in further land distributions by limiting to 500 jugera the amount of public land any man might rent. Thus the plebeians gained legal recognition for their claim to political and civil equality and some measure of economic relief.

We may conveniently anticipate, and add that in 287 the plebeians by a very peculiar method used their power to establish equal manhood suffrage in legislation. They compelled the legislative assembly, which voted by classes based upon property, to recognize as of equal standing the tribal assembly which voted by wards, apparently inviting the patricians who were of course a small minority to participation in the tribal organization. Thus this state within the state grew, by absorbing the patrician element, to be the very state itself; thenceforth tribunes could call the populace to-

---

judicial actions on infringements of the law which, if accurate, imply that the traditional account is correct. In VII, 16, he reports that Licinius was himself fined for possessing a thousand acres in 357, and in X, 13 (298 B.C.) that very many persons were fined *quia plus quam quod lege finitum erat agri possiderent;* cf. X, 23; X, 47 (*damnatis aliquot pecuariis*), seems to refer to the same law.

The law well corresponds to the economic situation of that time as we now know it. Land was deteriorating in value and some landlords who were consequently introducing cattle raising must have sought for extensive leases. The poor had already learned the advantage of land distribution but had of course sustained many losses in the Gallic invasion. We need not assume with Niese that the law presupposed a great number of latifundia at this time, for the existence of a few might suffice to induce preventive legislation.

gether under their presidency to decide the policies of the commonwealth. This was victory more than complete, and had Rome remained a state of small size, whose problems the populace had dared to settle single handed without the advice of the senate, Rome, like the Greek city-states, would henceforth have provided an example of a pure democracy.

In the light of this evolution we may recur for a moment to the land distribution of 393 whereby all citizens secured an allotment of seven jugera from the captured Veian territory immediately north of the city. To the wealthy landholders, of course, the allotment brought little of value; they probably sold their portions or leased them. To the proletariat, however, it gave in those days of hand-tools and intensive culture enough for a livelihood. To the state it meant that through a period of gravest dangers Rome was to be provided in these working landowners with a sound body of patriotic and reliable citizens. These aided her for some time to avoid the immobility of an absentee landlord class and the listlessness of peasant-tenants or their substitute, the farm slaves.

The Romans knew as well as we of course that the working landowner on his small farm was not always progressive. A master farmer like Cato, instructed in the agricultural lore of the Greeks and Carthaginians, could doubtless plant more wisely and secure greater returns by adapting his crops to the soil and to wider market needs. Like the Renaissance advocates of the enclosure system in England he knew that there was an economic advantage in concentration. Furthermore he must have found that the division of the Veian land into small plots destroyed the possibility of operating the extensive drainage tunnels which had been dug through large tracts of that territory.[15] Individual holders of small lots would hardly take care of their segments when unable to control the current above and below, and co-ordinated efforts were probably out of the question.[16] At any rate the tunnels fell into disuse, and the total of production must have fallen also.

However, maximum production was never an ideal of Roman statescraft. The senate usually considered the value of its citizens from the point of view of military and political needs, and the democratic element looked of course to social as well as economic amelioration. Obviously a homogeneous citizen-army was highly desirable in a small state as poorly protected as Rome. To constitute such an army it was necessary to have a large proportion of responsible property owners for whom the defense of the state was a matter of personal interest. On that idea the army had been built for centuries. It was equally important that the nation should have a large group of self-supporting

[15] There are still many traces of these drainage tunnels to be seen in the valleys near Veii, especially toward the north where the land is hilly; they have also been reported in the neighborhood of Bieda further north, *Röm. Mitt.* XV, pp. 185-6.

[16] There seems to be a reference to this difficulty in *Digest*, 39, 3, 2, 1.

citizens whose opinions and sympathies were stabilized at election time by contentment and faith in the existing order. These were everyday doctrines at Rome, and few statesmen permitted themselves to advocate in the senate economic advantages of a landlord system over the political and social advantages of the system based upon the working proprietor. If the former system nevertheless emerged victorious in the end, it was not for want of comprehension and interest but rather because the force of economic laws withstood the application of such remedies as were then available. That Rome bore so well the shock of the Gallic invasion, that she passed without bloodshed through the broils of the class struggles, survived the revolt of the Latins, and had the prudence to devise the liberal and flexible constitution which enabled her to unite Italy in an effective federation, all this seems now in no small measure due to the habit of providing by land-distribution a solid and interested citizen-body from the proletariat.

In the above summary the slow evolution of plebeian civil rights has for unity's sake been considered simply in connection with agrarian problems. Near the end of the crisis the economic problems were not a little complicated by the entrance of a new factor, the establishment of a state mint, which by the issue of money, not hitherto used, for some time upset the stable economic system of Rome, brought on financial upheavals, and quickened the course of the revolution.

The precise date at which Rome instituted a mint is

now difficult to determine. The Romans, who were prone to credit all their institutions with great antiquity attributed the innovation to Servius Tullius. But the designs upon the earliest coins are now definitely assigned on artistic grounds to the fourth century.[17] If the prow,[18] which serves as the emblem upon the first coins, has reference to the colonization of the seaport of Ostia, which dates from about the middle of the fourth century, we have in this first issue an explanation of several peculiar financial measures that followed immediately. In 352 a bankruptcy commission[19] was appointed; in 347 the legal rate of interest which had for a century stood at 8 1/3 per cent. was halved, and in 342 the taking of interest was absolutely forbidden. The laws look very much like an excited effort on the part of a government inexperienced in financial affairs to curb the evils which result upon a sudden "inflation" of currency. It is clear that the first issue of currency in an age that had been accustomed to barter must have

[17] See Hill, *Historical Roman Coins.*

[18] The arguments for the dates of Ostia I have given in *Class. Phil.* 1919, p. 314. The statement of Festus, who says the colony was subsequent to the first building of the village, is supported by the facts that its citizens belong to two different tribes and that its government has a double set of officials. See Taylor, *Cults of Ostia.* Recent excavations have revealed a city-wall which shows the workmanship and the material prevalent in the fourth century, see *Am. J. Arch.,* 1918, 182. It is usual to refer the "prow" to the capture of Antium.

[19] The bankruptcy law, Livy, VII, 21; the laws on interest, VII, 27, and VII, 42, to be read with Tac. *Ann.* VI, 16, and Appian *B. C.* I, 54.

acted as does a heavy over-issue to-day and upset the peaceful tenor of the market. It must have stimulated buying and invited new trade to the city, it must have facilitated borrowing for new ventures, not to speak of needless and perilous ones; and since prices tend to increase with the quantity of currency there were doubtless many miscalculations and numerous failures. How this situation quickly led to such financial crises as Livy records can readily be conceived. The laws that were passed to meet the stress show that the lower classes were gaining an everincreasing influence over the government. It was only three years after the prohibition of interest that the bold plebeian leader Publilius Philo passed the laws that cancelled the privilege of the patricians in the senate to veto legislation.

Statesmen, however, learned that in forbidding interest they had only increased the difficulty: later notices show that the old legal rate was soon accepted; and when presently conquests in Latium and Samnium opened up new lands for colonization the surplus currency was doubtless absorbed and the financial equilibrium re-established.

CHAPTER IV

NEW LANDS FOR OLD

THE intensity of the effort to reclaim small bits of eroding land was a proof of overpopulation and of a dangerous drain upon the productive qualities of the soil.[1] The danger of soil exhaustion was peculiarly great in Latium for several reasons. The soil there had not had a long time for accumulation. Along the extensive ridges of lava that radiate from the Alban hills toward the Anio, along the Appian way, and down toward Ardea, the surface was so hard that soil-making was well-nigh impossible. In such places the plow cannot now be driven. A mere scratch in the thin turf exposes the lava. In other places the conditions were more favorable since the ash and tufa are fairly productive for plants of powerful roots when covered with a humus of proper physical consistency and containing some nitrogenous matter. The surface was, however, new and therefore thin everywhere except in alluvial valleys. To add to the unfortunate conditions, the ash had fallen unevenly in knolls that time has not yet shaped down into a peneplain. In consequence the Campagna presents to the abrading rains of winter a very uneven surface, and when the Latin settlers had once stripped the turf and forest from that surface, the

[1] See chapter I.

thin soil was in danger of washing away. It is not surprising that the Latin farmer found it necessary to entice the thieving rainwater into underground channels with the utmost speed. The surface loam was very precious and must be saved. Notwithstanding his efforts, however, the exhausting harvests and the continual erosion did their work, and agriculture in Latium was threatened, and with it the thick adornment of prosperous Latin villages. The situation could well be illustrated by the history of agriculture in the sandy districts of central Pennsylvania, where the traveller to-day passes through large areas of country almost uninhabited though well studded with barns and farmhouses now abandoned and falling into ruin. Here the settlers of two centuries ago found a rich but thin alluvial soil lying over a subsoil of sand. A century of reckless tilling drew great wealth from the soil, but when that had been exploited the land was of little value and the farmers left it.

The situation in Latium never grew equally desperate, nor will it, since the subsoil there, even though slow to yield its wealth to the feeble roots of mere annual vegetation, is nevertheless comparatively rich. Yet, to judge from the constant cries of distress reported by the early books of Livy, the fifth and fourth centuries before our era were years of increasing poverty. To add to the desperate situation, the extensive forests[2] which had insured rainfall well into the

---

[2] Nissen, *Italische Landeskunde*, I, 432. The U. S. Forest Service has proved that a large percentage of rainfall is due to

summer and had helped husband the moisture in the dry season were ever giving way to the axe. The pressing demand for land resulted in the clearing out of every tract that could be made arable; the abundant population laid large demands upon the forests for lumber; and commerce, as we have seen, carried Latin timber as far as Greece, now well stripped of trees. The deforestation of the Volscian mountains on the south of the Campagna resulted in the ruin of that whole region, for the rains washed the mountain sides clear of soil, carried down the detritus into the flat plain below, choked up the courses of the streams and turned what was once the garden spot of several large cities into malarial marshes, a pest not only to its own dwindling population but also to villages as far off as Satricum and Astura. Norba, Cora, Setia, and Privernum dwindled down to unimportant hamlets. The same process of deforestation of the Sabine hills turned these also into bare rocks. Precipitation decreased, the dry seasons grew in length, the rain that fell found its quick course to the sea, and Latium became gradually the semi-arid plain that it is to-day.

While this change was in process the farmers naturally sought for remedies. There was scarcity of manure because during the very intensive tillage when every acre was in use it had not been profitable to keep cattle, since beef was rarely served as food, and horses

water-vapor given out by forest trees. *N. Y. Times*, Aug. 20, 1926.

were not in general use. When, however, many farmers found the loam too thin for further cultivation they had no choice but to seed their fields into pasture land, since turf could at least protect whatever loam remained. A few oxen were needed as draft animals, and the wealthy lords of the city provided some market for the meat. Sheep were also in demand for wool, though this had generally come by barter from the mountain pastures that were fit only for sheep-raising. Goats might be raised for milk and cheese.

The chief difficulty for the shepherd and herdsman was the lack of grass in July, August and September, which necessitated the laborious work of cutting leaves from trees.[3] However, in the fourth and third centuries, when the neighboring mountain pastures of the Volscian and the Sabine hills fell within the political sphere of Rome, a profitable combination of summer and winter pastures became possible. Whether it was the Latin landlord who sought to tide over the arid summer by resorting to the mountain pastures in dry season, or whether it was, as in the middle of the nineteenth century, the Sabine flock-owners who discovered green and warm winter pasturage for their flocks in the abandoned farms of the Campagna, we do not now know. But when once the discovery was made the Latin landlords were quick to seize the opportunity to find a now profitable use for the land that would no longer yield a reasonable harvest of grain. The earliest record we have of Roman slaves in great numbers

[3] Pliny, *H. N.* XVIII, 314.

shepherding on the mountains near Rome dates from the Second Punic War[4] but since such notices are incidental and rare we need not assume that the custom was then of recent date. He who has had the misfortune of trying to make his way from Tivoli to Rome against the endless procession of sheep going mountainward during the first week of July knows well what Horace[5] meant when he wrote:

Jam pastor umbras cum grege languido . . . quaerit.

This change, however, had serious consequences. Profitable sheep- and cattle-raising required capital, if indeed pastures were to be provided in two regions; and obviously, since the shepherding of a hundred sheep required little more labor than the care of half a dozen, the poor farmer with his small plot fell quite behind in the competition. Thus the small farmers gradually yielded ground to the master who could command the capital of large-scale ranching; and a general "enclosure" movement began at the expense of the grain fields. Again, since little skill was required, slaves were bought to care for the herds, and henceforth an area of a thousand acres, which in the days of profitable tillage had supported a hundred peasant families, now fell to the charge of a few foreign slaves living at random. The depopulation of the Campagna proceeded apace.

[4] Livy, XXXII, 26.

[5] Horace, *Carm.* III, 29, 21; cf. Varro, *R. R.* II, 1, 16; II, 2, 9-11; 5, 11; *L. L.* V, 36; Pliny, *Epist.* II, 17, 28.

Another industry presently hurried the process of crowding agriculture out of the Alban region. Here the abrasion of the soil had been most rapid because the slopes were steeper, but it was discovered that while the weak roots of annual plants like wheat and barley could no longer cope with the soil, grape vines and olive[6] trees could readily nourish themselves even in the tufa and ash that remained. All that is necessary is to hack out and crush the tufa and plant the roots deep with a handful of loam for the plant to feed upon when young. When the plant grows strong it finds its own nourishment where grain fails in the struggle. From that time to this the vineyards and olive groves have never disappeared from the hills and valleys about the Alban lake. Obviously this industry also was developed by the men of wealth who could afford to wait five years for the first vintage and fifteen years for the first returns on their investment in the olive groves.

[6] The festival of the Vinalia was recognized in the calendar of the regal period, but wine was not much used in the oldest cults. At the time of Pyrrhus the vineyards of the Alban hills are mentioned, Pliny, *N. H.* XIV, 12. In classical times the vine was cultivated farther down into the plains than it is to-day, for it is mentioned as a product even of Ardea (Colum. III, 9), Gabii (Galen, 6, p. 334), and other places now used solely for grain or pasture land.

The olive was imported later, its culture being connected with Castor and Pollux. Pliny quotes the price at Rome for 249 B.C. as being 10 asses for 12 lbs.—a very high price (XV, 2). Plautus' (*Capt.* 489) joke about the "combine" of oil merchants in the Forum implies that olive oil had become a staple of the market before the second century. Latium, however, did not raise a surplus for export until Cicero's day.

It is customary to say that when Rome gained possession of Sicily in the first Punic war and thus inherited from Carthage the grain tithes of that island she destroyed agriculture in Latium by flooding the market of the Latin farmer with cheap grain. But is it probable that the Roman landlords, who after all controlled the state, would have adopted a policy so ruinous to their own interests? Or is it likely that they were so stupid as not to see that this would be the result of bringing the Sicilian tithes to Rome? Is it not far more reasonable to suppose that the process we have sketched had actually progressed far by the middle of the third century, that Latium had already become a failure as a grainland, that many of the landlords had already turned to other industries, and that Sicilian grain filled a need already keenly felt?

The momentous changes here sketched in brief compass were the work of a long period from the fifth to the second century. They necessitated of course a constant reshifting of a population which we have found reason to believe was very dense in the sixth century. A similar exhaustion of the soil in Greece somewhat earlier had driven large hordes to colonize foreign lands and had turned many into commercial and industrial enterprises which revolutionized such cities as Athens and Corinth. Rome sought neither remedy directly. Her citizens did not abandon Rome for foreign lands, nor did Rome turn to manufacturing and commerce, although there seem to be signs in the building of Ostia and in the legislation of Appius

Claudius[7] that there was for a while a tendency in that direction. The surplusage of Roman population found an outlet instead in the territorial expansion which set in under the vigorous democratic leaders that came to the fore in the middle of the fourth century, soon after the plebeians had won their contest for the consulship in 366. In 343 the Romans aided the Campanians in driving back the Samnite mountaineers. The war resulted after two years in an allied victory through which Rome received some territory north of Campania for colonization. The year after this war the Latin peoples revolted from Rome's hegemony and, being defeated, were incorporated into the Roman state, part as full citizens, part for a probationary period as non-voting citizens. There were of course losses of men on both sides, and some land was confiscated and settled by Romans. In 328 a new Samnite war broke out which gradually spread through the whole of central Italy including the Etruscans, Umbrians, and Sabine peoples. For forty years there was almost constant warfare. This was finally followed by the war with Pyrrhus whose defeat left Rome the

[7] Meyer, *art. Plebs* in Conrad's *Handwörterbuch*, expresses the belief that when Appius (about 312) built the aqueduct into the lower sections of the city, paved the Appian Way, and permitted the *liberti* to register their vote in whatever ward they chose, he intended to encourage and to give political power to an industrial proletariat. In view of the present state of our archaeological knowledge of the period the theory seems somewhat to overleap the evidence.

recognized leader of a federation extending from the Arno throughout the whole of Italy.

This era of territorial expansion followed as we have seen a period of over-population and land hunger which had expressed itself constantly in a clamor for economic and social amelioration. Historians who have written of the period have always been disposed to conclude that land hunger was the driving force which led to the expansion. Possibly this conclusion is correct. There can be no doubt of the desire for more land. An agricultural people when hard pressed economically thinks in terms of territorial expansion, and the Romans though very legalistic were as quick as many other peoples have been to take mortal offense at a neighbor's behavior when they need their neighbor's food. However, we have no right to be induced to this conclusion either by the short-circuited argument of *post hoc ergo,* nor by an *a priori* faith in the economic interpretation of history. It is only fair to point out first that the Roman people who had for centuries to defend their titles to desirable plain-lands against the inroads of hungry mountaineers had thereby developed to a maximum the lowlander's sense of property rights and justice.[8] It is not by mere chance that Rome's civil code has been adopted by all the world as the basis of law. Moreover a careful study of Rome's method of utilizing her victories reveals the behavior not of a land-hungry bandit but of a far-seeing political

[8] In *Roman Imperialism,* chapters III and IV, I have tried to explain Rome's foreign policy for this period.

organizer. A parcel of land was often appropriated by way of indemnity, and it was frequently a fertile plot which would invite and retain its colonists, but the individual portions were generally very small, just sufficient for a military post, and among the settlers was always included a fair proportion of the allied peoples. The new settlements of the fourth century show unmistakably that the government kept needs of the state foremost, not the cry of citizens for new allotments. The first settlements were made at the seaport towns of Antium and Tarracina which had exposed Latium to the raids of sea rovers, and of Greek and Etruscan fleets. But only three hundred men were sent to each, enough presumably to take political control and command the ports; and the allotments consisted of a few acres per man. Colonists were next settled on some land of Privernum to control the pass over the Volscian mountains behind Tarracina, land which was too exposed to the malaria of the Pontine marshes to be chosen as highly desirable for economic reasons. Above Capua in the territory taken from the Sidicini, allies of the Samnites, the Latin colony of Cales was planted. It contained 2,500 settlers, partly Romans who gave up their citizenship for the Latin status, and partly Latin and Campanian allies. Cales in fact is an instance of the typical border colony that Rome favored. Good enough land was chosen to induce the settlers to remain and guard a perilous spot, Romans and allies were mingled in recognition of mutual rights and to serve as a cohesive group in the federation, and the situation

was selected chiefly for its strategic value: Cales
guarded the inner road between Rome and Capua, and
it separated the Samnites from the newly subjected
Aurunci. Similar military colonies were planted at
Luceria, Suessa, Interamna and Alba. Finally the
Falernian fields above Cumae where the coast road
debouches into Campania was taken and settled by
Roman citizens. The reason for the appropriation
was partly strategic, partly punitive, for the inhabitants, apparently an old enclave of Etruscans,[9] had
aided the Samnites against Rome. The land was indeed
excellent, but had good land been the chief concern,
Rome need not have sent her citizens one hundred
miles away.

These are the settlements made in the period of
expansion during the fourth century and they are fairly
representative of Rome's policy for the next century
as well. The only difference is that in the third century
the settlement of Romans alone is of infrequent occurrence, the Latin military colony becomes the standard
type, and some lands, such as the Ager Gallicus, fail
for a long time to find takers. These are all indications
that by the third century Rome suffered not from land
hunger but from a scarcity of men needed for her task.

An adequate statement of how far Rome's expansion
was conditioned by economic pressure it would be hazardous to attempt without a complete review of the

[9] Vergil, *Aen.* VIII, 724, makes Halaesus, a Faliscan, the leader
of the troops of the ager Falernus; see Deecke, *Rosch. Lex. sub
voc. Halaesus.*

whole history of Rome's foreign policy. The close connection between the economic revolution and the
political expansion cannot be denied. We may at least
say that the over-population of Latium apparent in the
early period and the distress of the people due to a
gradual deterioration of the soil played an important
part in setting into activity the instincts and impulses
which led the government into an aggressive foreign
policy in 343; subsequent ventures, and the possession
of a dense population of farmers enabled the government to build up an irresistible army which made conquest relatively easy. The wastage of the wars however and the requirements for military colonies at
strategic points soon absorbed the surplusage to such
an extent that the third century discloses an insufficiency rather than a congestion of population. Furthermore the evidence shows clearly that the government
from the beginning was controlled by a well-ordered
policy which considered political and military needs
paramount and that it never betrayed these to the
exigencies of the economic pressure exerted through
individual citizens.

It is equally manifest however that the political
expansion of Rome reacted permanently upon the economic life of the people. The constant availability of
good lands which the state desired to have occupied
against possible encroachment always attracted men
and capital not otherwise occupied. Thus the Romans
now felt no incentive to try new enterprises, to develop
industries or to enter commerce on land or sea. During

this period of expansion Rome almost isolated herself from transmarine influences. The contact with the outer world that Etruscan agencies had formerly encouraged was weakened. Temples built at Rome in the sixth century had been almost Ionic in style but the art of the fourth century shows few traces of contemporaneous Aegean influence.[10] The rude masonry of yellow tufa that remains from this period shows that Rome had ceased to follow the progress of Greek art; not till the second century did Roman architecture become aware of how far it had been outdistanced. In industrial arts the story is the same. Praeneste, the inland hill-city only twenty miles away, developed in the third century a group of silversmiths whose skill and artistry are still a source of pleasure.[11] It is hardly due to mere chance that Roman crafts of the period reveal none of this skill, since both cities were equally Latin. The explanation of Praeneste's new development probably lies in the fact that the city had limited its territorial bounds by a treaty of "equality" with Rome which tied it for all time to the possession of some fifty square miles and compelled its surplus energies to find expression in industry. It might have been well for Rome had she to some measure been forced back upon her inventive skill in the same way. But by the results of Rome's expansionistic ventures her citizens, always invited to settle new lands and to

[10] Pinza, *Bull. Com.* 1912, 53.

[11] See Matties, *Praen. Spiegel*, on Praenestine metal work.

invest their excess capital in real property, became for all time farmers and real estate capitalists. Necessity, the mother of crafts as well as of arts, never forced them into apprenticeship in those occupations that develop the love for artificial beauty and train the instincts for commercial enterprise.

CHAPTER V

ROMAN COINAGE

THE history of Roman coinage[1] reveals one of the most interesting attempts in financial experimentation that can be found, an attempt to provide with but little use of gold—which was far too scarce in early Italy for purposes of coinage — an adequate currency for a state growing by leaps and bounds, to establish for foreign trade an acceptable medium of exchange that might compete with the issues of hundreds of neighboring states, and to keep the coins of the two metals, silver and bronze, at a reasonable ratio despite the fluctuation of prices in metals.

Our first surprise is that Rome managed to do without coins till the middle of the fourth century,[2] though

[1] Head, *Historia Numorum*[2]*; Hill, *Historical Roman Coins;* Grueber, *Coins of the Roman Republic.* The standard works of Babelon and Mommsen serve as good introductions. Haeberlin's *Systematik der ältesten röm. Münzwesens,* 1905 7, is an original contribution to the history of Roman coinage, but is faulty especially in its treatment of historical facts. My arguments for the view that the Roman system was bimetallic are presented in *Classical Philology,* 1919, 314.

[2] See end of chapter III. Mattingly has proposed to assign the Romano-Campanian coinage to the period of the Pyrrhic war (*Numis. Chron.* 1924, 181 ff.). No weighty argument for this drastic proposal has as yet appeared. See also Sydenham, *Aes Grave.*

neighboring Etruscan cities had been minting money
for more than a century, and the Greek cities of Southern Italy and Sicily for more than two centuries. This
dilatory behavior cannot be explained on the assumption that coins of other states may have flowed in sufficiently to supply the want, since the early treasure-
troves of Latium disclose very few foreign coins. The
only explanation is that Rome—as indeed the extant
fragments of her early art imply—had quite fallen out
of the currents of world-trade after the Etruscan
princes had been banished, and that the sluggish agricultural economy fared satisfactorily with ordinary
bartering supplemented by the use of copper weighed in
the balance. It was only after the new democratic
element, which gained its first decisive victory over the
aristocracy in 366, demonstrated its interest in commerce by founding a maritime colony at Ostia that the
state undertook to coin money; and then only bronze
was issued, and in bulky one-pound pieces (called
asses), in uncial fractions of the pound, and in mul-
tiples of the pound.

Bronze was indeed the only metal coined at Rome
for the next eighty years, during the whole period of
rapid expansion that made her supreme in Italy. However a few years after this first issue, when Rome sent
her armies into Campania to aid in checking Samnite
invasions, her generals found themselves in contact
with Greek and Oscan peoples who used silver currency. In order to buy army equipment from them it
was necessary to have an abundance of silver money;

and the soldiers must also have desired their pay in a currency that would be respected in the cities where they were billeted. Silver was accordingly provided for use in Campania, though there is now some question as to how it was issued. Since these silver didrachms bear the name *Romano*, though their workmanship proves them the product of the Capuan mint, Mommsen held that Capua as a dependency of Rome struck the coins at Rome's orders and for Rome's convenience, and he therefore considered them of Roman mintage issued from a subsidiary mint. It is now generally thought however that Capua was still sovereign at that time. Capua therefore seems to have lent her mint to the Roman generals who issued military currency — as Flamininus did later in Greece — or she accepted a contract from Rome to issue silver for Rome's southern trade, just as certain Campanian mints afterwards coined money for Cora, Cales, and Suessa.[3]

The pieces in question were double drachms of the size which was then generally current in Campania. They weighed about 7.58 grams, so that the single drachm was considered to be 1-72 of the Oscan pound of 273 grams. On what basis it exchanged with the Roman bronze *as* we are not told. If bronze then exchanged with silver at the ratio normal later of 1 : 120, exchange must have been a cumbersome pro-

[3] See *Roman Imperialism*, p. 41. Haeberlin follows Mommsen in thinking Capua a dependency; Babelon, I, p. xxix, calls it a military coinage.

cess since the silver piece would then be worth 3 1/3 bronze *asses*. But it is possible that bronze was then worth a trifle more and that three *asses* bought a didrachm.

Why the government did not bring this silver coinage to Rome during the fourth century it is difficult to understand. The scarcity of these coins on Latian soil, while Capuan copper coins came in abundance, would seem to indicate that Rome did not encourage their circulation northward. Could it be that Rome, taught by the financial troubles that followed her first coinage of copper, decided for the present not to introduce silver at home? That seems not unlikely, for we can hardly ascribe great financial experience to the simple legislators who forbade the charging of interest on money.

About 312 B.C.—if the wheel on the Romano-Campanian coin refers to the construction of the Appian Way—the size of the silver didrachm minted at Capua was reduced from 7.58 grams to about 6.82 grams, an act that must have displeased the Campanians among whom the coin was meant to circulate. Rome could hardly have done this unless her position in Campania had been strong both politically and financially. It is plausibly assumed that Rome could have ventured upon such a move only after Capua had committed acts of disloyalty to the league as she did in 312, and had in consequence been relegated to a somewhat inferior position. Rome's reason for reducing the coin may have been to establish a convenient rate of exchange with the bronze *as,* her standard coin, at a ratio between silver and bronze of 120 : 1.

This slight change is interesting because its effects soon proved to Rome the force of "Gresham's law" that, other things being equal, an inferior coin tends to drive out one of superior value. What happened was that Rome presently came, in the conduct of the protracted Samnite War, into direct trade relations with Lucania and Apulia where the currency of the South-Italian Greeks had hitherto dominated, and where her new didrachm, which was about 15 per cent. lighter than the Tarentine coin generally used, threatened to drive the latter out of circulation. Tarentum[4] retorted with a similar reduction of her own coin. The incident demonstrates how powerful Rome was becoming in the South.

About 300 B.C. the bronze *as* which was still the standard coin at Rome was gradually reduced to about half a pound, and the fractional coins proportionally. This act is explained by Mommsen as an effort to relegate bronze to the position of token money.[5] His theory however involves several difficulties. Bronze was still the trading metal in the Roman market and

---

[4] Haeberlin, *op. cit.* p. 24; Evans, *Horsemen of Tarentum*, p. 138; Regling, *Klio*, VI, p. 519.

[5] Haeberlin, *op. cit.*, p. 44, interprets it as an attempt to relieve debtors and therefore ascribes it to the year 286 B.C. when the plebeians seceded to the Janiculan hill. This seems to me wholly unacceptable. In view of the rise of commodity prices at the end of the fourth century, the date should not be placed later than 300 B.C.

there is little evidence that enough silver had come to Rome to take a dominating place. Throughout the Republic moreover Rome shows a great dislike for fiat money, making time and again a desperate effort to keep bimetallism[6] intact and her coins in both metals at par value. Finally the bronze *as*, being a crudely molded piece, could very readily have been counterfeited and would doubtless have been if the metal in it had represented only half of its market value, for it must be remembered that the *as* was still a rather valuable coin, worth a third of a double drachm or a tenth the price of a sheep. A far more reasonable explanation seems to be that bronze like all other commodities was rapidly rising in value throughout the Mediterranean world because of the enormous treasures of silver and gold that Alexander the Great had recently found in the Orient and set into circulation. The price lists that can be made from the temple records of Delos[7] for the fourth and third centuries B.C. demonstrate the fact that during the half century that followed Alexander's conquests practically all commodities more than doubled in price. And while we have no record of the price of raw copper, there is no reason to suppose that it was an exception. The reduction

[6] Especially in the most important currency reforms of 312, 269 and 217 B.C.

[7] Reinach, *L'histoire par les monnaies;* Glotz, *Le prix des denrées á Délos* in *Jour. des Savants*, 1913, and *Ancient Greece at Work*, London, 1926.

in the size of the bronze *as* seems therefore due to a rise in the price of copper.[8]

However this new coinage of half-pound asses, brought out about 300 B.C., was by no means permanent. The successive issues of the first thirty years of the third century provided coins of constantly diminishing weight until the *as* fell to two ounces, *i. e.,* a sixth of a pound. Again the arguments just given preclude the assumption that the bronze coin was giving way to silver monometallism. It may seem drastic to posit a threefold rise in the value of copper in the first thirty years of the third century, but we have recently seen an equally startling rise[9] in the price of copper produced in two years by causes not wholly unlike those then prevailing. The condition of the copper market was indeed peculiar. The steady demand for the metals during the long Samnite War was doubtless draining the market, since copper was then more extensively used in wagons, ships, war-engines,

---

[8] The effort to preserve bimetallism by changing the weight of one of the coins had been tried repeatedly in Greece. The coinage of Agathocles of Syracuse furnishes a good example of about the same date. In order to meet the fall of price in gold from 15 : 1 to 12 : 1, he reduced his silver coins from ten to eight litrae. Modern states have acted similarly. In 1864 France reduced her fractional coins because of the influx of gold from Californian mines; three years later she reduced the two-franc piece to the position of token-money, and presently abandoned bimetallism completely. Had France waited a few years till silver was discovered in Nevada the process might have been reversed.

[9] Copper in the American market rose from 12 cents per lb. in 1914, to 36 cents in 1916. In 1919 it returned to the prewar price.

harnesses, shields, etc., than later. But the real crisis
came in 296 when the Samnites secured the support of
the Gauls and Etruscans. Then Rome's supply which
had come almost entirely from Northern Etruria must
have been completely cut off. During the next year
Rome cleared the North of enemies, but the source of
supply again fell into the enemies' hands between 285
and 280, while Rome's needs for the metal were increasing by the extension of the war north and south.
Under such conditions a threefold rise in the price is
less strange than what happened to the metal in 1914-
1916 A.D.

Pliny[10] has by chance preserved the old item of information that the Romans in 280 B.C. when they
captured the Etruscan city of Volsinii carried away as
booty some two thousand bronze statues and he cites
a Greek author who joked about Rome's making wars
for love of art. But there may have been more than
mere humor in the remark. Doubtless many of those
portrait busts went into the furnace to compensate for
the deprivations of years. When in 269 Rome re-
formed her coinage on a new system she was able to
restore the old ratio of 120 : 1 which had for some
years fallen to 20 : 1. This was of course made possible by the re-establishment of peace-prices throughout Italy and by the acquisition of large quantities of
metal in her capture of Volsinii and Vulci in 280. And
the process was doubtless aided by the fact that Greek
trade and industry had now so far assimilated the

[10] *Hist. Nat.*, XXXIV, 34.

extra currency of the last century that the prices of commodities had now generally fallen back to those prevailing before Alexander's conquest.

After the wars with the Samnites and Pyrrhus had ended in complete victory in 272 Rome found herself the dominant power of a confederation that included the whole of Italy, and yet her currency consisted of a Greek silver coin minted for her by a dependency and a crudely molded bronze coin issued at home. Obviously the time had arrived for a more adequate and dignified system. In 269 a thoroughgoing reform was undertaken, the old coinage was discontinued, and the denarial system was instituted at Rome and at several branch mints throughout Italy. This new currency was conceived on sound ideas, adequately managed, and soon gained respect throughout the Mediterranean basin. In the first place the new Roman pound (the Attic pound of 327 grams) which had gained favor in Central Italy was now substituted as a standard of weight for the Oscan pound which was about one sixth lighter. It was regularly divided into 12 ounces, or 288 scruples. The two-ounce bronze *as* (48 scruples) which had been found a convenient size was adopted permanently into the new system. However since peace-prices had restored to 1 : 120 the ratio between bronze and silver this new piece was worth only about one sixth of the war-time *as* of two ounces. For a standard silver coin a four-scruple piece, the denarius, was adopted. This was the size of the Athenian drachm and therefore somewhat heavier than the

Romano-Campanian drachm (4.55 grams instead of 3.80 —). The adoption of so large a coin would obviously entail a loss to Rome in South-Italian trade if merchants began to exchange the Greek and the Roman silver at par, for the cheaper money of the South might threaten to drive the larger pieces into the melting pot. But Rome apparently decided to take the risk for the sake of a sound and respected currency. At best Rome might be strong enough financially to win in the competition;[11] at worst she might use political pressure to suppress the mints of the south. Whether she used this power we are not told; at any rate the southern silver mints closed one by one during the century probably from financial incapacity to compete. Since the ratio of exchange between the metals was now $1 : 120$, the four-scruple silver coin was worth ten of the 48-scruple bronze asses and the silver coin was accordingly called the *denarius, i. e.,* the ten-piece. A one-scruple piece of silver was also issued which was of course worth two and one half asses and therefore called a *sestertius*. Various fractions of the bronze *as* were also struck.

Strange to say, later Roman writers who lived when the Emperors were alloying and debasing the coinage

[11] To tide over the season of confusion, and doubtless to call attention to the superior value of the denarius, Rome continued to issue from the Capuan and some other southern branch-mints silver coins of the old weight (3 and 6 scruples) which were called *victoriati*. They probably exchanged with the denarius on the basis of 4 to 3, but they bore no mark of value and were treated as Pliny says *mercis loco*.

of their day so misunderstood this great reform as to
suppose that the adoption of the two-ounce *as* was an
act of audacious debasement. Pliny[12] indeed goes so
far as to say: "Thus a profit of five-sixths was made
and debts were cancelled to that extent." Nothing of
course could be farther from the truth. In the new
system the government issued both silver and bronze at
market value, and, if anything, it sustained a loss by
adopting a denarius which was heavier than the
drachm-pieces with which it was likely to compete. As
for debts these were probably calculated in silver and
would naturally be computed in the intrinsic values of
the respective issues. The fact that the new bronze *as*
was only one sixth of a pound could therefore do no
harm. The word *as* simply meant a "unit," and the
Roman law courts were too respectful of property
rights to be misled by a mere word into permitting the
repudiation of debts. Those who had fallen into debt
in terms of the old drachm and asses could readily be
made to compute it in terms of the new denarii and
asses; the process could hardly have been more difficult than when after our Revolution old contracts
stipulated in pounds sterling had to be settled in terms
of dollars and cents.

The charge of debasement came so natural to historians who had endured the evils of imperial currency

[12] Pliny, XXXIII, 44-45; cf. Festus (Lindsay), 470, 87, 468.
The last reference in particular which ascribes the change to the
Second Punic War shows that Festus was capable of serious
blunders. Apparently there was no trustworthy history of coinage available in the days of Pliny and Festus.

that they employed it to account for almost every change in the Republican coinage. As a matter of fact while many autocrats both Greek and Roman debased their coins for the sake of profit, Greek and Latin republics never did except under very strong pressure. The Roman people at this time had little to gain from such an attempt. The neighboring states would at once have discovered the deception and have refused to accept the coins at face value; while at home the people who received the currency from the state as pay for army service—a large proportion of the citizens—for war materials, and for public contracts, were also members of the assembly that had to authorize such an act. They obviously were not likely to favor it. The situation in the Empire when alloying became prevalent was wholly different. Then the largest debtor, the one who had to pay the vast sums of the state budget, was an autocrat and could profit temporarily by paying those sums in cheapened money. Furthermore since the Empire extended over most of the world of commerce, almost all the trade was "domestic," and it mattered little whether or not the rest of the world refused to accept the imperial coin. The situation resembled that of medieval England where the silver "pound" gradually sank to one fourth its size because trade was then largely domestic. With the growth of foreign trade in Elizabeth's time the coin came into competition with foreign issues and then reductions ceased. It is well therefore to scrutinize all statements charging a reduction for fraudulent purposes during the Republic. Most of them are due to misattribution of a later evil. Only one or at most two early instances of such an attempt seem now to be probable, and they were quickly checked because of protests.

The most interesting of all of Rome's experiments in finance is perhaps the act of 217 B.C. by which the *as* was reduced to one ounce,[13] the silver denarius pronounced worth sixteen asses instead of ten, and gold issued in pieces worth 20, 40, and 60 sesterces. Pliny's[14] statement reads characteristically: "When Hannibal was pressing the Romans hard in the dictatorship of Fabius Maximus, the *as* was reduced to one ounce and it was decided that the denarius should exchange for 16 asses, the quinarius for eight, the ses-

[13] Pliny, XXXIII, 45; Festus (Lindsay), 470. It seems likely that Pliny in referring the law to the dictatorship of Fabius is to be preferred to Festus who ascribes the law to Flaminius. The latter was slain at the battle of Trasimene lake which brought on the crisis. Later authors who assumed that the law had a populistic purpose would naturally hit upon Flaminius as the proposer. Zonares, VIII, 26, seems also to believe that the law was intended to relieve debtors.

[14] Gold had been issued once by the Romano-Campanian mint before the denarial system. That was also at a critical moment, perhaps when the treaty was made with Carthage in the Pyrrhic war, 279 B.C. The coin represents the act of striking a treaty. Historians usually assume that this coin was issued about 300-290, since its value (4 scruples of gold = 30 asses) seems to coincide with the libral *as*. But if we are right in holding that copper rose in value so that the new semilibral *as* was worth as much as the old libral *as* this argument falls, and the gold coin may readily be assigned to the time of the Pyrrhic war.

tertius for four.   Thus the state made a gain of a half,
but in paying military wages one denarius was still to
be given for ten asses."   This measure is surprising if
it was meant, as Pliny says, to repudiate state debts by
one-half, since Fabius Maximus was of all men a
sound aristocrat.   Festus attributes the law to the
democratic leader Flaminius, implying that the measure was of a revolutionary nature and meant to help
individual debtors.   Apparently authorities were at
odds for an explanation, and well they might be.

Let us consider what the law effected.   It was passed
in 217 after the Roman armies had been almost completely annihilated by Hannibal.   Huge armies had to
be raised at once, Rome had to be fortified, fleets had
to be built, there was need for very large issues of
currency, and Hannibal held Etruria, the source of
copper, while currency as always happens in times of
invasion was disappearing into hiding places.   It does
not seem likely that the law was meant to relieve private debtors, for the state had recently allotted the
Ager Gallicus.   Nor is it easy to believe that the state
passed that law for the sake of repudiating its obligations, since the state had no debts at that time, it explicitly raised the soldier's pay to cover the difference
between the old and the new coin, and on all the contracts necessitated by the defeat it would in any case
have to pay at market prices.   We must conclude that
Pliny and Festus are again projecting late theories.
What Fabius was attempting to do was clearly to increase the volume of currency by every means pos-

sible. Of course issuing two small coins instead of one large one could not materially aid, but the new coinage did more than that. It recognized the war-time appreciation of copper and thus saved the amount of this appreciation for the treasury. The ratio of exchange was now 112 : 1, hence an ounce of bronze was worth about one-sixteenth of a four-gram silver coin, the denarius therefore was slightly reduced in size and pronounced, as indeed it was, worth 16 of the asses. There was no deception in either issue; both were meant to pass at market value, and as the state raised the pay of soldiers to conform to the new coin, the courts doubtless saw to it that all old contracts were equitably settled by the proper computation. The advantages to the state were numerous. In the first place, now that Rome had to buy war supplies abroad, she had a silver coin nearer the size of the Cartha-ginian and the more prevalent Greek drachm, and this effected a saving; then as noted above, the act took advantage of the appreciation in the price of copper. Finally by issuing smaller coins the state enticed back to the mint the old currency which was disappearing into hiding. The sole disadvantage, beyond the labor entailed, was that henceforth the denarius was not equated with ten asses as its name implied but with sixteen, thus destroying the convenient decimal sys-tem of the earlier coinage. It is probably for this reason that business men began to calculate their ac-counts in sesterces, now worth four asses.

The gold coins issued at this same time were the

first real Roman issues in that metal. Since the one-
scruple piece was marked xx (sesterces) and the new
silver sesterces weighed about five-sixths of a scruple
the rate of exchange must have been about 1 : 16 2/3.
This rate seems high, for in Greece during this same
period gold generally passed at the rate of 1 : 12.
When we consider however that Italy was poor in
gold, that the purpose of the issue was to provide as
much currency as possible at a time of severest stress,
we cannot but conclude that the rate was moderate.

It is of course unfortunate that the decimal system
was abandoned, but it is difficult to see how in such a
crisis the state without the aid of a well developed
credit system could have proceeded more wisely to
keep its metal in circulation, to expand its currency to
meet enormous demands, and still to hold its issues in
three metals at market rates when the exigencies of
the war had raised the commodity price of copper.

The system adopted in 217 remained in vogue into
the Empire except that the gold coins were soon withdrawn from circulation and the issue of bronze asses
was suspended from time to time, and the weight of
the *as* was during the Social war reduced to half an
ounce. What purpose governed this last reduction
cannot be determined, since we do not know the market value of copper[15] at the time.

Rome's currency system was of course not wholly

[15] See Grenfell and Hunt, *Tebtunis papyri*, I, Append. 2, and
Mitteis-Wilcken, *Chrestomatie*, I, lxiv, for conflicting theories,
also Segré, *Circolazione Monetaria*.

satisfactory. The necessity of frequently changing the size of the *as* because of the fluctuations in the market price of copper must have caused trouble in business; but gold was too scarce at least in the earlier day to trust as a standard, and its adoption might have led to worse evils. Possibly a silver monometallism would have been better, but it is doubtful whether the hard-headed Roman populace could have been made to accept bronze coins of fictitious value any sooner than they did. A second deficiency was the irregular way in which money was put into circulation. Since a free and unlimited coinage of silver and copper was out of the question, the size of the issues was determined by the consuls and senate, and these could hardly have had any good criterion for judging when more currency was needed. Doubtless many a financial crisis was due to the irregularity of the issues, especially as the banking and credit system developed very slowly. Yet there was perhaps a flexibility which there might not have been if Rome, like some modern states, had permitted the chance output of gold mines to determine per capita circulation.

At any rate the history of three centuries of efforts in yoking together two such unmanageable metals as bronze and silver, in adapting the currency to the needs of a rapidly expanding empire, and in keeping it withal sound and respected is very creditable to the Republican statesmen. The three centuries of selfish manipulation by the autocratic emperors that followed brought the coins down to less than one fiftieth of their one-time value, thereby destroying the returns of all trust-funds and charitable foundations.

Desirable as it would be, it seems impracticable to estimate the value of Roman money in terms of modern standards. To be sure if we might attempt a purely statistical calculation without raising the question of what ought to enter into the cost of living, we might draw up a brief though wholly inadequate comparative list of Roman and modern commodity prices, and this would show that gold bought considerably more of the poor man's necessities then than it has in recent years. The gold in Cicero's day bought[16] twice as much wheat, rye, and cheese, about the same amount of salt-fish, three to five times as much of the common vegetables, and six times as much dried beans—these were the poor man's staples—as it did in 1910—to adopt a year of normal prices. Cheap wine and oil, both necessities of his diet, could be had at about one-third the amount that the modern laborer at Rome had to pay before the war; shoes and coarse wool were about one-fourth the price.

In the case of metals, gold bought somewhat less silver—the rate of exchange varying from 12 : 1 to 16 : 1—twenty-five per cent. more copper, but only about one-fifth as much iron. The rich man had his ordinary labor at about one-tenth the modern price, but he had

[16] For prices see chapter xv, Schulz, *Sokrates*, 1914, 75, Glotz, *Ancient Greece at Work*, p. 357 ff., Segré, *Circolazione Monetaria*. Cavaignac, *Population et Capital*, 88 ff., deals too boldly with hypothetical statistics.

to have much more of it. Beef, pork, ham, mutton, and fowl, which the poor man could not afford, were sold at about one-half of the prices current in 1910. The better grades of wine and oil, and imported table delicacies of all kinds do not seem to have been cheap. House rents, for which we have few statistics, varied then as now according to other considerations than capital cost. Cicero's house in the exclusive section of Rome was far from new, but it cost 3,500,000 sesterces (about $150,000); Sulla when a poor but respectable youth had rented a flat for $150 a year, and there were apparently miserable rooms to be had for workmen at a dollar per month.

This enumeration of course does not lead us far, but it sums up the material on which historians arrive at the convenient and statistically true, though woefully misleading, generalization that gold in Cicero's day had about three times the purchasing value that it had at the beginning of our century. This statement should not be made without immediate modification. In the first place Rome's was not a gold standard; if the small amount of gold then available had also been called upon to serve as the basis of currency its price would certainly have risen very much. Hence a comparison is at once vitiated for any estimate of the currency. Moreover given commodities do not hold the same relative position in an ancient as in a modern list of utilities. Iron for instance was ordinarily of far less consequence in ancient life than it is to-day, and it was very costly. Labor which was a larger item to those who could employ it was shockingly cheap. Finally prices were less stable and varied more than now according to the distance of the place of production from centers of trade, while wars and famines interfered with prices more frequently, and relief in times of stress was apt to be dilatory. For instance, some extremely low prices are quoted by Polybius as prevailing in Spain and Cisalpine Gaul. These however by no means represent normal rates, but rather conditions in frontier agricultural lands where a primitive self-sufficing economy still persisted, where commerce had not yet regularly entered to take the surplus product, and where currency was seldom seen.

It is also well to keep in mind that slavery placed so wide a chasm between the upper and lower classes of Rome that hardly a single necessity of a workman's budget would recur in the list of the wealthy man's necessities. Even bread, which must have taken fifty per cent. of a laborer's salary if he had a family of four to provide for, could hardly have constituted a half of one per cent. of Cicero's annual expenses. And this leads to the greatest difficulty in attempting a comparison of value. While it is true that the laborer's denarius bought two or three times as many bare necessities as in 1910, it is true largely because he had to confine himself to a few of the cheapest articles that must be had if he were to keep alive. It would not have been true if he had attempted to enjoy the variety of food, clothing, and the amenities that the modern man must have, for then he would quickly have included a grade of articles that were as expensive as now. In the case of the wealthy man it is by no means accurate to say that gold bought two or three times as much as now, for he needed many articles and much service for efficient existence that because of cumbersome transportation and lack of machinery were very costly. Cicero's journeys on official business by private carriage, yachts, and hand-borne litters, his mail which had to be sent by private couriers, his skilled stenographers and copyists, his private attendants who were needed in the lack of street guards, were necessities and very expensive ones. His ground rent in the section of Rome where he must live does not seem cheap to the modern Roman. His furniture, plate and house decorations were doubtless as heavy an item as they would be to-day because the application of slow hand-labor, even though the labor was cheap, made them expensive. The sum of 100,000 sesterces (about $4,000) which he had to expend annually for his son's education at Athens does not really represent modern amenities, conveniences and luxuries amounting to three times $4,000. The need of having individual teachers in a day when there were no organized universities, of employing personal attendants, the necessity of food, clothing, and apartments befitting his position, the cost of travel, of manuscript books, etc., removed him from the market where cheap necessities could be had. For Cicero a pound of Roman gold probably bought little if any more than its present-day equivalent.

CHAPTER VI

The Establishment of the Plantation

In 264 B.C. Rome came to the parting of the ways, and with characteristic enterprise chose the way that led into deep forests without signposts. For the first time she acquired non-Italian territory in contesting the possession of Sicily with Carthage. The real significance of the step rests in the fact that she found and without fully comprehending it adopted in Sicily a non-Roman theory of sovereignty[1] which in time completely changed her political ideals, and, permeating her code, made her over into an imperialistic power. In the past Rome had built up a federation of autonomous states which had surrendered their political hegemony without the payment of a tribute. In Sicily, she found that the overlord, Carthage, claimed to be a master who could exact tribute from her subjects. This profitable theory, Carthage and the Syracusan tyrant, Hiero, seem to have adopted from the kings of Egypt and Syria who had inherited it from Alexander, as he in his day had adopted it together with his theory of divine rights from the Persian

[1] I have attempted to sketch the political aspects of Rome's conquest of Sicily in the *Cambridge Ancient History*, vol. vii, (forthcoming). See Carcopino, *La Loi de Hiéron* and Rostowzew, *Stud. Röm. Kol.* (but I find no evidence that the Romans during the Republic considered stipendiary land as Roman public land).

régime. By virtue of it the Carthaginians had imposed in Sicily tithes on grain and fifths on various other products of the soil, while the lands of which they had taken complete possession they rented out to the highest bidder or cultivated as state's domain.

How far thoughts of transferring this profitable possession to themselves counted with the Romans in inducing them to enter the dangerous hazards of a war with Carthage, we can hardly decide. Polybius states that when the senate hesitated to act, the chauvinists urged the popular assembly to consider the material advantages that would follow, and perhaps it was the tribute which they had in mind. The senate, it must be added, however, acted with reluctance and for two years sent such small forces to the front, that there was apparently on their part no immediate intention of conquering a new province: to them it seemed enough if Messana were protected so that the straits might be kept out of Carthaginian control.

Those who looked for material advantages from a war were never more deluded. A constant struggle of twenty-four years ensued in which Rome drained her resources to the last drop. Every available man was used on land or sea through interminable campaigns till her fields went to waste and debts outstripped the returns of scanty crops. To keep up a fair quota for her army Rome at the end of the war admitted into citizenship the Sabine and Picentine people, running the imaginary walls of her city-state across Italy to the Adriatic.

Rome won in the end, and took over Carthaginian Sicily with most of the lucrative dispositions of the former owner, but she did not for the present evict any of the landholders nor send any colony to the island. The reasons are patent. The drain upon her population had been so severe that it would have been no easy matter to find volunteers for a colony so far distant. Nor could the state have made use of a military colony of the usual type. Nothing but a legion of professional soldiers would serve the purpose since here the conquered were to be kept in subjection as tributaries whether or not they wished it.

The annual tribute that Rome collected amounted to about one million bushels of wheat, which was brought to Rome and sold on the market for the account of the treasury. Since this amount was probably enough to supply at least half the needs of the city of that day, it would be interesting to know what the farmers of the vicinity thought of this competition of the state with their market. Unfortunately our meager sources have left no apposite comment. It is impossible to believe that if the landowners had seriously objected the urban tribes, being only four, could have out-voted the rural tribes in favor of cheap grain. Since the exaction of tribute in kind continued and so far as we know no effort was made to divert the produce to other markets we may conclude that much grain was actually needed. If so, conditions in Latium had already shifted toward the position they held in Cato's day when grain culture had given way largely to pasturage, wine and olive-growing. The process, in so far as it was not complete, must of course have been accelerated by the deluge of Sicilian wheat. From that time one province after another was exploited to feed the growing population of the city, and central Italy could never again win the position of a cereal-producing region.

In 232 Flaminius, a bold precursor of the Gracchi, re-asserted the doctrine, adopted after the fall of Veii, that public lands should be employed for purposes of social and economic amelioration rather than rented, as the senate desired, to endow the governmental treasury. The land in question was the Ager Gallicus which Rome took from the Senones when in 285 they attempted to repeat the memorable raid of a century earlier. At that time the land had been left undivided for want of takers, and had probably been leased in large lots to grazers. As the city grew, however, senators who were in general the class that could carry such investments had naturally found the leases profitable. But their arguments against Flaminius were not wholly based upon personal considerations. As experienced administrators they saw of course the advantages to the state of having a steady and reliable source of income for the treasury in addition to the real-estate tax, and they could question with sincerity the wisdom of a doctrine whose implications would inevitably phrase themselves in the theory that the state owed all its citizens a means of livelihood. How severe the demands for new distributions may have been we cannot conjecture, but it is quite possible that in the years of casting up of accounts after the long Punic war, many peasants lost their properties in the mortgages incurred while they had been in foreign service. At any rate the contest was a bitter one before Flaminius finally secured a majority vote in the tribal assembly for his proposal. Polybius,[2] writing later when the city was drifting toward the Gracchan maelstrom, and adopting the interpretation of the law as he found it in the aristocratic writer, Fabius, cynically remarks that this was the beginning of Rome's downfall, and he adds, what seems to be an echo of senatorial invective, that it was the cause of the Gallic wars of the Po valley that followed. Later writers generally adopted this verdict, for the effective historians of the republic who have put the stamp of their own bias upon republican history were nearly all members of the aristocracy. And this is the reason why the whole career of this original though over-impetuous leader[3]

[2] Polybius, II, 21, 7; the sentence probably belongs to a late revision of his work by the author. See also Cicero, *Cato Maj.* 11, and *Brut.* 57. The tract is sometimes called *Ager Gallicus et Picenus* because the Picentines seem to have possessed it before the Gallic invasion. On the law of Flaminius, see Cardinali, *Studi Graccani*, and Münzer *art. Flaminius* in *Pauly-Wissowa*.

[3] It was Flaminius who built the via Flaminia, which served both as a military road towards Gaul, and a highway of the colonists to Rome. The man's interest in industrial questions is revealed in his support of the *lex Metilia de fullonibus* regulating the fullers' gilds (Pliny, XXXV, 197) and in his approval of the Claudian law which prevented senators from engaging actively in foreign commerce. The second great playground of Rome,

is everywhere stained with whimsical accusations. An important immediate result of this law was that Rome again turned her surplus energies to land development, although the opening of a rich province outside of Italy should have attracted attention to the profits of commerce and industry.[4]

The Second Punic War which was fought on Italian soil wrought terrible havoc upon the chief industry of the people and thereby accelerated the processes that we have already noticed. For more than twelve years the battle lines swept back and forth over the villages and fields of central and southern Italy. Cities surrendered to the seemingly stronger contestant for self-protection, only to be sacked in vengeance when captured by the other. Whatever contestant retreated, grainfields were burned for military reasons, vineyards and orchards cut, and the cattle driven off. The inhabitants who escaped scattered to the four winds, many abandoning Italy permanently for Greece. Many of the famous cities of Magna Graecia came out of the war with a few hundred famine-ridden weaklings huddling together along the ruins of the city walls.

The vigorous part played in the Second Punic War by Marseilles suggests the inference that economic causes were far more important in bringing on the

the Circus Flaminius, built by him, attests his interest in the urban populace.

[4] Since Claudius and Flaminius saw fit to prevent senators from engaging in maritime commerce, we may infer that some at least were entering this field at the time.

conflict than Livy supposed. Marseilles had had many
trading-posts on the coast of Spain whither her merchants had attracted the products of the whole peninsula. Obviously, when Hamilcar and Hannibal marched
northward from New Carthage cross-cutting all the
old trade routes Marseilles .found that Spanish products began to flow southward toward the Punic ports
rather than eastward. And since Carthage whenever
possible monopolized the commerce of her possessions
the success of Carthage in Spain would obviously result in the complete exclusion of Marseilles. It is
therefore very likely that it was Marseilles that first
tried to check the Carthaginians, and failing this, did
her utmost to excite the Roman Senate to activity in
her favor by exaggerating the reports of Punic designs
against Rome. The Ebro treaty and the Saguntine alliance may well be the results of Massiliot diplomacy.[5]

After the war, came problems of reconstruction
which were of course far beyond the resources of the
enfeebled and debt-burdened state. The few men who
could be induced to consider new allotments in colonies
were gathered together and sent to frontiers demanding immediate protection. Thus Cremona and Placentia were repeopled as a bulwark against the Gauls,
and a few hundred citizens were found for each of
several ruined harbors of the southern coast, now
exposed to raids and invasions.[6] Even for these south-

[5] Frank, *Roman Imperialism*, 121 ff.

[6] The maritime colonies, planted apparently in view of a possible invasion of Antiochus in conjunction with Hannibal, were

ern points the requisite three hundred citizens could not always be supplied, so that Thurii and Vibo were settled as Latin colonies, and non-Romans were also included in some of the others.

Vast areas of devastated lands at less vital points could obviously not be cared for at present. These the state took possession of, partly because they were without claimants, partly, in accordance with the new theory of sovereignty recently adopted in Sicily, because they were forfeited in title to the conqueror. What was to be done with these vast areas, aggregating a total of perhaps two million acres,[7] at least half of which was arable? Obviously the state pursued what seemed to be a reasonable policy in offering it in large lease-holds to Romans who had the capital requisite to make use of it. By this method at least there was some hope of redeeming the land, for with the scarcity of settlers and the lack of capital available for buying it outright, the only other alternative would have been continued desolation and consequent lawlessness and brigandage. Under the law public lands could be thus leased in blocks of five hundred jugera per holder, or a thousand jugera for citizens having two children. Intensive cultivation to be sure was out of the question in such blocks, for labor was scarce and with the means of transportation then available grain

---

Sipontum, Croton, Tempsa, Buxentum, Salernum, Puteoli, Liternum, Volturnum, Thurii and Vibo. Citizens of Fregellae are known to have shared in the colonization.

[7] Beloch, *Bevölkerung der Griech. Röm. Welt.*

could not profitably find good markets. But the land could at least be turned into ranches since cattle raising might be conducted with the aid of a few slaves and the product be brought to market with little difficulty. Even on these terms much land found no renters, and the censor's bureau seems, pardonably if not wisely, to have permitted enterprising renters to exceed their allotments of the legal five hundred jugera if they so desired, and in many cases also to have connived when such renters let their cattle graze on less desirable lands lying unleased in the vicinity. Thus large tracts of public lands which for the time being were not otherwise of any service, came in time to be enclosed in the original holdings without good and legal title. It was a procedure which has found many parallels in the land-record offices of our own Western states. Here as there the practice was not only excused but even encouraged by public opinion, since those nearby saw nothing but advantage accruing from what is popularly called the "development of natural resources." Later after the population had grown and prospective settlers were clamoring for new allotments, a reaction set in demanding the "conservation of natural resources," and some of the officials were thrown into prison for permitting what public opinion had heartily approved of.

Needless to say, when Rome recovered from the dire effects of the war, when the population began once more to increase and fill up the interstices, though this required more than one generation, it was found that the state's hasty liberality had been imprudent in its failure to impose due restrictions. Ranches had spread over lands fit for agriculture; slaves imported from the East were thriving where citizen-soldiers should be growing up for service in time of need;[8] territory that might have been available for colonization by Rome's overflow of children was found occupied, and capitalistic farming, which even under normal conditions outstrips small-lot culture, had been entrenched by a state act. After such leaseholders had established a further equity on unreclaimed possessions by many investments and improvements, a demand on the part of the tribal assembly for a return to the theory of Flaminius might well precipitate a very dangerous revolution. The germs of the Gracchan sedition were inherent in the inadequate reconstruction policy adopted after the Punic war.

A brief account of the agricultural methods in use upon a moderate-sized plantation may serve not only to describe Rome's chief industry but to illustrate an ordinary Roman's methods of dealing with practical problems. We are fairly well informed about agricultural practices by the instructive, if garbled, treatise written by Cato[9] in the second century B.C., the some-

[8] Appian, *Bell. Civ.* I, 7, states that the squatters preferred slave to free labor both because slaves could not be levied for the wars and because there was profit in their offspring.

[9] The orthodox theory that Cato's book is an abstract of Mago's large work is not probable. Africa demanded "dry-farming," Italy did not. I have here used imperial writers only on technical points where old methods continued. Cato wrote at the begin-

what longer work written by Varro a century later, and the full and charming treatise of Columella composed in the first century A.D. Valuable data are also found in Vergil's Georgics and in Pliny's encyclopaedia. Since the orthodox system was already in vogue in Cato's day, and later works reveal merely an extension of the system with a few changes adapted to new needs we may, if some caution is used, supplement Cato's account by use of the two later authors.

In speaking of the plantation system in Italy we do not mean to imply an approach to the capitalistic methods found in the "bonanza" wheat-farming of our Western states, where success has depended upon the extensive use of labor-saving machinery capable of being employed upon level areas of rockless loam. Italian agriculture, even when specializing in cereals, continued for obvious reasons to use the methods of intensive farming. In the first place even before Cato's day the need for fertilizing had become imperative in central Italy, and manure was not to be secured in unlimited quantities nor applied without much labor. Secondly central Italy has little land suited to the use of machinery. When the landed proprietors of Latium to-day employ large gangs of laboring men, women, and children to spade, hoe, and cradle the grain by

---

ning of olive and wine culture; Varro has an added interest in orchards and cattle raising; Columella comes at the beginning of a reaction against slave labor, but in general the methods of intensive capitalist farming persist. See the excellent study of Roman agriculture in Heitland, *Agricola*.

hand it is not wholly due to lack of intelligence and capital. The wooden plow, the exact counterpart of the one described by Vergil is still used in various parts of the Campagna, where there is need of a modest implement that is willing to dodge stones and slip harmlessly along the surface if the soil is thin. Such plows cannot turn the soil; hence cross-plowing, hand work with the mattock, and reharrowing are necessary. All this means that in the several processes of soil-preparation an abundance of laborers was required, and since they were at hand they were also used for the harvest and the threshing, where machinery might have been invented to do the work more quickly. In a word the methods employed on the grain plantations were quite the same as those of the small plot; the difference between the two lay largely in the consequences to society in that latifundia substituted a herd of slaves for citizen farmers.

The typical villa was a large rambling structure containing granaries, wine presses, and vats in one part, the working quarters of the slaves in the other, and a second story comfortably fitted out to receive the master when he had time enough from affairs of state to take his brief vacations in the country. The management of the estate, which probably consisted of a compact farm of from 100 to 300 acres, was entrusted to a reliable slave "vilicus" and his wife. If ordinary farming was attempted, a troup of forty or fifty slaves was not too large. The farmer usually specialized on one crop, the purpose being to produce a handsome clear profit for the owner's account from a large bulk of one product, besides devoting some portion of the ground to various side products which would keep the slaves alive and meet the simpler needs of the villa.

A typical wheat plantation would engage a large band of slaves. In the autumn there would be plowing and cross-plowing, a slow process, for oxen walk very leisurely and insist upon resting frequently; but the ancient thought as did Walter of Henley, that the ox was preferable to the horse, being "mannes meat when dead while the horse was carrion." Indeed cattle-raising produced milk and cheese and beef besides draft animals for the plow, and if the beast plodded slowly, slaves' time was after all not expensive. A second or even a third plowing was necessary with the poor instrument used, and if the soil was a meadow just broken the turf had to be crushed with a mattock wielded by hand. Then the land was contoured[10] as it still is to-day, with gullies about twelve feet apart in order to keep the roots out of standing water during the long rainy season of winter, which threatened to rot the grain. All this required slow hand labor. In the spring when the rains ceased and the scorching Italian sun began to bake the ground, bands of slaves came out to weed and to hack[11] the ground between

[10] Plowing: *Columella*, II, 4, 3; Fairfax Harrison, *The Crooked Plow, Class. Jour.* XI, 323; Contours: Varro, *R. R.* I, 29 (quo pluvia aqua delabatur); Col. II, 4, 8; 8, 3.

[11] The hoeing was done two or three times: Cato, *R. R.* 37, 5; Pliny, XVIII, 184; Col. II, 11, 2. The Italians continue the practice, but I have never seen it done in America in the case of wheat.

the plants so as to break up the capillarity near the surface and prevent the subsoil moisture needed for the roots during the dry month before harvest from evaporating. At harvest, as is often done to-day, the tops were cradled and hauled to the granary first, and then the rest of the stalk at a second cutting. The straw served as thatch for the slaves' huts, as litter for the cattle (with an arrière pensée on the compost heap) and also to some extent as fodder. Finally the threshing was done by means of flail and winnow. The slaves had to live, and might as well be kept busy.

The labor of fertilizing[12] the field could of course not be neglected. So important was this item that the keeping of cattle was largely justified on the score of the manure; one head provided for half an acre of ground. In the Republic no chemical fertilizers were known, but in the Empire the use of chalk and lime was introduced from Gaul.

To provide the running expenses of the villa, to keep the slaves occupied between regular tasks, and to make use of waste products, some subsidiary crops

[12] Fertilizing. See *art. Düngung* in *Pauly-Wissowa;* The Greeks and Romans were skilful in the use of nitrogen-fixing legumes and clovers; Cato, 37, 2; Columella, II, 15; XI, 2, 44; Pliny, XVIII, 134; Varro, I, 23, 3; Alfalfa (medica) came to be thoroughly appreciated in the early Empire. Vergil, *Georg.* I, 215, and Varro, I, 42, both mention it, while Columella, II, 10, 25, is very enthusiastic about its power to enrich the soil. Servius, in commenting on the Vergilian passage, says that in his day it covered the whole of Venetia. Its importance as a fertilizer has hardly been appreciated by Simkhovitch in his article on *Hay and History* (*Pol. Sc. Quart.*, 1916).

might be cultivated. A row of willows[13] in the marsh supplied twigs from which slaves wove baskets during rainy weather; a grove of elm and poplars furnished wood for the kitchen fire, for the villa's pottery where wine and grain jars were made (volcanic alluvium makes fair redware), for the lime kiln, and provided leaves for the cattle. The slaves had of course a garden plot for cabbages, turnips, and other cheap vegetables. Pigs might be kept if oaks were near; they grew rather thin on mere kitchen leavings, weeds, and roots, and to bring a good price they needed a modicum of acorns. Sheep cropped the rough land and the olive orchard, and produced work at the loom for the slave women who were too old for heavier work. If the master was enterprising he might raise fowl also. Varro[14] knew a farmer who sold home-grown poultry and fish for $25,000 a year, and another who raised thrushes by the thousand which brought him fifty cents a piece. Pea-hens were worth several dollars each and brought good profits. In general, however, the

[13] Cato, I, 7, gives his preferences of products on the farm in the following order: (1) vinea (if the quality is good), (2) hortus (if one can irrigate), (3) salictum—apparently for basketry in fruit-bearing countries, (4) oletum, (5) pratum, apparently for fodder, (6) grain, (7) timber for fire wood, (8) arbustum—probably a combination of orchard and garden, (9) oak forest for timber and swine-raising. Pliny however (18, 29) quotes Cato as advocating cattle raising above all. How, *Class. Rev.* 1920, 178, suggests that Pliny is here referring to a conversation reported by Cicero, *de Off.* II, 89. Cato apparently had Latian and Sabine conditions in mind when he advocated grazing.

[14] Varro, *R. R.* III, 2, 14-17.

landlord insisted upon the use of his land for the particular purpose to which it was adapted. A self-sufficing "home economy" did not satisfy the capitalist, who looked upon his farm not as a home but a source of income. If it suited his ledger best he was even willing to send the slaves' food and clothing[15] out from the city to his farm.

Wheat-raising could of course not be continued for several successive years without exhausting the soil; hence when it was the staple product, rotation of crops relieved the strain. The portion used for wheat one year would be sown with rye, barley, or oats the next,[16] and every third or fourth year beans, peas, alfalfa or some other leguminous crop that brought back nitrogen to the soil was substituted. Sometimes green crops of this kind were plowed under to enrich the soil, or instead the ground might be allowed to stand fallow for a year as rough pasture (seeding was too expensive), and the sheep turned in to graze.

It must not be supposed that any large portion of the western Italian slopes continued cereal culture regularly into the first century. Obviously even with cheap slave labor, when provincial dues came into Rome in the form of sea-borne grain, expenses often threatened to overbalance receipts. When in Augustus' day Dionysius came to Rome he says he found the whole

---

[15] Cato, 135. Many of the things that slaves could make at the villa, such as rakes, mattocks, wine jars, baskets (Varro, I, 22) and even slaves' clothing, Cato apparently bought in the city.

[16] Pliny, *H. N.* XVIII, 187; Columella, II, 9, 4, and II, 12, 7-9.

country a garden; but he was a Greek accustomed to a land of limestone rocks. What Dionysius probably saw was an unusual number of vineyards and orchards of olives, figs, apples, peaches, plums, cherries, and almonds, many of which, as in Campania to-day, admitted some cereals and vegetables between the rows. These combination orchards and gardens are possible in the bright sunlight of Italy where lighter crops ac·tually benefit from shade. The elms,[17] poplars or fig trees were set out in rows about forty feet apart and on these the vines were trained. The fig trees justified themselves in their fruit as well as in propping the vine. Poplars and elms were liked because they did not shade too heavily and their leaves were pruned for fodder. Thus by planting grain and vegetables between the rows of elm-propped vines, the farmer found that the smaller plants thrived better, he enjoyed the advantages of a diversified crop, he did not have to wait for a return on his capital until the vines were full grown nor suffer a complete annual loss when hail ruined his crop of grapes.

Often sheepraising was combined with olive production since sheep could pasture on the grass that grew between the trees, but it proved possible also to raise cereals in the olive groves. Where land was rich and irrigation was feasible, as in Campania,[18] a constant succession of grains, legumes, and vegetables, three

[17] See art. Arbustum in Pauly-Wissowa; Varro, I, 7, 2; Pliny, XVII, 202; Columella, II, 9; V, 9, 11.

[18] Strabo, IV, 3.

crops per year, could be produced between the rows of vines. There however Vesuvius had fertilized the soil with a beneficent rain of rich volcanic detritus and the streams of the Apennines supplied an abundance of water to the very level plain; but Latium and Tuscany were not similarly blessed. On the whole the Roman farmer seems to have been very skilful in the use of manures, nitrogen-producing legumes, and in the proper rotation of his crops; he also proved through the centuries versatile enough in shifting the emphasis between cereal culture, grazing, and fruit raising so as to permit his tired land periods of recovery. Although as we shall see later, Italian agriculture ultimately failed to meet the demands of Rome, it is very doubtful whether it was the native farmer who deserves the blame for the failure.

CHAPTER VII

INDUSTRY AND COMMERCE

DURING the fifth century when Rome's political power was slipping out of hand it was hardly to be expected that she could retain her hold upon the commerce and industry developed under Etruscan princes. Indeed during that time the industrial class probably diminished rather than increased, for the slow-moving revolution which ended in the plebeian victories of 339 does not in any real way resemble the socialistic outbursts of an urban industrial proletariat. The inference is sometimes drawn from the vast space cinctured by the Servian wall that the city was very populous and, by implication, that large numbers of its citizens were engaged in productive occupations. The wall, however, took its long course partly because it could thus avail itself of certain convenient escarpments partly because various sacred shrines upon the outlying hills laid claim to protection. What uninhabited spaces it thus included, we cannot say. At any rate it would be very hazardous to estimate its population from the area enclosed by the walls.

Later, in the fourth century, there are political measures of a new color that imply, at least temporarily, the influence of an urban democracy. The famous

Appius Claudius,[1] whose sympathies for the urban poor are revealed by his construction of an aqueduct to the workingmen's quarters and his support of a freedman, Flavius, for a curule chair, seemed to aim at universal individual suffrage in his attempt to remove property qualifications for voting by allowing the city proletariat to register in any ward of the city, a measure which, since voting took place in the city, would have made the industrial class dominant in many of the wards. The proposal was rejected by the next censor, but the attempt of Claudius would seem to prove that at the end of the fourth century there existed a considerable class of men engaged in other than agricultural pursuits.

When, however, we look about for the products of this putative industry, they are difficult to find. There are no chance references in Greek authors pointing to the purchase of Roman goods, and there are very few articles found outside of Latium that permit the assumption of Roman origin. In pottery, for instance, the native ware[2] that appears in the Esquiline graves of that period is inordinately poor, certainly it could not have found a market abroad. The better ware is generally Campanian and Etruscan. A single exception to the rule, if it be one, is the pair of vases found at Falerii[3] with a Latin inscription. The work is good but the archaeologist insists that if it was made at

---

[1] Reforms of Appius Claudius: Diod. XX, 36; Livy, IX, 46. See also E. Meyer, *Art. Plebs* in Conrad's *Handwörterbuch*.

[2] Pinza, *Bull. Com.* 1912, p. 24.

[3] Helbig, *Führer*[3], II, 1799 b.

Rome, it was by no native, a sufficient comment upon the state of Rome's industry. There exists to be sure a very finely engraved bronze box, the well known Ficoronian cista, which bears the explicit testimony: "Novios Plautios made me at Rome."[4] Apparently artists were working at Rome and in some instances creating ware of good quality, but here as in the case of the vases the theme and workmanship are un-Roman. Such industries, however, did not spring out of Roman needs, they were transplanted and apparently died with the generation that happened to bring them to Rome. Aside from these two instances we can point to only a few coarse vases of Latin manufacture which somehow got into Etruscan trade; and this occurred at a somewhat later time than the fourth century.[5] After so meager a harvest of evidence, we seem forced to the conclusion that the industrial class, such as it was, could hardly have supplied a vast market. Probably there were only the men needed to make clothes, shoes, and armor for Rome's expanding armies, wagons, plows and hoes for the farms, pots and pans for the kitchen.

Indeed the fourth century was not one of industrial progress anywhere. Greek cities were only marking time after the disastrous Peloponnesian war, and the

[4] *Novios Plautios med Romai fecid.* Helbig suggests that the name is apparently Campanian, and that the locality would probably not have been mentioned had it been the artist's customary abiding place, Helbig[3], II, 1752.

[5] Helbig[3], I, 565: cf. *Mélanges d'arch et d'hist.* 1910, p. 99.

new commercial activity that sprang up with Alexander's release of Asiatic resources was not yet in evidence. Etruria dulled by the loss of Campania and Latium on the south and of the whole of north Italy was no longer providing a rich market for the Greeks, and suffered in addition through the financial weakness of the Greek cities that had at least purchased her ores and metal-work.

The quickening of commerce that followed Alexander's conquest brought little of permanent value to the central Mediterranean. It was largely a feverish activity stimulated by an inflated circulation which did not last, since the source of the new wealth was not a permanently producing industry. During the century that the new-found hoards dribbled out of the commercial currents again, the full temple accounts of Delos,[6] which note so meticulously every obol of receipt and expense, mark with a melancholy monotony the dulling of life through the cheapening of wages and the product of labor. As for Rome it is significant that Claudius' reform did not succeed and that it was not soon proposed again. At the end of the century and at the beginning of the next the heavy demand for men for the army and the colonies[7] removed all need for a socialistic political program at Rome.

In the two succeeding centuries we do not find evidence of any marked change in the nature of production at Rome. Doubtless the amount of ordinary ware

[6] Glotz in *Jour. des Savants*, 1913, p. 206.

[7] See chapter IV.

produced at home increased with the growth of the city—ancient transportation was too costly to make commerce in cheap wares profitable—but of goods worthy of export we do not hear. The only difference now is that work previously performed by free labor began in the second century to fall into the hands of slaves, which of course tainted manual work to such an extent that the poor citizen, if he could not secure a plot of land, must perforce to save his self-respect stand idle at the state crib. The slave who became the new man of industry had no choice but to work in silence, and so the voice that had spoken for the urban industrial class in political gatherings was henceforth silent.

For a long period Roman commerce fared no better than industry. In the West, Marseilles, Carthage, and such Italiote-Greek cities as were not "protected" to death by Greek and Syracusan tyrants held the field of legitimate commerce, while minor cities like Caere and Antium, deprived of strong political authority, fell back upon privateering. Roman trade, not having the stimulus of an aggressive production seeking an outlet, and discouraged by the neglect of an agricultural nobility which scorned it and in treaties with commercial states even betrayed it for political advantage, made no permanent progress. By the treaty of 348 a Punic trader had free access to the markets of Latium,[8] but a Roman, should he care to compete, was excluded from three-fourths of the Carthaginian domain; and

[8] Polybius, III, 24.

the senate had, in return for what privileges we do not know, signed away the Roman trader's right to sail along the Italian coast east of Tarentum. It was at about the time of this treaty that a colony was planted at the mouth of the Tiber.[9] Hitherto the sea craft that succeeded in crossing the bar at the mouth had to pull up against the vigorous Tiber current for fifteen miles, but sailing boats were seldom manned with oarsmen enough for that task. A harbor provided a transfer station at the river mouth where vessels of deep draft could either unload into storehouses by means of barges, or transfer a part of their loads to lighters,[10] take on oarsmen, and proceed to Rome. This first colony was indeed very small, apparently not over six acres. But it seems to have sufficed for a long time. Not till Gracchan days are there signs of expansion. Then it is likely that the tribune, who was not afraid of paternalistic experiments, put in state granaries here, though he seems not to have deepened the harbor.

During the Hannibalic war it was necessary for the state to have goods transported to the armies in Spain, Sardinia, and Sicily.[11] To draw out sufficient Roman shipping for this purpose the government offered to insure the ships and cargoes, making bargains with

[9] See chapter III, end

[10] Dion. Halic. III, 44; Strabo, III, 5. Ships of 3000 talents (less than 100 tons) could not enter the Tiber in their day, whereas ordinary merchant ships of the Mediterranean were from three to five times that size; Torr, *Ancient Ships*.

[11] Livy, XXIII, 48, 49; XXV, 3, 4; Polyb. I, 83, 7.

three corporations on those terms. The venture was not entirely successful, however, for the companies tricked the state by collecting insurance upon rotten hulks. After the war Rome continued to need grain transports for the armies that were operating in Greece and Asia, and we may assume that these engagements aided in introducing Roman merchants into the eastern field of commerce. That field, however, was already occupied by clever Greek and Syrian traders who knew the language, the whims and the needs of the eastern customers, as no Roman could. Apart from state contracts therefore the Roman merchants made little progress.

Nor did the state seem willing to patronize or advance the interests of the Roman merchant except in so far as the immediate needs of the commissary department required. Before the Punic war a democratic assembly forbade senators[12] to own vessels of sea-going capacity. The reasons for this measure have been widely discussed. Were the people afraid that the senators might waste public funds in harbor improvements? A few years later a censor was accused of contracting for docks at Tarracina because he owned estates nearby.[13] Or could it be that the com-

[12] Livy, XXI, 63, explains that it was passed because it was unseemly for senators to engage in gainful occupation. The maximum specified was 300 amphoras = about 225 bushels of wheat. The Claudian law was strongly supported by the radical democrat, Flaminius, which seems to imply that the restriction was not imposed wholly out of respect for old Roman *mores*.

[13] Livy, XI, 51, 2.

mercial corporations were already strong enough to
demand and secure monopolistic privileges? Such an
hypothesis is supported by no other evidence. Livy's
explanation that the Romans considered gainful occupations below the dignity of a senator is doubtless the
true one, and Caesar's[14] re-enactment of the law shows
that time did not alter the sentiment. Beneath this
sentiment there probably also lay the practical consideration that senators were needed at home in the service of the state: indeed a senator always required for-
mal permission from his government before he could
travel beyond the call of a summons to the curia.

When we review the second century, therefore, a
period in which Rome's commercial interests are popularly supposed to have gained such influence in politics
as to have caused the destruction of Carthage and
Corinth,[15] we find upon examination of our sources
practically no Roman trade of importance, and certainly no evidence except in the Gracchan days that the

[14] Digest, 50, 5, 3.

[15] Mommsen, *Rom. Hist.* III, 238; Heitland, *The Roman Republic*, II, 156. My point of view, presented more fully in *Am.
Hist. Rev.* 1912-13, 233, is defended by Holleaux, *Rome, La Grèce
et les Mon. Hell.* 85 ff. See also Hatzfeld, *Les Trafiquants italiens
dans l'Orient.* Rostovtzeff, *Soc. and Econ. Hist.* p. 21, reverts to
the old theory that the Roman wine and olive growers urged the
destruction of Carthage in order to remove competition in these
products. Since Carthage did not then have enough land to support herself (the *fossa regia* lay only fifty miles west of Carthage)
and was importing wine, and since the Romans left intact the
best olive country of the Liby-Phoenician towns there seems to
be no support for this hypothesis.

state cared to encourage Roman traders. After Hannibal met defeat Rome still permitted Carthage to close
its seas,[16] a fact that reveals an unconcern almost in-
credible; and when Carthage finally fell in 146 Rome
provided no harbor in Africa for her own province,
permitting Utica, a free city, to inherit the trade and
even to handle the produce of such Romans as settled
in the new province. In the province of Sicily Rome
established no port-exemptions or preferences for herself.[17] In the allied city of Ambracia[18] by the treaty of
189 Rome asked indeed for customs immunities but
explicitly provided that these should also be extended
to all the allies, including in the provision the Greek
trading cities of Magna Graecia which were Rome's
real commercial rivals, if indeed Rome had any commerce at the time. Similarly though Rome had helped
her ally Marseilles to subdue the hill-tribes of Savoy in
135, and by her joint signature to the treaty aided
Marseilles in establishing her wine trade in the subdued
country,[19] she nevertheless refrained throughout her
career from imposing similar provisions in favor of
her own commerce, whether in Spain, Africa, Asia, or

[16] Peter, *Hist. Rom. Frag.* p. 273, fr. 9.

[17] The request of Rhodes for permission to buy grain in Sicily
in 169 is sometimes taken to imply a general control of the trade
in Sicily, Polyb. 28, 2. However this request was made when
Rome was at war and needed the grain. Cicero (Verr. V, 145
and 157) shows that commerce in Sicily was generally free.

[18] Livy, XXXVIII, 44.

[19] See *Roman Imperialism*, p. 280. Cicero, *de Rep.* 3, 9 (dra-
matic date 129 B.C.) lets a critic of Rome cite a prohibition of

her own Gallic provinces. Again, upon giving Delos to Athens after the third Macedonian war, Rome stipulated that it should be a free port for all nations. Rome's advantage doubtless lay in securing a place where her armies and navies when engaged in the East might procure supplies at reasonable prices. But the commercial profits fell to the numerous traders of Greece, Syria, and Egypt who soon made Delos an important trading center. It is merchants from these places that occupy the most space on the numerous Delian inscriptions of the second century. To be sure the names of not a few Occidentals also occur but upon examination these prove to belong to south-Italian

---

wine-raising in Savoy as Roman. This criticism was of course answered in the next book, which is lost. The fact that Marseilles took and kept the hostages after the war in Savoy shows that the treaty was merely underwritten by Rome. Rostovtzeff, *op. cit.* p. 22 goes so far, on the basis of this meager evidence, as to speak of "the prohibition of vine-planting in the newly acquired western provinces of Rome." There was no such prohibition for Spain, see Pol. 34, 8; Varro I, 8, 1; I, 31, 1; Strabo 3, 2, 6; 3, 4, 16. Proconsular Africa is too dry to raise much wine, so that we hear little of it there, but *Bell. Afr.* 43 and 67 prove that viticulture was not prohibited. As for Gaul, Diodorus, V, 26, held the opinion that it was too cold for vines north of Marseilles, and Varro I, 7, 9 says that in going to the Rhine he has seen places where there were no vines, but that implies that vines did grow in others. Neither author seems to be aware of a prohibition. In Strabo's day, IV, 1, 2, there were vineyards in the Cevennes. There is in fact no evidence that Rome forbad vine or olive culture anywhere during the Republic. Later Domitian limited viticulture in Italy as well as in the provinces, but seems to have relented.

Greeks and Campanian traders,[20] until some years after the province of Asia was acquired. Very few Roman merchants had any share in the great prosperity of the island before that time. Finally we may recall that during the Republic commercial interests at Rome were not powerful enough to procure the slight appropriation necessary to make a road-stead at Ostia capable of accommodating sea-going vessels.

Until the Emperor Claudius improved the harbor of Ostia all the larger vessels put in at Puteoli,[21] a hundred and fifty miles from Rome. Indeed the ancient world has no record of any state of importance so unconcerned about its commerce as was the Roman Republic.

In the preceding pages the inference has continually been drawn that Rome's constant acquisition of new lands turned men and capital away from commerce and industry into fields more congenial, and that herein lies the chief reason for Rome's circumscribed economic interests. It may be well to consider more fully how this restriction reacted upon society in such a way as to create peculiar moral inhibitions and even social groupings by the aid of which the natural economic evolution that we have traced justified itself to the

[20] Hatzfeld, *Bull. Corr. Hell.* 1912 and *Les Trafiquants italiens.* 1919. The sacred island was a Mecca for pilgrims from all Greek cities, and as such had a just claim to a free port.

[21] For Puteoli as a harbor in Cicero's day see Cic. *Verr.* V, 154; *In Vat.* 12; *Rab. Post.* 40; *de Fin.* II, 84, and Strabo, IV, 6. It will be recalled that even St. Paul on his way to Rome disembarked here and made the rest of the journey by the Appian Way.

Roman consciousness. Such a consideration may reveal the reasons why the *a priori* methods of interpreting historical development by means of generally accepted economic and psychological maxims must be applied to Roman history only with great reserve. It will be noticed particularly that those forces which in modern societies find effective expression through universal suffrage and a ready hearing through facile means of communication then failed frequently to reach even the organs of government. In the Roman Republic it is not safe to infer that a great need or a strong desire felt by a certain class or group eventually manifested itself in a governmental act or law.

For instance, the laboring classes which are now strong enough to modify to their advantage practically every financial, industrial, or commercial bill passed by a modern law-making body, could in Cicero's day exert but slight pressure upon the government. There the laboring man was either a slave whose voice was never heard, or a client who, considering his own advantage, voted as his patron told him. Even if he chose to vote independently his ballot was usually cast in one of the four city wards with those of ex-slave offspring. He could not organize to elevate his economic position, though a free man, for slave wages and slave conditions of life determined his own. In a thousand years of Rome's history there is not one labor strike recorded. He got only what the ruling powers saw fit to give him, and that usually was charity at most. In a word he had great needs but he had no way of exerting effective pressure upon the government to procure what he needed.

When we turn from the employee to the employer, we again find a similar difference between Roman and modern conditions. Whereas in a modern industrial state the business man has come to be the controlling power not only in society but in the government, he was at Rome so far from being a leading citizen that even Cicero, who needed him for his *concordia ordinum,* found it possible to discuss whether he was quite respectable.[22] Cicero concluded that he was! But Cicero was equally sure that any man who went to the provinces on a business tour lacked the instincts of a true Roman: a worthy citizen could hardly leave the center of civilization for mere financial reasons. If wealth had been able to gain for men social and political prestige at Rome, the nobility could not have excluded capitalists from the Senate as they did till Caesar's day. The *novus homo* seldom made his way to the consulship, and, when the miracle was performed, it was not through financial power but through forensic ability or military prowess. The Roman Republican government was in fact blind to the political value of a soundly based industry and commerce, and failed to appreciate the relatively few Romans of ability who engaged in these pursuits. It might have devised tariffs and subsidies in aid of those who were facing foreign competition, but it did not. A lobby of manufacturers and shippers in the Roman Senate is

[22] Cic. *ad Quint.* I, 1, 15; *de Off.* I, 151; *Pro Flacco,* 91.

quite inconceivable to one who knows Roman society and manners intimately. There was economic conflict enough, but the pressure was seldom exerted through political channels: apparently in this case it was the social caste-system that acted as a barrier.

To be sure the man of wealth gained some recognition in a limited field, that is, where the civil service needed him. Since the Roman Republic with its frequent changes of executives could not build up permanent bureaus and boards for revenue-collecting and public works, it needed the capitalist to carry the contracts, and for this service it was willing to grant him a title, a ring, and a seat in the theater. Consequently the *equites* became a well organized political influence in the last century of the Republic, and latterday expansion was in some measure attributable to this class. But it is interesting to note that in this particular instance social position was gained through semipolitical service to the state, and that this position was definitely conceived of as quite inferior to that of the ruling nobility.

The agricultural class on the other hand was very powerful during most of the Republic. The farmers and land-owners were probably in control of all the rural tribes, and their interests often coincided with those of the senators, who usually owned large tracts of land. It is rather surprising therefore that we never hear of laws to protect Roman farm produce. However, even if we cannot find in Roman legislation any traces of positive measures in favor of the farmers, we may perhaps attribute to their predominance the apathy of the government to industrial and commercial needs, an unenlightened revenue system, a cumbersome financial policy, and the exclusion of the intricate problems that generally arise from economic conflicts.

However, it was difficult to secure common action on the part of the farmers. Being without ready means of transportation, they had to consider the advantages of the market nearest at hand, and thus this group readily split into various diverse factions, each moved by different interests. Perhaps this is why we can point to so little positive legislation that clearly bears the granger stamp. The influence of the landed class showed itself early in a desire for safety on the border and consequently well ordered relations between tribes. As has often been said, the prospering farmer in the open plains had all to lose and nothing to gain from a state of border-brigandage, so that he became a convert to faith in the sacredness of vested interests. Then he organized his military machine and struck back at the raiders till he converted them to his views—not forgetting to exact an indemnity, and, in special cases, applying the doctrine of dreadfulness. The economic factor was therefore of great importance in shaping the Latin federation, but that does not imply that it was or could be organized to secure immediate economic ends.

The nobility which directed Rome's policies could of course usually express their desires in action, and their economic interests, which were fairly uniform, were probably not neglected. We have seen that they paid far too little heed to the needs of industry and commerce on the one hand, and of the laboring classes on the other. To their own desires they were naturally not so heedless, though we need not assume that these desires were always of a material nature. The average Roman noble was rather hard and practical, prudently calculating, not very sentimental, but on the whole fairly just. Material interests were very important to him, for he must conserve his property qualifications or fall below his class. For this purpose he needed to have his lands well managed and to receive legacies from his clients. But the motives that might influence a senator were many and various. Now it is plausibly said that, since man is engaged in acquiring property most of his waking hours, he naturally employs to the same end what political power he may have. If we are to apply this test to the Roman senator, however, we need to keep in mind that most of the influences about him were not of an economic nature. He was not a business man, and he spent very little of his time with his own material concerns. Problems of state and judicial or legal service usually engaged his attention, so that his daily concerns naturally kept him less occupied with the economic viewpoint than is true of men in general, and since he held his seat for life he did not have to serve the material needs of a constituency in return for votes.

Since the economist takes cognizance of environment, we may consider how this affected the Roman senator.

From boyhood he lived in the presence of the *imagines* of his ancestors. Some of them had died on the battle field, some had triumphed, some bore names that were inscribed upon laws, and treaties, and dedicated temples. There were among them consuls, judges, orators, governors of provinces—there were no captains of industry. They had won the *memoria sempiterna* that Roman history held before man as his highest goal. Could the sons of a noble pass daily before those statues and not be kindled with a yearning for *gloria? Nullam enim virtus aliam mercedem laborum periculorumque desiderat praeter hanc laudis et gloriae*—a sentence that had not yet lost its meaning even in the days of civil strife that made the best of men cynical. No people has ever more treasured the glories and the virtues of ancestors. The nobles themselves wrote the nation's history: Fabius, Cincius, Postumius, Cato, Piso, Fannius, Sempronius, and a score of others. They embodied their deep respect for brave deeds in their institutions: the *laudatio funebris,* the triumphal arch, the honorary dedications, the heroic burial, the pomp of triumph, and all the rest. To catch the spirit that entered these men one must read Vergil's "masque of heroes" or Livy's epic of seven centuries. The irresistible determination, the power of self-control, the stolid puritanism, as well as the hardness and self-sufficiency of the native old Roman were racial qualities, a part of the blood inheritance transmitted after centuries of hard-handed struggle had weeded out the unfit. In the old Roman noble that inheritance was

not so diluted that his *virtus* did not quickly respond to
the appeal of ancestral memories. It was not till the
civil wars cut down the old race, emancipation and immigration mixed the blood, and overmuch prosperity
induced parasitism, that time-honored ideals went for
nought.

As we have said, daily occupation with the political
and diplomatic problems of state somewhat blinded the
Roman noble to the economic point of view. He dealt
with the intricacies of a hundred treaties made with
free, allied, and tributary states; he must consider the
state's relations with scores of tribes in every degree
of civilization or barbarism all along the border; there
were always provinces to keep satisfied, governors to
appoint and supervise, armies to levy, shift, and direct.
All these matters involved niceties of legal interpretation, of etiquette, position and honors. Engaged in
these problems he grew legal-minded and pompous,
but he was hardly likely to become obsessed with the
ideal of a "business administration." That the Roman
Senate never devoted half enough attention to economic questions is largely due to this preoccupation
with diplomatic, political, and ceremonial concerns.

Finally, the desire to conserve their own position and
power, the *auctoritas senatus,* both for the sake of personal prestige and for the pecuniary advantages which
the position entailed, taught the nobility to maintain
a conservative régime. If, for instance, some individual consul advocated a war of expansion the Senate
was likely to oppose him. The aristocracy had in fact

learned early that when a small city-state extended its boundaries too far, a large army was needed to hold the empire, and a popular leader of the army was a menace to aristocratic control.

It would seem, therefore, that Rome was one of the states where the normal economic pressure generally met with strong counteracting forces. The laboring man could not reach the attention of the governing class, the industrial interests were weak and their value underrated. The farmers were so separated geographically that their interests failed to coincide, and the nobility were so pre-occupied with purely administrative problems and so jealous of their own prestige that they gave little thought to economic measures. In general it must be said that the Roman economic problems were unusually simple. The gradual conquest of Italy and the provinces more than occupied the surplusage of capital and population so that there was no crying need for industry and commerce. The returns from the simple investments in land and in capitalistic enterprise sufficed to keep the people in prosperity, and presently in flabby desuetude. The intricacies of our economic system, therefore, never threw their inordinate strain upon the government of Rome; and the charge that Livy and Tacitus wrote political history because they were "economic-blind" misstates the case: they wrote as they did because they grasped clearly the essential facts of Roman society.

CHAPTER VIII

THE GRACCHAN REVOLUTION

THE middle of the second century B. C. found Rome in a ferment of discontent. Under the leadership of the philhellene aristocracy the state had engaged in entangling alliances throughout Greece and the East which were now compelling Rome to decide whether she would endure daily insults as a "friend" or assume control. She chose the second alternative though with many misgivings; for the senate dreaded the military power that empire necessitated, and the democratic leaders feared the power and prestige that would accrue to the senate from provincial administration. In a word, questions of foreign policy had become so hopelessly interwoven with every domestic problem that the simplest reform could not be discussed on its merits. The irritating questions of government threatened to divide Rome into hostile factions.

By this time too the very stock of Rome had begun to change, not through immigration but through the accretion of manumitted slaves and war captives. Doubtless the jibe of Aemilianus overshot the fact when he claimed that he had led to Rome in chains the hordes that now validated the revolutionary bills of Gracchus. But the phrase would have passed as pointless had there not been much truth in it. That reform

127

through orderly compromise now gave way to revolution through bloodshed is largely due to the displacement of real Italic peoples by men of Oriental, Punic and Iberian stock.

Finally the evil consequences of the over-benevolent leasing system now began to lower over the whole land. The lease-holders had soon gained possession of all vacant lands thereby precluding new distributions to a growing generation. But more than that, holding an advantage over the settlers who tried to work their plots by precarious hand-to-mouth methods, they even encroached upon and gained possession of many such holdings. For the sixty years before the Gracchan reforms, during a period when war casualties counted for little, the citizen-population of Rome increased not at all. Apparently the peasantry lost courage and withdrew to the provinces, or into the uncounted riff-raff of the cities.

It was a young aristocrat, Tiberius Gracchus,[1] the friend and associate of a group of moderates that read

[1] The chief accounts are found in Appian, *B. C.* I, 1-26, and Plutarch's lives of Tiberius and Gaius Gracchus. Greenidge and Clay, *Sources for Roman History*, have a convenient collection of most of the other ancient references. The introductory chapters in Greenidge, *A History of Rome*, give an admirable review of social and economic conditions. His chapters on the Gracchi, and those of Heitland, *The Roman Republic*, II, are the best surveys of the Gracchan reforms. See also E. Meyer, *Kleine Schriften*, p. 383; Cardinali, *Studi Graccani*, 1912; De Sanctis, in *Atene e Roma*, 1920-21; Von Stern, in *Hermes*, 1921; Münzer, art. *Sempronius*, in Pauly-Wissowa. The fragments of the Gracchan speeches are collected in Meyer, *Orat. Rom. Frag.*, and Haepke, *C. Semproni Gracchi fragmenta*.

Stoic philosophy at leisure moments, who had the
courage and faith to attempt agrarian reforms which
seemed to promise social and political amelioration.
He had observed while travelling through Etruria, that
the plantation system fed upon slavery which he,
keener visioned than his contemporaries, held to be an
evil in itself. In his election speeches, fragments of
which have survived, he argued that such a system
could not provide the strong body of yeomen needed
by the army of a growing state. But he went further
and appealed to humanitarian ideals as well, and,
adopting a social theory then gaining support among
Greek publicists, he assumed that the state owed to its
citizens in return for loyal services a parcel of land
on which they might earn a livelihood. His proposal
was to reclaim the public lands that were held contrary
to the quantitative restrictions of the old Licinian law,
and to distribute these in small lots to Roman citizens
as inalienable leaseholds at low rentals.

The senators discussed the bill and rejected it. They
argued the injustice of reasserting a claim to lands that
the state had overlooked for generations, that had in
fact been improved at no little expense by the holders
and had to some extent passed by testament or purchase to others. They also reminded the Italian peoples who had been admitted to such lands that if the
Gracchan measures were adopted they would probably
lose their holdings to Roman citizens, and that a Roman
commission would probably not give allotments to
them.

Tiberius, balked by the senate, revived the long dor-
mant provision of the constitution of 287 which permitted a referendum[2] to the plebeian assembly of
legislative proposals. When, however, he called for a
vote, a fellow tribune, Octavius, as was his legal right,
interposed a veto. Tiberius refusing to be blocked then
proposed a measure legalizing the "recall' of tribunes
who acted contrary to the wishes of their constituents.
The measure passed amid cries and charges of rebellion. Forced through as the measure was without adequate constitutional justification, the act was near
rebellion, and few there were who later revived the
precedent. But Tiberius' instinct was right. The tribune was not originally intended to be a magistrate of
the state, but rather an advocate and patron of a class
or of individuals and as such subservient to the needs
of his constituency. Furthermore the enlargement of
the board of tribunes to the unwieldly number of ten
had not been intended to provide division within the
board but only to extend its capacity for action over a
large area. After tribunes began to sell their services
to checkmate each other the original purpose of the
board was defeated, and only by reducing its number
virtually or actually to one could its efficiency be restored; that at least the introduction of the "recall"
would accomplish. In any case the assembly had been

[2] F. F. Abbott, *The Referendum and Recall among the Ancient
Romans*, Sewanee Review, 1915. The theory of the recall was
again successfully applied in Cicero's day: Asconius, *In Cor-
nelianam*, ed. Kiess. p. 64.

empowered by the constitution of 287 to try whatever legislative experiment it might desire, though it was in duty bound to employ less abridged methods than Tiberius used on this occasion.

Thus by revamping the machinery of popular sovereignty Tiberius passed his drastic agrarian law. He had a judicial commission elected with powers to examine and adjudge titles and to distribute the lots. The senate still attempted to impede the execution of the law, and indeed after the death of Tiberius succeeded in nullifying the powers of the commission, but some of the boundary stones erected by it are still in existence, and if Mommsen's contention is correct that an increase of 73,000[3] names on Rome's census list of the year 125 B. C. betokens an increase of approximately that many land-holders, the committee must have worked with great success. Fate has generously spared a milestone[4] erected by the consul Popilius, the chief opponent of Tiberius, on which he had inscribed the

[3] See Mommsen, *Rom. Hist.* III, 335. Beloch, *Die Bevölk.* p. 308, questions this interpretation because he believes that the citizen-rolls included only property owners, whereas these allotments were technically leaseholds. But it is now clear that all male citizens were supposed to be registered (*Roman Census Statistics, Class. Phil.* 1924, 329). Since few proletarians had been levied for army service before the Gracchan period, no serious effort had been made to enroll them in the census; but these new leaseholders would certainly be desirable for army service and were doubtless listed on the census rolls. Tiberius in fact had urged his reform partly on the basis of military needs.

[4] A milestone in Lucania on the new military road leading from Capua to Sicily. The sentence reads: Eidemque primus fecei ut de agro poplico aratoribus cederent paastores. C.I.L.I, 551.

surprising record: "I first compelled the grazers to give back the public land to tillers." One is almost tempted to hazard a guess that some sarcastic workman inserted the line for amusement. But perhaps Popilius was after all a shrewd politician who knew when to steer with the wind.

Tiberius' attempt to secure re-election resulted in a riot in which he was killed, and his work soon came to a stand-still. His brother Gaius, however, reached the same office in 124 and continued the work with a widely expanded program. He at once re-enacted his brother's agrarian law and put it into operation; he secured corn doles for the poor of the city at half-price; he had the tax-collection of the province of Asia auctioned to corporations of knights; one bill deprived the Senate of its usurped power to appoint judicial committees, another deprived the senators of the right to sit as jurymen or judges in the courts, transferring this office to the knights; and finally he proposed an extensive plan of colonization, and promised to support a bill granting Roman citizenship to the Latins and ultimately to all Italians.

Gaius Gracchus is still an enigma to us since the documents upon which our later sources rest were all written in the bitterest spirit of partisanship whether for or against the tribune. From the fragments of his speeches[5] quoted verbatim, though often excerpted with evil intent, it is clear that he sometimes acted in

[5] Meyer, *Orat. Rom. Frag.* pp. 224 ff., Haepke, *C. Semproni Gracchi fragmenta.*

the spirit of a party leader, who could when need arose propose measures of little general value in order to gain adherents and strengthen his *bloc*. That he even struck at his opponents in a purely vindictive manner seems demonstrable from his own words. These facts however must not be allowed to weigh seriously in the judgment of his main program or in the interpretation of doubtful points. In pagan Rome, not yet very far from the age of the vendetta, vindictiveness under the sting of a brother's murder was accepted as reasonable and, in fact demanded by considerations of *pietas*. The only question that concerns us at present is whether the pursuit of vengeance blurred the vision or misdirected the ultimate blow when the great task of reform called for completion. And it must be admitted that no legislative act of his actually passed which was not fully justified from the point of view of his program.

As for the intrusion of party politics, we are seldom able to say what measures were merely means to an end, intended to be annulled or neutralized after the goal was reached. The monthly distribution of corn to the poor at half price was cited by his opponents as a case of mere bribery. This may be correct. But, it is also possible that Gaius instituted this measure by way of temporary relief to serve only until he could secure support enough to scatter the poor in the country by further colonization. Meanwhile the cheap grain served as part pay for work in the numerous enterprises in which he employed the urban laborers. It is, however, not unlikely that this was a frank experiment in state socialism suggested perhaps by his Stoic mentor, Blossius. We know that the theory that the state owed its poor a livelihood had become current in the East in the dreary days of the third century when Greece was slowly dwindling to futility.[6] And if Gracchus was touched with such humanitarian ideas the temptation was great, for the granaries of the state were full of wheat from Sicily which belonged to the people. They had but to vote a distribution to themselves of their own property. Why should they go hungry when the decision to open their own storehouses lay in their own hands?

The experiment to be sure led to disastrous results both in neutralizing the success of the Gracchan colonial schemes and, since few statesmen later dared oppose the charity, in a continued pauperization of the Roman populace. But the first experimenters in social legislation readily fall into errors, and recent experience has proved that states which have to face the exigencies of strenuous military duties take short cuts to the winning of a contented and well fed populace,

[6] Ditt. *Syll.*[3] 976; Rostowzew, art. *Frumentum* in *Pauly-Wissowa*, VII, 139. The Stoic philosopher Blossius, the teacher and companion of the Gracchi, seems to play the same role of social reformer in connection with his pupils that Sphaerus did who a century before encouraged Cleomenes to divide all property in Sparta. The Gracchi might also have learned of such movements in Greece from their personal conversations with Polybius, who was deeply interested in the career of the strange Spartan king. Cicero, *De Off.* II, 80, implies that the Gracchi followed the example of the Spartan kings: ex eo tempore tantae discordiae secutae sunt.

regardless of the future consequences to the general
morale.

Two other measures are usually credited to partisan
spirit, the transfer of jury service from the senators to
the men of wealth, the equites, and the displacement of
the native tax collectors in the province of Asia by
Roman publicans who gathered the dues by contract.
A fragment of a speech by Gracchus proves clearly that
in the former case the author fully realized that it
would create a division[7] between the nobility and the
knights, as of course it did. The significant political
consequence of the law which Diodorus[8] and other
critics of Gracchus emphasize, namely its effect in placing provincial governors at the mercy of the publicans,
could hardly have been contemplated or indeed foreseen
at the time of its passage, since that far distant result
was made possible only by the slowly accumulated effects of the contract law.

Gaius clearly had in view the curtailment of senatorial power, but if we bear in mind his peculiar faith
in business men and business methods we can readily
believe that Gaius desired most of all to elevate that
class in popular esteem by some form of official recognition and to enlist its good will and practical experience in public service. And though the record this
class afterward made as jurymen probably fell below

[7] Cic. de Leg. III, 9; Diodorus, XXXVII, 9.

[8] Diodorus, XXXV, 25. Diodorus followed Poseidonius who
represented the point of view of the Greek provincials and of the
Roman nobles with whom he was on friendly terms.

his expectations there is no evidence to show that it performed these services with less honesty and efficiency than the senators.

The collection of Asiatic tithes by contract, though like all work done by political contracts it led to much corruption, brought in a larger and more dependable revenue than could have been procured through the agency of local authorities, usually unfriendly, and too far distant to watch. Naturally a well organized civil service bureau, such as the empire finally provided, would have been more considerate of the taxpayer. But this was not yet possible since the republican constitution was based upon the idea that magistrates should hold office for but one year, and, obviously, important departments of state, being at the mercy of each administration, could hardly be durable under such a system. Political critics never tire of rehearsing the evils of the contract system, which is still perforce so largely used in modern democracies. To Gaius Gracchus the introduction of the contract was of course a step toward efficiency. He found that the tribute of Asia instituted a few years before was dwindling partly because some districts were incapable of financial administration, partly because the most capable of them would shirk the burden under any pretext. If he knew—as any Roman of experience must have known from complaints against the publicans engaged in Italy—that the companies would occasionally fall into the temptation to defraud and extort moneys, nevertheless he had reason to trust in the supervision of the proconsul or in the power of some Roman tribune to bring the guilty to punishment. At any rate both these measures reveal in Gracchus a faith and deep interest in the possessors of wealth, a trait that we have discovered some trace of in Appius Claudius and Flaminius, but hardly elsewhere.

It was the same sympathy with the commercial classes that led Gaius to conceive of a new class of colonies,[9] nothing less than seaport colonies, not this time simply to protect landing places against incursions, but to encourage Mediterranean commerce. When in 146 the great port of Carthage was destroyed the senate had been so negligent of commercial interests as to leave the new province of Africa dependent upon non-Roman ports like Utica for ingress and egress. This deficiency Gracchus proposed now to remedy by planting a citizen colony at Carthage. Tarentum also, partly ruined by the Punic War, was to have a colony of picked citizens who might develop the port to its old-time splendor. The need here was great since a large part of the recently allotted lands lay in southern Italy. A third colony of selected citizens was sent to Scylacium opposite Vibo, perhaps in response to the advice of merchants who preferred to have a portage there rather than risk the troublesome sail around through the straits of Messana. It will be remembered that Rome still found it practicable to get much of its merchandise by land transport all the way from Pu-

---

[9] Plut. *C. Gracch.* 6, 8, 10; App. *B. C.* I, 23; Livy, *Epit.* 60; Vell. II, 7. See Hardy, Six Roman Laws, p. 73.

teoli! In all these measures the tribune may have had the advice of the best business intelligence, since in his vast enterprises he constantly came in contact with men of large affairs.

The proposal upon which the young enthusiast went down to defeat—a proposal offering mere justice without any material benefit to the voter—was a bill giving citizenship to all possessors of Latin rights and *Latinitas* to all other Italians. His enemies saw in this a scheme merely to create a new electorate bound to him alone, though it is difficult to see why he should put in jeopardy his present support for a new constituency if power was his object. His purpose in this measure was partly to place the Italians in a fair position with reference to the agrarian law, partly to bring all Latins under the protection of the civil courts when suffering from the abuses of irresponsible Roman officials. Moreover, his outspoken interest in a sound citizen-body from which to draw soldiers for the army and his dislike for the freedman class that threatened to dominate the city justify the belief that he also saw in the measure great advantages for Rome.[10] The bill, however, raised unfulfilled hopes in the Italians, and its defeat hastened on the Social war.

[10] It is difficult to believe that a man of such clear vision as Gaius Gracchus could have intended to extend the franchise throughout Italy without taking the obvious step to make it effective by placing ballot boxes in every municipality. We have no direct proof of such intentions, but when Caesar, who borrowed many ideas from the Gracchi, took the first step in that direction just before his death by ordering the municipal census registry to be recorded at Rome, we may well conjecture that Gaius Gracchus had entertained some such plan. A single

The Gracchan reforms did not save Rome from the deserved penalties of her misdeeds. The more important measures were obstructed, those that passed were either modified by the senate or administered with so little of the spirit of the author that their benefits were largely neutralized and their evils exaggerated. The actual results belied all hopes and intentions. The agrarian laws doubtless improved central Italy and relieved Rome temporarily, but, left incomplete, they sowed the seeds of the Social war, whereas the continuation of the corn-doles soon brought the city to a worse condition than before. The *equites* were recognized in affairs of state, and this should have broadened the economic outlook of Roman statesmanship. Unfortunately when met and obstructed at every turn by the jealousy of the old aristocracy, they degenerated into a selfish faction satisfied to become parasites of the financial bureau, growing fat upon whatever capitalistic investments the new contract system threw in their way. The re-introduction of the principle of popular sovereignty was excusable only if the electorate could have been enlarged as the Gracchi intended. Without that reform the Roman populace was coming to be incapable of self-government, not to speak of the government of a world. And the breach

primary assembly for the whole of Italy was of course preposterous; men will not travel three hundred miles by horseback to vote. When Gracchus proposed the extension of citizenship there was no need to risk defeat for his bill by speaking of the next step, especially as the method of balloting could subsequently be changed by a censorial decree.

in the constitution produced by the attempt could not readily be healed when once the populace had thus recovered the machinery that made them all-powerful. The rehabilitation of the plebeian assembly therefore led directly to the civil wars and the Caesarian autocracy.

Of immediate interest to economists as a result of these contests are the elevation of the capitalist-mercantile class to a position of power in the state and in its financial enterprises, the closing of Italian lands for colonization, which directed capital into other channels, and the acceptance of the policy of state-charity for the poor of Rome which placed industry in the city at a discount for all time.

CHAPTER IX

The New Provincial Policy

During the Gracchan revolution Rome had acquired a peculiar province in Asia, and had opened the province of Africa to settlement in a new manner. These innovations were soon to bring private interests into politics, and it is not long before these interests influenced the course of territorial expansion.

The last of the Attalids had given his kingdom to Rome by will, a logical act since by far the larger part of the kingdom had been pared off from the Seleucid realm and assigned to Eumenes II by Rome. The new province of about 60,000 square miles was a social patchwork, the nature of which no Roman governor would even attempt to comprehend. Roughly one might divide it into two parts: autonomous Greek cities along the coasts and rivers, and a great number of petty agrarian fiefs of semi-free natives living in villages.[1]. The king of course had claimed ultimate ownership of such fiefs or at least the right to assign them at pleasure, but his profits from them had not been large, apparently a tribute of one-tenth of the value of the crop. The tenants usually held hereditary leases paying presumably about a half of the crop to the

[1] Ramsay, *Cities and Bishoprics*, 10 ff.; Cardinali, *Il Regno di Pergamo*, 96 ff., 173 ff.; Rostovtzeff, *Röm. Kol.* 253 ff.

feudal lord, and in addition were bound to devote a certain number of days to the cultivation of the lord's private land. The lord held his equity by purchase or as reward for service in the army or at court, and his fief was frequently hereditary and transferable, but subject to the good will of the king. There was, therefore, a well-developed feudal system throughout the rougher country, inherited through the Seleucids, Alexander and the Persian kings.

An inscription—dating about a generation before the Romans came—gives a good insight into the conditions on one of these estates.[2] It is the record of a mortgage in which Mnesimachus, presumably a favorite of the king, who holds his land in fief, pledges his equity as security for a loan of about $6,000, made him by the Temple of Artemis. The king, the landlord, and the many peasants all claim to different degrees possessory rights in the land. The territory, besides containing two small freeholds of about fifteen acres with six slaves, consists of five villages, the inhabitants of which are royal quasi-serfs, and two separate plots that are subject to a tribute payable to the king. Since this royal territory must provide a living to the peasants of the five villages besides a stipend (probably about a tenth, but payable in money) to the king, the landlord's returns could hardly have been more than a third of

[2] Buckler and Robinson in *Am. Jour. Arch.* 1912, 12 ff.; Wilamowitz dates this inscription in the second cent. B.C. (*Gött. Gel. Anz.* 1914, 89). The editors' interpretation of the statistics (p. 73) need revision.

the produce; but it was considerable since it sufficed to cover the mortgage recorded. The instrument does not state what his rental was, for it was probably the percentage that was customary in the region. It merely mentions somewhat loosely "dues rendered by the peasants in money and in labor" and "other revenues accruing from the villages." In other words the lord of the manor received a cash rental from the land, as well as certain days of work from the peasants to be expended upon his private allotment which he held in fee, and in addition he seems to have had the right to farm out concessions in the villages. There are other[3] inscriptions that prove this the normal condition throughout the non-Greek portion of the kingdom.

As for the Greek cities, several had been free and immune from stipend since the days of Alexander, and some from the time that Rome assigned Seleucid territory to Eumenes, but there is also evidence that on some the Attalids had gradually imposed stipends,[4] though not heavy ones, in return for protection. And it is also apparent that the cities usually owned villages of subject natives who paid tribute to them, as other villages paid tribute to the king.

In addition there were many old temples[5] which

[3] Cardinali, *Il Regno di Pergamo*, 182 ff. (with some confusion of royal estates with *ge basilike*) and Rostovtzeff, *Röm. Kol.* 240 ff. (where *idia* should be translated "special" not "private"); Cf. the gnomon of the Egyptian *Idios Logos* in P. Meyer, *Jur. Papyri*, No. 93.

[4] Cardinali, op. cit. p. 177.

[5] Rostovtzeff, in *Anatolian Studies Presented to Sir Wm. Ramsay*, 370.

owned territory on which semi-free peasants and
temple-owned slaves worked the land, for the temples
of Asia usually held property and disposed of large
sums of money. Several of these temples were immune from the royal stipend, but not all. In some
cases the king had assigned them stipendiary land, in
others they had acquired it by purchase; in such
cases they were held responsible for the stipend.
Finally the king owned[6] and exploited by use of his
slaves some royal estates, parks, gardens, and mines,
as well as factories where rugs (an old industry in
Anatolia), tapestries, parchment and the like were
manufactured under royal management.

Such was the strange inheritance. What would the
government of the Roman Republic do with this Asiatic
confusion? Would it preserve a feudal system and
recognize the fiefs by the side of free cities and theocratic estates, and would it continue to own the factories and become a large manufacturer as well? The
evidence regarding Rome's procedure is all too slight
and there is much diversity of opinion as to the actual
purport of what we have. In fact the Roman parties
quarrelled over the disposition of the property and in
the confusion they came to concern themselves about
the profitable exploitation rather than a reasonable
development of Asia.

It is clear that Tiberius Gracchus intended to convert
the king's movable and personal property into cash at

[6] Cardinali, *Il Regno*, 188 ff.; Rostovtzeff, in *Anatolian Studies*,
375.

once to pay for some of his expensive reforms.[7] He was killed, however, before he could bring the requisite administrative bill before the assembly. The senate[8] accordingly assumed its old functions in provincial affairs and sent out a commission of five senators to study the situation and propose a proper form of government. When they reached Asia they found that an illegitimate son of Eumenes had laid claim to the throne and raised a large army of slaves and semi-free peasants, presumably on promises of freedom and land. It is significant that he met with greatest favor among the barbaric mountaineers of that part of Anatolia which did not belong to the kingdom. After several successful battles he was taken captive and Aquilius was sent with a new commission to organize the province. This commission seems to have given liberty and immunity to the Greek cities, as Attalus had requested in his will.[9] Apparently the temple territories were also left immune from taxes.[10] There is no evi-

[7] Livy, *Ep.* 58; Plut. *Tib. Gracchus*, 14.

[8] Greenidge, *A Hist. of Rome*, 175 ff.; Chapot, *La province d'Asie*, 18 ff.

[9] Liv. *Epit.* 59; App. *B. C.* V, 4; However the Pergamenes overstepped their authority in presuming to give freedom to the king's slaves (Ditt. *Or. Inscr.* 338) and the commissioners disregarded their decree. It seems that a few communities were placed in the stipendiary class at once for having supported Aristonicus.

[10] The Romans seem at first to have been meticulous in the treatment of the temple properties. Strabo, 14, 1, 26, speaks of territories which the kings had taken but the Romans restored. We also have an inscription in which the people of Ilium express gratitude to the Roman censor of 89 B.C. for restoring sacred properties; Ditt. *Or. Inscr.* 440, with notes.

dence that any change was made in the crown lands in
which the semi-free villeins paid stipends, a large part
of which was controlled in old fiefs by wealthy lords.
To be sure we do not hear of feudal service on such
lands under Roman sway during the republic, but it
was not like the Romans to alter[11] native custom sud-
denly. The stipend was to be collected as before and
sent to Rome presumably by a questor under the supervision of the propraetor. The personal property of the
king was of course taken, the royal farms and gardens
becoming *ager publicus*. The factories and mines[12]
were probably closed, for the slaves were transported
to Rome. The senate would hardly care to enter into
industrial enterprises. The commission also proposed
to cut down the province into manageable proportions.[13] It advocated giving the whole of Phrygia to
the King of Pontus, and the mountain regions of Caria
and Pisidia were left to manage themselves. Apparently the senate did not intend to assume a task that
would require standing armies, and it was not inter-

[11] We must however not too readily assume that Roman pro-
consuls would recognize the institution of corvée, since the Greek
landlords and not the state benefited by it. It would to a Roman
seem a very illiberal practice. Aemilius Paulus, when propraetor
in Spain (189 B.C.), seems to have liberated the native serfs of
Punic Hasta, but that may have been for services rendered.
On the other hand Varro, *R. R.* I, 17, seems to imply that forced
labor was in his day customary in Asia, Egypt, and Illyricum.

[12] The quarries of Phrygian marble at Synnada were not extensively worked till the days of Augustus, Strabo, 12, 8, 14.

[13] E. Meyer, *Die Grenzen Kleinasiens*, 1925.

ested in possible commercial exploitation. If the province paid its own way while giving Rome a position of vantage in Asiatic politics, that was all that could be asked.

But Gaius Gracchus was not so hesitant. When he became tribune, and had spent large sums of the treasury on roads, streets, harbors and granaries he became aware that the Asiatic stipend, exacted with some lenience by the propraetor's questor, dwindled far below what had been expected. He also was too much of a democrat to comprehend why the Greek cities of Asia, which Rome long ago had taken from Antiochus, should go immune while the peasants continued to pay the old stipend. And he saw no reason for throwing away Phrygia. Since the knights had shown themselves efficient contractors at Rome, they might well be employed for the farming of the Asiatic taxes. This method would bring in the funds at once when wanted, it would please the knights, it would take the financial responsibility away from the governor of the province, and lastly it would enable Rome to institute taxes in kind which would be less burdensome to the peasants in lean years. And so by a vote of the assembly the senate's settlement of Asia was revised, the cities were subjected to the tithe on their landed territories (which of course were relatively small) and Phrygia was brought back into the province.[14]

It is the common opinion at present that in this settle-

[14] App. *B. C.* V, 4; Cic. *Verr.* 3, 12; Diod. 35, 25; C. Gracchus, *apud* Gell. 11, 10.

ment the Roman government took the legal view that
the vast rural regions of Asia which had been stipendiary and considered "crown land" by the kings of
Pergamum now became Roman *ager publicus*.[15] This
theory is very difficult to accept. The time came perhaps during Caesar's dictatorship or Augustus' régime
when the Roman lawyers devised the doctrine of
dominium in solo provinciali. The date of this interpretation cannot now be established, but there is no
trace of it in the treatment of Asia during the Republic.
To be sure the territory of Carthage had become *ager
publicus* in 146, but Carthage had been taken after a
long siege and treated as war booty. Even when
Caesar conquered Gaul there is no evidence that the

[15] This view has been widely accepted from Rostovtzeff, *Röm.
Kol.* p. 287 ff. but without substantial evidence. Strabo, for instance, does not say that Cato sold the *chora basilike* of Cyprus;
the *agri Attalici* of the Chersonese are classed by Cicero (*Leg.
Agr.* II, 51) among kings' estates, not among crown domains;
we do not know of "several procurators" of the Emperor Augustus in Asia; and finally the view that the patrimonial estates of
the Pisidian region derived from *ager publicus* through Antony
is not supported by any evidence. We have as yet no evidence
of *ager publicus* passing directly into imperial estates in the early
Empire. Where we can trace such estates they come by inheritance or confiscation from the estates of wealthy landlords. It
is far more likely that these imperial domains derive from the
confiscations of the Claudian emperors as did those of Africa.
The suggestion of Ramsay, *Cities and Bishoprics* 10 ff., developed
by Cardinali, *Il Regno*, 182 ff. that these domains grew by the
seizure of sacred lands is also unlikely. Finally Cicero's list
(*Leg. Agr.* II, 49-51) of public lands that might be sold in the
East proves that not even Caesar's party had in 63 B.C. adopted
the theory that stipendiary or decuman territory was *ager
publicus*.

conquered territory was considered a Roman estate. It is, therefore, very probable that Rome continued to levy the Attalid tax in Asia as she had the Hieronic tithe in Sicily without examining the Oriental theory of royal ownership, and that the land was simply considered decuman and stipendiary rather than *ager publicus*. In other words Rome took as public land in Asia only the estates which the king had owned in a private capacity and had given to Rome with his personal property.

However, though the extensive crown-lands were thus removed from the temptations of demagogues, there were enough seeds of contention in the possible exploitation of the tax-contracts to keep senate and knights embroiled. Even Gracchus, it seems, had intended that Phrygia should be an untaxed protectorate, but the knights gained entry in a few years and were not ordered to desist. They also made constant difficulties with the Greek cities, prying into their accounts to find out whether any parcel escaped attention, and no less into the temple-estates, which had held lands from the kings. Our records show that the Roman censors had to intervene time and again in behalf of the natives, but somehow the knights constantly enlarged their field of operations. To taxpayers who fell into debt they would lend money on mortgages at high rates and foreclose at the first opportunity. The Roman propraetors were constantly called upon by distressed natives for protection against unjust estimates (for the law was not drawn up with the

meticulous care of the Hieronic code in Sicily), and if
the propraetor proved unfriendly to the knights, a
charge might be trumped up against him at Rome[16]
where the court panels now consisted of knights. Nor
must it be supposed that the propraetors were always
blameless. They gradually assumed the right to station detachments of troops in the cities at the expense
of the cities. What the propraetor could in this way
save from the appropriation made by the senate for
the maintenance of his army he might turn back into
the treasury; but there are instances on record of
agreements between the praetor and the questor to
withhold such sums for their own use. Thus it was
that the privilege of exploiting Asia became lucrative
and led to quarrels between the senate and knights as
to the control of the courts at Rome.

While Rome was occupied with the social war in
89-88 B.C., Mithradates, the ambitious king of Pontus,
seized the opportunity to over-run and plunder the
province. He and his partizans put to death about
80,000 Italians found there. Many of these were of
course tax collectors, accountants in the service of the
tax farmers, besides agents and laborers who had to
collect, store, and dispose of the enormous quantities
of grain and fruit which the tithe produced. A chance
remark of Posidonius[17] to the effect that the Italians
in question tried to escape detection by doffing the
Roman garb which they had "recently assumed" indi-

[16] As in the case of Rutilius Rufus: Liv. *Epit.* 70; Vell. 2, 13.

[17] See note 21 chapter XV.

cates that most of them were men whose citizenship dated only from the end of the Social War. They were probably Greek and Oscan Italians who had gone into service with the Roman companies because they had long engaged in trade in the east and were acquainted with its language and customs. It is probable also that some of these south Italians had taken themselves off to the province, as many took to piracy, when the Social War broke out, in order to escape participating in a dubious contest. To what extent citizens of Rome had migrated to Asia by this time we cannot say: some there would certainly be, but their number could not have been large.

This raid in which Greek cities were compelled by Mithradates to share was the beginning of a series of disasters to Roman capitalists as well as to Asia. Sulla did not improve conditions when four years later in order to pay his army—now no longer recognized by the democratic government at Rome—he demanded the immediate cash payment to himself of the tithe for the five years of delinquency and in addition a "war-indemnity" to be paid in installments, making a dreadful total of 20,000 talents.[18] And to get this money he did not employ the Roman tax gatherers, but divided the province into districts which he held responsible each for its definite share.[19] Every community

---

[18] Appian, *Mith.* 62, Plut. *Sulla*, 25.

[19] Cic. *ad Q. Fr.* 1, 1, 33; *pro Flacco*, 32; Plut. *Luc.* 4; Cassiod. *Chron.:* XLIV regiones. Lucullus was left by Sulla to gather the cash contributions and the installments directly by districts.

had of course to find the money as best it could, mort-
gaging its public buildings, harbors, and common lands.
The temples which carried on an extensive banking
business doubtless took such mortgages so long as their
funds lasted, but it would seem that Italian bankers
and Roman knights became heavily involved in Asiatic
loans at this time.   One wonders how the tax was
gathered in the old fiefs in the rural districts where
the tenants seldom saw money and had but little grain
after paying their tithe to the state and their rent to
the lord.   The lords of the manors must have had to
meet the payments for their tenants.   Many must have
mortgaged their estates to agents of Roman capitalists,
and since Mithradates was still near and Sulla was
setting off for Rome with his army the risk was hazardous and the interest rate unusually high, rising in
some instances to forty-eight per cent.   In such conditions the debts increased rapidly and the agents of the
Roman knights were soon at hand placing new loans
as the installments came due.   In fourteen years the
debt of 20,000 talents had thus risen[20] to 120,000.
Meanwhile every time Mithradates stirred a shiver ran
through the banking quarters at Rome, and when he

During this period and at least for the collection of the tribute of
five years the contract system was in abeyance.   Since Sulla
abolished the censorship it is not unlikely that it was his intention
to dispense with the contract system altogether, as I suggested
in *Rom. Imperialism*, p. 326.   Holmes, *The Roman Republic*, I,
p. 395, does not think Sulla made a permanent change.   The
knights were back in Asia in the year 70 at any rate.

[20] Plut. *Luc.* 20.

invaded Bithynia in 74 there was a panic.[21]   Faith in
the senate's willingness to protect Roman investments
had overreached itself.

The senate assigned one of its favorite members,
Lucullus, to take charge of the war, though his province was Cilicia.   When he had driven the enemy back
he looked into the affairs of the suffering province and
issued a proconsular edict that won him the abiding
hatred of the money-lenders.   He fixed[22] the maximum
interest rate at twelve per cent., and canceled all interest that exceeded the amount of the principal, which
—since the debts had now run about fifteen years—
had the effect of reducing the actual return on the
original loans to about six per cent.   Then by imposing a tax on slaves and on houses, but limiting annual
exactions to a fourth of the crop, he arranged to have
the residue completely wiped out in four years.   However the relief had been long delayed, and there can be
no doubt that many mortgages had been foreclosed.
In the correspondence of Cicero during the middle
decade of this century there is abundant evidence that
many Romans had come into possession of estates in
Asia.[23]   We may suppose that various cities had in
their distress surrendered some of their lands, but the

[21] Cic. *Imp. Pomp.* 15-19.

[22] Appian *Mith.* 83; Plut. *Luc.* 20-23, Cic. *Acad. Prior.* II, 3;
Ad Att. V, 21, 11-13.

[23] Cic. *Quint. Fr.* I, 2, 6-10; *Fam.* I, 3, 1; XIII 43; 44; 45; 55;
56; 57; 66; 72 (Caerellia); *pro Flacco*, 31 and 70; Verr. II, 1,
69, 73-74, etc.   Cf. Früchtl, *Geldgeschäfte bei Cicero*, 1912.

landlords who had to face the responsibility of financing their tenants must have suffered most, and many of them doubtless surrendered their properties to the Roman creditors. Such land continued of course to pay the tithe to the Roman treasury, but it stands to reason that powerful Roman landowners could not be exploited by the publicans in the manner that natives had been, and thus an economic counter-force hostile to the publicans gradually grew up at Rome. How these diverse interests gained expression in politics at home and exerted pressure on the government to extend the empire eastward we shall discuss in the next chapter.

The province of Africa dates from the fall of Carthage in 146 B.C. The province as we have only recently learned[24] was at first very small, and half of the province taken was left to old Phoenician towns that were made autonomous and permitted to keep their territories—in fact with considerable additions. The boundary of the province was drawn about fifty miles west of Carthage to pass east of Vaga and Thugga. Thence it came eastward as far as Apthungi only thirty miles from the eastern coast, whence it ran almost due south to Thenae, just skirting the territories of the free Phoenician cities of Hadrumetum, Leptis, Thapsus, and Acholla. What Rome actually had to dispose of was only the square of about 50x50

[24] The boundaries and early Roman settlements of Africa I have discussed with references in *Am. Jour. Phil.* 1926, 55-73.

miles near Carthage (about a twentieth of the area of New York state), and even here the free town of Utica with its territory cut out a segment.

Since Carthage was destroyed and those who had not fled to Numidia were swept off as captives, Rome, following an old Italian custom in regard to war-booty, declared the territory public property. Rome, in need of money, had tried to sell this land as private tax-paying property,[25] but with little success. The native Berber population of small farmers and shepherds who still lived here and there in the hilly country north, west and south of the plains were accordingly encouraged to stay where they were, being made stipendiary as they had been while subjects of Carthage. We find later that several native villages remained and prospered.

In 122, since much of the good land still lay fallow, Gracchus[26] sent a colony here of about 6,000 settlers, giving each man a surprisingly large lot of 200 jugera (about 130 acres). It had been usual to give only twenty and thirty jugera in Italy; apparently Africa was not very attractive to Italians. Probably four-fifths of the plain-land was thus disposed of in free gifts.[27] This land was now private property to be held in full title, and as in Italy without payment of taxes. On the death of Gracchus the senate annulled

[25] See *Lex. Agr.* C. I. L. I, 585, l. 78.

[26] Liv. *Epit.* 60; *Lex. Agr.* C. I. L. I, 585, l. 59; Oros. V. 12.

[27] See Barthels, *Bonn. Jahrb.* 1911, for the colonial survey; and Cichorius, *Röm. Studien*, p. 113, for the colonial commission.

his colonial organization, but gave title to the settlers, and we may presume that a large proportion of them remained.

There was still vacant land, presumably less desirable plots in the hills. The censors of 115 accordingly decided to rent this out on five-year tenures[28] at whatever rental they could get, the price naturally varying with the quality of the land. Romans, Latins, or natives could bid for it and the questor of Africa would have charge of collections which were to be turned over to publicans. This presumably disposed of what was left over, for the agrarian law[29] of 111, of which we have a large part of the text, confirmed previous dispositions and sent commissioners to Africa to record titles and settle disputes. This law speaks of four important groups of land: that which had been sold after the war to be private tax-paying property (a very small portion), that which was left in the hands of stipend-paying natives (some villages in the hills), that which was given outright in large farms by Gracchus, and the residue which was rented on five-year contracts by the censors of 115. As regards this last class the clause was added that the rental was not to be increased; it therefore became practically fixed and the renters were doubtless to remain as long as they proved to be satisfactory. The senate was apparently tired of conducting a troublesome real-estate business and wanted simplicity and continuity of policy.

[28] *Lex. Agr.* op. cit. 1.85.

[29] C. I. L. I, 585, 45-96. Also in Hardy, *Six Roman Laws*, p. 35.

The third class—of Gracchan colonists—was the most important, for they held excellent land in large farms. These men were now fairly wealthy landlords. In Italy, a farmer, with the tools and intensive methods then in vogue, seldom took the burden of more than ten or fifteen jugera of arable land. On the large Gracchan farms the owner must have needed a great deal of labor, and since the farming population was gone and the land had lain fallow for a generation, he must have resorted to the use of slaves. Since we find few traces of expensive Roman villas in this area, we can not be far from right in assuming that the owners generally went to live in Utica (as later in Carthage), conducting their farms through slaves under the management of a slave steward. This then was a peculiar area under the so-called *Jus Italicum* where extensive estates grew up on tax-free private land as in Italy, and there were very few regions like it in any of the provinces.

A second region[30] (an area of about twenty-five miles square) just west of the old Gracchan colony had a similar history. It is the tract that lies between Vaga and Thugga on both sides of the Bagradas river. It was hilly, with considerable unarable rock land, and subject to erosion, but blessed with a better rainfall than Carthage. Since the *fossa regia* drawn by Scipio in 146, which was the original boundary of "Africa," has now been found to run several miles east of Thugga, this tract must at first have belonged to Masi-

[30] See *Am. Jour. Phil.* 1926, 55 ff.

nissa's kingdom of Numidia. But it had been cleared,
terraced, and planted with great success by the Carthaginian landlords, and after them by Masinissa's
Numidians. During the Jugurthine war, 109-7 B.C.,
Metellus and Marius campaigned in this region, which
they found very prosperous. Marius, who had promised land to his recruits, doubtless had this country in
mind when making his promise, for he swept off several villages, and when his campaigns were over his
political henchman Saturninus[31] enacted a bill (100
B.C.?) giving lands "in Africa" for distribution to the
Marian soldiers. That this was the very country appears from the fact that at least two places within the
region, Uchi Maius and Thibaris, later assumed the
name *colonia Mariana*. New excavations will probably disclose inscriptions of the same kind in other
towns. Though the fact is not mentioned in our scanty
sources, we may assume that at the same time this
colonized area was at once incorporated in the African
province, and as it can be shown that the new provincial line ran down straight south from Thabraca and
east of Bulla Regia and Sicca we may consider this
tract between the old and the new boundary as the
Marian tract. There is a peculiarity about the political
organization of the region which indicates Marius' old-
fashioned system of settlement. His settlers were not
organized in urban communities—Appian tells us that
he had recruited largely from Italian farms—but by

[31] "*De Viris Illust.* 73; Sall. *Jug.* 87; C. I. L. VIII, p. 2590,
and no. 26270.

rural townships (*pagi*) as were the colonists of Campania after 211 B.C. Several towns of the region, notably Uchi, Thugga, Thignica, Agbia, Numluli, and Avenensis have a *civitas* of native villagers with Roman accretions and by its side a more important township (paganal) organization of citizen settlers.[32] Since according to later usage in Cisalpine Gaul the *pagani* are the barbarians and the *civitas* the Roman urban settlement, the real significance of this institution has escaped notice.

For the peculiar economic history of this district—which became in later days the region of the most famous of the imperial domains of Africa—this colonization of Romans on large lots about a group of Libyan villages proved to be of the utmost importance. It enabled the settlers to find skilled, acclimated, and willing tenants, thus freeing them from the cost and inconvenience of procuring slaves in great quantities; and this in turn developed a peculiar villa-system which was wholly different from the homeless latifundia that spread over the Gracchan tract in time. How many soldiers accepted lots here we are not told, but since the soldiers had seen the prosperity of the region we may suppose that many were willing to come. Since we are told that the lots were 100 jugera each we can estimate that five thousand or more might well have found arable land in the square of 25x25 miles that makes up the well-known region of imperial

[32] See the inscriptions in C. I. L. VIII for the differentiation of *pagus* and *civitas* in the places named.

estates. The land was doubtless given in full title, rent free and tax free, as lands in Italy had usually been bestowed. The natives that were left were of course stipendiary, and their tax seems to have been an eighth of the crop.

In the empire this appears from inscriptional evidence to be the region of large estates.[33] In view of the fact that these lands were tax-free and that the labor problem was permanently solved, the growth of large estates was to be expected. The original lots were large and invited extensive capitalistic ventures from the first. Though Marius had drawn largely on farmers, it is likely that the changes in climate and soil soon resulted in an economic differentiation, and we may well believe that some of the veterans failed, sold out and moved to more congenial surroundings, or upon loss of their property accepted tenancies from the more successful. At any rate vast estates absorbed smaller ones very quickly here. Since there was no large city in the vicinity the successful planter was apt to build his house on his farm, and, of course, proportionate to his success and ambition. About the house he employed the spare time of personal slaves to farm a portion for his own use and pleasure while the larger portion would be rented out in convenient plots to natives, who were abundant. When his wealth permitted he might decide to live in Carthage or Rome. He could employ a steward to manage the property,

[33] *A Commentary on the Inscription of Hr. Mettich;* in *Am.Jour. Phil.* 1926, p. 153.

or, since there were trustworthy citizens in the region, he might place one of these as head-tenant (conductor) who would make his profits by farming the home grounds, and would collect and market the owner's shares as a part of his work. It is this method of using *conductores* which has seemed so strange to historians who are acquainted only with Roman agricultural conditions, and they have long discussed the origin of the system. But when one observes the circumstances out of which the system grew, it proves to be wholly natural and logical.[34]

We have then two tracts in Africa, the Gracchan and the Marian, where tax-free land was held in fee with the same rights as in Italy but rarely elsewhere in the Roman world. Naturally these tracts became very desirable in the eyes of Roman investors, and it was not long before an "estate in Africa" became a synonym of wealth.[35] And here developed a system of tenantry, especially on the Marian tract, where there

[34] It has been customary to assume that the peculiar social and economic institutions found in this region derived from Hellenistic practices. It is far more probable that they developed out of local conditions as I have tried to show in *Am. Jour. Phil.* 1926, pp. 55-73.

[35] Horace, *Carm.* I, 1, 10; III, 16; *Sat.* II, 3, 87; Roman landowners in Africa during the Republic are mentioned in Nepos, *Atticus* 12 (Julius Calidus); Cic. *pro Cael.* 30 (Caelius); *ad Fam.* 12, 29 (Lamia, the Saltus Lamianus is later imperial), etc. There were three hundred Roman citizens at Utica who had contributed to the senatorial cause against Caesar. From this group Caesar exacted in 46 B.C. a fine of a hundred million sesterces (about five million dollars), which is evidence of large property-holdings there. Caes. *Bell. Afr.* 90; cf. Plut. *Cato*, 30.

were available the native renters of which we hear a great deal in the domanial inscriptions of the Empire.[36] The rest of the province of Africa was not of great importance during the republic for most of the arable part was held by the Punic cities, and the stipendiary villages in the hill-country paid fixed stipends to the government without the intervention of the publicans. It is not till Caesar refounded Carthage and annexed Numidia that Africa began to be reckoned as one of the important provinces.

Of conditions in the province of Spain during the republic we shall speak later. The province of Sicily concerned the Romans but little during the second century except in so far as decuman grain, about a million bushels a year, came to Rome. As a large part of this was used by the armies, and the Latin fields were producing less than enough for the growing metropolis the effects of this importation were not serious. Since the regular association of knights had no share in the collection of the tithes, Roman investors were for a long time not attracted to Sicily. Furthermore, since tithe-free land could be had in the rich Po valley in fee, the stipendiary lands of Sicily were not attractive to immigrants from Italy. Rome had not yet invented the legal formula that provincial land was public property,[37] hence not even Gracchus assumed the right to

[36] See chapter XXI.

[37] The Rullan bill of 63 B.C. proposed to dispose of all public land. Cicero, in discussing this bill in his three speeches, de Lege Agr., clearly shows that the agri censorii, not the tithe-paying areas, were concerned. On agrarian conditions in Sicily see Scalais in Mus. Belge, 1922.

seize lands for colonization here. The native land-lords, mostly Greeks and some ex-Carthaginians, continued to concentrate their holdings of decuman lands, employing slave labor more and more until the devastating servile wars of the post-Gracchan period impoverished a number of the lords by the destruction of the crops and the loss of their slaves in battle. There are signs that South Italian Greeks immigrated into Sicily and to some extent displaced bankrupt natives, especially during the dread years when the social and civil wars threatened to spread all over Italy. The evidence of this consists especially in the names of Roman citizens and "knights" with Greek cognomina that crop up in the Verrine orations. In the year 70, when Cicero took up the case of Sicily against Verres, the arable land was still devoted chiefly to grain culture, for the Roman purchase of a second and third tithe removed the surplus and kept prices high. We now find that despite the burden of the tithe, Roman citizens were beginning to purchase or rent lands in the island while others were entering business and taking tax contracts. Cicero's letters of the middle of the century prove that this number was then increasing. However, cereal culture has its limits when kept up consistently. In the days of Caesar and the early empire we hear little of Sicilian grain. The surface soil had doubtless deteriorated and a change to horticulture which taps a deeper stratum of soil, and to pasturage, which stops erosion and gives some respite to the soil, was essential here as elsewhere—at least for a time.

CHAPTER X

FINANCIAL INTERESTS IN POLITICS

After the death of Gracchus the dread of civil war
for a time sobered the tempers of both parties whenever questions of domestic policy arose. The assembly
let itself be cajoled into acquitting the consul, Opi-
mius, when he was brought to trial for disregarding
the Sempronian law which prohibited the passage of
the *senatus consultum ultimum*. In return the senate
recognized the settlement of Asia, the contract system,
the equestrian jury panels, the land distributions and
unfortunately also the corn doles. In the period of
adjustment that followed, however, the senate was able
to carry a number of amendments to the land laws,
each concealing some desired clause within the legal
verbiage that carried the concessions desired by the
Gracchans. The purpose of the first[1] was to permit
the alienation of the allotments. The followers of
Gracchus had no objection to this. Many had found
their assignments hidden away in rough mountain
country, scores of miles from congenial society. For
the raising of grain, vegetables or fruit, such lots were

[1] Appian, *B. C.* I, 27; Cic. *Brut.* 136, and the *Lex Agraria* of
111 B.C. (C.I.L. I, 585) tell us the little we know about these
laws. Hardy's commentary on the *Lex Agr.* in *Six Roman Laws*
is convenient. See also the article *Leges Agrariae* by Vancura
in Pauly-Wissowa.

too far from the market; to plant vines or olives on them would require more capital than they possessed, and for ranching the plots were too small. Naturally there was a demand for the right to sell, and senators who had ranches in the neighborhood were glad to buy these properties if they could be had in fee and at a low price.

A second law, attributed to a tribune of the year 118, was also in the nature of a compromise. It abolished the agrarian commission and recognized the holdings of public land within the legal acreage as private property, though subject to tribute (probably of a tithe). The income from this tax was to be used in public charity, apparently in support of the corn dole. It is likely that the holders of public land were more than willing for the present to continue to pay the tithe in return for the assurance that the annoying commissioners would forever disappear and that no new tribune could ever propose to distribute their holdings. There might still be lawsuits regarding their boundaries but the Roman praetor and not men chosen by the assembly would preside at such trials.

Then in 111, when the senate considered itself secure in control, the extensive agrarian law of which we have spoken was passed to dispose of all disputes as to property rights that might arise through obscurity in the preceding laws, and to codify in affirmative form all the implications of the laws then in force. In addition the important clause was inserted that the tribute on the holdings confirmed by the Thorian law should be abolished. This measure, therefore, specifically confirmed legal, tax-free ownership in fee in all parcels assigned by the Gracchan allotments and also in the occupied public land within the legal acreage. It retained as public property the Campanian lands untouched by Gracchus, it confirmed the Gracchan requirement of road-work upon those who had accepted lots with this stipulation, it recognized the legal status of the public mortgages entered into during the Second Punic War, and finally it established strict rules regarding the use of the community grazing grounds.

This was presumably to end all contentions; but it appears that after it was passed the landlords asserted themselves too boldly, for two years later when the people had been stirred to great anger by the mismanagement of the Jugurthine war, five tribunes carried a new law[2] (of which we have sections 53-5), providing for various official surveys under commissioners, and also for the organization of self-governing communities among the lot-holders with powers to settle boundary questions within their respective communal boundaries. Presumably the landlords were included in these municipalities and made amenable to the decisions of their town meetings. Therewith agrarian

[2] *Lex Mamilia Roscia Peducaea Alliena Fabia*, in Bruns Fontes[7], p. 95. Fabricius in *Sitz. Akad. Heidelb.* 1924-5, 1, has proved that this is not a Julian law but belongs to Mamilius, the famous tribune of 109 B.C. We have only three clauses preserved by the agrimensores. Since these are numbered 53-6, the complete document must have been extensive. The name of Mamilius is enough to vouch for the democratic intent of it.

agitation in Italy came to an end for the present. Even Marius when he promised land to his volunteers realized that the land must be found in Gaul, Sardinia or Africa, and not in Italy.

The contest of the parties was from this time on rather intermittent, breaking out only when chance offered a plausible advantage to either party. The failure of the conservative party leaders in the Jugurthine war (111-107 B.C.) gave the popular party an excuse to appoint Marius as general[3] and thus disregard completely the senate's time-honored prerogative to select the general by lot. And since Marius made up his army by recruiting volunteers[4] instead of accepting the draft of the censors, it is apparent that the year 108 established two precedents that boded ill for the old constitution.

In 106 the senate plucked up courage to attack the court panels. The equestrian jury was being used too effectively as a club over provincial governors who attempted to curb the exactions of the publicans in their provinces. Charges of misgovernment could readily be trumped up against unfriendly governors and when brought to court these men had no chance with equestrian juries. The senate convinced the people that injustice was being done and the law was revised so as to admit senators with the knights on the panels.[5] Unfortunately, Caepio, who had proposed the

[3] Sall. *Jug.* 73.

[4] Sall. *Jug.* 86; Val. Max. 2, 3; Gell. 16, 10, 10.

[5] Obsequens 101; Cic. *pro Cluent.* 140; *Brut.* 164.

revocation, disgraced himself the next year in the
Cimbrian war, and in the consequent revulsion of feeling the knights were able to restore the Sempronian
jury.[6] On such turns of chance great issues were
decided.

It is doubtless to the business classes concerned with
Asia that we must attribute the effort made in 103 to
clear the seas of pirates,[7] for the democrats won the
elections that year. The pirates came largely from
Cilicia, which had been free from surveillance ever
since Rome annexed Asia without assuming the burden of governing the southern portion. Rhodes was
no longer in a position to restrain these venturesome
sea-rovers; Rome had long been engaged in the Jugurthine and Cimbric wars, while Mithradates was hiring
them from time to time in privateering expeditions on
the Black Sea. Hitherto few Romans had engaged in
commerce on the seas, but now that the Roman contractors were receiving the Asiatic taxes in produce
which they had to market, they were keenly interested
in seeing their cargoes safe even when these were sent
in foreign ships. Antonius was accordingly sent with a
fleet to clear the eastern seas, and this he quickly did.
Cilicia was then declared a province, that is, a district
under permanent military supervision, and the seas
remained safe until the Social war necessitated the
concentration of Roman forces in Italy.

The riots of the group which supported Saturninus

[6] Cic. *Verr.* I, 38.

[7] Livy, *Epit.* 68; Obsequens, 104.

and Glaucia in 103-101 have no real economic significance. Personal political ambitions, employing Gracchan precedents, account for them; and even Marius,
impatient with the unjustifiable promises of public
property in return for political support, added one
more precedent to block popular control by recognizing
the validity of a Senatus Consultum Ultimum.[8]

In the year 90, after futile efforts for fifty years to
obtain Roman citizenship, the Sabellic tribes of Italy
issued a declaration of independence, formed a republican government of their own,[9] armed themselves to
defend their liberty and called, though in vain, upon
the other peoples of Italy to follow their example.
Their grievances were varied. As inferior allies of a
state now grown monstrously large, they were constantly being called upon to serve in wars not of their
making and not to their apparent interests; and their
soldiers had to endure the strictest military discipline
without the protection afforded by citizenship. They
had no share in the stipends that flowed to the Roman
treasury from conquered peoples, in the grain that was
distributed to the populace of the capital, or in the
offices, emoluments and honors that came to the governing people. Their rights to public land in Italy had
been disregarded in all the agrarian laws that had been
passed, and worst of all to a sensitive, liberty-loving
people, they were no longer treated as equals in personal contacts.

[8] Livy, *Epit*. 69; Cic. *pro Rabir*. 20.

[9] See Domaszewski, *Bellum Marsicum*, Sitz. Akad. Wien, 1924.

Their request for the franchise had been supported from time to time by democratic leaders, Gracchus and Drusus both risking their lives in the issue; but the masses of voters in the city, who knew that their own power would be diminished by the extension of the franchise, could never be made to grant it. From time to time there were also many individual senators who favored it as a just measure. Progressive enfranchisement had in fact formerly been an aristocratic policy. But now that this policy was associated with the hated name of Gracchus, the instinct to protect the senate from possible "contamination" found an excuse in the claims of party loyalty, and a large majority of the senate opposed enfranchisement. The knights were also divided, with a heavy majority in the opposition. It is possible that an aversion to sharing the profits of state-contracts with Italians who were wealthy enough to claim equestrian rank influenced many of them, but of this we have no information.

The Social War (90-89 B.C.) does not directly concern us. Rome was able to break up the costly rebellion in two years only by promising to grant the franchise throughout Italy. The sequel, however, involved measures of vast economic consequence. The senate after having promised the franchise to all Italians as far as the river Po, insulted the new citizens by grouping them all in ten new wards so that despite promises their influence would be completely lost at elections.[10] To be sure the Italians cared little

[10] *Schol. Bob.* on *pro Archia* 7; Vell. 2, 20; Appian, *B. C.* 1, 49.

for the trouble of going to Rome to vote, and they had gained the standing in the army and in the courts which they desired, but this act of treachery enraged them. A tribune, Sulpicius, became their spokesman and appealed to the people to support a bill granting an equal apportionment of Italians[11]—and for good measure of all freedmen—throughout the thirty-five wards. The populace of Rome (except for the freedmen) were listless regarding this proposal till Marius promised to support the bill in return for a commission as the supreme commander in the Mithradatic war, just declared. The assembly passed the double measure. Sulla, who was consul and had the command of the army by allotment, declared the change of command illegal, as indeed it was, marched on Rome "in defence of the constitution," ordered the senate to outlaw Sulpicius, Marius, and their agents, and then departed for his province. The Italians of course were now thoroughly convinced that the Roman senate was their inveterate foe. Marius who had escaped, returned, called the Italians to his support, captured Rome and sated his hatred in a terrible proscription. The popular party, however, notwithstanding their recognition of the Italians as citizens, did nothing to hasten their enrollment.[12] Four years later Sulla came back from the east with his victorious army. His subsequent proscription of political opponents resulted in the death

[11] Livy, *Epit.* 77; Appian, *B. C.* I, 55; Plut. *Sulla*, 8.

[12] See *Roman Census Statistics from 225 to 28 B.C.*, in *Classical Phil.* 1924, 335.

of thousands and his confiscation of lands from dis-- affected communities disrupted large areas of Italy. The war of pacification which he carried on against the Italians, who centered on him their hatred for the treacherous deception of 88, devastated much of Samnium and Etruria. When presently Sulla imposed his aristocratic constitution he deliberately omitted the censorship so that the new citizens had no means of enrolling for the elections. While there were at this time fully two million citizens in Italy entitled to the vote, the census of the year 85 registered only 390,000, and no new registration was made till Sulla's constitution was overthrown in 70 B.C. It has been suggested that the civil war of Marius and Sulla was in reality a continuation of the "Social War." It would be more consonant with the facts to say that the Social war resulted from the clogging of the political machinery as a result of civil hatred, and that this hatred had now dragged the whole of Italy into a prolonged contest of parties.

The Social and Civil wars brought no benefits. The sturdy Samnite and Marsian peasants suffered severely, and ranches now spread into districts where careful terrace-farming in the hills had formerly supported a healthy population. Sulla's colonization of his troops on confiscated lands did not greatly change the aspect of the Etruscan and Campanian towns, for his was a draft-army of citizens; but these soldiers had not been trained for agricultural work during ten years of very ugly fighting in Italy and in Asia. To be sure in some cases large estates were cut up into small lots again, which in itself was not an evil, but if we may judge from the experience of Praeneste,[13] where within twenty years the landlords were back in control, the distribution of the land had no permanent effect. And a great many of the dispossessed of Campania took to brigandage and buccaneering, and many drifted to Africa and Spain, joining the rebel armies which Pompey later subdued. The disaffected who remained in Italy made up a large part of the rabble that Catiline later gathered to his standard. And finally there was a decided shift in property and political influence from family to family, especially under Sulla's régime, for he not only destroyed his enemies but confiscated and sold their properties so that their families were reduced to penury.

The conservative constitution of Sulla lasted but eight years after his death, and it would not have survived so long had not the power of the knights been shattered by the proscriptions. In the year 71 Pompey and Crassus, both intimately connected with the class of property-holders, stood for the consulship on a program that provided some check to aristocratic predominance. They promised to restore the tribunician power as a balance to senatorial administration, to admit the knights with the senators to the jury panels, to check senatorial misgovernment in the provinces, and to re-establish the censorship. The purpose of the last measure seems to have been in part to have

[13] Cic. *Leg. Agr.* II, 78.

a new census so that the large body of Italians who had failed to be inscribed on the citizen-rolls might at last get recognition, and in part to loosen up the machinery of provincial tax gathering.   After winning the elections, Pompey and Crassus kept their promises, and the old democratic constitution was practically restored.   However, nothing was done to introduce ballot boxes in the municipalities for national elections, the one measure that might have made Italy an effective body of voters.   Not till Caesar's day were the local censors of the municipalities made a part of the censorial machinery[14] for the enrollment of citizens, and even then these censors were permitted only to register the citizens.   They were not empowered to conduct the elections throughout Italy.   So determined

[14] V. Premerstein (*Die Tafel von Heraclea*, in *Zeit. Sav.-Stift.* 43) has demonstrated that the Lex Julia Municipalis is one of the laws which Caesar left in incomplete draft at his death and which Antony later issued among the "acta Caesaris" with the approval of the senate.   An important clause of this law (11.142-156) stipulates that the Roman censors shall enter on their state records the rolls of citizens made by the municipal magistrates of that year.   Since up to that time citizens had to go to Rome in order to enroll, and since the state had no great interest in the enrollment after the Italian tribute and the regular conscription had been abolished, the census for some time had been far from complete.   If Caesar had had any intention of preserving republican institutions he would at this time have taken the next logical step and empowered the municipal magistrates to record the voting for Roman magistrates at the local elections, thus giving the Roman franchise normal value throughout Italy. Had Gaius Gracchus been able to carry his reforms to a natural conclusion, this stage might have been reached in his day and the Republic might well have been saved.

were the Romans—even the democratic leaders—to hold the deciding power in the hands of those who lived near the capital.

The financial interests now felt strong enough to ask a favor. The piracy that had been encouraged in the east by Mithradates, and had spread to the west by the accretion of Campanian and Greek adventurers during the Social and Civil wars, had been but partially checked by Servilius, who in 76-5 destroyed some of their strongholds in Cilicia. The seas were still unsafe for those who had business in the East. When the senate offered no relief, Gabinius carried the bill to the assembly which then empowered Pompey to build a vast fleet and clear the seas. The senate objected, ostensibly on constitutional grounds, and found a tribune to veto the bill, but the knights were determined and resorted to Gracchus' device of calling upon the assembly to depose the tribune. The bill then passed. Pompey did the work with exemplary speed, and recognizing that the buccaneers were no more at fault than the government which had neglected to police the seas, he established the captives in colonies and turned them into useful farmers.

The success of this enterprise encouraged the knights to propose that Pompey be placed in command of the war against Mithradates. Lucullus was recalled, partly because of his merciless treatment of the creditors in Asia, partly because his stern discipline had brought his soldiers to the point of mutiny. Pompey had pleased the knights not only by his consular

program in 70 but also by his good work in clearing
the seas. He had also made a province of Cilicia,
thereby indicating that he believed in expansion—
which meant new contracts. Such a man could be
trusted to open Bithynia and Syria and perhaps all of
Mithradates' great domain to exploitation, and he
would certainly not follow Sulla's example in imposing state exactions through the senatorial quaestor, or
Lucullus' drastic way of protecting the natives by can-
celing their debts to Roman capitalists. If the senate
were allowed to complete the war, there was no doubt
that if new provinces were taken (and Bithynia must
at least be included since it had been given to Rome
by testament) the tribute of such provinces would be
confined to reasonable stipends to be gathered by the
questor according to the original senatorial plan for
Asia. Furthermore if such a settlement were made,
the province of Asia might be placed permanently on
the original basis. The bill was introduced into the
assembly by a tribune and strongly supported by
Cicero,[15] the most effective speaker of the day. Cicero
had admired Pompey from the time when the two
young men had served together on the staff of Pompey's father. Cicero was too young to know what the
contract system at its worst could be, for he had
grown to manhood under the Sullan régime, and his
experiences in the Sullan days had given him cause to
advocate a democratic administration.

[15] Cic. *pro Imp. Pomp.* The campaign of Pompey is well
described in T. Rice Holmes, *The Roman Republic*, vol. I.

Pompey secured the command and justified the hopes of his supporters. Bithynia, Cilicia, and Syria were organized as tribute-paying provinces like Asia; Pontus was included in Bithynia; Galatia and Cappadocia were reorganized as stipendiary kingdoms, and Armenia, though left independent and tax-free, accepted the position of a buffer client-state. In the midst of all this territory there were also a number of petty princes and high-priests of small temple-states who were confirmed in their offices, placed under the protection of the provincial governors, and ordered to pay tribute to Rome. The annual revenues that accrued from these new dependencies almost doubled Rome's public income.

Pompey's administrative measures in the new provinces reveal primarily an interest in the revenues to be collected. In his triumphal procession he had a tablet carried containing the names of thirty-nine cities[16] which he had founded. The purposes of his "policy of urbanization" have been much discussed. It is questionable, however, whether we should speak of a policy here or at any rate attribute to Pompey a peculiar faith in urban culture. If we review the conditions which Pompey found in various parts of the new provinces we shall see that his reasons for building cities were influenced by diverse local conditions. We do not hear that he founded cities in the province of Asia where the largest areas of rural peasants were to be found, or in Galatia where the tetrarchs managed

[16] Plut. *Pomp.* 45; App. *Mith.* 115.

well, or in Lycia where a responsible league governed. In the barbaric Pontus, which was taken from Mithradates and assigned to the province of Bithynia, he divided the whole territory into eleven districts and if there was no suitable city to serve as a central and responsible administrative center of a district, he naturally founded a new city or raised some village to the proper dignity. In such instances market places and public buildings would be contracted for and the populace of the vicinity would be invited to come to this new center so that the city might be assured some power, revenue, and promise of abiding vigor.[17] Pompey's real object doubtless was to create strongholds, centers of trade, and above all tax-gathering units with which the knights' associations could enter into negotiations in collecting the tribute. Tribute could then be gathered with less cost to the knights, and with more justice to the natives. These cities were then included in the province of Bithynia where urban centers were already in existence and local self-government generally prevailed.

In Cappadocia the purpose of the city-building was somewhat different. This kingdom had been devastated by Mithradates, and 300,000 of its citizens carried into captivity into Armenia. The captives had to be brought back and given homes, and as the bankrupt

[17] Strabo, 12, 3, 1; Cumont, *Studia Pontica* for the new cities in Pontus; Strabo has some notes on Pompey's methods: 11, 8, 4, (Zela); 12, 3, 30, (Magnopolis); 12, 3, 38, (Neapolis); 12, 3, 28, (Nicopolis); App. *Mith.* 115 mentions the city of Mazaca in Cappadocia.

king, Ariobarzanes was to be nursed into a tribute-paying client he must be provided with a respectably organized kingdom. It was a question of sheltering his subjects in places that would be secure from attack and that would also invite trade and agriculture. It would seem that Pompey himself lent the king considerable sums of money—at a high rate of interest—with which to put his kingdom into working order.[18]

Syria, finally, offered a large number of peculiar problems of its own.[19] The earlier Seleucids had long ago preferred to build cities and draw definite tribute from them rather than gather petty rents from scattered areas of crown-lands. But when the later Seleucids lost their power the kingdom fell apart, and the lawless Arab tribes of the Hauran and of Coele-Syria overran many of the old communities, the Maccabean government took possession of the Hellenic cities of the Decapolis and of the Palestinian coast, and the folk of the edge of the desert took to nomadic life. The only wise course for the Romans to pursue was to check such disintegrating tendencies, as the earlier kings had done, and the cure in each case consisted in creating a strong line of responsible urban centers. Rome profited at once in that the tribute could now be more easily secured without the wastage of revenue that would otherwise have gone to the support of

[18] Cicero, at least, was collecting for Pompey in 50 B.C. from the son of Ariobarzanes, *Ad Att.* 6, 3, 5.

[19] On Pompey in Syria see Plut. *Pomp.* 39-41; Appian, *Mith.* 106; Strabo, 16, 2; Josephus, *Antiq.* 14, 3-4.

sheiks and petty kings. It is very doubtful whether in
all this Pompey considered the cultural advantages of
city life or aimed at systematic Romanization through
city foundations.[20] His purpose was a more immediate
and practical one. And yet when Pompey's work was
done, though he had not excluded the publicans from
the new province, he had so organized the communities that the publican societies had in fact less power
to harm these cities than they had had in the province
of Asia.

The hypothesis that Pompey considered the stipendiary "crown-lands" of the deposed kings as *ager publicus* cannot be proved and is not plausible. He seized
the personal and real property of the kings in Bithynia,
Pontus and Syria, and turned these over to the treasury of the Roman people,[21] but the vast expanses of
rural tracts that by eastern custom had been called
crown-land and subject to royal tribute he apparently
classified as private stipendiary land, and on this the
peasantry was apparently not disturbed. Such at least
is the plain inference to be drawn from Cicero's discussion of the Rullan bill (63 B.C.) which proposed
to sell all public land in the provinces for funds with

[20] T. Rice Holmes, *The Roman Republic* I, 211, and Rostovtzeff,
A Social and Economic Hist., seem to overemphasize the cultural
motive.

[21] The treasures and booty turned into ready money were considerable; the Roman treasury received 20,000 talents (Plut.
Pomp. 45), and to the soldiers and officers were distributed 16,000
talents in bounties (App. *Mith.* 116). Some idea of the personal
property of Mithradates is given by Appian, *Mith.* 115.

which to purchase land for needy citizens in Italy. In his enumeration of public lands[22] he mentions a number of plots that had formerly belonged to the Roman peoples, that is, some *ager publicus* in Sicily, the lands from which Servilius had removed pirate tribes in Cilicia in 75 B.C., the Attalid estates in the Chersonese, the royal estates of Philip in Macedonia, the very sites of Corinth and Carthage destroyed in 146, the personal estates of the king of Cyrene, and the *ager publicus* near New Carthage in Spain, which had been Punic public land. In the new provinces he mentions only the *regios agros* of Mithradates in Paphlagonia, Pontus, and Cappadocia, and those of Nicomedes in Bithynia. The inclusion of only the site of Carthage in Africa and of merely the territories of a few destroyed cities in Cilicia is proof enough that stipendiary land was not at this time included in the term *regios agros*. And again it ought to be quite clear that if the oriental theory of state ownership had been adopted, we should be driven to the supposition that Rullus and his backers, Caesar and Crassus, were proposing to sell more land in the provinces than the complete acreage of Italy itself. We must, therefore, assume that the phrase *agri regii* is not a translation of *Chora Basilike,* but that it refers simply to personal properties of the kings. We can, accordingly, comprehend why the Rullan bill did not mention Syrian lands at all. The fact is that the Seleucids had quite regularly followed the policy of assigning private as well as

[22] *Lex Agr.* II, 48-50.

crown-lands to communities from which they took
stipends, and the small estates which they had retained
had doubtless been seized by cities or peasants in the
anarchic decades of the last futile reigns of this house.
In Syria it is apparent that there were no extensive
agri regii and the stipendiary lands Rome left to the
communities. In the shaping of the new provinces of
the East, therefore, it is clear that Pompey as well as
the Roman government recognized the peasants and
private landlords as the owners of the fields which
they cultivated, and left them in undisturbed possession
although demanding a tribute from them. And it is
also clear that only the lands that had actually belonged to the personal estates of the kings were placed
at the disposal of the censor of the Roman people.

It is a curious fact that Pompey's great service to
the equestrian corporations ultimately cost him heavily.
The taxing companies of the several provinces became
so powerful that in the year 61 they united to compel
the senate to remit a third of their pledged sum on the
plea of poor crops in Asia. When the senate refused,
Caesar gained the support of the knights by promising
the desired remission in case he won the consulship.
He kept his promise and permitted this great combination of capitalists to exploit the provinces for ten
years;[23] and when Pompey broke with Caesar, taking
his stand with the senate, Caesar, because of this act,
held the allegiance of a large group of knights through
the civil war.

[23] Laurent-Vibert, in *Mélanges, École de Rome*, 1908, 172.

While Pompey was still in the east a dangerous conspiracy under Catiline broke out at Rome which threatened to end responsible government. It did not rise wholly out of economic distress though its leaders wished to be considered benevolent reformers. The disaffected classes ready for revolution were large, to be sure, but the remedy proposed by Catiline—a reallotment of properties—was the very thing that had caused most of the distress which he pretended to bewail. Catiline found many followers in northern Etruria and Picenum where Sulla had dispossessed whole cities of Marian sympathizers and reduced them to the "Latin" status. These are doubtless the people whom Sallust mentions as having lost their citizenship. Many of Sulla's own colonists, who had been given the confiscated tracts, had failed as farmers and were now ready to take their chances at a second re-distribution. The old war wounds of Italy, however, were not chargeable to the present government, and in any case the cure lay not in more civil war. Rome's standard method of dealing with such evils was to let migration to the provinces, urban corn doles, and time's slow adjustments bring alleviation, and this method might well have sufficed once more. Catiline also counted upon the dispossessed Marians of Praeneste, where all the land had been distributed to Sullan partizans, upon the hordes of slaves who shepherded the vast ranches of southern Italy, and upon the urban mob, consisting of broken men who were simply existing on the public corn doles. However very few of these really cared to fight for a change of government. When Catiline faced the enemy he had only a little over three thousand men in his ranks.

The fact is that there was no serious economic crisis, and that conditions were actually better than they had been since the end of Sulla's raids over Italy twenty years before. The tension was political rather than economic. The senate and the people were each day becoming more conscious of the fact that their claims were inconsistent and that whether a democracy or an oligarchy was to control the republic would have to be decided by force. Moreover they all feared that Pompey on his return would decide the question by arms as Sulla had done. The senate was in haste to establish itself in power, since it feared that Pompey's decision would be favorable to the democracy; while the young democratic leaders, Crassus and Caesar, wished to gain complete control of their party before Pompey came to assume that leadership. And behind all the anxiety, haste, and fear lay the memory of how Marius and Sulla had used their armies to reshape Rome to their whims. Intransigent refusal to amend the constitution and reach any reasonable compromise, and the dangerous precedents set by Sulla were the mainsprings of war rather than any material pressure. Catiline was at first less a reformer than a brainless tool of leaders who expected to use and then remove him. The utter inadequacy of his intelligence for the task set him is shown by the manner in which he betrays his own selfish motives in a letter to Catulus:

"Enraged by the insults and injuries heaped upon me, since I have been denied the rewards of my labors and failed to obtain an office of dignity, I have, as is my wont, espoused the cause of the unfortunate,—not because I could not pay my debts out of my own property, but because I saw unworthy men honored by high office." From his own words we infer that he espoused the cause of the unfortunate because a *novus homo* like Cicero won the consulship which he, a patrician, had failed to attain. In the aristocratic re-action which followed this wild attempt at revolution, the senators overestimated their popularity and abused their power. And Julius Caesar taking advantage of their folly gained for himself a military command with which he finally made himself the master of Rome.

CHAPTER XI

Public Finances

The Roman was a practical businesslike person in the management of his private concerns, but in the management of public finances his instinct for efficiency was neutralized, as happens in all democracies, by the pressure of friends seeking special privileges, by lack of a stable and durable policy in the ever-changing government, by want of any scrutinizing and controlling supervision, and by a popular demand for amiable rather than officious magistrates. Frequently therefore the Oriental despots whom Roman governors displaced in the East had been better managers than their successors. Their kingdoms had been their private possessions: they had accordingly chosen efficient men to manage the satrapies, had removed those who failed, and had continued in office the successful officials until they became specialists in their respective tasks. The Roman democracy on the contrary worked upon the theory that any citizen of good family could serve the state in any capacity. An eligible young man began his career as an official of the treasury for one year, then after a year's rest, if he pleased the voting populace, he had charge, as aedile, of some division of the public works, an office which under ordinary circumstances admitted him to the senate for life. After another year's rest he might be made a judge in one of the important praetorian courts, whether or not he had studied law. Indeed one of the reasons why Roman civil law freed itself so readily from outworn legal conceptions, and kept its feet on the common-sense ground of equity was just that normal men of affairs presided in the courts over juries of men of similar stamp. But the system for obvious reasons failed to create an adequate criminal law. The official was then given a year's practice in managing one of the smaller provinces; after which if the people so disposed he might for a year become the supreme magistrate of Rome. Thereafter he would be put in command of an important province for a year, from which he returned to Rome to live the rest of his days a respected senator and aid in the direction of the imperial policies of Rome. Obviously such men received a very wide experience, but they were specialists in nothing in particular, and the knowledge they gained must frequently have come through sad mistakes committed in all kinds of offices for which they were not half fitted until it was time to depart for the next position. The system provided an excellent training school for retired senators, it did not make for skilful government. In the early days when the city was the state and when the citizen who paid his taxes could see day by day how the state moneys were being expended, no great evil could result for long. What might happen later when unprotected provinces far from Rome were placed at the free disposal of such men is well enough illustrated by the stories that have made the name of Verres·a proverb.

In the early Republic national expenses were but trifling. The few magistrates served their year without salaries. To be selected by popular acclamation was flattering enough to evoke a year's public service without further reward. The army also served gratis: only property owners were called to arms and they presumably had sufficient interest in the protection of their homes and properties to fight without pay. As for equipment the heavily armed first line and the cavalry were selected from the wealthier men who could best afford to equip themselves. Public work like wall-building[1] was done by the citizen-army as a part of its duty, roads and streets were graded by the property owners at public command. The early temples seem largely to have been provided by the sale of booty. And this brief list runs the gamut of the early state's needs. Rome had not yet outgrown the conditions of tribal life where common action, so difficult to secure, confined itself to the mere physical defence of the group, leaving all questions of moral, intellectual, and social welfare to the devices of the family and the interested individual. New functions the Roman government assumed very slowly and reluctantly. Thus for instance it was not till the day of autocracy that the state considered itself under any

[1] For example, Livy (VII, 20) says that the soldiers after their campaign of the year spent the rest of their time repairing the walls.

obligation to supervise or encourage education, even
as in modern times the most liberal governments of
Europe have been the most dilatory in accepting such
non-political burdens.

The first demand for a well-stocked treasury came
with the long war against Veii. The year-long service
in the army with the consequent neglect of farms and
business necessitated the introduction of a regular
stipendium. At first this was very trifling, little more
in fact than enough for the soldier to pay for his
rations, but it marks the time from which a tax had
to be levied upon Roman property. This annual tribute[2] seems to the modern not very large, frequently
not more than a mill per cent. And even this was at
times restored[3] to the taxpayer, if war indemnity and
booty sufficed to permit repayment. This tribute was
a uniform property tax. On real estate[4] it was levied
on the *ager Romanus,* that is, upon all land within the
bounds of the city-state proper as far as the ward-
divisions extended, and was levied even if a non-
Roman acquired such property. In addition to this all
Roman citizens whether living at home or abroad were
subject to a tax on all other property as well, as for
instance on cash, slaves, cattle, implements and furni-

[2] Livy, XXXIX, 44: his rebus omnibus terni in milia aeris
adtribuerentur; Livy, XXIII, 31: eo anno duplex tributum
imperaretur.

[3] Livy, X, 46; Pliny, *N. H.* XXXIV, 23.

[4] See Marquardt, *Staatsverwaltung,* II, 167, 168; Lecrivain, art,
Tributum, Daremberg-Saglio.

ture. The property of widows and orphans, not at
first on the citizen census list which had been made up
for military purposes, was later subjected to a tax
that was set aside for the equipment of cavalry.

The Samnite wars, long protracted through desolate
regions and necessitating a reorganization of the army
with new equipment and much road-building, entailed
heavy taxpaying for long seasons. The First Punic
War also proved extremely expensive, especially because of the heavy losses of the navy. Seven hundred
ships of war were lost in battles or in storms. It is
not surprising that at the end Rome not only exacted
an indemnity from Carthage—though it amounted to
but a fraction of the cost—but also adopted from her
the new theory that subjects should share with citizens
the costs of government. The Sicilian tithe of course
very materially relieved the strain upon the treasury.
In the Second Punic War however this tithe did not
even suffice to feed the armies in the field. Taxes
were doubled and trebled. New super-taxes on in-
comes were added, free contributions asked for, public
works were let on credit and loans were floated on the
security of Rome's public lands. Indeed at that time
the administration of the Roman exchequer assumed
the aspects of a modern national treasury. But the
Roman Senate disliked arrears and complicated financing. As soon as possible after the war it liquidated
all outstanding loans by surrendering the mortgaged
lands to the creditors, at first reserving the right to
reclaim them at a revaluation, later conceding even

this privilege. Thus the treasury got rid of its loans
and thereafter succeeded fairly well in keeping a surplus account. Finally in 167 B.C. the accumulation of
a large surplus from state mines, from indemnities
and war booty, and an accession of regular income
from Spanish tribute and from the rental of the Campanian and other public lands in Italy placed the treasury in such a strong condition that the direct tax upon
citizens was discontinued.

In Cicero's consulship, before Pompey had added
the new eastern provinces of Syria, Bithynia and
Pontus, we are told that Rome's public receipts were
about 50,000,000 denarii,[5] or about ten million dollars.
The bulk of this sum came from provincial taxes, but
smaller amounts were received from the rental of
Campanian public land, public mines in Spain and
Transpadane Gaul, fishing rights on lakes, rivers, and
on coasts, and a salt monopoly, a five per cent. tax on
the price of manumitted slaves, an occasional tax of
five per cent. on inheritances, and from port duties
levied at harbors, usually of from two to five per cent.
These port duties were not conceived of as protective
tariffs. They were too low to serve such purposes,
and were in fact collected as regularly on exports as
on imports. The Empire indeed developed a system
of tariff-districts so that goods which were shipped a
long distance were apt to pay duty more than once.

Of the ten million dollars provided in Cicero's day
the larger part came from provincial tributes which

[5] Plut. *Pompey*, 45.

differed in amount and method of collection according
to the treaty or exaction made at the time of conquest.
Sicily with its tithes and rents on public lands provided
about one tenth of this, the tithe alone amounting to
about one million bushels of wheat. Asia furnished
one and a half million dollars in Hadrian's day after
Caesar had somewhat lightened her burden. Perhaps
we may estimate two millions for Cicero's day. Since
enlarged Gaul provided two millions in the Augustan
period, a half million will be a generous estimate for
the small province of Narbo. In comparison with
these provinces, if we consider size, productivity and
the conditions of conquest of each, we may venture to
assume about one million dollars from Spain, apart
from her mines, a half million for Sardinia and Corsica, a million for Africa with her public lands, a million for Macedonia, and half a million for Cilicia. The
other revenues mentioned may well account for some
three million dollars.

To these amounts Pompey added the revenues of
Syria, Bithynia, and Pontus, amounting to about six
million dollars; Caesar conquered Gaul thus adding at
least one and one half million, and Augustus annexed
Egypt which, being largely royal property and consequently now completely at the disposal of the treasury, brought in a full ten million dollars.[6] If we add
to these some minor taxes instituted by Augustus we
find that the Empire during the first century had an
annual budget of about thirty million dollars or less

[6] Strabo, II, 118, and XVII, 798.

than eight per cent. of the annual budget of the City of New York!

These provincial tributes varied in nature and manner of collection, since Rome frequently tried to adapt her methods to those that had already been in vogue. In Spain for instance Carthage had imposed a light burden in order to make her conquest easy, and Rome in order to invite the people to a new allegiance during the Punic War had lightened rather than increased the burden. Hence a definite amount was agreed upon for each community and the towns collected these dues without the interference of Roman publicans. The stipendium of Spanish communities was equal to about half a tithe.[7] In Sicily,[8] except in the case of several friendly cities which were left immune and of public lands which Rome had inherited from the former sovereign or expropriated at the time of conquest, the grain lands were subjected to tithes, fruit lands to double tithes, and pasture lands to a cattle head-tax. These tithes were estimated jointly by the community and the Roman official, and the collection contracted for accordingly. Since, however, the law required that the contract should be let in Sicily, the community could protect the interests of its citizens by bidding for the contract, and this was frequently done. To be sure Roman and Italian business men who often engaged in collecting port-dues and in renting the public land in Sicily might also enter into the bidding, and being

[7] Livy, XLIII, 2, 12.

[8] Rostowzew, *Art. Frumentum*, Pauly-Wissowa, VII, 152.

men of ready capital they came to capture many contracts which they managed to make lucrative. In the days of Verres these men had been so favored by the Roman questor on the island that Cicero in gathering evidence for the prosecution found Roman knights engaged in oppressive exactions in several cities.

After the contract law of Gaius Gracchus, Asia fared even worse. Here there were legitimate objections to a fixed annual amount, since years of drought and incursions from the East made such payments impossible at times. A tithe on the actual crop, whereby both parties shared equally in the uncertainties, was therefore in theory a fairer tax. But many communities[9] of the interior had little experience in management and failed to bring in their quota. Furthermore the produce was not needed at Rome and the transporting and disposing of it proved irksome. Gracchus therefore, to ensure a reliable income to the treasury, decided to throw the speculative risks upon capitalistic companies which might care to take the business of collecting[10] and disposing of the tithe. The censor auctioned the complete prospective tithe to the highest bidder. The companies that secured the contract gathered the requisite capital by issues of stock, which because of the risks involved were put out at attractive rates of interest. These stocks were widely bought at Rome, and as a result complaints of extortion on

[9] Cic. *Ad Quint.* I, 33; qui pendere ipsi vectigal sine publicano non potuerint.

[10] Rostowzew, *Geschichte der Staatspacht, Phil. Supp.* IX.

the part of Asiatics met with less sympathy on the rialto at Rome than they might otherwise have done. Sulla, after himself robbing the province, relieved it somewhat by substituting fixed charges, but Pompey, under pressure of the equites who had supported him in politics, reinstituted a modified form of the Gracchan system,[11] and this lasted until Caesar abandoned the worst features of the contract system. In the empire when it became possible to organize permanent civil service bureaus, the contract system was gradually displaced everywhere by officials responsible to the Emperor.

Corresponding to this income were the expenditures for the state bureaus, public works, cults, corn-doles, the army and the provincial government. Since magistrates served without pay, administrative expenses were still low, but the office-forces and bands of public slaves were increasing in size. Little was spent on police or fire departments before Caesar's day. One wonders how long a modern city would last with the kind of police protection that Cicero had. Some charges fell on the treasury for games. Public works, as for instance the building and repairing of roads and aqueducts, walls and public buildings, frequently re-

---

[11] Rostowzew, ibid., p. 357; cf. Josephus, *Antiq.* XIV, 10, 6; Cic. *prov. cons.* 10; *Ad Att.* V, 13; V, 16; VI, 1, 16; *Ad Fam.* XIII, 65; *Ad Quint.* I, 35; *Pro Flacco*, 32. Caesar remitted about a third, converted the rest into fixed amounts of money which the cities henceforth collected: Plut, *Caes.* 48, 1; Dio, XLII, 6; App. *B. C.* V,4.

ceived outright a fifth or a tenth[12] of the year's income
to be assigned by the censors. Temples as in the past
were often built by victorious generals from booty,
and sometimes also endowed by them, or kept in repair
by their descendants. But at times the state itself
built temples and paid for special devotions requested
by the pontiffs. The corn-doles instituted by Gaius
Gracchus required in Cicero's day about a million dollars[13] annually. From this the fifteen bushels of wheat
allowed to each man who cared to stand in the bread-
line were supplied at a fraction of the cost. Clodius in
his bid for popularity passed laws that nearly doubled
this expense.

The armies and the provinces however devoured the
greater part of the state's income in these troublesome
days, and some provinces cost the state more than they
provided in tribute. The senate never admitted the
need of a standing army, always dreading a repetition
of its abuse by men like Marius and Sulla, but the
warfare in Spain, Africa, and the East continued inces-
santly and the senate was compelled to hand on standing armies from one pro-consul to another. As each
soldier received 120 denarii per year as pay the salaries
for a legion exceeded $100,000, and the annual ex-
penses of a legion doubtless reached double that
amount. From incidental remarks in Cicero's letters
we find that even in normal times Syria, Asia, Bithynia, Africa, Spain and Cisalpine Gaul had at least three

[12] Livy, VI, 32; XL, 46, 16; XLIV, 16, 9.

[13] See Marquardt, *Staatsverwaltung*, II, 116-18.

legions each. At least twenty legions were therefore in service. Wars called for new and extra levies though at such times neighboring legions might be brought to the point of immediate danger. Pompey received six million dollars—more than half the year's income—to prosecute the war against the pirates in 67, and in 55 he was voted a million dollars annually for Spain, largely for the sake of matching his forces with those that Caesar had in Gaul. Piso, Caesar's father-in-law, received an equal appropriation for the comparatively peaceful province of Macedonia in 58, but the Senate in this case probably intended Caesar's relative to come back with a handsome surplus for which he need make no accounting. Indeed at this time the Senate had adopted the theory that nobles who had served the state all their lives gratuitously ought to receive in their last office as provincial governors a large appropriation to indemnify them in part for past expenses. Cicero at the end of his term in Cilicia, a province of very modest proportions, had a surplus of a hundred thousand dollars still unusued from the senatorial appropriation, and an equal sum left over from provincial dues. He did not put it in his own pocket, which awakened some unfavorable comment. A paragraph from Augustus' account of his reign[14] will give a better insight than can any general statistics into the extraordinary expenditures which the new empire assumed in its efforts to please the populace.

"When consul for the fifth time I gave each and

[14] *Res Gestae Divi Augusti*, 15-17.

every Roman plebeian four hundred sesterces (about
$20) from the spoils of war; again in my tenth con-
sulship I made to every man a special gift of four hundred sesterces out of my own estate; in my eleventh
consulship I twelve times distributed food, buying grain
at my own expense; in the twelfth year of my tribunician power I again gave four hundred sesterces to
every man. These donations have never been made
to less than 250,000 men. In my twelfth consulship I
gave sixty denarii (about $12) apiece to 320,000 of the
city plebs. When consul for the fifth time I gave
to each colonist of my army 1,000 sesterces ($50) from
the spoils. About 120,000 participated in this triumphal donation. When consul for the thirteenth time
I gave sixty denarii to the plebs who were at that time
receiving public grain; of these there were a little more
than 200,000.—

"To acquire lands for soldier-colonies I paid 600,-
000,000 sesterces (thirty million dollars) for Italian
farms and 260,000,000 sesterces for land in the provinces . . . and to soldiers whom I sent back to their
native cities I gave gratuities amounting to 400,000,000
sesterces, etc."

Rome's method of exploiting mines of precious
metals and useful ores for the benefit of the treasury
requires a more explicit statement than could be given
above in the general review of the state's sources of
income. The ancient state's need of precious metal
for purposes of coinage early begot a more or less conscious theory that veins of silver and gold were public

property to be treated as discovered treasure. Philip
of Macedon worked the rich gold mines of Thrace on
the state's account, Athens, the silver mines of Laurion,
and Carthage, those of Spain. The Roman government
of the Republic never consistently claimed possession
of such subsoil treasure as a matter of course: Crassus[15] and other wealthy Romans owned rich mines in
Spain, and the state even sold to private individuals
various properties it could no longer exploit with
profit. But the Senate did from time to time, when
the need was great or when the opportunity favored,
betray a strong interest in acquiring mines and working
them for the account of the treasury. The Spanish
placer-mines which for a while during the second century B.C. brought the state nearly two million dollars[16]
annually may have been upon public land inherited
from Carthage. It seems however that when Rome
came into possession of a new province the mines
whether in public or private lands were apt to be taken
over for the public account.[17] If ores were afterwards
discovered the state probably did not claim ownership,
at least during the régime of the Senate.

We still possess fragments of the regulations under
which some silver and copper mines of Spain were
farmed out by the emperors, and since the contract
system was here used and the mines had then long been
worked we can apply most of the specifications to the

[15] Plut. *Crass*. 2; Diod. V, 36; Digest, 27, 9, 3.

[16] Polybius, according to Strabo, III, 2, 10.

[17] Strabo, IV, 6, 7 and 12.

Republican situation.[18] Here we find that the whole mining region, including the town itself, was state property under the supervision of an imperial procurator. Whoever wished to take a mining claim must first pay a stipulated occupation price, after which he must begin work within twenty-five days. On beginning work he had to pay the state or give proper security for the price placed on the mine by the procurator, this being fixed at one-half the estimated value of the ore. On payment of this price the contractor received the possession of the mine so long as he worked it faithfully without a respite of more than six months. Abandoned mines could be occupied on the same terms. In addition to the mining rights however the state also established and rented out a great many concessions in the town. It controlled a public bath, the exploitation of which was auctioned to the highest bidder under very strict rules regarding its management: the concessionaire must contract to keep the bath-tubs full of warm water every day throughout the year, must polish the metal work once a month, must admit women from daybreak till one o'clock daily at the price of one cent, and men from two till eight o'clock at half that price.

The state also controlled a public shoe shop, a barber

[18] At Aljustrel, *Lex Metalli Vipascensis*, C.I.L. II, 5181, and a fragment of another regulation which may be found in *Rev. Arch.* 1906, p. 480. See Bruns, *Fontes*[7], pp. 289-295. Since Strabo, III, 2, 10, informs us that private contractors were working these mines in his day we may assume that the plan originated in the republican period.

shop, a laundry, and an auction room, the concession-aires of which had a monopoly of such work in the town but must provide what was required at prices fixed by the state's procurator. School teachers alone had the free range of the town and paid no fees. The work in the mines was largely done by slaves; but the rules regulating penalties for thefts of ore on the part of miners specify free men as well as slaves.

CHAPTER XII

THE PLEBS URBANA

THE direction which industrial development takes depends in large measure upon the amount and nature of the available labor and the condition of the society out of which this comes. Our Southern States secured negro slaves because they could be profitably employed in the hot toil of tobacco and cotton lands, but the masses of slaves when once there practically conditioned the further economic development of the South for decades.

Preliminary to a closer study of the industrial innovations of the Ciceronian period it will therefore be pertinent to try to analyze some of the social changes taking place in Rome's lower strata. It is generally recognized that the independent house-holders of the Latin stock had materially decreased in numbers after the Second Punic War, and that their place was filled with slaves and slave offspring. How far this process had gone during the Republic, we shall attempt to discover.

When Cicero was canvassing for the consulship in 64, his brother wrote him an interesting pamphlet on practical electioneering methods in which he reminds him that "Roma est civitas ex nationum conventu constituta,"[1] and that a candidate must be careful of

[1] *De Petitione Cons.* 54 and 29.

his behavior toward his slaves and freedmen, for these have no little power in influencing the vote of the populace. It is in the light of such chance remarks that one may comprehend the stormy riots and the bloodshed so frequently mentioned during the last days of the Republic, and the power of popular leaders like Clodius who gained such strength through his patronage of labor gilds that neither Caesar nor Pompey dared interfere with him. How Rome's body of citizens had come to be a "conglomerate of all nations" is however not so readily explained, since, after all, citizenship had not yet been given to any people outside of Italy. The evidence that we now have seems to indicate that immigration played a relatively small role in this change, but that the transmutation of stock was due to the growth of a class which had come up from slavery.

The wars of Rome were largely instrumental of course in destroying Italy's native stock.[2] The Second Punic War alone with such disasters as Trasimene Lake and Cannae accounted for a loss of perhaps a third of Rome's citizens. The succeeding wars in Greece, Asia, Spain, against the Cimbri and the Allies were severe enough to keep the manhood of Italy down. And what cost more than actual casualties during this period was the constant retention of about twenty per cent. of the young men of marriageable age in military service, so that the chances of family life decreased to that extent. On the other hand dur-

[2] See Park, *The Plebs in Cicero's Day*.

ing the period when the best of the native stock was being drafted for service, slaves and freedmen lived in security at home constantly multiplying in numbers.

The fact that after the Second Punic War the areas of vacated lands were being occupied for ranches and plantations manned by slaves contributed to the same result. Indeed as Appian[3] dryly remarks the landlords preferred slaves to free labor, since free men were liable to military service, while slaves were left alone, and could therefore be depended upon. His words are: "The landlords used slaves as laborers and herdsmen fearing that if they used free men these would be drawn into the army. The ownership of slaves itself brought great gain *from the multitude of their children,* who increased because they were exempt from military service. Thus the powerful ones became enormously rich and the *race of slaves multiplied,* while the Italian people dwindled in numbers and strength being oppressed by penury, taxes, and service in the army. If they had any respite from these evils they passed their time in idleness, because the land was held by the rich who employed slaves instead of freemen." The redundancy of Appian's phrases does no more than justice to the deluge of evils that he describes.

The new generation that grew up, excluded from opportunities to acquire land in Italy, drifted into the back eddies of urban slums or emigrated to the new provinces that were constantly being opened,[4] and such

---

[3] *Bell. Civ.* I, 7.

[4] The Roman governors found enough Roman citizens resident in such provinces as Spain, Asia, and Africa to levy a legion of

men were to a great extent lost to Rome's body of citizens. For forty years[5] after the Second Punic War there was despite a constant manumission of slaves but a slight increase of 1.3 per cent. annually in the citizens' rolls, and thereafter for thirty years, a period during which Rome added Macedonia, Africa, and Asia to the Empire, there was an annual decrease of one-fourth of one per cent.

A complete statement of the causes of decline in population would necessitate a discussion of the Malthusian law, the social evil, birth control and much else, and for these problems we have of course but few data. Some considerations however may be indicated in passing. There is the striking fact which all readers of Rome's literature quickly notice that of the many families of which we have fairly good records in literary notices few contained more than two or three chil-

---

them in time of need: see for example Cic. *Ad. Att.* V, 18, 2; Caesar, *Bell. Civ.* III, 4, 3; *Bell. Alex.* XXXIV, 5. Cf. Kornemann, *art. Conventus*, Pauly-Wissowa.

[5] Beloch, *Bevölkerung der Griech. Röm. Welt*, 347, gives the census list with some revision as follows:

203 B.C.		214,000
193 "		243,000
173 "		269,000
168 "		312,000
163 "		337,000
153 "		324,000
141 "		327,000
131 "		318,000
125 "		394,000

See Frank. *Census Statistics, Class. Phil.* 1924, 329.

dren. This fact accords with evidence provided by the thousands of tombstone inscriptions recording the names of parents and their children. Confirmation comes also from speeches like that of Metellus inveighing against race-suicide, from the legislation of so many of the emperors who tried by tax exemptions or by censorial compulsion to induce or compel the citizens to consider the political necessity of a sound and increasing progeny, and finally from the blunt statements of historians who record the "lamentations of the poor, saying that they were reduced to childlessness[6] because they were unable in their poverty to rear their children." For the empire during which we have fairly full records of the more distinguished families we are enabled even to reach definite statistics[7] regarding the amazingly rapid decline of the old stock. For instance, of the forty-five patricians in the senate in Caesar's day only one is represented by posterity in Hadrian's day. The famous Aemilii, Fabii, Claudii, Manlii, Valerii and all the rest, with the exception of the Cornelii, have disappeared. Augustus and Claudius raised twenty-five families to the patriciate, and all but six of them vanish before Nerva's reign. Of the families of nearly four hundred senators recorded in 65 A. D. under Nero all trace of a half is lost a generation later, and not a few of those surviving live on only through the adoption of children. Of course members of the aristocracy suffered severely under the political tyranny of that

[6] Appian, B. C. I, 10, applying to the time of Tiberius Gracchus.

[7] Stech, Klio, Beiheft X.

century, but most of this result is after all directly traceable to voluntary childlessness.

It should not be too hastily assumed that this was accomplished by means of the old Indo-Germanic practice of *expositio*. This custom was not as prevalent at Rome as might be inferred from Plautus, whose plots are almost wholly Greek in origin. It may well be that in early Latium the period of overpopulation had brought such economic hardship as to reintroduce and excuse a practice which many branches of the race had sloughed off when emerging from barbarism. But Roman law never permitted the exposing of any normal male child, and a count of the children, male and female, recorded upon tombstones reveals the fact that the numbers were nearly equal, and that therefore female children were reared as were the male.[8] That the custom was not completely discountenanced however helps us to comprehend how public opinion could early blink at the fact that Roman families were shunning the burden of parenthood.

Of much greater importance than *expositio* are certain social conditions of the time. After the Punic War the old religion, which had once encouraged large families by stressing the supreme importance of ancestor-worship in the continued happiness of the parent in after-life, counted for little among the upper classes; moreover a society in which the young men

[8] The detailed study of the inscriptions here employed may be found in the *American Historical Review*, 1916, 689-708. This study has been discussed by M. L. Gordon in *Jour. Rom. Studies*, 1924, 93. See also Nilsson, *The Roman Empire*, 1926.

spent their prime in the army and came back experienced men of the world to enter into domestic life was apt to have unrestricted patience with the canker of prostitution. Finally it must be remembered that Rome and Greece were the only two nations before the nineteenth century in which many individuals reached a condition of pampered ease, of rational self-control, and of sophisticated freedom from instinct-born folkways which played havoc, as these things now do, with the devices of natural evolution.

That the native stock dwindled is clear from all the evidence. The question of what took its place is pertinent. Immigration accounts for a very small part. Labor in Cicero's day was so largely servile that this element which to-day moves most freely in response to economic needs, was then moved and controlled by capital in the form of slaves. The free man was generally too poor to shift for himself. Furthermore neither Italian lands which required capital for development nor the city of Rome, which had no industries not in servile hands, could attract the foreign workman. And to live in semi-idleness at Rome upon the grain provided by the state required the status of citizenship; and this a foreigner could seldom acquire. South-Italian Greeks who received citizenship after the Social War were practically the only non-Romans who could avail themselves of this, and as we shall see they apparently scattered into the provinces to act as middlemen between Roman capitalists and the Greek-speaking East. In the early Empire for which inscriptions provide much information, we find at Rome exceedingly few names that bear the regular forms of nomenclature of non-Romans. The small shopkeepers[9] and traders of Rome prove to be largely non-Italian, but an examination of their names shows that they are freedmen rather than free immigrants. Only in some of the learned professions[10] and arts—in medicine, teaching, painting and architecture, for instance—and in some occupations that required versatility and cunning, like those of the low comedians and acrobats do inscriptions and letters record a few foreigners; but even in these they had to compete with intelligent freedmen who had been given for purposes of profit a specialized training by their masters.

Slaves were of course available in great numbers.

[9] Parvan, *Die Nationalität der Kaufleute.*

[10] Juvenal, III, 76:

> "While every land—daily pours
> Its starving myriads forth, hither they come
> To fatten on the genial soil of Rome,
> Minions, then lords of every princely dome,
> Grammarian, painter, augur, rhetorician,
> Ropedancer, conjurer, fiddler and physician."

One might infer from Juvenal's lines that these were free immigrants, and of course the casual observer had no way of knowing, but the inscriptions prove that men of this class were frequently slaves and freedmen. At Rome slaves could not be recognized as such. When a senator once proposed that slaves be given a distinctive dress, the Senate defeated the measure fearing that the slaves might become dangerous if they came to realize their great number, Seneca, *de Clem.* 1, 24. Cf. Tac. *Ann.* 4, 27; Ibid. 13, 27; "most of the knights and many of the Senators were descendants of slaves."

The more docile ones were supplied by the Greek markets where the Greeks in their economic decline sold
their unprofitable chattels and for which they presently
began to breed and train new generations of slaves as
they found the demands of the West worth supplying.
Throughout all that vast area of misruled Asia Minor
also where petty kingdoms kept up a constant warfare,
hordes of captives and kidnapped children of the various Oriental races were brought to the block by traders
and pirates. Strabo[11] remarks that on the slave market of Delos ten thousand slaves per day were frequently sold. Rome's generals also brought in vast
numbers of captives, many of them savage warriors
who could be used only in heavy labor under close
watch or in chains. The glut of Sardinian captives[12]
became proverbial. A hundred and fifty thousand
Epirotes were brought in by one raid. Pontus provided
large numbers of captives in the campaigns of Sulla,
Lucullus, and Pompey. When Carthage fell a large
part of its population was sold into captivity. The
Cimbri taken by Marius, assigned naturally to the
heavy work on plantations, made up the backbone of
Spartacus' army a few years later. And so the dismal
story goes. Such were the laborers on the land and in
the industries of Cicero's time. And these were generally permanent accretions, for Rome's extremely
liberal policy in manumitting slaves and giving them

[11] Strabo, XIV, 3, 2; Diod. 36, 3.

[12] War captives. See Koeser, *De Captivis rom.*, Livy, XLI, 28;
XLV, 34; Appian, *Lib.* 130; *Mithrad.* 61 and 78, Livy, *Per.* 68.

citizenship with freedom made it possible for the conglomerate stock to liberate itself with unusual ease and
to merge into the citizen body of Rome. Thus slaves
not only supplied the demand for labor but the sons of
slaves spread out into the trades and crafts that required civil standing, and in Cicero's day it was these
people who already constituted the larger element of
the plebeian classes.[13] To reach more definite data on
the proportion of this new stock in Rome's population
is difficult since no ancient author has chosen to give
the complete census figures then available. The best
that can now be done is to draw upon such facts as may
be derived from Roman inscriptions, keeping well in
mind that these inscriptions come largely from the
Empire and that some reduction must be made for any
inferences applied to the late Republic.

As is well known, the voluminous Corpus of Latin
Inscriptions contains in the sixth volume the full text
of all the sepulchral inscriptions of Rome, more than
twenty thousand, and it may fairly be assumed that
these, numerous as they are, record a representative
list of Roman names of average type for the first three
centuries of the Empire. Now a Roman tombstone
may reveal many secrets. The name alone is often
eloquent. In its official form it shows whether the
bearer is a slave, an ex-slave, or citizen-born. In the

[13] See Chapter XVII. Even the laws of the early Empire designed to restrict manumission were seldon enforced. Indeed no
one was interested in enforcing them. The *Lex Salpensana* proves
that owners could legally manumit practically without limit,
C.I.L. II, 1963, ¶28.

case of citizen-born, the cognomen, if foreign, seems to betray ignoble or at least non-Roman ancestry. The stone is also liable, when it records the names of parents, children, or relatives, to disclose useful information regarding the status of the family and hence, by inference, of the individual.

Furthermore the Roman, proud of any petty office he has held, is sure to record the honor, and such offices and occupations to some extent make known the class and rank of the holder. In a word, a careful study of the numerous sepulchral inscriptions can furnish important data for estimating the character of Rome's population.

There has been some doubt as to whether the foreign cognomen is a safe criterion for judging the bearer's origin. If, however, one considers the inscriptions in which both parents and children are named, one finds that the second generation is remarkably fond of changing a foreign sounding cognomen into one of respectably[14] native appearance. Martial of course commented upon this, as upon all else, and his epigram on the Syrian barber, Cinnamus, who transformed himself into Cinna, a name of unsuspected purity, has had many a congener in recent numbers of *Punch* and *Life*. This process of Romanizing names and choosing distinctly Roman cognomina for children is so very pronounced that we may safely infer that the foreign names had no good repute even among the lowly. When the latter occur, they may be taken as proof that

[14] *Am. Hist. Rev.* 1916, p. 693, for the full evidence.

the ancestral tree had its roots in foreign soil. And when the name is Greek, as a very large proportion of slave and freedmen names actually are, we may also infer that the bearer came from or at least by way of that part of the slave-producing world in which Greek was the language of commerce, that is Asia Minor and Syria.[15]

By using all the criteria just enumerated and applying them to lists of persons who actually resided[16] at Rome with their families, and not to mere transients, and by including in the list the Latin slave names, like Salvius, Hilarus, and Apparatus, that were avoided by freeborn citizens we reach the surprising conclusion that nearly 90 per cent. of the population permanently resident at Rome in the Empire bore the taint of foreign extraction.

The question then arises whether it was possible for this foreign and servile population to multiply and to merge into the civil population of Rome. In the absence of evidence to the contrary, the assumption has prevailed that in the city at least work in aristocratic households was so exacting that slaves could seldom have been allowed the privilege of family life, and that the masters could not afford the cost or the waste of service involved in the rearing of slave children. This

[15] The evidence is collected in Bang, *Die Herkunft der Röm. Sklaven*, Röm. Mitt, 1910 and 1912.

[16] See *Am. Hist. Rev. Loc. cit.* I have included children of ten years or less, who presumably were born at Rome, but of other slaves and freedmen only such as revealed a near personal relationship with some resident of Rome.

assumption however proves to be erroneous. The sixth volume of the Corpus of Inscriptions fortunately records names taken from the extensive burial grounds and urn-depositories of several aristocratic households, and these prove that the slaves even in such well-organized establishments usually married and were well-nigh as prolific in offspring[17] as the average Roman of free station. Livia's dressmaker married her butler, Octavia's hairdresser was the wife of her keeper of the plate, Statilius' messenger courted the spinning maid, and so on the lists run. To be sure the percentages of offspring are not as large as in average Roman families, but when we consider that the slave child often failed for reasons of expense to receive the honor of an inscription, and furthermore that such children were often perforce separated from their parents and therefore not recorded with their parents the general conclusion just hazarded will not seem an overstatement.

That slaves usually married and had goodly families not only in the country, as Varro and Appian[18] both remark, but also in the urban households is then evident. A concomitant fact important for our purpose is

[17] *Am. Hist. Rev.* 1916, 697-8.

[18] Varro, *R. R.* I, 17, 5; II, 1, 26; II, 10, 6; Appian, *B. C.* I, 7; Columella, I, 8, 18; Hor. *Epode*, II, 65; Livy, XXII, 11, 8; Nepos, *Atticus*, 13, 4. Somewhat to our surprise, the laws which were invented for the encouragement of large families favored freedmen and freedwomen as well as the native stock. By the *lex Aelia Sentia* a freedwoman of "Junian" standing could become a full citizen by giving birth to a child, and a freedwoman who had four children was released from the guardianship of her patron, Gaius, I, 29, and III, 44.

that the Romans were exceedingly liberal in the practice of the manumission of slaves, so that this stock
soon became an integral part of the citizenship. The
facts about manumission are so easily accessible in the
works of Friedländer, Dill, and others that we need
not attempt to describe them here. The processes are
well known. Frugal and ambitious slaves, particularly
the quick-witted Orientals, could save enough in a few
years to buy their freedom. Many were given their
freedom because of good service, many were set up in
some petty business upon a percentage of profits and
hence earned their liberty; very many were set at liberty by testaments of their masters. Such freedmen
would usually labor to win the liberty of their wives
and children, if that had not already been secured, and
thus there was always a horde of freedmen, whose
children possessed full civil liberty, who assumed
Roman names, dress, and manners, and were ready to
found new houses that might some day vie in splendor
with the nobility of ancient days.

Nor is it to be inferred that the picture we have
given of a wholly changed race was true of the city
alone. Tacitus speaks only of the metropolis as the
"cesspool of the world," and indeed Rome was naturally more affected than the rest of Italy. But no
region of the West really escaped the process of
change. Not only do the other important cities of
Italy, like Beneventum, Milan, and Patavium, reveal
a strikingly large proportion of non-Italian names in
their cemeteries but the very core of central Italy

whence the hardiest soldiers were once drawn seems to have become largely foreign; a careful reading of the inscriptions of the Marsi and Vestini will allay the most obstinate doubts on this point. In a word, the whole of Italy as well as the Romanized portions of Gaul and Spain were during the Empire dominated in blood by the East.

And it is accurate to say "the East." An analysis of the given names of the slaves and freedmen of Rome reveals that seventy per cent. are Greek; the indices of the same class for Latium outside of Rome give sixty-four per cent. Greek. Even Cisalpine Gaul, the region where one would expect few Oriental slaves and numerous Northern ones, proves to yield forty-six per cent. Greek names. And it must not be forgotten that many freedmen of Eastern extraction had already acquired pride enough to hide their condition by substituting Latin for Greek cognomina, so that our percentages do not by any means overstate conditions.

It will probably always remain a problem why the Oriental stock continued predominant when in fact the Gallic, German and Dacian wars furnished so very many captives for the block at Rome. The explanation doubtless involves to some extent practices well understood at Rome but which have not happened to be recorded. Perhaps slave-capture and kidnapping persisted in the East during the Empire to an extent that has not been surmised. Perhaps the expanding economic prosperity of the West drew the surplusage of slaves from a decaying East, and perhaps also the

Eastern trade encouraged the rearing of slaves for the Western market as one of the regular products for export. As for the northern war-captive we may surmise why this race soon vanished. A chance remark of Caesar[19] for instance reveals the fact that Cimbric war captives were the mainstay of the slave revolt under Spartacus. Those revolters were of course wiped out in the hopeless contest. And this may give us a clew to further surmise. The Gallic and Germanic war captives were hardly suited to the household duties which provided the best opportunities for survival. Rude and strong, they were probably sent to the roughest service in the mines and in the galley. There they worked themselves to an early death knowing nothing of wife and offspring and caring for nought but possible revenge and improbable escape.[20] Their course was soon run. That inscriptions say little of them is not to be wondered at. Such we must assume were in part the conditions and practices that eliminated the Northern captive and encouraged the multiplication of the Oriental. At any rate the testimony of the inscriptions that the latter overwhelmed Rome cannot be disputed.

It would be interesting to know how far the social transmutation we have tried to follow accounts for the fundamental changes in the Empire. Was not absolutism inevitable when the Italian, who had so equably combined liberty with law, gave way to impulsive and

[19] *Bell. Gall.* I, 40, 5.

[20] Strack, *Hist. Zeitschrift*, CXII, 9.

passionate races[21] that had never known self-government? Did the emotional and mystical religions of the East spread westward and capture the Roman empire as the Orientals who lived by faith and intuition displaced the rationalistic Occidental? Did the literature of the later day lose its originality because a new people came to copy its forms without comprehension of its spirit? Did Rome's capacity to govern fail because the people of the iron will, indefatigable purpose, and prudent vision that had built the state bequeathed its government to men of softer fibre? Such questions lead far afield, but the questions themselves indicate the direction that historians may expect to take in accounting for some of the economic changes of the Empire.

[21] In *Pro Flacco*, 17, Cicero characterizes with much amusing exaggeration the *ingenita levitas et erudita vanitas* of the Asiatic Greeks, making the striking statement that "whenever our political assemblies are thrown into confusion it is usually people of this race that have caused it."

CHAPTER XIII

Industry

RECENT students of Roman industry have disagreed fundamentally regarding its scope, its aims, and processes, some[1] comparing it with the primitive methods of an undeveloped rural society, and others applying to it the language of the intricate industrial system of modern times. This disagreement is of course largely due to the inadequate information found in the ancient writers, who were for the most part statesmen interested in political history and who concerned themselves little with the occupations of slaves and freedmen. Except for some agricultural treatises, the volumes of Frontinus on Rome's water supply, and a few books of Pliny devoted to the technical methods of production, Roman writers have left the economist to the mercy of parentheses, obiter dicta, and the mute objects brought to light by the excavator's spade. If progress

[1] Cf. Rodbertus, *Jahrb. f. Nationalök.* IV, 341; Bücher, *Entstehung d. Volkswirtschaft*[4], 1904, p. 117. The opposite view is held by E. Meyer, *Kleine Schriften*, pp. 79 ff. and 169 ff. The advocates of both views have gone to untenable extremes. Gummerus, art, *Handel und Industrie* in *Pauly-Wissowa* is reliable. In the following five chapters the material is drawn largely from the period of greatest industrial activity in Italy, that is, the last half century of the republic and the first century of the empire. Only the earlier jurists are cited.

is to be made in this nebulous subject a patient reckoning with the evidence of archaeology is essential.

It is my intention in this chapter to examine several typical industries, especially those that have provided some record of themselves in the form of trademarks and maker's signatures,[2] in order to procure definite data regarding the scale of production, the degree of centralization, the extent of the market, and the class of people involved in the production of them. In the next chapter by way of corrective and a supplement I shall attempt a survey of the economic structure of Pompeii, the only Roman city that has survived to such an extent as to permit a reliable reconstruction, and to this I shall append a summary of such conclusions as seem to be justified.

It may be said at once that in general the Roman producer was much nearer the consumer than he is to-day, that the handicraftsman who sold in his small artisan-shop the product of his own labor was the typical maker and merchant and that a fullfledged factory system of production emerged only in certain favorable circumstances. What these were may be gathered from the examination of the individual industries which follows.

The table-ware that was most popular in Augustus' day was a *red-glazed pottery* ornamented with designs in low relief and called, after the most important city of manufacture, Arretine ware.[3] It frequently

[2] Such inscriptions have been collected in the fifteenth volume of the *Corpus Inscriptionum Latinarum.*

[3] See *C.I.L.* XV, 702 and XI, 1081; Chase. *Catalogue of Arretine Pottery* (with bibliography), 1916.

bears the stamp not only of the manufacturer but also of the particular craftsman who designed the piece, or rather the mold from which the piece was turned; for the processes were those of mass-production in a factory rather than of individual craftmen's shops. The designer, for instance, produced a variety of stencils, probably in clay, with patterns of leaves, geometrical designs, or human figures posturing, etc., and with these he would stencil running friezes, not into each bowl, but into a mold which could serve for the production of hundreds of bowls. The designer was a trained craftsman who could model in clay and who had some taste in the composition of patterns, but we need hardly suppose that he was an original artist like the men who so frequently produced exquisite work in the famous Greek vases, since in Arretine ware the patterns were usually borrowed from those of silver plate.

To judge from the instances in which we can actually apply a test to the form of the signature,[4] the designer was usually a slave or a freedman. If the designer was a slave we may be fairly sure that the ordinary laborers were. The owners of the factories were of course Roman citizens, but it is surprising how frequently they bore a foreign cognomen, a fact which implies that they or their ancestors of no remote date

[4] See *Am. Hist. Review*, 1916, p. 693, for criteria; also Oxé, *Rhein. Mus.* 1904, 108. The pottery produced at Cales two centuries earlier was designed almost wholly by the shopowners who were free citizens, see Pagenstecher, *Die calen, Reliefkeramik*, p. 148 ff.

had come up from slavery. Indeed some of the owners appear to be the very persons who designed the patterns of an earlier style, an indication that slave-artists sometimes secured their freedom and a sufficient competence to gain possession of their master's factories.

The extensive proportions of some of the factories are proved beyond a doubt. So, for instance, the ware of certain firms has been found, not, to be sure, over the whole Roman world—for each firm seems to have supplied the regions opened by the natural arteries of trade—but at least over half the Mediterranean basin. Indeed for one period it is true that the potteries situated in three districts, i. e., near Puteoli, at Arretium, and in the valley of the Po, supplied the whole demand for moderately good table-ware throughout the Empire, excepting only the southeast. The scale of production[5] is also indicated by the great number of workmen engaged in certain firms. That of Cornelius, for instance, has provided the names of some forty designers. To be sure, they were not all contemporaneous, but at any rate a single designer could keep a large number of mixers, potters and furnacemen busy, since presumably he merely made the molds and touched up the designs. Calidius Strigo had at least twenty designers, Perennius as many, and there were a dozen other firms of goodly proportions at Arretium.

[5] *Notizie degli Scavi*, 1896, p. 455, describes a large pottery. The mixing vat had a capacity of 10,000 gallons. The Gallic potteries also produced on a large scale: Déchelette, *Les vases céramiques de la Gaule*, p. 91; Hermet, *Les graffites de la Graufesenque*.

Finally, mass production with a view to extensive trade is disclosed in the establishment of branch factories in Gaul and elsewhere, the purpose being, of course, to save what was in that day the heavy item of freight. Indeed the home factories were eventually put to rout by these new ones, whether because the clays of Gaul were better, the makers more enterprising, or the provincial market more conservative when fashions began to change in Italy. So, for instance, a consignment of red ware that had reached Pompeii shortly before the eruption — the box had not yet been opened — contained more Gallic pieces than Italian, although the box had apparently been packed at Rome.[6]

In this industry, then, we find the machinery of an extensive factory production of articles intended for wide distribution. Of course the student of Roman society sees in this instance an exception to, rather than an example of, the usual rule, but it is apparent that conditions here favored the development of large-scale production. Two elements were of prime importance. One was the quasi-trade-secret involved in the making of the paste, for, though there was no copyright and this particular clay could be and in fact was manufactured in several places, exact knowledge of a rather intricate formula was after all essential. Secondly, a designer of some skill, training, and taste was required; consequently competition could not spring up over night, and the expense of keeping a skilled designer naturally suggested the advisability of

[6] Atkinson, *Jour. of Roman Studies*, IV, 27.

gathering under him enough unskilled labor to occupy
his time. Hence it is that this industry developed in
a way that was rather unusual in the Roman world.

By way of contrast both in workmanship and in
conditions of production it is interesting to compare
the manufacture of another article of pottery, namely,
the ordinary *clay lamps*,[7] millions of which must have
been manufactured every year and sold for a very few
cents apiece. Many of these lamps have a little decoration, but seldom does a pattern show any real artistic
worth. They were turned out in molds by an ordinary potter, and the clay paste was little better than
that used in good roof-tiles. Furthermore, they were
so cheap that it would hardly have been worth while
to ship them any considerable distance. To be sure,
the recurrence in all parts of the world of certain
types of lamps bearing a well-known firm-name succeeded until recently in deceiving archaeologists into
thinking that certain firms commanded the trade over
wide areas. But it has now been proved[8] by measure-
ments that the greater number of these lamps came
from local potteries that simply used various shapes
successively popular at some center like Rome, importing the originals and using them, firm-name and all,
as molds. Since, then, in the absence of protective
copyright, there was here no difficult formula or trade-
secret to aid in excluding competition and no great

---

[7] *C.I.L.* XV, 784; Fink, *Sitzungsb. Akad. München*, 1900;
Loeschcke, *Keramische Funde in Haltern*, p. 210.

[8] Loeschcke, *op. cit.* p. 210.

economic inducement for gathering considerable labor, the industry scattered in such a way that local potteries usually supplied the needs of each community. Concerning the class of labor used we have some indications. The firm-names are usually in briefest form, a cognomen alone, though in early examples good Roman gentile names occur. Judging from the frequency of Greek cognomina we may suppose that the potteries which produced these cheap wares fell into the hands of the class that in general managed Rome's industries, at least in the Early Empire, i. e., the freedmen.

Certain developments of the *glass* industry in Augustus' day[9] bring us back to conditions not unlike those of the red-glazed pottery. Glass-making apparently grew out of the art of surface-glazing in Egypt at a very early age, and in Roman times the glassware of Alexandria, chiefly mosaics of varicolored glass pastes, was shipped the world over. It is likely that there were very large factories in Egypt, but since the ware bears no trade-mark and since it was successfully copied at Rome and elsewhere, we are quite unable to determine the proportions of such factories. There is, however, a translucent glass of Rome, usually figured and signed, and apparently made with the blowpipe, that provides some little information of value. When Strabo says that in his day certain new inventions at Rome had greatly increased the production of

[9] Kisa, *Das Glas im Altertum*, pp. 261, 702; Eisen, *Am. Jour. Arch.* 1916, p. 143; Morin, *La Verrerie in Gaule*, 1913; *C.I.L.* XV, 871.

glass and brought down the price to a cent or two per article he may well be referring to the discovery of the process by which a bubble of glass paste was manipulated with the aid of a blow-pipe. It is obvious why this method revolutionized the production of clear glass. Hitherto for the making of bottles and for many shapes of beakers a new mold had to be shaped for each individual article, a labor-consuming process, and one which, because of the sand and clay of the mold, left the article far from clear. With the blow-pipe a permanent outer mold was used which might contain the figured pattern—figures were the fashion in all wares of Augustus' day—and the glass-blower with the use of his pipe could force the paste to fill the mold and assume the pattern desired. The product was clearer and smoother and the work was far more rapidly done than by the old method. It is not surprising that the makers of the new glass, inartistic though it was, showed such enthusiasm over the new process as to put their names in prominent letters upon the pattern. The ware, which can readily be distinguished, is not only found widely distributed, but the maker's name is printed in Greek as well as in Latin, apparently on the supposition that the articles would find a wide sale.

Here again, as in the case of Arretine ware, conditions favorable to monopolistic production existed. Whether or not modern methods can extract glass paste with ease from the sands and pozzolanas of Italy everywhere, it is clear from Strabo and Pliny that the ancient glass-maker had great difficulty in finding a tractable sand. This alone prevented much competition. Moreover, the new invention made a peculiar distribution of specialists necessary. Hitherto the workman who handled the hot glass paste at the furnace must also be skilled at molding it quickly into the desired pattern. By the new process one designer could shape any number of exterior molds, and any number of glass-blowers might produce the articles on these molds, given only special skill in glass-blowing. Thus again it was good economy to gather labor into one place and about one designer.

There is one additional fact of interest here that deserves mention in passing. The manufacturers of this glass bear Greek names and call themselves natives of Phoenician Sidon. It may be that some of the factories were in Sidon; at least Ennion's work is found mainly in that region. On the other hand, the work of Artas, Neikon, and Ariston appears mostly at Rome. Either we are dealing with an eastern product that captured the trade of Rome, or, what is more likely, we are dealing with skilled artisans and manufacturers who, realizing that Rome offered the best market, set up their main factories in Italy. Perhaps these are the factories on the Volturnus River mentioned by Pliny.

The *brickmaking*[10] *industry* was another which tended toward factory and monopolistic methods at

[10] *C.I.L.* XV, 1.

Rome, though for a very different set of reasons. During the Republic the industry found little encouragement. Public buildings were largely made of tufa-blocks, and when concrete was introduced it came to be lined with stone, large blocks or small squares set in cement. Clay was burnt chiefly for roof-tiles. In the early Empire till Claudius' day the stone facing and opus reticulatum still continued in vogue, though broken roof-tiles were also introduced for the facing of concrete walls. In the reign of Claudius, however, brick-facing became more general so that brickyards had to supply new forms in addition to the roof-tiles. It was in Nero's reign, especially when, after the great fire, a large part of the city had to be rebuilt, that the brick industry came to its own. It is evident that the brick kilns then in existence had to supply an inestimable quantity of material for the facing of concrete walls, and brick-faced concrete remained the standard material for construction thenceforward.

There were of course both centrifugal and centripetal forces in this industry at Rome as elsewhere. The recipe was centuries old, and by no means a secret. Furthermore, good clays for bricks were abundant. To be sure, the excellent Pliocene shales behind the Vatican that now feed the great kilns of Rome seem not to have been exploited to any great extent in ancient times, but the alluvium of the Anio and of the Tiber which combines the limestone silt of the Apennines with the volcanic pozzolanas of Latium still produces some of the finest red bricks of Rome, and here,

to judge from the texture of the old bricks and from
the brick stamps, were the chief yards of ancient
Rome. That supply was inexhaustible and could not
well be controlled by any single firm.

Since the product was too heavy for ready transport, it was not easy for a firm to secure control of the
trade over large areas. Only in very few instances do
the ancient brick stamps appear widely distributed.
Bricks from Roman yards were of course barged down
to Ostia, and some wares of the Campanian and even
the Ligurian and Gallic coasts went by sea to Rome's
seaport and vice versa, possibly as ballast. Yards on
the Tiber above Rome, even a hundred miles away,
gained a market down the river, and when a particularly good article was desired by a nobleman for his
Alban villa he would pay the expenses of a costly
transport from the metropolis; but this list fairly completes the cases of trans-shipment.

And yet certain brick firms at Rome grew to immense proportions, owing possibly to a capacity and
ability to grasp the opportunities offered. Interesting
in this connection is the growth of the property of the
famous Gallic orator, Domitius Afer. Arriving at
Rome a poor man in the reign of Tiberius, he gained
wealth and political position by his remarkable gift of
speech, ready wit, and calculating devotion to the
reigning prince. Like any Roman ambitious to establish a social position, he invested in landed estates, and
it was probably in this way that he became an owner
of a brickyard, since tile-burning was still looked upon

as a legitimate branch of agriculture and therefore respectable beyond the run of ordinary business. The times were auspicious, for bricks were just working their way into fashion. Afer's adopted sons and heirs, Tullus and Lucanus, profiting doubtless by the devastating fire that destroyed most of Rome, perhaps also skillfully using for business purposes the political influence which they both inherited from their ennobled father, extended their enterprises enormously, acquiring, as their trade-marks show, the yards of several different estates which they finally conducted under a score of managers. There is hardly a public or private building of importance during their period—an epoch of enormous building activity—where their trade-mark is not prominent, if not predominant, among the brick stamps found. These, by the way, are the properties which formed the main group of the imperial yards of a later day, for they passed by inheritance through the hands of Lucilla, the daughter of Lucanus, to her grandson, who became the emperor Marcus Aurelius. In his day, indeed, the brickyards of Rome had largely become imperial property, well-nigh an imperial monopoly, a situation which, however, was largely due to the accident of intermarriage between the families that owned the chief yards at the beginning of the second century and the succession by due inheritance into the family of the Annii.

It is deserving of notice that brickmaking is practically the only industry at Rome in which the aristocrat does not hesitate to display his connections with

the profits of a factory. The reason probably lies in
the associations with agriculture already mentioned.
The Roman noble was supposed to be a landlord, and
it was always proper for him to be intimately acquainted with all the processes of agriculture and to
develop all the resources of his land, be this by grain-
or stock-raising or by turning a clay bank into a tile
yard. Indeed Asinius Pollio was one of the first nobles
at Rome to have his name stamped upon tiles which
he apparently made at his Alban villa, and there is
little reason to doubt that the tiles bearing the name
of *Tuli* from the vicinity of Tusculum were made at
the favorite Tusculan villa of Cicero.

This fact again explains a peculiar business practice
in the association of the owner and slave-managers of
such factories, for brick stamps usually indicate the
names of both the owner and the superintendent of
the yard, the latter invariably a slave or freedman.
The practice of course simply continues the conditions
that regularly held upon the large landed estates. The
landlord at this time seldom leased his lands; he rather
cultivated them himself, placing a trusted slave or
freedman in charge of his property, a position of considerable responsibility and dignity. It is apparent
that the superintendent of the brickyards who was permitted to stamp his name upon the brick with that of
his master corresponds in every way to the *villicus* of
the estate.

Regarding the manufacture of *metal-ware* a few

definite facts can be elicited from ancient writers, and in the case of bronze and lead-ware, from producer's signatures. Wrought *iron* and steel of excellent quality were made and used in arms and agricultural implements, but since the valved bellows had not yet been invented a thorough melting of iron ore was not yet possible. The Roman manufacturer[11] therefore did not know of cast iron, the cheapest and most serviceable form of the metal. In lieu of thorough smelting he had to content himself with the expensive product that could be procured by patient and reiterated forging on the anvil. Delian price lists quote iron at about six dollars per hundred weight, which seems very high when we consider that the Roman procured his copper at very little above the modern price.

In Cicero's day there seems to have been a very remarkable concentration of iron production at Puteoli. Italian iron ore came then as now from the island of Elba off the Tuscan shore. The ore dug there was brought to the mainland and "roasted" until the mass "resembled sponges" with such heat as could be produced in low furnaces. At the time of the Second Punic War,[12] the Etruscan cities still held possession of the iron industries of Italy, producing great quantities of arms and implements; but in the second century

[11] Jullian, Art. *Fabri*, Daremberg-Saglio; Blümner, *Technologie*, IV; Cou, *Antiquities from Boscoreale*, Chicago, 1912, describes farm implements from the villa of Helius Florus.

[12] Livy, XXVII, 45. The town was dead in Strabo's day: 5, 2, 6. The vast heaps of slag are now being resmelted.

Puteoli captured the trade and the industry. Here, according to Diodorus,[13] manufacturers gathered great numbers of smiths who wrought the crude metal into "arms, mattocks, sickles and other implements," which merchants bought and carried into all parts of the world. That Puteoli succeeded Tuscany[14] is not surprising when we consider her wealth of fuel in the Phlegraean fields, her excellent harbor, her position near the richest agricultural land of Italy where iron tools were especially used, and her place as a distributing center for the armies and navies of Rome.

The language of Diodorus might lead the unwary

[13] Diodorus, V, 13. In Cato's day Cales on the border of Campania produced good iron ware. The industry may have spread from there to Puteoli. Of course excellent steel was also made in Spain, Noricum, and in Anatolia, in articles which the Romans always imported in quantities.

[14] Pliny's chance remark that an old decree of the Senate had forbidden mining has led to much futile guessing (Pliny, *N. H.* III, 138; XXXVII, 201). The iron mines of Elba were being worked in Strabo's day, and doubtless were worked as long as they proved profitable. It may be that the Senate had once ordered the mines closed in the third century when the Gauls invaded Italy and found arms in northern Etruria. It will be remembered that Porsenna had previously forbidden the use of iron in Latium except for agricultural implements. Needless to say the Senatorial decree must have become a dead letter as soon as the Roman confederacy had complete control of Italy. The law limiting the output of gold at Vercellae, also quoted by Pliny (*N. H.* XXXIII, 78), was probably intended to prevent a sudden fluctuation of prices such as had taken place when gold was discovered at Aquileia (Pol. XXXIV, 10). Such gold placer-mines did not continue to produce long, and no repeal of the law was therefore necessary, a thing which seems to have misled Pliny into thinking these laws were still in force in his day.

into assuming a real factory system in this industry, as indeed it does justify us in applying to it the terms of capitalistic industry and international commerce. But we must not infer too much. Since the furnaces could not produce a thoroughly molten ore in large quantities, cast-iron implements which might have been made *en masse* were of course out of the question. Every iron and steel implement was accordingly the product of repeated heatings and forgings on individual anvils. There was therefore in all probability little division of labor, and little use of labor-saving machinery except such as any simple smith would employ. If some manufacturers, as Diodorus implies, took advantage of Puteoli's excellent position, to gather there under one roof a large number of skilled smiths, slaves or free, they might well be called capitalistic producers, but the essential elements of a factory system, such as we have found in the pottery and glass industries, cannot without further evidence be assumed.

In these circumstances it is not surprising that all the large cities reveal in their inscriptions the fact that individual producers of iron implements continued to prosper everywhere.[15] They were the artisans who

[15] *C. I. L.* VI, 9886, 2196, 1952, 9442, 9260; II, 3357; X, 3984, 3987; Cic. Cat. I, 8, mentions a house at Rome *inter falcarios*. The Roman gild of *fabri* is mentioned in *C. I. L.* VI, 1892. Pompeii seems to have had hardware stores without forges; probably most of the iron ware of that town was supplied from the factories of Puteoli.

Varro also mentions travelling smiths that went from farm to farm, and some landlords found it worth while to own slaves trained as smiths, see *C. I. L.* VI, 6283-5, and Cic. *Pro Plancio*, 62.

kept a small shop with a single forge where with the aid of an apprentice-slave or two they made their own specialty and sold it. In the Vatican gallery there stands a typical illustration of such a shop represented upon a tombstone.[16] On one side is pictured the smith forging a blade, on the other he is seen by the side of a small rack of knives and sickles making a sale to a customer. Nothing could better illustrate the general condition of Roman industry. Very many of the tombstones of Roman artisans reveal this same system prevailing in the iron trade in that they mention the special craft of shield-maker, sword-maker, sickle-maker, helmet-maker, and the like.

In the production of arms and armor the participation of the government altered conditions in the trade, but this probably did not interfere seriously with private enterprise until late in imperial times. Every army[17] had its group of smiths behind the lines not only to make the artillery of the army but also to mend shields, swords and helmets and to supply spear-points in great abundance. But the artisans at home, during the Republic at least, did no little work in filling the demand for arms since every legionary soldier[18] had to provide himself before departure with a helmet, a breastplate or coat of mail, a standard sword, and a steel-pointed lance. It is probable too that the ar-

[16] Amelung, I, 275.

[17] Vegetius, II, 11; Livy, XXVI, 51; XXIX, 35; Polyb. X, 17.

[18] Tac. *Ann.* I, 17.

mories[19] which every municipality of any size kept
well stocked against sudden riots or invasions bought
their supplies from private shops or large producers.
At any rate the armamentarium[20] of Pompeii which
was recently found had no place for production in the
vicinity. In the late Empire, as is well known, the
government assumed the task of producing all the arms
and armor needed by its forces and erected for the
purpose large state factories in several cities throughout the Empire.

The manufacture of *bronze* and copper-ware[21] on
the other hand seems to have developed a real factory
system, at least in Capua. At the end of the Republic
and in the early Empire there was being produced a
great abundance of bronze utensils frequently of
seemly shape and artistically ornamented, such as
wine-containers, platters, ladles and bowls, not to
speak of kitchen pots and pans, and all of these bear
producer's names which recur with remarkable frequency. This ware, quite uniform in workmanship,
had been found in abundance not cnly in Italy[22] but

[19] Cic. *Pro Rab.* 20; Tac. *Hist.* I, 38.

[20] *Notizie degli Scavi*, 1916, p. 432. Della Corte, *Juventus*, p. 60,
thinks it a *scola juventutis*.

[21] See Willers, *Bronzeeimer von Hemmoor*, p. 213; *Neue Untersuchungen; Studien z. Griechische Kunst*, p. 156; Mau-Kelsey,
Pompeii, pp. 369-79, for illustrations. See also Pliny, *N. H.*
XXXIII, 130. Winter, *Die Hell. Kunst in Pomp.* IV, 29, thinks
that the best of this ware came from Alexandria and the Greek
cities of southern Italy.

[22] *C. I. L.* XV, gives the Roman inscriptions.

everywhere in Germany and as far north as Scotland, Sweden, and Finland. It is probable that we should look to Capua for the source of these articles. There the Etruscans in the earliest times created a bronze industry; there Cato[23] advises his readers to buy "bronze buckets, containers for wine, oil and water, and all other copper ware"; there Pliny says the best copper-ware of his day was still produced, and it was there that medieval churches had their *campane* made. The conjecture that Capua was the producing center of the widely scattered ware has practically been proved by finding on Capuan tombstones the frequent occurrence of the family names which these articles bear: Cipius, Oppius, Nasennius, and others.

Willers, who has studied this ware, believes that the producing factories were large enough to employ thousands of workmen. Considering that during the Middle Ages copper utensils were remelted whenever found, the survival of many dozens of specimens throughout Europe might perhaps justify his conclusion. He also seems to be justified in employing the term "factory." The process of production involved in making these articles was more elaborate and required a greater number of special artisans than in the iron industry described above. The metal was melted, mixed with proper proportions of tin or zinc, cast in molds that only trained artists could produce, and then submitted to trained artisans who polished, carved

[23] Cato, *R. R.* 135; Pliny, *N. H.* XXXIV, 95; cf. Horace, *Serm.* I, 6, 116.

and forged. Here there was surely not only the investment of large capital but the far-reaching division of labor which characterizes the modern industrial factory.

The reasonable surmise has been made that the existence of these foundries at Capua made possible the extensive employment of bronze in the statues, busts, and objets d'art which have been found in abundance at Herculaneum and Pompeii. To be sure, archaeologists[24] are still prone to ascribe many of these to the studios of Athens, but busts of men like Caecilius Jucundus, the Pompeian banker, prove that native work of very good quality could be produced in the vicinity. It is not improbable that in Cicero's day and during the century following the Capuan foundries cast a large number of statues for Greek and Campanian artists residing at Naples, and that much of the work usually assumed to be imported may soon be accepted as native. Certain it is that much of the beautiful metal furniture of Pompeii, the bronze lamp stands, tables, braziers and tripods, which have influenced later decorative art to such an extent, was made possible by the high development of the bronze industry at Capua.[25]

[24] Deonna, *Statuaria* in Daremb.-Saglio; *Jour. Hell. Stud.* 1903, p. 217.

[25] Unfortunately we have no way of determining what class of labor was used in this Capuan industry, since we do not know whether the signatures belonged to the factory owner, the designer or the workman. It is not unlikely that in Campania

In the manufacture of *water pipes*—usually made of lead—the factory system however failed to emerge, despite the fact that large quantities in standard sizes were frequently needed. Here we get our information partly from Frontinus' business-like account of the water supply of Rome, but mainly from the stamps upon the pipes which indicate their owner and maker.[26] In general, the imperial water-bureau provided for the main aqueducts of Rome, and for the distribution of water to all public places, that is, to the imperial palaces, to the public baths and gardens, and to a large number of free public fountains whence the poor carried their water. In Frontinus' day the bureau owned some seven hundred slaves to do the requisite work, a part of which consisted in making and laying the lead pipes of the public service; indeed such pipes usually bear the name of the maker besides those of the water commissioner and the emperor. And here it is interesting to find that the bureau not infrequently had to employ the services of independent plumbers,[27] as Frontinus himself implies in his statement that he is compelled to let contracts for part of his work.

At Rome, however, the larger number of pipes was contracted for by private individuals who had pur-

---

where Greek ideas still largely prevailed many free workmen labored in the shops, especially since frequent expropriations by Sulla and the triumvirs had removed many natives from the land.

[26] *C. I. L.* XV, 906 ff.

[27] *C. I. L.* XV, 7279-83, 7289, 7309. Compare 7325 with 7523 and 7333 with 7409.

chased the right to tap the public water-main, a group that included most of the well-to-do of the city. Such pipes were quite regularly stamped with the owner's name in order to afford ready identification in case of repairs—for often several lines lay parallel to each other under the street. Usually the maker also took this occasion to have his own name recorded. Now these names reveal some singular circumstances. From the great mass of material recovered and the numerous names recorded, it does not appear that any one firm secured large contracts or tried to build up a stock for large orders, although Frontinus shows that certain standard sizes were in demand. A maker's name in fact very seldom recurs in two widely separated regions of the city, and furthermore when a contract is large it is apparently divided among several plumbers.[28] Moreover it is clear that the names occurring upon the pipes were almost invariably made a part of the original mold, which indicates that the pipe was made to order and that no stock was accumulated. The system in vogue therefore was this: small shop-owners with a few slaves, with no large capital, and with few facilities, took the orders when they came, bought the metal,[29] melted it and rolled it into plates which were cut into the requisite strips and soldered into pipes, and finally laid and connected

[28] C. I. L. XV, 7369-73.

[29] Lead was very cheap, since most silver mines produced more lead as a by-product than the market needed. Pliny, XXXIV, 161, quotes the price of pipe-lead at one cent the pound.

these. That is to say, the plumber was also the maker of the pipes. Why this time-consuming system was conserved it is difficult to understand. Of course since the city laid few mains, and the private citizen who desired water had frequently to conduct it for long distances, it was exceedingly important that the owner's name should be stamped in enduring form, a point certainly secured by this system; but other ways of attaining the same result are conceivable. It would seem that the inertia of this industry is simply an illustration of how tenaciously the small-shop system conserved itself against obvious economic inducements toward centralization—a phenomenon too well known and recognized to need further illustration.

That the people engaged in this trade, if independent shop-owners, were frequently freedmen, or of the same general class as freedmen, is shown by the frequent recurrence of the Greek cognomina. Often indeed they were simply practicing a trade which as slaves they had learned in the imperial or municipal bureaus. Thus the plumber who laid the pipes of the great villa on the Appian way[30] was an imperial freedman, and at Ostia several plumbers bear the descriptive name of Ostiensis in lieu of family names.

Finally, diverse tendencies of industry may be illustrated from the activities of the jewelers and *goldsmiths*. There is no evidence that wholesale production played any part in this trade. Rings and pendants

[30] *C. I. L.* XV, 7799.

and ornaments of precious stones[31] were generally made and sold in small shops, though we sometimes hear of *negotiantes* who apparently were not artisans. Since the raw material was costly, an extensive system of custom-production usually prevailed, and we frequently hear of individuals bringing their old gold or uncut stones to the gold-smiths to have them made into jewelry.[32] But this was by no means the only practice. The cases of lawsuits cited by the jurists[33] also imply that goldsmiths were at times handicraftsmen who owned their raw material; and the tombstone of many jewelers which record large legacies[34] or enumerate long lists of freedmen who had once served them prove that these men often possessed considerable wealth. In this industry furthermore, as in many others, wealthy patrons often equipped an artisan's shop for a skilled slave or freedman, as a profitable way of investing capital. An inscription[35] raised by such a patron to the memory of his freedman reads in part:

"To M Canuleius Zosimus—The patron to his freedman. He did nothing contrary to the wishes of his patron. Though he always had

[31] Gummerus has recently discussed this matter in *Klio*, vols. XIV and XV.

[32] Plautus, *Men.* 525; *Digest*, 19, 2, 31; 34, 2, 34; 41, 1, 77; 19, 22, 1. Diocletian's edict assumes custom work in this industry, but at a very late date when free labor was being suppressed.

[33] *Digest*, 19, 5, 20, 2.

[34] *C. I. L.* VI, 2226, 9433, 9544-45, 9547, 9950, 30973.

[35] *C. I. L.* VI, 9222.

much gold and silver in his possession he coveted none of it. He excelled in carving Clodian ware."

Closely related to the jewelers, sometimes identified with them, were the *gemmarii,* cutters of intaglios and cameos.[36] In ancient days this art assumed very significant proportions for the reason that every man of the least consequence must have his own signet ring, and in the later days of the Republic the aristocratic Romans commanded the services of the very best gem-engravers for these seals, many of which are still treasured as works of exquisite art. There are of course all grades of work. Dioscurides, who was summoned from the East to make the imperial seal, was looked upon as an artist of high rank, and he doubtless did not need to keep a shop. He is a fair instance of the Greek and Oriental artisan who drifted to Rome with the tide of wealth. At the other extreme are the craftsmen known from humble tombstone inscriptions who designate themselves as gem-engravers[37] from the "Sacred Way," the jeweler's street. Here was apparently a row of shops where such craftsmen took orders and worked. Their names seem to indicate that they were freedmen. Possibly they had been trained as slave apprentices and had saved enough by extra labor to purchase freedom and set up shops of their own. Finally, there is a peculiar group of signa-

[36] Furtwängler, *Antike Gemmen.* p. 300, and plates 49 and 50. See also *Arch. Jahrb.* 1888.

[37] *C. I. L.* VI, 9433-6, 9545-49, 33872.

tures written in Greek, though with Latin praenomina. Presumably these designate men who were also immigrant artists but who had gained citizenship—the right to use the Roman form of name—by direct gift of the state, perhaps in recognition of their work. That is to say, they use the Roman praenomen to distinguish themselves from the freedmen, but write the name in Greek as a means of suggesting the fact that their work is not the ordinary crude native cutting. The signatures seem to indicate that for one fine craft at least Rome had to draw largely upon the artisans of Greece and the East. The more ordinary grades of work fell to the slave apprentice, and the business of the small shops was conducted here, as in other trades, by the freedman class. Production on capitalistic lines was naturally out of the question, not only because customers insisted upon having the special attention of some recognized artist, but because most of the work had to be done to order.

CHAPTER XIV

INDUSTRY, *Continued*

INFERENCES drawn solely from the larger industries must perforce lead to conclusions that are partially incorrect. It is fortunate therefore that we are enabled by the survival of the skeleton of Pompeii to examine in some detail the economic structure of an ancient town and thus to round out our conceptions of industrial conditions. Pompeii was not in every respect a typical Roman city. A small seaport town, it doubtless served commerce rather than industry. Living in a region that was still half-Hellenic in Cicero's day its inhabitants had learned to look upon manual labor with a kindlier eye than did the old fashioned nobility of Rome. But the difference should not be overemphasized. The dominant class in Pompeii's politics and society were the well-to-do land-owners who had descended from Sulla's Roman veterans, and these of course had brought Roman folkways with them. The differences in size caused no great dissimilarity in their economic régime: a city of twenty-five thousand souls was rather more significant in those days of evenly distributed production than it is now. If we could recover a few blocks of a typical street of Nero's Rome, we should find difficulty in distinguishing its system of shops and booths

from that of Pompeii. The picture of the city disclosed by the diligent Italian excavators may with
this word of caution be used to illustrate Roman
economics.[1]

At Pompeii, as was usual in the ancient walled
towns where space must be carefully husbanded, shops
lined all busy thoroughfares, while houses of residence
subsided to the centers of the blocks.[2] Since this system obtains throughout the city we may examine a
typical insula,[3] No. 2 of Regio VII, in order to trace
some lines of connection between the industries and the
social classes. The insula contains about forty shops
and booths strung out mainly along the busier streets—
Stabiana and *Augustali*—beside some ten residences
crowded into the center with hallways usually opening
into one of the quieter streets. The first large house
on via Stabiana (No. 6) belonged to Paquius Proculus.
a very popular baker, who reached the high office of
the duumvirate apparently by an overwhelming majority,[4] and was proud enough of the fact to have his

[1] The official reports of Pompeian excavations are not adequately published from the historian's viewpoint. Very often
objects of little artistic value are not reported though they might
prove of great use to the student of economic and social history.

[2] Recent excavations at Ostia have revealed a few tall apart-
ment houses. There were probably many in Rome during the
Empire. In such blocks there were but few shops.

[3] See map in *C. I. L.* IV, Suppl. II; Niccolini, *Le case ed i
monumenti*, II, 42-5, and III; Fiorelli, *Descrizione di Pompeii*
p. 184; Della Corte, in *Rivista Indo-Gr-It.* 1920, p. 117; Engelmann, *Fuehrer durch Pompeii*, 1925.

[4] *C. I. L.* IV, 1122.

portrait, genial, and sufficiently apologetic if rather
unintellectual, painted, apparently in white toga, upon
the wall of his tablinum.[5] With this house he combined the adjacent one, sacrificing the gardens of both
for the mill and workrooms of his bakery. And yet,
though the owner was willing to live within sound of
his mills, he did not choose to display his wares directly in the five shops that lined the front of his
home. These shops are all independent of the house.
To judge from an election notice[6] which appears
nearby, Proculus owned a fairly large bread and cake-
shop in the opposite corner (Reg. IX, 3, 10) to which
also was attached a bakery with five mills. Here there
was less danger perhaps of flecking his judicial toga
with the dust of his calling. Be that as it may, it is
interesting to find that *duumvir juredicundo* actively
engaged in an expanding business of milling and baking. He may fairly represent the prosperous industrial
class to which the petty aristocracy of Pompeii's municipal officials largely belonged.

No. 11 is a house of moderate size which was turned
into a dyeing establishment in the early empire when
the clothing industry became important in Pompeii.
It is indeed characteristic of the conservative industrial
tendencies of Pompeii that the proprietor did not build
a place to suit his needs but installed himself in a house
built for domestic use, where, of course, the rooms
were by no means adapted for his purposes. The pro-

---

[5] Mau-Kelsey, *Pompeii*[2], p. 477.

[6] *C. I. L.* IV, 3651.

prietor, like Proculus the baker, apparently used part of the house as a dwelling-place.

The next residence of note is No. 16. It is spacious, contains a handsome peristyle, and has supplied several noteworthy frescoes to the Naples museum.[7] Its owner seems to be M. Gavius Rufus, a man of some wealth. What his source of income was we do not know; his house is not physically connected with any shop or booth.

Next door (No. 18) lived C. Vibius, probably he of the cognomen Severus, since the dozen election placards of Vibius Severus are all found in the immediate neighborhood. If so he also entertained the ambition of becoming duumvir. He too turned the rear part of his house into a workshop, for the chambers beside the peristyle were used as store-chambers whence there was direct communication with the shop upon the back street.

N. Popidius Priscus dwelt in the next house (No. 20, Casa dei Marmi[8]), the largest and most handsomely decorated in the block and apparently long in the possession of the family, since the family name appears in Oscan on an old stone inscription in the peristyle.[9] Yet the source of this display is readily disclosed to anyone who will follow the three several doors that lead from the house to various shops in other parts

[7] *Naples Mus. Cat.* Nos. 1381, 1383, 1385.

[8] Helbig, *Wandgemälde*, 475; Della Corte, *loc. cit.* p. 113.

[9] There were magistrates of this family before Sulla took the city; Conway, *Italic Dialects*, 61.

of the block. Indeed there was found in the house a
bronze stamp such as bakers use to trade-mark their
cakes, and this stamp bore the name of Popidius. The
excavator was therefore not surprised to find a door
leading from the atrium of this house into a prosperous bakery at the corner. Here were five mills of
the usual type made to be worked by horse-power, a
cunningly contrived machine for kneading dough, a
bakers' oven having a capacity of perhaps two thousand loaves per day, and a number of cake forms, but
no display counters nor doors inviting the purchaser.
Popidius may have had his sales-shop elsewhere, or
he may have disposed of his wares at wholesale. But
this was not his only investment. In the rear of his
house a door led to a spacious barroom (No. 47) with
many wine jars and a hospitable double door upon the
street. Finally another rear door led to a complex of
rooms (No. 38) which appears to have constituted a
workshop terminating in two salesrooms upon the
street—but we do not know what was produced and
sold here. Whatever the various sources of his income,—and he may well have been a landowner also—
the sum total was not small, judging from the mag-
nificance of his house.

No. 35 is a house of moderate size which is characteristic of a very large class of houses at Pompeii, in
that it connects directly with two workshops upon the
street, Nos. 27 and 30. The former contains a fixed
workbench and a small furnace in one of its two small
rooms, but there is nothing in No. 30 to indicate the
character of its products.

Such were the houses that hid within and fed upon the encircling row of petty shops bordering the four streets. They give us a picture—proved true to type by the study of other blocks—of a society somewhat less provincially aristocratic, a trifle more worldly-wise, than that which Rome's staid literature deigns to notice. These men who had their courtyards decorated with marble cupids and fauns, their dining-room walls frescoed with legends from Homer and Euripides, the men whom their fellow-townsmen elected to the highest municipal positions[10] of trust and to expensive honors, these leading citizens of Pompeii were, to some extent, her prosperous bakers, potters, and tanners, and they did not scorn to draw their livelihood from shops and booths if only the accumulated profits summed up large enough.

But the greater number of doors in this block lead merely to independent one-, two- or three-room shops and other small shops connected by a stairway with a balcony room or two. Here it was that the "other half," or rather the other nine-tenths, lived packed in the narrowest of quarters with the typical work- and

---

[10] We know the houses of several other magistrates and candidates: Vedius Siricus, *duovir* in 60 A.D., lived at Reg. VII, 1, 47, well known for its mosaic of *Salve Lucru* (see Overbeck-Mau, p. 320); L. Popidius Secundus, an *Augustianus* and *duovir*, lived in the beautiful "house of the citharist," Reg. I, 4; M. Lucretius Fronto in Reg. V, 4, 11; Bruttius Balbus at Reg. IX, 2, 16; Cuspius Pansa, four times *duovir*, in the modest house at IX, 1, 22; Albucius Celsus in the "house of the silver wedding" (Mau-Kelsey, p. 301); and Trebius Valens in the charming house recently found at Reg. III, 2, 1 (*Notizie*, 1915, p. 416).

salesrooms upon the street. These are in fact the very essence of ancient industry with its inordinate number of petty specialists. Their purpose is often betrayed by two distinguishing marks: some remnant of a workbench, forge, or furnace, which proves the inhabitant an artisan, and a peculiar wide lintel with grooves, which shows that in the daytime the shop stood wide open to invite customers. The well-known picture of the cupids as goldsmiths[11] gives precisely the right conception of this kind of industrial life. Various little workmen are busy at the furnace, the anvil, and the workbench, but at the center one of them is engaged in making a sale. Except for the fact that Pompeii had a greater proportion of non-slave artisans than the metropolis, these combination workshop-salesrooms were typical of all normal Roman industry. It was from shops like these that the Roman usually got his shoes and his togas, his jewelry and his lamps, his furniture, the ornaments of his house, and his kitchen utensils.

The first impression then upon walking around any normal block at Pompeii is of a busy hive with countless small cells where poor artisans make and sell their few specialties, but where the space within is occupied by prosperous men who in part direct and live upon the fruits of this petty industry. A larger survey of the whole city, however, will lead to a more complex definition of the city's industrial life; and for such a survey it is of first importance to examine the articles

[11] Mau-Kelsey, p. 334.

of commerce discovered in the shops and in particular the articles that bear inscriptions and trade-marks. The ordinary terra-cotta tableware[12] was certainly imported. A large part of it came from the well-known potteries of Arretium, while the firms of Puteoli[13] and Capua and the new potteries of Gaul supplied the rest. There is no evidence that Pompeian potteries made any "Arretine" ware. Indeed even the simple *mortaria*[14] that are so numerous in Pompeii were generally imported. At least many of them bear the mark of famous Roman tile-makers whereas none has a brand known from native ware.

On the other hand all the very crude and bulky terra-cotta articles such as tiles[15] and wine jars were made nearby. In fact the ware of L. Visellius, most popular at Herculaneum, is the only one that extends freely over several Campanian towns. It is noteworthy also that while more than fifty producers supplied such ware only two or three makers are represented by any considerable number of stamps. There was therefore no monopoly in these articles. It is very probable that, as at Rome, tile-making was con-

[12] *C. I. L.* V, 8055-6; Atkinson in *Jour. Rom. Studies*, IV, 27.

[13] *Bull. dell' Instituo*, 1875, p. 242; Pliny, *N. H.* III, 82, mentions the pottery of Puteoli that was made from clay found on the island of Ischia. Cumae and Sorrento also produced this ware (Martial, XIV, 102, and Statius, *Silvae*, IV, 9, 43). Cf. Dubois, *Pouzzoles Antique*, p. 121.

[14] *C. I. L.* X, 8048.

[15] *C. I. L.* X, 8048-52.

sidered practically a branch of agriculture and that any farmer who found that he had suitable clay was apt to burn tiles and jars for his own use and also if convenient for neighboring customers.

The splendid silver plate[16] that the rich Pompeian set upon his table was in large part the product of Campanian shops. The only piece of the Boscoreale trove that bears a maker's signature is a mirror signed by a Roman citizen, presumably of freedman stock, M. Domitius Polygnos; all the marks of ownership are Latin; and two of the finest cups portray Augustus and Tiberius in scenes taken presumably from Roman triumphal arches.[17] If these excellent pieces could be made in Italy, the rest may well have been, though of course some of the patterns are obviously Alexandrian. Even Pompeian craftsmen may have produced work of this kind, for there were silversmiths[18] in the town. Perhaps we may go a step further and say that the production of such ware had passed to a large extent out of the hands of independent handicraftsmen into the control of large producers. If in such shops the principle of division of labor had been introduced so that each workman performed a set task instead of producing complete articles, we can explain why so few of these elaborate pieces are signed, why themes and designs from Egypt, Syria, and Rome occur side by side, why on certain pieces the engraving, the

[16] For the Boscoreale treasure see *Mons. Piot.* V.

[17] Mrs. Strong, *Roman Sculpture*, p. 83; Pliny, *N.H.* XXXIV,47

[18] A *caelator* is mentioned in *Notizie*, 1912, p. 69.

molded design, and the emblemata often fail to har-
monize, and finally why Italian inscriptions mention
specialists in silver-work who obviously were tied to
some very circumscribed part of the work, as for instance, the *figurator,* the *flaturarius,* the *tritor,* the
inaurator, and the *caelator.*[19] Pliny indeed seems to
refer to shops of large output when he complains that
the fashion in silver plate changed, demanding *nunc*
Furniana, nunc Clodiana, nunc Gratiana[20] It is doubtful whether individual craftsmen could so have influenced the market.

What has been said in the preceding chapters regarding the iron and copper industries is in accord
with conditions at Pompeii. The city was too near the
iron and bronze factories of Puteoli and Capua to
necessitate much native work in these articles. Instead
of many small shops that combined production and
selling therefore we find what seem to have been general "hardware shops" which had no forge or workbench.[21] In such places are found despite centuries of
looting a few farm implements, locks and keys, kitchen
utensils, pieces of harness and even bronze trinkets and
cheap objets d'art.

Where and how the great abundance of very elabor-

[19] Schreiber, *Alexandrinische Toreutik,* p. 132; Drexel, *Bonn.*
Jahrb. 1909, p. 179.

[20] Pliny uses the phrase *genus officinae* in this passage (*N. H.*
33, 139); however individual craftsmen would naturally accept
the styles set by large producers. One such smith at Rome (VI,
9223) claimed preëminence in *caelatura Clodiana.*

[21] *Notizie degli Scavi,* 1912, pp. 143, 181, 333, 355; 1913, 31.

ate Pompeian furniture was manufactured we are of
course not told, nor does any of it bear tell-tale factory
signatures. Many of the simpler pieces were doubtless
made in petty shops, but the excavators have not yet
unearthed any shop so equipped as to be able to produce the better articles. The beds, chairs and table-
couches certainly required skilled craftsmen of many
arts for their production,[22] and the requisite raw materials could not have been assembled without the outlay
of considerable capital. The legs of these pieces, generally of wood, required the turning lathe, usually
skilled hand-carving, and often the craft of the intarsia
worker. The frames, if of wood, were frequently
inlaid with figured bronze and silver, chiseled ivory,
or at times with tortoise shell or precious stones. The
headrest and back were often veneered or inlaid, and
the decorated metal braces usually took the forms of
finely wrought horses' heads, dolphins, satyrs and the
like, figurines that were sometimes molded, sometimes
beaten out or carved by hand. Even if some of the
metal ornaments could have been ordered from the
foundries of Capua, this kind of furniture implies the
existence of elaborate factories that employed many
craftsmen skilled in all kinds of wood and metal work.
The combination of carved marble, fine woods and
wrought metals in tables, stands and candelabra also
points to factory production. Perhaps the Roman inscription (CIL. vi, 9258) mentioning a gild of Neapolitan citron-wood workers may be taken as a clue to

[22] See Ransom, *Studies in Ancient Furniture.*

the location of the important industry near Pompeii.
That intarsia furniture was imported to Rome in large
quantities from some such center we may infer from
the existence at Rome of a strong gild of *negotiatores
eborarii et citrarii* whose statutes we still have in frag-
mentary form (CIL. vi, 33885).

In wheat milling and breadmaking, as we have seen,
wholesale porportions were reached, though in the
nature of the case the trade could not well spread beyond the confines of a city, and "town economy" was
a necessary result.   Certain it is that very few Pompeian homes had ovens for the baking of bread, though
it is possible of course that some of the large ovens of
the city were for community use, as is frequently the
case in Italian cities to-day. What so quickly central-
ized this trade in large shops despite the abundance of
house servants, we are not told, but presumably the
scarcity of fuel and the failure to invent an adequate
method of milling the wheat may explain it. At Rome
also as we may infer from inscriptions[23] and from the
elaborate frieze on the bakers' tomb still visible at
Porta Maggiore wholesale bakers quickly captured the
trade of the city.   During the Empire however the
government there took charge of the business when it
decided to distribute loaves of bread to the poor instead of grain.

There must have been some wholesale trade in

[23] *C. I. L.* VI, 22 and 1002. The large gild mentioned in VI,
1739 was under state control.

wine,[24] since the trade-marks upon the amphorae bear witness to the importation of Coan, Cnidian, Sicilian, not to speak of Falernian and Cumaean brands. Perhaps Cornelius Hermeros was a wholesale wine merchant,[25] since his mark occurs upon several brands of imported as well as old domestic wines and other "bottled goods." However, no large wine dealer's storehouse has as yet been discovered in Pompeii, and among the thousand or more marks repetitions of names are relatively so infrequent that it would be quite misleading to assume an organized system of middlemen wine dealers. Judging from the frequency with which estates[26] are named upon the jars we should attribute the personal names and initials partly to owners of vineyards and partly to responsible *villici* of wine-producing estates.[27] We may conclude therefore that wine was usually supplied to owners and private cellars directly from vineyards, just as the wine growers of the Alban hills even now send their cartloads to Rome every morning. At Rome the trade naturally assumed larger proportions both because of

[24] *C. I. L.* IV, 5510-6600.

[25] Wholesale dealers are mentioned on 5535 (the *princeps libertinorum* of *C. I. L.* IV, 117) and 5526. One jar (5894) bears the marks of the shipping office: *in nave Cn. Senti Omeri, Ti Claudi Orpei vecta.* Pompeian wine was also shipped to Rome, and the trademark mentioned by Pliny ("Trifolinum," *N. H.* 14, 70) has been discovered (IV, 5518).

[26] For example, in the house of the Vettii, these jars are marked, respectively, *de Arriano, de Asiniano, de Formiano.*

[27] Cf. *C. I. L.* IV, 5778 (L. Arellius Successus), and 6499.

the demand for great quantities of imported brands and because of the necessity of carrying large stocks on hand. What quantities had to be available at times may be realized when we read that on the occasion of triumphs it was not unusual to distribute several hundred thousand gallons of wine to the populace in one day.

Olive oil, like wine, was generally distributed at Pompeii in moderate quantities by the grower to the petty retailer with little interposition of oil merchants. No store chamber of large capacity has been found in the city and the oil jars lying about the small shops usually bear the names of nearby plantations. There is a hint in Cato[28] that oil production had once tended to fall into the hands of a special class, for he speaks of contractors who would buy the crop on the trees, harvest it, and manufacture the oil. Possibly the Italian farmers were at that time not yet thoroughly familiar with the approved processes of manufacture, or it may be that the product was not then readily marketed, since olive oil was still considered something of a luxury. However when, by the invention of the screw-press, a cheap and easily manipulated oil-press could be installed on any plantation, the grower usually pressed and distributed the oil, and the situation which we find at Pompeii doubtless became normal. Rome, of course, presented peculiar conditions. Since wealthy epicures demanded the best products of South Italy,

[28] Cato, *R. R.* 144. He generally assumes, however, that the owner harvests the crop.

Spain and Africa, there developed whole gilds of *olearii negotiantes*. In the Empire the demagogic princes began to interfere both with the trade and with the production of the vicinity by distributing largesses of oil to the populace, until finally they were compelled to assume complete control of the oil trade in the city. The mountain of broken jars behind the emporium called Monte Testaccio—which the Italian army used as a station for anti-aircraft guns during the Great War—is in part composed of casks that brought these government requisitions from Spain and Africa.

Large-scale factory methods are well illustrated in the production by the wealthy duumvir Umbricius Scaurus and his freedmen of the famous fish sauces called *garum*[29] and *liquamen*. The constant discovery at Pompeii of jars bearing the familiar trade-marks of this producer proves the magnitude of the business, and the prominence of his mark shows how nearly his firm secured a monopoly of the trade at home. Here too is one of the few Pompeian products that reached a foreign market. Pliny knew the garum of Pompeii as one of the three best known brands and indeed a jar marked *gar. Pompeian.* has been found at Rome.[30] Despite the success of Scaurus, however, there were epicures in his native town who craved the best brand,

[29] *C. I. L.* IV, 5657 ff.

[30] Scaurus, however, seems not to have brought the whole industry under one roof. There are several brands, e.g., *G (ari) F(los) ex officina Scauri; ab Umbricia; ab Umbricio Abascanto; G. F. Scauri ex off. Agathopi.*

the garum of the large joint-stock company of publicans in Spain.[31] A jar bearing this trade-mark was found in the house of M. Gavius Rufus.

We are far from well informed about the organization of the clothing trade in the Roman world, and it may be that Pompeii will some day provide the essential facts for solving the problem. The mountains between Pompeii and Amalfi must have furnished pasture[32] for thousands of sheep, and that the city became an important center in the clothing trade in Campania is shown by the number of well-equipped fulleries that took possession of old-fashioned houses in several parts of the city. In the Middle Ages when the manufacturing of clothing first emerged from the stage of household production it often happened that the wool grower, or the weaver, or the fuller assumed the role of entrepreneur and organized the trade of a country district by purchasing the wool and directing it from spinner to weaver and so on from house to house until the finished article was ready for the market. When presently an export trade developed the drapers or cloth merchants further organized the trade

[31] Pliny, *N. H.* XXXI, 94; Martial, XIII, 102. This firm was probably the corporation of publicans that bought the fishing concession on the Spanish coast, and then proceeded to pack and distribute the product of their fisheries. There are very few instances of such producing corporations on record.

[32] Seneca (*Nat. Quaest*, VI, 27) mentions the herds of sheep on these mountains. To assume with M. Rostovtzeff that Pompeii was the woollen market for Apulia is to mistake the scale of Pompeian production.

and brought the goods together in a community hall, like Blackwell Hall in London, where individual purchasers might choose their goods, and whence the agents of the drapers' gild might go to offer the surplus on the foreign market for the common benefit of all the gild members. Large factories seldom arose until the invention of machinery required the collection of the various craftsmen at some common point where the requisite power could be had.[33]

At Pompeii it is evident from the ubiquitous whorls and weights that spinning and weaving remained in the household; and the list of assignments scratched on a pillar of the house of Terentius Eudoxus[34] shows how the eleven slave maids of one house employed their spare time. Indeed so long as the very simple processes of spinning and weaving could conveniently utilize the unoccupied energies of such housefolk, which would otherwise go to waste, it is clear that there would be neither a demand for high-power machinery nor the possibility of large-scale production in factories. This explains why gilds of spinners and weavers did not arise in ancient Italy.

With the subsequent processes of cloth-making however it was different. Homespun direct from the household loom was now no longer used even by people

[33] See Ashley, *The Economic Organization of England*, p. 90.

[34] Insula VI, 13, 6; cf. *C. I. L.* IV, 1507; similar graffiti have been found recently in excavations not published, e.g., Reg. IX, Ins. 12, on Via Abondanza. The wall paintings of IX, 7 nearby also indicate an interest in the clothing industry.

of moderate means. It had to be sent to the fuller who put it through an elaborate treatment of cleansing and bleaching,[35] of stamping, carding, and shearing. Then the dyer, whose work might or might not be done in the fullery, finished the cloth into a delicate product of which the figures in Pompeian wall paintings give a faded impression. At Pompeii the fullery with its expensive system of vats, its complex trade-processes, and its group of skilled workmen may fairly be called a factory; but it is at once characteristic of the ancient conservative methods that no fullery outgrew the relatively narrow confines of the ordinary dwelling-house.

And yet at Pompeii the fullers seem to have taken an unusual step toward the organization of the whole trade. In the early Empire, Eumachia, a generous priestess, built an extensive hall near the forum for the use of the fullers.[36] This building is certainly not a fullery, and it can hardly be anything but a hall for sales-booths, like Blackwell Hall in London. In other words it is very likely that, as often happened in England, the fullers, who were the last to handle the cloth in the process of manufacture, bought the stuffs outright, finished them, and became the distributors as well. So far we may safely go, but we do not yet know whether the fullers ever attempted to organize the whole trade by purchasing the raw wool and contracting for the spinning and weaving of it. Nor do we know whether, like the drapers' gilds of England,

[35] Pliny, *N. H.* XXXV, 198.
[36] Mau-Kelsey, p. 110.

they ever attempted to market their goods abroad through corporate agents.

In this trade again Pompeii seems to represent the normal practice in the Roman world. Roman authors generally assume that maid-servants of the households occupied their spare moments with spinning and weaving;[37] there is no evidence of clothing factories in Italy,[38] we have no mention of gilds of weavers or spinners in our inscriptions, while the fullers' gilds were among the most important ones. Indeed several cities besides Pompeii possessed special buildings for them,[39] while Rome granted them certain exemptions from the public water-rents.[40] To be sure we may not

[37] Friedländer, *Sittengeschichte*, I, 462; Varro, *Men. Sat.* 190; Colum. 12, praef. 5-9. Cato's farm was equipped for weaving but Cato preferred to buy the clothing from the city (*R. R.* 10, 5; 14, 135); perhaps this particular farm had no sheep. Gummerus, *Klio, Beiheft* V, has generalized too boldly from this instance. Atticus, who owned large sheep ranges in Epirus (Varro, *R. R.* II, 10, 11), apparently had the wool woven on his estate, Cic. *Ad. Att.* XI, 2, 4. In Sicily Verres found that good stuffs were produced in many wealthy households, he accordingly requested them to produce tapestries for him, Cic. *Verr.* IV, 58.

[38] An exception may be found in the wholesale remaking of cast-off clothing by *centonarii*. Perhaps several of the workmen mentioned in Roman inscriptions (*C. I. L.* VI, 7861, 3, 4, etc.) labored in such a factory since they are all freedmen of a certain Octavius. A few weavers' gilds were found in Anatolia where there probable was factory production of tapestries, and in Gaul where military cloaks were apparently produced in quantities, Waltzing, *Corpor.* II, 153; IV, 95.

[39] *C. I. L.* X, 5682; XIII, 3202; IX, 2226.

[40] *C. I. L.* VI, 266; 10298. The fullers were of course also the laundrymen of ancient times.

assume that the well-to-do at Rome and other large cities continued to wear "homespun" to any considerable extent. But much good cloth could doubtless be selected by the fullers from the products of the household looms and when skilfully fulled, carded, and dyed, be marketed as wholly satisfactory cloth. For the fastidious there were always the imported[41] stuffs from the Egyptian state factories, the hand-worked fabrics of Anatolia, the choice purples of Syria, and the "Coan Silks" of the Greek islands. For the manufacture of garments there was no need of an extensive industry, since most garments were simple pieces of cloth that came from the loom in almost the form in which they were to be worn.

The shoe trade at Pompeii as everywhere was in the hands of individual shoemakers who were generally considered men of very humble station. There was apparently a gild of them in the town and several of their shops may be identified. The shop of Insula IV, 3, is typical, where the cobbler eked out his small profits by serving as portier. At Rome the *sutores* seem to have drifted down to the "shoemakers' ally" in the Subura in great numbers, and their row of shops may be restored in imagination by any one who has tried to buy a pair of shoes from the street racks in the cobblers' quarters of Athens or the Souks of Constantinople. A gild[42] of those who specialized in wom-

---

[41] See Chapot, *Textrinum*, in Daremb.-Saglio; Wilson, *The Roman Toga*.

[42] The Collegium fabrum soliarium baxiarium centuriarum III (*C. I. L.* VI, 9404). Wholesale trade in leather is attested by the third century inscription, VI, 1117.

en's footwear at Rome claimed some three hundred members, a sufficient proof of the minute distribution of the trade.

By contrast the tanner who supplied the leather to the shoemaker was a far more important personage. Tanning could not profitably be done on a small scale since the space and the apparatus needed for the curing of a few hides could quite as well serve for curing large amounts, and some ready capital was needed to tide over the time required in the curing. It may well be that the large tannery[43] found in Regio 1, 5, of Pompeii was able to provide all the leather needed by the shoe and harnessmakers of the town. Here is an instance where economic considerations inherent in the nature of the industry quickly made for large-scale production.

As for agriculture, we have long known from the famous treatises of Cato and Varro that farming had to a wide extent become a capitalistic enterprise by the middle of the second century B.C. We are now able to restore the picture of a typical plantation from the remains of a farmstead at Boscoreale,[44] two miles beyond Pompeii. That the owner was a practical farmer is clearly apparent from the abundance of farm implements, wine vats, and the like. That, however, he was

---

[43] Mau-Kelsey, p. 395.

[44] *Monumenti Antichi* VII. For other villas near Pompeii see Barnabei, *La Villa di P. Fannio Sinistore*, 1901, and *Notizie*, 1898, p. 495; 1899, pp. 15, 297, 392; 1910, p. 139; 1921, 415 ff; 1922, 459; 1923, 271, also Rostovtzeff, *Social and Econ. Hist.*, p. 496.

a man of urban breeding and social connections, with wealth enough to gratify very fastidious tastes, is proved by the fact that his silver plate is now reckoned one of the special treasures of the Louvre.[45]

Whatever other plantation owners may have done, this landlord, from the point of view both of production and of consumption, was a part and parcel of the world's commerce and industry. So-called domestic economy has no place in his system of householding. He produced a few specialties for the market with a view to profit, caring little whether or not he succeeded in satisfying the needs of his household from his own estate. The main part of his farm was devoted to vine culture, as two strong presses and a storeroom of jars with a capacity of nearly twelve thousand gallons testify. That there was also provision for some olive growing is shown by a mill, a press, and jars of a few hundred gallons' capacity. Little provision was made for stock raising and there was apparently small need for hay. A survey of the implement room is instructive. The abundance of hoes and picks and pruning hooks as well as the absence of scythes and hammers and shears indicate the narrow limits within which the work of the farm was confined. A small mill and oven show that there was grain enough for home use, but nothing has been found to bear out the orthodox assumption that a house of this sort should have a staff of slave women spinning and weaving. Since the soil near Vesuvius was too rich to be given over to pasture

[45] *Mons. Piot*, V.

the farm probably produced no wool, and the clothes
were probably bought. Moreover, the supposition that
large plantations were independent of the market in the
matter of labor and implements seems to break down
here. It is hardly necessary to mention that the house
was built by skilled masons, as the fashionable type of
reticulate masonry indicates, frescoed by an expert
painter from the city, decorated with terra-cotta ornaments, and fitted up with standard bathtubs and an
elaborate hot-water system that must have required the
services of Pompeii's highest priced plumbers. These
things are in harmony with the silverware, the artistic
bronzes, and the modish furniture. But even the implements of the stockroom are of the standard forms
made by skilled artisans, the pottery bears the factory
stamp, and the bricks bear trade-marks known from
Pompeii. In fact the landlord had proceeded far beyond the earlier practices of agriculture according to
which the householder adapts his system of livelihood
to the production of his farm. This man's connections
with his land were quite incidental. To him the land
was a factory for the production of a special article
from the profits of which he could make a living. And
he lived upon his farm, when he did, only because he
chose to be near his business or because he liked the air,
not because it gave him his bread and cheese and
homespun.

Such was the economic structure of the city, and
this determined the social system. In the first place
agriculture must have been the most respectable occu-

pation at Pompeii as at Rome, and there can be little doubt that it was a portion of the land—the vineyard of the Vesuvian slopes and the rich vegetable gardens below—rather than the shops of Pompeii which Sulla distributed among the veterans in 80 B.C. During the early years when the city government was controlled by the colonists these must have held all the higher offices; to that class must have belonged the Holconii, the Quinctii, and the numerous other magistrates whose liberality evoked inscriptional records. Yet, as we have seen, the profits of industry were frankly acknowledged, as witness the *Salve lucrum* of Vedius Siricus, the ubiquitous trade-mark of the fish packer, the tile stamps of Saginius and Eumachius, and the mills of Proculus, for all these men were elected to the magistracies. If Caecilius Jucundus, the banker-auctioneer, who lived as luxuriously as any of these, failed to reach the duumvirate, lack of respectability could hardly have been the reason. He probably fell under the provisions of the *lex Julia municipalis* which disqualified the praeco[46] for municipal office, apparently in order to keep the "contractor out of politics."

Of course much of the profitable business must have been carried on by trusted freedmen, as Cicero's letters prove that it was at Rome, but at Pompeii where many of the natives were Greeks and still bore Greek cognomina it is not an easy matter to recognize liberti by

[46] The business accounts of Jucundus (*C. I. L.* IV, Supp. I.) show that he not only took municipal contracts but also acted as agent in placing such contracts and in farming public revenues.

means of the nomenclature. At any rate on the streets
of tombs the most elaborate monuments are as likely
as not to boast the honors of a sevirate, thus betraying
the rank of a freedman.

Slaves of course shared in the industrial life of the
city and not only manual but also administrative work
was intrusted to them. Very often the signacula, the
seals and stamps used to brand goods and legalize documents, bear the name of a responsible slave as well as
that of his master. The loaves of bread now in the
Naples Museum for instance are marked *Celeris Q
Grani Veri ser* (*CIL*. X. 8058, 18).

If we may judge from election notices, however,
Pompeii seems to have had a comparatively large free
population. The gild members who explicitly support
candidates are not only the prosperous fullers, the mill-
ers, and the bakers; they are owners of small shops like
the aurifex and the veterarius, the petty merchants of
stalls and booths like the pomari and the unguentari,
and there are also the workmen's groups of dyers (of-
fectores and infectores), the porters (saccari) the harvest hands (vindemitores), and the woodworkers (lig-
nari). To be sure such election posters do not permit
the inference that every supporter is a citizen, but there
would be little point to these announcements if the
labor gilds consisted largely of slaves.[47]   That there

---

[47] Della Corte, *Case ed abitanti a Pompeii, Neapolis*, II, 152.
The usual inference that the gilds were "in politics" is by no
means justified. The "election notices" were posted as adver-
tisements by the candidates. In every case where it was possible
the candidate tried to make the advertisement effective by an-

was a large free population of poor workmen may also be inferred from the inordinately great number of petty barrooms and lunch counters. The scores of these places in existence could only have been supported by poor but free folk who were in a position to spend a few sous daily for tidbits. Some of these laborers were independent craftsmen who managed their own small business in front of their two- or three-room houses; others were clients of the well-to-do. A very large number were ex-slaves whom after manumission their former master set up in some shop, usually on a percentage basis. Such freedmen probably occupied the shops and booths connected with several of the larger houses in the block surveyed above.

We have now reviewed the methods of Roman industry and attempted to observe their application in one city. It is obviously the part of wisdom not to compete with economists who have attempted to describe this intricate situation in one all-inclusive formula. However, bearing in mind that everchanging forces were constantly producing new conditions and that the data are nowhere adequate to justify final conclusions we may be permitted to attempt a classification of the factors that now encouraged now circumscribed the growth of Roman industries.[48]

---

nouncing the support of those who occupied the house or shop on which the advertisement was painted. Such a notice however does not necessarily imply a greater enthusiasm for the subject of the advertisement than does a modern placard at the grocer's lauding the merits of some breakfast-food.

[48] C. I. L. VI., 6213-6440.

The simple economy of the primitive household may have existed in the mountains of Italy in Cicero's day, but few traces of it can be found. The Roman farmstead was often meant to be "self-sufficient," to provide for all its needs and to possess slaves who could perform the technical as well as the ordinary work. When, however, this was the case, the self-sufficiency was not a mark of primitive conditions—as in our own frontier life—but rather of an elaborate capitalistic economy in which the fastidious landlord could afford to satisfy his every whim.

In the cities we find an industrial system which in many respects resembles that of early nineteenth-century New England where the native artisans of inland towns not yet connected by steam power produced most of the articles needed by each town. However, many of the Roman cities were now growing large and the number of wealthy men who demanded and could pay for luxuries and delicacies far exceeded that of our early Republic. To gratify these an extensive commerce had long existed, and in some lines of production industries aiming at a wide market had already arisen.

The forces that worked in favor of large-scale and monopolistic production differed but little from those of a similar tendency to-day. The possession of a new device of glass-blowing seems to explain the success of the Sidonian glass-makers, who apparently erected a factory on the Latin coast; the accumulation of skilled workmen and artistic designers at places providing a desirable clay enabled the Arretine potters to capture the trade of half the world; and similarly the possession of good recipes gained a wide market for certain food specialties like fish delicacies and prepared brands of wine. The production of silver and bronze-ware tended to concentrate, partly because a combination of many highly trained molders, designers and engravers was required, partly because the expensive raw product demanded capital. The same is true of many kinds of furniture that required skill in working expensive woods, metals, and marble. The extension of the fulleries and tanneries illustrates how mass production was encouraged when chemical preparations and apparatus not easily procured by the public were required. In wholesale breadmaking the centripetal forces were the desire to save labor and space, the increasing cost of fuel, and the difficulty of procuring flour in the home. To some extent certain towns specialized in iron-ware. Here doubtless the problem of fuel reckoned in the account, and it may also be assumed that the irregularity of the demand for arms and armor, and the seasonal suspense of the trade in farm implements discouraged the individuals who had not the capital to wait for the market; ordinary cutlery which found a steadier sale was doubtless produced to a considerable extent in small shops. Finally the behavior of the brick monopoly at Rome illustrates the chance aid that an industry might receive from such an accident as the great fire which threw enormous contracts in the way of a few men who had the facilities for production ready when needed.

A genuine factory system did not, of course, fully develop in all of these lines, but division of labor and the employment of some labor-saving machinery and technical processes were present in the production of silver and bronzeware, pottery, glassware, furniture, bricks, and some table delicacies; while in most of these instances there is evident a capitalistic production having a world-wide trade in view.

Certain centrifugal forces on the other hand were still very strong. With the slow transportation of that day perishable goods could hardly pass from town to town. With the concomitant cost of transportation heavy articles of low value like cheap earthen-ware could not advantageously be shipped. Lack of patent laws must also have retarded concentration since new processes quickly became the property of any rival. The heaviest drag upon industry, however, must have been the all-dominating slave system. The abundance of slaves enabled fastidious householders to have everything possible done in their own houses in accordance with their personal tastes. Among the slaves of Statilius Taurus, the magnificent friend of the Emperor, we find trained slaves engaged not only in performing extravagant personal services but in making articles that the industries of Rome might well have supplied: smiths, fullers, tailors, spinners, weavers, shoemakers, masons, cabinetmakers, carpenters, workers in marble, and others. This was hardly a condition calculated to help the marketing of factory-made goods. Moreover a plentiful supply of cheap labor discouraged a demand for new labor-saving devices which might have created new products for a potential market, and might also have tended to the accumulation of expensive tools and trade-secrets to the benefit of industrial concentration. For instance the invention of a valve in the bellows used in iron furnaces to create a continuous blast, an improvement that any intelligent and interested workman might have conceived, would have revolutionized the iron industry by making smelting and casting possible on a large scale. But the slaves who performed the work were not expected to bring quick interest to their tasks. Finally, the general disrespect for industry, due partly of course to a conservative devotion to land found in all aristocratic societies but indelibly fixed by the association of industry with slavery, turned aside the capital and the intelligence of strong Romans which might otherwise have flowed into industrial development. It now seems a fair conclusion that Roman industry had reached as high a degree of advancement in Augustus' day as it was likely to do so long as slavery persisted.

CHAPTER XV

CAPITAL

FROM the point of view of the modern world the capitalist had a thorny path to tread during the late Republic. The semi-aristocracy of wealth, flattered when needed in the civil service, or in the formation of a political *bloc,* was generally at warfare with the Senatorial nobility after the Gracchan turmoil. Gaius Gracchus, to be sure, strengthened the hands of the knights and united them with the popular party for an onslaught upon the Senate. In turn the Senate made peace with them in 64 in its eagerness to protect vested interests against Catiline's rebellion. For a season between 70 and 66 they seemed to be the dominant power, forming the backbone of the coalition that broke the Sullan constitution in 70 and directed an aggressive foreign policy in 67-6. But this temporary success is not to be attributed to equestrian popularity or leadership. Indeed, Roman history does not point to a single effective leader trained in business. The Sullan constitution, out of date when adopted, was doomed to failure in any case. It gave way at the first attack, when Pompey accepted the position of figure-head in a revolt that most of Rome desired. Crassus manipulated the political moves, Cicero coined the necessary phrases, and the knights provided the funds. Three years later the knights had their reward when the same elements combined in a demand that Pompey clear the seas of pirates, so shamefully permitted by the Senate to prey on commerce, and the year after commissioned him to destroy Mithradates and organize the East into a series of provinces which would be open to commercial "development."

To this extent the capitalistic interests played the political game with some success and profit. Nevertheless Romans were never allowed to forget that political considerations were and must be paramount and that wealth must be subject to political needs. Sulla in 82 proscribed 2,600 knights and confiscated their property in order to fill the treasury. When furthermore he laid an indemnity of twenty million dollars upon Asiatic cities for acknowledging Mithradates and the cities had turned to Roman capitalists for a large part of the amount, Lucullus, acting for the Senate, presently permitted them to repudiate most of the interest charge, thus throwing the burden of Sulla's theft largely upon the shoulders of the knights. In 43 again the triumvirs after raising an army of forty legions by extravagant promises of bounties threw the principal burden of payment on those who had wealth. Two thousand knights were proscribed under pretext of disloyalty and their property taken for the account of the treasury.[1] It is not surprising that Roman business men usually

[1] Many Roman landowners who were not themselves accused of disloyalty lost properties that they happened to possess within the confines of municipalities which were punished by wholesale expropriation.

preferred to avoid politics, and that they made their investments if possible in far-distant real estate or in noiseless private banking. The feeling grew strong in those days of civil war that while money might be power it should not measure itself with political power, and that vested interests, so strongly supported by the old aristocratic code, had few rights that were sacred in the eyes of the government if held by a class not in sympathy with the government. This condition continued into the Empire. Whereas capitalists continued to gather vast sums from all the empire into their private coffers at Rome, they remained at the mercy of imperial tyrants who when driven to bankruptcy preyed upon them and confiscated their treasure under whatever pretext, as the easiest method of balancing their ledgers.[2]

The surplus capital of the Romans, as we have noticed, had for centuries followed the expanding armies inland. Time and again when the population of the city became dense and there were signs of a drift toward the sea or toward commercial outlets, a new advance on the border had required military colonization, and the familiar call of the land that Romans were accustomed to heed turned men inland once more. It is a situation that reminds one strongly of the opening of the American frontiers, which permitted our once flourishing merchant marine to decay and tem-

[2] See Pliny's famous statement (*N. H.* VI, 35) that Nero, finding half of the province of Africa in the hands of six planters, confiscated their lands.

porarily stemmed the current of New England industries. When in the second century however Rome's armies went beyond Italy, annexing Spain, Greece, Africa, Southern Gaul and parts of Asia, the settler did not follow with the same alacrity. The land among strangers did not seem to offer a congenial home to the average Roman, and even Gracchus found little support for foreign colonies.

In Italy, however, Roman wealth must have expanded rapidly as measured by the census rolls. Beloch[3] estimates that the land in Italy thrown under Roman cultivation by the expropriations of the Punic war and by the seizures in the Po valley doubled the former acreage, making the total of ager Romanus about fourteen million acres, which at the very modest price of fifty dollars[4] per jugerum usually given for unimproved land totals a billion dollars in soil value alone. This would give a high per capita property rating for the 320,000 citizens of Gracchus' day. When we remember that large landholding was already the rule we may be sure that there were many thousand Romans who were well-to-do.[5]

[3] Beloch, Bevölkerung, 388.

[4] Columella, III, 3, 3, places this value on ordinary unimproved Italian farm land. The figure is rather too low than too high for Cicero's day when Varro's account shows a very active interest in farm lands.

[5] Before the Second Punic War there were nearly 20,000 citizens possessing a knight's census. We are not told that this was then placed at 400,000 sesterces, but it may have been, since Polybius (VI, 20) implies that the knights' census was higher than that of the "first class." See Marquardt, Staatsverw., II, 331.

Ready capital may however have been scarce. The typical farmer seldom went to the bank; the turnover of money is exceedingly slow in agriculture; the strong box in the *tablinum* could take care of the surplus until the owner found another neighboring patch in which to invest. Later this process extended into the provinces. Always did the surplus of the average Roman lie easiest that found its resting place quickly in some real estate. Cicero's properties were mainly in farm and city holdings, Atticus had large estates in Epirus and Italy, Varro in Campania and Apulia, Caesar's prefects, men like Labienus[6] and Mamurra, who were enriched by booty, at once invested in land. Cicero's civil suits usually had to do with titles to land in Gaul or Etruria or Lucania, and his letters of recommendation are full of references to large estates in Greece, Sicily and Asia.[7]

In the last century of the Republic, however, not a little capital found new outlets, especially in the management of state contracts, in money lending and banking, and in trade. The activities and importance of the state contracts are apt to be overestimated because, having a general interest, and being the concern of every citizen, they form the topic of the political

[6] The Caesarian partizan attacked by Catullus in Carm. 94, 105, 114 and 115 is Labienus; see *Am. Jour. Phil.* 1919, 396.

[7] Cf. Cicero, *Pro Flacco*, 70; *Pro Caelio*, 73; *Ad Fam.* XIII, 69; 72; 38, 11; VIII, 9, 4; *Pro Quinctio, Pro Tullio, Pro Fonteio, De Lege Agraria*, passim. Cicero, *De Off.* I, 151, naïvely suggests that the merchant may deodorize his profits by investing them in a plantation.

harangues and letters of the day. Indeed our news-
papers give more space to one million dollars invested
in municipal contracts than to many hundreds of millions invested in other enterprises. As a matter of fact
the actual capital engaged in public contracts probably
did not reach one per cent. of the amount invested in
real estate in the city of Rome. Of the ten millions of
state income that we have estimated for Cicero's day
two-thirds at least did not pass through the hands of
the publicans. Asia was the only province that had
been wholly abandoned to them, and in other provinces
like Sicily, Spain, Africa, and Gaul, they collected only
the less lucrative revenues. The construction of public
works like aqueducts, roads, and harbors brought
profit at times, but such works were subject to precise
estimates of cost and close supervision; the work was
almost invariably well done and without the odor of
dishonest spoils. Whoever will take the time to examine the pavement of an ordinary Roman highway,
or the remnants of the docks of an old Roman harbor,
or the imposing arches of Republican aqueducts still
standing on the Campagna will conclude that even
political contracts have at times been honestly filled.
The collection of port-dues could usually be checked
by ship invoices since the cargoes at most ports passed
at a low and uniform rate. Pasture dues also depended
upon a simple count of cattle and must have caused
little confusion of accounts. In the estimate of tithes,[8]

[8] The companies were generally rather small, specializing in
one form of taxation as *portoria*, or *scriptura* or *salinae*, etc. The

however, many companies were caught in vicious
thievery. The calculation was difficult, the provincial
could not take his appeal to Rome without great cost,
at Rome he seldom found a patron who cared to waste
time on an unsympathetic jury in his behalf, many of
the jurymen were apt to hold shares in the company
of contractors, and the provincial governors, though
often hostile to the financial group, usually preferred,
sometimes with their eye on political preferment, not
to incur the enmity of a company. Many cities were
robbed, some resorted to bribing the collectors or the
governors for self-protection. Very often in lieu of
efficient management of their own finances they borrowed money at unreasonable rates from the official
collectors with which to pay the taxes due. Thus the
evils of the vicious system raised a stench to heaven
before Caesar put an end to it. The system certainly
worked as much wrong in that far off province of
Asia as it did for instance in France before the Revolution, where we are told that the cost of collecting
often amounted to as much as the sum which reached
the exchequer.

The wounds of Asia must not however all be laid to
the bludgeons of the companies. The aristocratic party
should have credit for a generous half of them. When
Sulla exacted his enormous idemnity of twenty million
dollars he laid upon the Asiatic cities a burden of debt

Bithynian company seems at one time to have consisted of an
inner group composed of members of several companies, Cic.
Ad. Fam. XIII, 9.

which kept them in arrears for a generation, and it
was the interest upon such debts that pressed them
even more than the annual tithes. Nor did senatorial
supervision always use reason in dealing with the companies. It was an old theory even in the days of
Polybius[9] that the companies should be encouraged to
bid with a narrow margin of receipts on the under-
standing that the Senate would remit a reasonable
portion in case of unforeseen disaster. Such contingencies frequently arose in the East where Parthian
raiders might drive off herds, burn the fields, and put
a temporary end to trade. But in the political squab-
bles of Cicero's days it happened more than once that
a clique in the Senate would effectively block any
attempt at remission and the companies had to bear
the complete loss. By that time the buying of shares
in the public companies had come to be looked upon
as a gamble which conservative men avoided[10] and the
business therefore fell to men of lower standards.
The companies in consequence exerted themselves to
cover their occasional losses due to war, bad crops, and
senatorial obstinacy, by extortion and deceit. Such
was the experience that led Caesar to place Asia in
the same position as the other provinces, and during
the Empire the companies are found in charge only of
the contracts in which supervision was readily exercised and extortion quickly detected. Henceforth little
capital was required in the concerns, shares were less

[9] Polybius, VI, 17.

[10] See Cic. *Ad. Fam.* XIII, 10, 2.

extensively held, and public interest seldom became such as to bring the companies to the notice of Roman writers.

Following the flag and the official tax gatherer went the *negotiator*,[11] the "busyman." The history of the word illustrates the history of business activities. At first, the word applies to men who went abroad to lend money where rates were high, to place mortgages, to buy land at bargain prices, and incidentally to do some trading if good profits offered. This indicates that the Roman had little control of the machinery of commerce; also that specialization in business had not yet progressed far. It was only in the Empire when various enterprises were better segregated, when banking in the province became less profitable because of a more stable régime, and when the Roman had a better command of shipping, that the word came to apply wholly to traders. It is with the *negotiator* of the Republic that we are here concerned. A typical example may be found in Cicero's client, Rabirius Postumus,[12] who in many respects reminds us of the American business adventurers that operate in Central American bonds, mines, and revolutions. Inheriting a fortune made in tax-farming, he continued to some extent to engage in the same business. But he also

[11] See Cagnat, *art. Negotiator*, in Darem.-Saglio.

[12] Fowler, *Social Life of Rome*, p. 91; Giraud, *Études Economiques*, p. 204; Tyrrell and Purser, *The Correspondence of Cicero*, II, p. xxx. Dessau (Hermes, 1911, p. 613) seems to be in error when he identifies Curtius Postumus with Rabirius Postumus.

extended his activities into regular contract work on a large scale, into lending money at high risks in the provinces, and even into shipping and trading. In 57 the King of Egypt, driven into exile by a revolution, came to Rome to appeal for aid, and when it was bruited about that Caesar and Pompey were inclined to support him Rabirius formed a partnership to equip the King with the needed millions, the King pledging his revenues against the debt. When the Senate obstructed a motion to give the King official recognition and support, the governor of Syria, a friend of Pompey's, received an intimation from adherents of Pompey that he might profit by escorting the King home even without a decree of the Senate. So the King was restored, and Rabirius went with him to see that the mortgaged revenues were used toward paying his debts. At Alexandria, to the astonishment of Roman travellers, Rabirius took his office in Greek garb at the custom house and managed the state monopolies in linens, cosmetics, bricks, beer, and all the rest: Puteoli was not a little amazed to find one day a whole fleet of Rabirius' come into harbor laden with precious Egyptian ware, paper, linen, and glass. The Senate in a rage at the success of the King despite its explicit veto took vengeance on the Syrian governor, who was tried and banished for his part in the affair. Rabirius was finally imprisoned by the King and escaped alive with difficulty. His lawyer claimed that he was a bankrupt. The Senate suspected, however, that the farcical denouement was invented by Rabirius and the

King to deceive the Senate and the angry Egyptians,
a not unplausible hypothesis. The adventurer was
apparently exiled from Rome, but Caesar found a
place for him in his commissary department during the
Civil War, where like most of Caesar's business agents
he was doubtless given an opportunity to fill his purse.
Such were in general the negotiatores of the late
Republic.

To make an estimate of the capital available for
large business undertakings would not be possible, but
it is fair to say that over-estimates are frequently
encountered. In the first place we do not know of
any very large fortunes actually made in commerce,
banking, or manufacturing at Rome. The large fortunes[13] mentioned—in two instances we hear of twenty
million dollars—were acquired by other methods and
were possessed by the ruling aristocracy or by freedmen who acquired their wealth by misuse of imperial
influence. Lentulus, credited with the largest sum,
was a senator who gained much of his wealth in opportunities afforded him by Augustus, presumably in the
purchase of confiscated estates and in military service.
Pompey, worth several millions, had profited from
very fortunate campaigns in the East, for generals
then, as naval commanders till recent times, secured a
portion of the booty taken in war. Pompey's business
manager, the freedman Demetrius, is said to have
gained very heavily from his business connections with
the general, and to have left a fortune of four million

[13] Marquardt, *Staatsverw.* II, 56.

dollars. Crassus, reputed the richest man of the Republic, left seven million dollars acquired largely from secret dealings in the real estate of those proscribed by Sulla. The three richest men mentioned in the first century of our era were three rascally freedmen of Claudius who traded on the influence and power that they acquired over Claudius, and over the Empire through him. Pliny[14] indeed mentions an Isidorus, a freedman in the time of Augustus who left large estates and herds besides a ready fortune of three million dollars. Perhaps this was acquired in trade, but we are not informed.

Corporation law did not in Republican times develop to the point where vast sums could be combined in ordinary enterprises of industry and commerce. Only in the formation of companies to farm public revenues and to operate public property like mines and salt works did the state permit and encourage full fledged joint-stock companies, associations that could accumulate considerable sums not only through the participation of members who held *partes* but also of stock holders who bought shares (*particulae*.) Yet such companies could not have been very large, since separate firms seem generally to have been organized at each census for the management of each subdivision (ports, pastures, tithes, etc.) of each province. Seldom did any annual operation of this kind require a capital of a million dollars. For the management of business

---

[14] Pliny, *N. H.* XXXIII, 135.

enterprises, partnerships[15] were often formed but they had slight protection in law and had to rely mainly upon the mutual good faith of the partners. They were of course dissolved by death or by the word of any member, and they were not protected by privileges of limited liability. One has but to read the brief paragraphs in Gaius, *De Societate* (III, 148-154) to realize how little Roman business relied upon partnerships and how incapable these were of undertaking enterprises like manufacturing or extensive banking which must depend upon a durable and legally protected corporation. As a matter of fact most of Rome's larger business enterprises seem to have been carried on by individuals who placed in the business only their own capital and what they might borrow on their personal credit.

The machinery of banking[16] also developed more slowly in the Republic than the growth of the state

[15] Illustrations of such partnerships are found in Cic. *Pro Fonteio, Pro Rosc. Com.; Pro Rab. Post.* For the law on corporations and partnerships see Gaius, III, 148-154, and *Digest*, especially 17, 2; 47, 22, 14, 1-4, and 3, 4.

[16] Byrne, *Titus Pomponius Atticus;* Früchtl, *Die Geldgeschäft bei Cicero*, 1912; Blümner, *Röm. Privat-altertümer*, 649. At Pompeii were found more than a hundred receipts of a small private banker, Caecilius Jucundus, who seems to have specialized in collecting moneys, auctioning slaves and chattels at a percentage of one or two per cent., and in farming the city's lands and town properties, *C. I. L.* IV, 1.
Many seals, made of thin plates of bone, inscribed with a name, a date, and the word *spectavit* in abbreviated form, have been found. They have been explained by Herzog (*Aus der Gesch. d. Bankwesens*) as seals of bankers' money-bags to guar-

would seem to require. The needs in the provincial field were largely met by the taxing societies which seem to have transported money and credits and by the Greek and South Italian bankers already in the eastern field. The vicious attacks upon property made in the civil wars of Sulla, Marius, Catiline and Caesar, taught Romans the need of keeping their accounts in the hands of trusted freedmen rather than in bank ledgers accessible to the agents of proscribing governments. Finally the lack of interest in business always betrayed by the landed aristocracy must be taken into account in explaining why the Roman government failed to follow the example of several Greek states and of the Ptolemies in chartering state-banks or at least in encouraging banking by instituting state supervision. Augustus, in fact, denationalized the banks in Egypt. There were however several important bankers doing business at Rome in Cicero's day though they seem to have been foreigners and Campanians. Men like Oppius, Egnatius the Spaniard, Cluvius and Vestorius, both of Puteoli, must have had large offices and were widely trusted. They received deposits on current accounts on which they paid interest, they lent money on notes, mortgages and on current accounts,

---

antee the amount and purity of the money enclosed. Cary (*J. R. St.* 1923, 110) has observed that many of the names seem to be of business men known from the inscriptions of Delos. The full significance of this new evidence is not yet known. Perhaps such seals were not only used at banks but also for sums sent to and from foreign shippers, and to and from estates in Italy.

and did some discounting. They bought and sold real
estate on their own account and as agents for others;
they did considerable business in money changing since
numerous foreign issues of gold and silver came to
Rome through foreign trade; they often kept expert
business agents at the disposal of customers, especially
men versed in provincial investments who travelled
extensively abroad. Cicero for instance gave the
agents of Oppius and Cluvius letters of introduction to
provincial governors, to use in their eastern affairs.
There was of course little of what we call syndicate
banking since industries had not as yet developed to
the point of requiring it, but in the placing of large
loans to foreign cities the bankers sometimes acted as
agents for wealthy nobles, and sometimes formed temporary partnerships. Finally some of them had
branches or correspondents in the provinces so that
bills of exchange could usually be procured for most
of the important centers of trade. It must be said
however that the business of foreign exchange was far
from systematized. Cicero for instance, when he
wished to establish a credit for his son in Athens made
over to Atticus his urban rentals at Rome, in return
for which Atticus gave his banker in Athens orders
to credit Cicero junior with the amount and to debit
the account of his income from the Epirote estate.[17]

For gauging the growth of Rome's foreign business
we have some data in the body of inscriptions found

[17] Cic. *Ad. Att.* XII, 32, and XIII, 37.

at Delos.[18]   In 169 after subduing Macedonia Rome
gave the island of Delos to Athens, requiring only that
the place be left a free port to all comers.   Since no
port dues were exacted, the shipping of the East soon
found it a convenient meeting place for trade.   From
the cities of the Black sea, from Syria, Egypt, and
Italy, traders came to exchange their wares.   Rome
found it a useful rendezvous when in the middle of the
century she had to deal with revolts in Macedonia and
Greece; and when Corinth was then destroyed, the
harbor of Delos was in a position to take its place as
the chief port of Greece for western shippers.   Twenty
years later Asia became a Roman province, and then
Delos naturally came to serve as a way-station for
Roman publicans who farmed the provincial tithes and
managed the royal estates.   Its market place was
chosen as a convenient one in which to dispose of the
products exacted in the province, and before the end
of the second century, as our inscriptions prove, Ital-

[18] Hatzfeld, *Les Italiens Résidant à Délos*, Bull. Corr. Hell
1912, and *Les Trafiquants italiens*, 1919; Frank, *Roman Imperialism*, 284; Roussel, *Délos, Colonie Athénienne*, 72 ff., who
gives an excellent map of the city. The traditional view, still
repeated by Roussel, 7 and 433, that Rome established a free
port at Delos to favor Roman commerce assumes an interest
that did not yet exist. Why did Rome then give the island to
Athens with the control of the sacred property in shops and
houses so necessary to commerce? Why did she not assume control of the harbor securing port exemptions to Roman traders?
Obviously the declaration against port-dues extended to all commerce and all visitors at the shrine, the natural privileges of a
sacred port which had regularly been manifest in the asylum
enjoyed even by hostile vessels in the harbor, see Livy, XLIV, 29.

ians had come to be the controlling element of the town. To be sure when we examine the names of these hundreds of Italians it is seen that they largely emanate not from Rome, but from the south, i. e., from Campania, only half-Romanized at the time, and from the federated Greek cities of Magna Grecia, which in all Roman treaties were given the same rights that were accorded to Romans. In fact, "Roman" associations (*conventus*) in foreign cities consisted at this time indiscriminately of all peoples from any part of Italy. The two groups of "Romans" at Delos that we can best identify, the bankers and the oil merchants, consist of south-Italians. The bankers are respectively a Greek from Syracuse, one from Tarentum, a Syrian who acquired citizenship in Naples, an Apulian, and a certain Aufidius Bassus who may or may not be a real Roman. The oil merchants, all from the south, are apparently men who sell the oil of south Italy on the eastern market.

Can it be that Rome after all had not yet entered either the commercial or the capitalistic field that her armies had opened, and that only those peoples who were already upon the high seas profited from the pax Romana and the "freedom of the seas" that followed the extension of Roman rule? It is clear that south-Italian merchants and the bankers associated with them were the first to profit by the extension of Roman rule eastward. The Greeks from Tarentum to Cumae had always loved the sea and engaged in trade and in ship-building. Indeed Rome had always relied upon these people to supply her vessels and seamen for the navy. Their merchant marine had therefore received all the encouragement that came from the upkeep of ship-yards and the training of seamen. Furthermore these Greeks who knew the language and customs of the Oriental peoples as well as of the Romans naturally became the middlemen between the East and the West.

Nevertheless it is difficult to believe that these Italiote Greeks could successfully have captured so much of the Delian trade from the practiced Syrians, Egyptians, and Islanders if they had dealt wholly with their own capital and on their own account. It is very probable that Romans of Campania were sup-plying some of the capital of the shippers who put out at Puteoli. The rather startling statement of Plu-tarch[19] that the elder Cato lent money in marine insur-ance partnerships may be explained in this way. Cato possessed lands in Campania where he came into con-tact with the numerous industries that centered about the harbor of Puteoli. Cicero[20] in his Verrine speeches and his letters reveals the fact that the Romans who engaged in business in Sicily and the eastern trade with Sicily were largely men like Vestorius, Granius, Clu-vius, and Sittius, whose base of operation was Puteoli.

The true interpretation of the Delian inscriptions re-lating to Roman business seems therefore to be some-thing like this. When Rome established her rule in Macedonia and later in Asia the trading and banking

[19] Plut. *Cato Maj.* 21.

[20] Cic. *Verr.* V, 56, 57 and 59.

between Rome and the East was at first done through
south-Italian business men already in the field, supported by some venturesome Roman capital. Then
when the contracts for the Asiatic tithes were let at
Rome, the contracting firms, which were obliged to
find a large personnel of clerks and agents who could
speak Greek and knew something of the East, must at
first have relied very heavily upon the business houses
of the South for their staff. Naturally the Roman
business managers who went to the province to supervise the work reported upon the new opportunities they
found there for lucrative investments and thus gradually drew Roman capitalists directly into the field.
At the time of Mithradates' raids in Asia and at Delos
few real Romans[21] seem to have been slain, but the
financial loss fell largely on the Roman forum.

Capitalistic ventures in the East were somewhat
uncertain, but capable under favorable circumstances

[21] The eighty thousand "Italians" slain in Asia by Mithradates
were indeed called *cives Romani* by Cicero (*de leg. Man.* 7), but
only for rhetorical purposes. Those of them that were not slaves
and freedmen were mostly South-Italian Greeks, as is revealed
by Posidonius (quoted by Athenaeus, 213 B), who says that to
save themselves "they assumed Greek dress and called themselves
citizens of their own native cities again." The explanation is that
the South-Italian Greeks had assumed (somewhat prematurely) the
Roman toga and Roman names after the passage of the lex
Plautia Papiria in 89. One year later, when Mithradates attacked the province, they renounced Roman citizenship for
safety's sake and reassumed their former status, which in most
cases must still have been their real legal status. The majority
of the 20,000 inhabitants of Delos at the time of its destruction
in 88 were Italian, according to Appian (Mith. 28).

of bringing good profits. Many bought real estate, available at low prices because of a generation of turmoil and dread of invasions. The Romans having faith that their rule would insure peace, stable government, and sympathetic courts invested where discouraged natives sold, and we find that many of Cicero's friends owned[22] plantations there.

More profitable however was money lending on the frontier where interest rates were high. At Rome where conservative courts had always protected property—indeed Sallust[23] complains that they were more concerned in supporting the laws of property than those of human rights—interest was usually stable and low, normally ranging from four to six per cent.[24] In Greece where vested interests were less considerately protected and a more venturesome spirit directed the money market, rates generally ranged from ten to twelve per cent. In Asia, where invasions, inefficient government, and indirect business methods made for insecure possession, twelve per cent. was a low rate even in times of peace. After the Mithradatic raids extraordinary inducements alone could lure money out of hiding, and Romans entered the market only provided the rates were attractive enough. The situation was not unlike that of our own frontier days when bankers who lent money in Boston and New York at

[22] Cic. *Ad Fam.* XIII, 69; 72; *Pro Flacco*, 14; *Pro Cael.* 73.

[23] Sall. *Cat.* 33 and 39.

[24] Billeter, *Der Zinsfuss.*

five and six per cent. asked twenty-four to forty-eight per cent. in the Indian and locust-ridden plains of the West and when even municipalities, since grown great and rich, were compelled to issue bonds at thirty-six per cent. In such circumstances senatorial edicts against high rates had little effect. Cicero's correspondence has left a notorious record of how the Stoic Brutus[25] exacted forty-eight per cent. in Cyprus. To be sure he was sufficiently ashamed of his act to attempt to conceal it, but not enough to make reparation when discovered by Cicero. Even at twelve per cent., the legal rate, the profits to Roman bankers were enticing when the establishment of Roman law-courts promised to protect investors, and hence large sums were placed through bankers and private agents with spendthrift kings, semi-bankrupt cities and individuals. The king of Cappadocia[26] owed Pompey and Brutus a sum that ran into millions of dollars, the king of Egypt as we have noted borrowed several million dollars from Rabirius and his friends. Cluvius[27] of Puteoli, lent heavily to five Asiatic cities placing not only his own funds but also those of Pompey and others. Lampsacus, Tralles, Sardes, Mylasa, Alabanda, Heraclea, are some of the other cities incidentally mentioned by Cicero that owed money to Roman knights. Before Pompey went East the cities

[25] Cic. *Ad Att.* VI, 1 and 3.

[26] Cic. *Ad Att.* VI; 1.

[27] Cluvius, Cic. *Ad Fam.* XIII, 56; Nicaea, Cic. *Ad Fam.* XIII, 61.

of Asia owed a total of forty million dollars, most of it doubtless to Roman capitalists. If this brought twelve per cent. per annum, private interests at Rome drew more than twice as much from this account as the treasury drew from the annual tribute.

That bankers in general were not held in very high esteem is not surprising. Respect for them has come only with their participation in promoting and organizing productive industries, for which there was as yet little opportunity at Rome, and in financing state debts, which Rome generally tried to avoid. As a matter of fact Romans were liable to come in contact with bankers too frequently as mere money-changers or as money lenders secretly accepting questionable risks at high rates from riotous youths not yet in possession of an approaching inheritance. The enormous debts of young nobles like Caesar, Antony, Caelius, and Curio raised an ill odor about the forum. Even in the legitimate investment business and the placing of loans bankers performed only the kind of service which most of the wealthy lords could procure through clever and trusted stewards. These stewards were generally freedmen, and the association of business with them did not tend to elevate the latter in the general esteem. Then, too, they were often asked by wealthy men like Pompey to place funds at good rates with hard pressed eastern cities and potentates, acting as agents in affairs that the noblemen might hesitate to carry out through their own stewards and in their own names. When such affairs were generally

talked of on the street they did not add to a statesman's dignity, and it is likely that Pompey, though he
wrote polite letters of thanks to his bankers, preferred
not to be seen chatting too intimately with them in the
Forum. Cicero whose political program called for a
close union between the nobility and the men of wealth
assumed more cordial manners, occasionally inviting
men like Vestorius to dinner, but he too adopted the
usual patronizing tone when in his private letters or
in his speeches before the Senate he spoke of *negotiatores, faeneratores,* and *toculliones.* Caesar who prized
business efficiency and gladly employed men of affairs
in the army organization admitted men like Balbus
into the Senate but he did not please the Senate in
doing so. When bankers like Vestorius, for instance,
stood well in the esteem of many Romans, the fact was
a special tribute to their personal integrity, to cultural
interests, and probably to a refusal to engage in trans-
actions considered questionable.

CHAPTER XVI

COMMERCE

SAINT PAUL'S journey[1] in custody from Jerusalem
to Rome was probably not unusually full of adven-
tures for one which included half the length of the
Mediterranean. To find a ship going Romeward his
centurion took him on board an Asiatic coasting
vessel at Caesarea, whence they skirted Syria and
Cilicia. At Myra they transferred to an Alexandrian
boat for the west. When the winds proved contrary
they decided to put in at Crete for the winter, but
were prevented by a storm which drove them help-
lessly up and down the Adriatic. Throwing overboard
some of the tackling, they finally reached the coast of
Malta where the frightened crew plotted to abandon
the two hundred and seventy-six passengers and make
for land in the life-boat, and were restrained only by
the soldiers who were on board. The ship struck the
shoals and its cargo of wheat was jettisoned, but to
no purpose. When the vessel broke, the passengers
had to make for land as best they could on pieces of
wreckage. They remained all winter at Malta sailing
in the spring by another Alexandrian ship that had
wintered there. Putting in first at Syracuse, then at
Rhegium they finally reached Puteoli, whence the pas-

[1] Acts 27 and 28. On commerce, see Charlesworth, *Trade-routes*.

sengers bound for Rome made the rest of the journey of one hundred and fifty miles by road. Alexandria is now considered to be about three days from Rome.

A very brief account of Cicero's crossing of the Aegean[2] a distance of some 250 miles, in sixteen days *sine timore et sine nausea* is given us in a letter to Atticus. Six days brought him the one hundred miles from Athens to Delos. "Sailing has not been all play, though it is midsummer. We reached Delos six days out from Athens. On the sixth of July we reached Zoster in a contrary wind that held us there on the seventh. On the next day we had a pleasant sail to Ceos, thence we continued to Gyrae in a savage though not adverse wind, and thence to Syros and Delos somewhat more speedily than we intended. You know yourself what the open Rhodian boats are like. Well I won't stir from Delos till the Peaks of Gyrae stand clear." Greek steamers now make the journey to Smyrna in one day.[3]

It is to be noticed that neither of these travellers had Roman boats. St. Paul took passage on an Asiatic and two Alexandrian freighters; Cicero out of regard for his station and his mission chartered a special boat,

[2] Cic. *Ad Att.* V, 12, cf. V, 13.

[3] These were of course slow journeys. Pliny, *N. H.* XIX, 1, says that in favorable weather Sicily could be reached from Alexandria in six or seven days and Puteoli in eight, and that six days might bring a sail from Cadiz to Ostia. When Cicero was proconsul in Cilicia he usually received his mail from Rome (via Brundisium—the Gulf of Corinth—Athens—Smyrna) in five or six weeks.

but it was apparently Rhodian. The fear of wind and
weather apparent in both accounts was probably not
due to ignorance of seamanship[4]—the Greeks fairly
lived on the sea—nor to the fragility of the boats; the
average large freighter was then a boat of two or
three hundred tons,[5] as large therefore as those in
which our early Salem skippers roamed to India and
China without a fear. The chief difficulty for the
ancient mariner resulted from his lack of a compass.
It was this that made him follow courses along well
known coast-lines and islands, which in turn exposed
him to frequent danger of shipwreck whenever storms
arose, and it was chiefly this which brought all shipping to a standstill in winter, when the sun and stars
were seldom visible.

Of the organization and methods of Rome's maritime trade in the late Republic we are not well informed. At Athens the situation can be reconstructed
from the cases of the Attic Orators whose orations are
full of references to shipping. Since Romans at this
time seldom engaged in commerce, the orations offer
practically no information. Some compensation is
afforded us in cases cited by the Jurists of the Digest.
These to be sure are somewhat too late for our imme-

[4] It is generally agreed that the Greeks and Romans knew the
art of tacking against adverse winds, cf. Pliny, *N. H.* II, 12, 8;
Lucian, *Navig,* 9.

[5] There are many references to boats of 10,000 talents, about
250 tons. The ship that carried the Vatican obelisk to Rome
seems to have had a capacity of 1,300 tons. Cf. Torr. art. *Navis*
in Darem.-Saglio; and *Ancient Ships*, 1895.

diate purposes, but since they reveal a logical development of maritime commerce from the situation de-
picted in Lysias and Demosthenes we may proceed by
way of striking a mean between the earlier and later
evidence and comparing our conclusions with such
casual references as we have from the Ciceronian age.
The Greek merchants[6] like our Salem skippers of
colonial days were usually independent ship-owners,
sometimes even ship builders, who "tramped" from
port to port with whatever cargo seemed to promise
best profits. They employed their own capital or sums
borrowed at high maritime rates, they personally conducted the buying and selling of their cargoes, and
when the season neared its end, they found if possible
a desirable cargo for the home port, whither they
repaired to await the return of the spring sun. Of
course they also "rented space," as they called it, to
merchants who filled orders for foreign consignees,
but this was considered a minor part of their business.
"Packet boats" with regular schedules or prescribed
routes seem to have been unusual. When such a trader
grew wealthy he was apt to acquire more boats in
which he placed trusted agents to do the same kind of
business for him. Since, however, these agents had
less discretion than the owner, and generally had to
be advised what courses to take and in what articles
to trade, the growth of such shipping houses tended
somewhat to reduce tramp-trading in favor of more

[6] Huvelin, art. *Negotiator*, Darem.-Saglio.

regular packet shipping. But progress along these lines did not continue far in Greece.

In Cicero's day the irregular service pictured by the Greek writers apparently still prevailed, especially in eastern waters where Greeks and Orientals seem to have dominated the seas.[7] The interesting mariner's guidebook called the *Periplus of the Erythraean Sea*[8] implies that the merchant trader of the old type dominated the Arabian, Persian, and Indian trade. Claudius' decree[9] in encouragement of grain importation leaves the inference that ship builders, ship owners, and grain merchants were sometimes identical. Trimalchio[10] is pictured as a merchant who built his own ships, and Philostratus[11] still assumes that the Greek

[7] In 59 B.C. Cicero assumes that the negotiatores who carry most of the goods through the harbors of the province of Asia are Greeks (*Ad Att.* II, 16, 4). In the Civil war of 49, Pompey thought he could starve Italy to submission (*Ad Att.* X, 8, 4) by seizing the ships of Alexandria, Colchis, Tyre, Sidon, Aradus, Cyprus, Pamphylia, Lycia, Rhodes, Chios, Byzantium, Lesbos, Smyrna, Miletus, and Cous (*Ad Att.* IX, 9, 2). In the Civil war of 43 Dolabella was able to collect a hundred freight ships of over 2,000 talents on the coast of Lycia in a very short time (*Ad Fam.* XII, 14; 15). Finally, though Claudius gave special rewards to Romans and Italians who entered the service of the annona, the inscriptions of the shipping companies stationed at Ostia show a preponderance of foreigners (*Bull. Com.* 1915, 187).

[8] Schoff's translation with notes may be consulted (Longmans, 1912). Cf. Kornemann, in *Janus*, 1, 54.

[9] Suet. *Claudius*, 19 and 20. See also Cic. De Off. III, 50.

[10] Petronius, *Satyricon*, 76.

[11] *Vita Apoll.* IV, 32, 2.

merchants accompany their cargoes from port to port. When however the Romans began to build ships and invest in foreign trade the more regular system which is illustrated in the Jurists made some headway. Ulpian and Paulus usually assume that the owners of vessels (*exercitores*) employ ship masters[12] (*navicularii*) who transport goods for, or as they call it, "rent space to," importers and exporters[13] (*mercatores*) very much as is generally done to-day. They even assume that ships often have regular routes,[14] engage in a definite line of business, and that some, like those running between Brundisium and Dyrrhachium, specialize in a regular passenger service.[15]

This advanced specialization and organization of the business was to be expected from the condition prevailing at Rome. When timber became scarce in certain centers of industry and orders had to be placed at more favored ones,[16] shipbuilding naturally specialized.

[12] *Digest*, 14, 1, 1, 3 and 7 and 12 and 15. Ulpian, however, knows of instances where the *mercator* is also *navicularius*, Digest, 4, 9, 7, 2.

[13] *Digest*, 14, 2, 2, 1; 14, 1, 1, 3.

[14] *Digest*, 14, 1, 1, 12.

[15] *Digest*, 14, 1, 1, 12. The passengers apparently had to carry their own food for the journey, 14, 2, 2, 2.

[16] The premiums offered by Claudius to Romans and Italians did not suffice, so that Nero had to extend premiums to foreign shipbuilders as well (Tac. *Ann.* XIII, 51). This was probably due to lack of timber in Italy. Ostian shipbuilders doubtless imported lumber from abroad, since the Ostian gilds of shipbuilders continued to flourish, *C. I. L.* XIV, no. 256.

Merchants who grew wealthy in trade and expanded their business far and wide naturally had to employ agents and super-cargoes to supervise a part of it. And this tended to create import and export firms that directed the course of commerce from land. When, moreover, the state undertook to encourage and insure regular shipping with the grain producing provinces in order to make certain of Rome's food supply, organized schedules[17] were established to so many important points that shipping companies could depend upon the service and conduct their business from their offices.

That Romans had some share in this development of the shipping industry is clear from the new methods introduced, but our explicit references are few. Cicero mentions a Lentulus[18] who owned ships that ran between Athens and Rome. Rabirius mentioned above seems to have had a "fleet" of ships, but this may have been connected with the royal monopolies of Egypt. In the Empire when the publican companies were no longer strong enough to engage sufficient grain ships for Rome's food supply, Claudius, as we have noted, tried to encourage Roman and Italian builders and

[17] The Alexandrian grain fleet is frequently mentioned, and the shipping companies that had their offices behind the theatre at Ostia seem also to have engaged in a very regular service, Calza, *Bullettino Com.* 1915, 187.

[18] *Ad Att.* I, 8; I, 9, 3. Cicero asked Atticus to ship him some statuary by these boats. The goods were later put off at Caieta near Cicero's Formian villa.

traders to supply the want.[19] That his offer did not suffice is evidenced by the fact that Nero presently had to offer tax exemptions to foreigners who would aid in this service, and the existence of several foreign companies at the offices of the Ostian grain bureau may be taken as a commentary on the failure of Claudius' measure and the success of Nero's.

If we wish to gain a fair idea of Rome's commerce before the Empire a convenient method is to study Rome's chief seaport of that time, the city of Puteoli,[20] on the bay of Naples. In the Second Punic War Rome was hampered in her operations against Hannibal at Capua by not having a port of her own in this region. Immediately after the war, therefore, she sent a small colony of three hundred men to the old town of Puteoli. This number was obviously just enough to guard the port; indeed the Senate apparently failed to comprehend the great possibilities of the place, for no land was given the colony on which it might expand or gain the support of a rural population of its own. Port dues were instituted but the shipping of the Roman colony at Capua was invited by placing another custom house between Naples and Roman Campania. Puteoli soon began to grow as a Roman port at the expense of Ostia even though it

[19] He offered ship insurance and certain civil rights to those who built large ships and engaged in importation of food to Rome for a period of six years. Suet. *Claud.* 19, 20.

[20] See the excellent history and description of Puteoli by Dubois, *Pouzzoles Antique*, 1907.

was a hundred and fifty miles further away. The chief
reasons were that the harbor was deep and sheltered,
and that ships could find some exports at Puteoli for
return cargoes whereas Ostia, near Rome, offered very
few. As we have seen, the iron industry of Populonia
moved to Puteoli and extended to the nearby towns of
Cales and Minturnae. The excellent bronze-ware
made at Capua was establishing a market all over the
North and West, and large quantities of it were
shipped especially to Marseilles, whence traders carried
it up the Rhone for wide distribution in Gaul and
Germany. It was also found that the volcanic sand[21]
of Puteoli (pozzolana) possessed excellent qualities for
the making of hydraulic cement and it was in demand
wherever harbors and deep foundations were to be
built. Sulphur from the Solfatara, and the earthen-
ware of Cales and Puteoli made from the clays of·
Ischia, likewise found extensive markets. Thus the
port grew steadily in importance, though of course,
because of Neapolitan competition, not very rapidly.
Lucilius[22] writing in the Gracchan days calls it "a
lesser Delos," and at the time Delos had perhaps ten
to fifteen thousand inhabitants.

The proximity of Puteoli to old Greek harbors like
Naples was on the whole an advantage, for it could
draw ships, experienced ship-builders and sailors from

[21] On the industries, see Dubois, p. 117.

[22] *Delumque minorem*, Lucilius, III, 123. In Augustus' day it
was the chief port of Italy, but even then the imports exceeded
the exports, Strabo, XVII, 793.

well equipped yards. After Rome acquired provinces in the East it could also find numerous Greek-speaking business agents and clerks for the publican companies, and the capitalists that turned eastward. Nor is it surprising that bankers like Philostratos[23] of Syria drifted to Naples to take advantage of these new Greco-Roman connections. Such bankers profited especially by writing marine insurance not only for Puteolan firms but also for foreign shippers whose return cargoes loaded at the harbor.

The Social War of 90 B.C. aided Puteoli in an unexpected way. This is indirectly revealed by the Verrine speeches of Cicero. It would seem that when such Greco-Campanian towns as Pompeii, Nola, and Abella were punished for their adherence first to the allied cause and later to the democratic party under Marius, many of the inhabitants took refuge with Sertorius in Spain. Later when this rebel leader began to lose power many of them, being accustomed to the sea, engaged as sailors wherever possible, not abstaining entirely from joining Spanish and Cilician pirates at times. Ultimately, great numbers drifted into the service of Puteolan shippers, so that when Verres undertook to apprehend at Sicilian ports such sailors as were accused of piracy there arose a cry[24]

[23] *Bull. Corr. Hell.* 1912, p. 67.

[24] Verr. V, 154. This, of course, explains how Verres put "Roman citizens" to death. They were probably former *socii* who might claim citizenship by the laws of 89 and 88. Verres was too much of a Sullan to recognize such claims in the case of *socii* who had taken to privateering rather than accept the decision of the social war.

from the firms of Puteoli that he was arresting their sailors, business agents and even members of the firms! The incident proves illuminating for the history of Puteolan commerce although Cicero did his best to conceal the disagreeable items of the story.

The city soon took on a semi-oriental appearance because the traders of all the great Eastern seaports like their successors of the medieval *fondachi* at Venice established agencies there. Such foreign colonies rented particular docks and warehouses, took possession of a separate quarter of the town, erected their own temples and had their own cemeteries. In the second century the "station" of the Tyrians[25] was still paying annual rentals and dues to the amount of 100,000 denarii, although the colony was "then far smaller than formerly." The colonies of Beirut, of the Nabataeans and of other peoples had temples of their own; the people of Baalbek had a cemetery of four acres; and dedicatory inscriptions erected by natives of Asiatic cities are very numerous. Such inscriptions at Rome's principal harbor raise serious doubts as to whether the Romans ever succeeded in becoming a seafaring people.

It is not our purpose to follow the vicissitudes of commerce through the Empire. Suffice it to say that when Claudius dredged out a good harbor at Ostia

[25] *Inscr. Gr.* XIV, 830. The inscription shows that the Tyrians had a similar *statio* at Rome. *Stationes municipiorum* are mentioned in Suet. *Nero*, 37. Cantarelli (*Bull. Com.* 1900, 129) has well compared these with the foreign *fondachi* at Venice.

and built jetties to keep the Tiber mouth clear, Puteoli lost much of its shipping and especially its grain trade. However the lack of return cargoes at Ostia still prevented that new harbor from monopolizing all the shipping. Many boats preferred to make port at Puteoli and send the goods bound Romewards by road or by small coasting vessels.

The trade of Italy was of course very unevenly balanced: even Puteoli in the best days of Campanian industry could never fill the ships that came in loaded.[26] Latium exported very little. Italian wines went eastward through Egypt, according to the Periplus[27] cited above, but these were doubtless Calenian and Falernian wines carried cheaply as ballast. The Alban varieties could not compete with the numerous good Greek brands. Latium began to export some olive oil[28] in Cicero's day, but this did not last long. In the Empire when Rome had learned the value of this article, very large quantities were imported from Spain and Africa. No manufactured articles of importance seem to have gone from Latium: in the long lists of goods enumerated in the Periplus Rome is not even mentioned. Campania exported chiefly iron and bronze-ware, some pottery, wine, olive oil, and Capuan ointments. The rich Po Valley[29] sent wine, pitch,

[26] Strabo, XVII, 793.

[27] *Periplus*. 6 and 49.

[28] Pliny, *N. H.* XV, 2.

[29] Strabo, V, 12.

lumber, grain, pork, wool and cloth chiefly to Rome,
and the jars that contained Venetian and Istrian products have been found far up in the valleys of the
Tyrol.[30]   Arretine pottery as we have seen also found
a market all over the western provinces until in the
early Empire the branch-potteries of· Gaul captured
the trade of the mother firms.   That completes the list
of important Italian exports.   Needless to say, in such
circumstances, Italy could not sustain an equilibrium
of trade.   Her ledgers balanced only because of the
large credit accounts on capitalistic investments and
the constant inflow of tribute.   Even then the government found the outflow of specie disturbing and had
to resort to desperate measures to keep it at home.   We
are reminded of recent governmental orders by the
law which Gabinius[31] had passed in 67 forbidding provincials to borrow money at Rome, and by the effort
that Cicero made in his consulship[32] to have custom
officials at Puteoli seize all silver and gold that was

[30] Dessau, *Inscr. Lat. Sel.* 8572; Charlesworth, *Trade-routes*,
23; Rostovtzeff, *Soc. and Econ. Hist.*, 534.

[31] Cic. *Ad Att.* V, 21, 12. The law was also meant to prevent
provincials from being able to misuse funds in influencing courts
at Rome. However, the attempts made to keep gold and silver
in Italy at this time seem to reveal the real animus of the law.
Cicero (*Pro Flacco*, 67) states that several consuls had tried to
prevent the export of silver and gold.

[32] *In Vat.* 12; cf. *Pro Flacco*, 67, which shows that efforts were
also made to prevent the hoarding of gold in temples. Perhaps
the Jews, when prevented from sending temple gold from Italy,
simply drew on accounts in the provinces, and the governors had
instructions to check this indirect drain upon the supply.

being taken out of the country. Such measures were of course futile in the long run. Pliny[33] a century later informs us that at least five million dollars per year went to China, India and Arabia for articles of luxury.

The principal imports[34] aside from grain originated in the East. The provinces of Asia and Pontus supplied some grain, salt-fish, timber, dried fruit, precious stones, wine, and the tapestries, draperies and rugs for which Anatolia is still famous. Syria sent much glass-ware from factories in Sidon and the famous purple dyes and cloths for which Tyre was noted. The linens of Byblus and Beirut and the cedar of the Lebanons were also highly prized at Rome. In times of peace Northern Syria tapped the caravan trade of Parthia whose merchants brought Chinese silk and Indian cotton, pearls, ivory and spices. To Gaza in the south came the Nabataean caravans bringing Arabian incense, spices, myrrh, and precious stones. The state factories of Egypt exported much fine cloth, glass and paper, and Alexandrian merchants expedited Ethiopian ivory, beasts for the games, and black slaves, besides transporting from the harbors of the Red Sea all the products of India and Arabia. This eastern sea trade received a great impetus from Augustus who, contrary to Roman traditions, adopted

[33] Pliny, *N. H.* XII, 84.

[34] This is but a brief summary of the articles that concerned Italy; see *Darem. Saglio art. Mercatura*, by Cagnat and Besnier, and Charlesworth, *Trade-routes*.

in Egypt the mercantilistic policy of the Ptolemies, so far improving upon it that the shipping of the harbor at Myos Hormos[35] on the Red Sea quickly tripled and quadrupled.

From the West came fewer finished articles but more raw products. Marseilles, then an independent Greek city controlled the trade of the Rhone, brought down metals, hides, rough wool, salt meat, cheese, slaves and amber from the north in return for Italian iron, bronze, earthen ware and the fine handiwork of the east. Her traders also brought tin from the British Isles by way of the Rhone and Seine. Further west the Roman colony of Narbo[36] established a new road by way of the Gironde in search for British tin, and tapped the mines of Aquitania. From Northern Spain came rich stores of metals and also finished products made of the excellent Spanish steel. The central portions produced good fabrics of wool and linen, and the south an ever increasing quantity of olive oil, wine, wheat, salt pork, fish, and leather, carried chiefly by the shippers of Gades.

Despite this great amount of trade, the machinery of transportation is so far from showing uniformity that we can hardly expect well organized systems of salesmanship and distribution, though in general we may

[35] Strabo, II, 5, 12; Herrmann, in *Zeits. der gesch. Erdkunde*, 1913, 771; Charlesworth, *Trade-routes*, 255.

[36] Cicero, *Pro Fonteio* and *Pro Quinctio* show that these colonists and Roman negotiatores are carrying on a large wine trade and an extensive banking and real estate business in Narbonese Gaul.

assume that every harbor had a wholesale market[37] where buyer and seller might meet. But the use of this market varied according to time and place. In the period when commerce was mostly of the "tramp" class, the condition which in fact created these market-places, the incoming merchant unloaded whatever wares he thought he might sell, and displayed them in the market while his ship stood at anchor. At the same market he could look over the wares of his competitors, buying and taking on board what seemed to him to promise good profits elsewhere. To the same market came of course the small shop keepers of the town to buy for their retail trade. In this system, which still prevailed to some extent in Cicero's day, middlemen buyers and salesmen were not essential. But there was an advanced stage of trade, already noticed at Puteoli, which also dispensed with middlemen to a certain extent. The Tyrian exporters, for instance, did not sail the seas with their cargoes, but rented ware-houses and dock space at Puteoli where their countrymen, agents or partners, received consignments, presumably displaying and selling their wares to retailers, in their local offices. They had a similar *statio* at Rome to which their Puteolan agents sent out such parts of the consignments as were destined for the city. Puteolan inscriptions prove that this system was used by many eastern cities. Indeed the Italian agora at Delos is apparently an instance of occidentals adopting the same system, and the *stationes*

[37] See Besnier, art. *Portus*, Darem.-Saglio.

of Ostia[38] were apparently erected by Rome for analogous purposes. With the development of the shipping business and the growth of exporting firms that operated from land, there doubtless also arose commission houses at the ports of entry though we are not explicitly informed about them.[39]

Of a developed system of salesmanship there is little trace, probably because there were few factories such as now send out salesmen and "drummers," and the general existence of market places created by a more primitive system generally brought the product to the buyer with sufficient success. There is, however, an indication that some factories did not have to bring their goods to the market place. At the potteries of Auvergne[40] have been found large invoices of goods that are thought to be orders placed by wholesale pottery merchants for manufacture and future delivery. If this be a typical case the buyers went to such factories as then existed and placed their orders.

In general it may be said that the producer was in that simpler day nearer the consumer than at present, that in foreign trade the shipper brought his goods to

[38] Calza, in *Bulletino Com.* 1915, 187.

[39] Probably some of the ἐγδοχεῖς of Delos were commission merchants, *Bull. Corr. Hell.* 1883, p. 467; 1887, 245 and 252. In some cases they are agents of the shippers.

[40] Déchelette, *Les Vases Céramiques de la Gaule*, I, 86 ff. The buyer in this case seems to have been a wholesale dealer and distributer of earthenware, probably the merchant spoken of in inscriptions as negotiator artis cretariae, *C. L. L.* XIII, 1906 and 6366; Hermet, *Les graffites de la Graufesenque.*

the harbor market-place for the retailer or consumer, and that to a far greater extent than to-day the producer of domestic articles was himself an artizan and shopkeeper who sold directly to the consumer what he made in his small shop. Middlemen[41] were relatively very few.

Freight and passenger rates seem moderate despite the high insurance and the slow movements on the sea. The reason was of course that ships were built and manned by cheap labor, and that port dues were generally lower then than in tariff countries to-day. A thousand bricks (over two tons) were sent from Athens to Delos (one hundred miles) for about fifteen to twenty drachms ($3-$4) which was about 25 per cent. of the purchasing price. For half a hundred weight of minium sent from Athens to Ceos the expressage was one obol (three cents). The freight of a

[41] Many of the negotiatores mentioned in imperial inscriptions are wholesalers who act as middlemen between large producers and retailers. As such we should probably class the following: neg. artis saponariae, C. I. L. XIII, 2030; neg. ferrariarum, X, 1931; negotians calcariarius, X, 3947; Notus . . . vendenda pelle caprina, IX, 4796; negotians coriariorum, VI, 9667, etc. However, shopkeepers sometimes style themselves negotiatores, e.g. VI, 9664; 33886.

The Jurists also speak of "circitores who sell or hawk goods for clothiers or linen weavers" (Dig. 14, 3, 5, 4). They resemble our peddlers and were very numerous, but the Jurists speak of them as being for the most part slave agents. The Jurists likewise speak of "slaves who are sent out to buy merchandise for their masters' shops" (Dig. 14, 3, 5, 7). The use of slaves in such capacities probably militated against the growth of a middleman system.

ton of stone from Paros to Delos[42] was twenty-five drachmas, but heavy stones were expensive to handle with the cranes of the day. In the third century A.D. wheat was brought to Rome from Alexandria for two cents the bushel, which is about the modern rate. In this case the ships were probably insured gratis by the state. Of course regular freight rates hardly came into consideration in a large part of the tramp shipping since the merchant went up and down the seas bartering with his own goods.

Passenger fares seem to us to have been very low. Passengers however appear to have been responsible for their own sustenance, the quarters were probably far from luxurious and of course loss of life by shipwreck unlike loss of freight entailed no financial loss to the carrier. The fare from Aegina to Athens seems to have been two obols, from Alexandria to Athens only two drachmas. One could cross the Aegean for four obols.

Did the Romans follow the suggestions of Gracchus and enter the commerce of the world that their armies had opened to them? If we gather all the literary references to Romans who are in business in the provinces and add the inscriptional records of *conventus*[43] of Romans abroad we must conclude that

[42] The freight prices cited for Delos are for the third century B.C.; cf. Glotz, *Jour. de Savants*, 1913, p. 16 ff.   Other items may be found in Böckh, *Die Staathaush. der Athener*, I², 76.

[43] Kornemann, art. *Conventus*, Pauly-Wissowa; Schulten, art. *Conventus* in Ruggiero, *Diz. Epig.*; Pârvan, *Die Nationalität der Kaufleute*.

many heard and obeyed the call. Cicero's speeches
Pro Quinctio[44] delivered in 81 B.C. and *Pro Fonteio*
given in 69 B.C. are evidence that the colony at Narbo,
founded for commercial purposes by Gracchan followers, had accomplished its purpose. It had un-
doubtedly succeeded in capturing the western Gallic
trade from Marseilles. The Gracchan colony in Carthage was deprived of its primary function when the
Senate stupidly refused to let a city be built that might
have become an excellent trading center, and thus the
chief commerce was thrown to independent African
cities like Utica. But the settling of the Gracchan
colonists is no doubt what accounts for the presence
of Roman traders in places like Cirta[45] during the
Jugurthine war. The Verrine speeches prove that besides money lenders and real estate speculators there
were also some merchants, especially Campanian ones,
in Sicily, despite the refusal of the Senate to allow
Roman publicans to exploit the tithe gathering.[46] The
entry of the Roman trader into the province of Asia

[44] Quinctius had been a partner of one Naevius in real estate
business, farming, cattle raising, and slave-trading near Narbo.
Fonteius was accused of having as governor of Narbonese Gaul
created difficulties for Roman traders by exacting unreasonable
duties on wine.

[45] Sallust, *Jugurtha*, 26 (*Italici*); 47, at Vaga; 64, at Utica.
See also "Caesar," *Bell. Afr.* 97 and 36. The *faeneratores* driven
from Sardinia (Livy, 32, 27) by Cato were probably Carthaginians.

[46] Rostowzew, *Staatspacht.*

to take advantage of the bargains offered by the tax gatherers we have already noticed.[47]

Despite the fact that the Senate did not care to procure preferential tariffs for Romans[48] they did have certain advantages in provincial trade. Not only did they possess the kind of prestige that comes from a strong nation's protection, a thing often neutralized by a haughty bearing toward the natives, but they had an advantage in the courts. Roman citizens, and somewhat to our surprise, other Italians with them, formed in foreign cities separate communities called *conventus*.[49] From this group the governor was required to draw his jurors. Thus they were generally assured a sympathetic hearing in their cases against natives, a fact that often secured them a trifle more than due justice, unless the governor was a very haughty aristocrat like Verres who carried to the province his Rome-bred animosity against business men. Such *conventus* of Roman and Italian bankers, publicans, traders, land owners, and ex-soldiers settled in the provinces, existed in almost every town of importance during the last years of the Republic. They happen to be mentioned in at least twenty-five cities of Asia,

[47] A typical trader is Falcidius (*Pro Flacco*, 91), who bought from the publicans the tithes of whole towns. Avianius mentioned in Cic. *Ad Fam.* XIII, 75, had gone into the Eastern grain trade after serving for a while on Pompey's official grain commission.

[48] Romans were exempted from the *octroi* duties of Ambracia by an early treaty, but so were all of Rome's allies as well. See Frank, *Roman Imperialism*, p. 279.

[49] See Hatzfeld, *Les trafiquants italiens*.

twelve cities of Greece, seven of Africa, five of Sicily, and three of Syria.

We must, however, bear in mind the definition of *negotiator* during the Republic. He was primarily a banker and land speculator, not a real merchant. We need also to remember what the survey of Asia, Delos, and Puteoli have taught, that even these capitalists are more often Campanians and Italiote-Greeks who became "Roman citizens" by the laws of 89 and 88, than representative Romans of the old stock, that many of the "Roman citizens" settled in the provinces are native ex-soldiers[50] who have attained citizenship by service in the army, that the trade which depended upon connections with the quasi-public tithe-farming was of a temporary character, and that we actually have very few references to Roman shippers like Lentulus. In other words, Rome's participation in commerce can all too readily be over-estimated if hasty conclusions are drawn from the existence of *conventus* and *negotiatores*.

In the East[51] references to Roman *negotiatores* and *conventus* dwindle very rapidly during the early Empire showing how slight was their hold upon the trade. Bankers and investors who had come in the train of publicans to profit from unsettled conditions appar-

[50] For example, the old soldiers called back to service in Macedonia and Crete, Caes, *B. C.* III, 4. Some of these were Italians who settled down in the country where they were discharged. Some were natives simply returning home after service in auxiliary forces.

[51] Pârvan, *op. cit.* p. 122.

ently did not thrive when the publicans were withdrawn and a reign of peace permitted the natives to stabilize their finances. The normal commerce of the East never got beyond the control of the natives, while the independent grain trade into which Romans had entered came to an end with the development of Egypt and Africa. Eventually the occidentals who had settled in the East—Italic Greeks, some homeseeking Romans and freedmen, veterans of the army, and members of Caesar's proletariat colonies—lost their identity and merged into the Hellenic population. It is surprising to find how soon the colonists at Corinth, Antioch and Sinope for instance became Hellenized and forgot how to use respectable Latin on their tombstones.[52] Roman investments of course remained in the East especially in latifundia accumulated by purchase or by the foreclosing of mortgages. But it is probable that their management was undertaken by native agents under the supervision of occasional visits from the Roman *dispensatores*. At any rate the East remains socially under eastern control.

In the rich province of Egypt annexed by Augustus Roman business made even less headway. The Ptolemies had so thoroughly organized the state monopolies and the Alexandrian trade for the benefit of the treasury that the Emperors saw no advantage in taking these things out of practiced hands. Roman business men found no bargains there and generally remained away.

[52] Robinson, *Ancient Sinope;* Hahn, *Rom. und Romanismus*, p. 95; Ramsay, *Jour. Rom. Stud.* 1922, 160.

In the West, however, the situation was at first more favorable to Roman enterprise. Here the conquerors met people in a lower stage of culture who were eager to learn their language, buy their wares, and adopt their manners. With the fall of Marseilles in the Civil War, Roman colonies like Narbo, Lyons, and Arles, became the centers of culture. From such places men went not only to lend money and buy land but also to direct trade by the numerous river boats of the Rhone, the mule-road over Tolosa (Toulouse) to Burdigala (Bordeaux), and to the merchant camps on the Rhine frontiers which supplied the traders in Germany. Many of these traders again bear Greek cognomina[53] as the ubiquitous freedmen generally did. Native Gauls also entered into the currents of traffic in great numbers, as the Celtic names show, but there were Romans enough, with the aid of a liberal naturalization policy on the part of several Emperors and the frequent establishment of Roman schools, to transform the West in time into a thoroughly Romanized country. By the fourth century it is likely that more people in Gaul than in Italy read Vergil and Cicero.

The imperial inscriptions[54] of the city of Rome go far to bear out the inference generally drawn from the pages of Cicero, that Romans were in general averse to trade. However much the great merchant was respected, the successful wholesaler is usually a man who has served an apprenticeship at retail trade, and

[53] Pârvan, *op. cit.* pp. 24, 25.

[54] *Ibid.*, pp. 41, 42.

for him Rome had little good to say. That is of course an important reason why there are so many colonies and stations of the foreign shipping cities at Rome, Ostia, and Puteoli, and also why so very many of the names of Roman wholesale dealers, *negotiantes vinarii, olearii, materiarii, vascularii,* and the rest, bear Greek cognomina. The freedmen were the folk who gained control here also. Acquiring their liberty through diligent and obsequious service they applied the skill they had acquired in managing some rich master's affairs and the money that the master willingly lent with a prospect of good returns, and pushed boldly into all the ventures that the land-loving Roman of the old school refused to touch. Typical of this class is Trimalchio who in Petronius'[55] sketch entertains his fellow freedmen over the cups with the rambling story of his ventures at the seaport town of Puteoli: "I too was once just like you, but by my ability I've come to this. It's brains that makes the man, all the rest is trash. I buy cheap and sell dear; others may have different ideas. I'm running over with good luck. As I was saying it's my careful management that has brought me all this wealth. I was only as big as that lamp when I came from Asia, in fact I used to measure myself by it every day. By heaven's help I became master in the house, and then I caught the fancy of my fool of a lord. So at his death he made

[55] Petronius, *Cena Trimalchionis*, 75-6. The translation is in part from Lowe's edition. It may be noted that the articles mentioned in Trimalchio's cargo are those generally exported from Campania. The scene is laid at or near Puteoli.

me co-legatee with the Emperor and I got a senator's fortune. But no one ever has enough. I wanted to go into business. To cut the story short, I built five ships, loaded them with wine—it was worth its weight in gold then—and sent them to Rome. Every ship was wrecked just as though I had ordered it; that's a fact. In one day Neptune swallowed up thirty million sesterces. Do you think I lost courage? No, by heaven, the loss only whetted my appetite as if nothing had happened. I built more ships, larger, better and luckier ones, so that no one should say I wasn't a man of courage. You know a great ship has strength in itself: I loaded them with wine again, pork, beans, perfumes and slaves. Then my wife did a respectable thing; she sold all her jewelry and dresses and put in my hand a hundred pieces of gold. This was like leaven to my fortune. What heaven wishes comes quickly; by one trip I cleared a round ten million. At once I bought back all the estates that had belonged to my master. I built a house and traded in cattle; everything I touched grew like a honeycomb. When I found that I had more than all the citizens of the town put together I quit the counter and set up my freedmen in business for me. Then I built this house. As you know, it was once a hovel, now it's fit for a god. It has four dining rooms upstairs, my own bedroom, this viper's sitting-room, a very fine porter's lodge, and spare rooms for guests. Take my word for it, if you have only a cent you are valued at a cent, but if you've got something you'll be thought worth something. So your humble servant who was a pauper has come to be a prince."

CHAPTER XVII

The Laborer

The universal law of inertia that makes of every man a potential parasite has generally led naïve thought to the inference that labor must be the penalty of sin imposed at the exit-gate of paradise. Ancient philosophers like Aristotle and Zeno while hardly satisfied with an explantion so simple arrived at an equally low estimate of a life spent in manual labor by dwelling upon the moral and intellectual futility to which years of constant drudgery led. And yet the ancient workman seldom committed suicide in despair. He possessed of course other saving instincts which provided him with unanalyzed compensations, and doubtless many a carpenter's son consoled himself with vaguely sensed beatitudes that seemed to pronounce a blessing upon the poor in spirit, the meek, the non-resisting, even though few such meditations have survived for us. Cicero, the Academic, and Posidonius,[1] the Stoic, merely repeated the aristocratic scorn for labor which their instinctive aversions and their experience in a society permeated with slavery seemed to justify.

Vergil here as so often questions the wisdom of his

[1] Cic. *Pro Flacco*, 18, Opifices et tabernarios atque illam omnem faecem; cf. *Cat.* IV, 17; *Acad. prior*, II, 144. Posidonius quoted by Seneca, *Ep.* 88, 21, *volgares et sordidae . . . opificum.*

age. He proves that he knows a gospel of work, in a
picture, not without humor, of Jove who, bringing to
the end the era of blissful idolence,[2]

> Shook from the leaves their honey, put fire away,
> And curbed the random rivers running wine,
> That use, by gradual dint of thought on thought,
> Might forge the various arts.

It was not without a conscious smile that he chose as
his illustration of a happy existence the ex-pirate
peasant who, "In pride of spirit matched the wealth of
kings." Vergil never forgot the simple people of his
native Mantua where a sturdy race still tilled the soil;
he wrote most of his poems near Naples where to judge
from his favorite illustrations he must have stopped
frequently before the benches of the smiths and shipbuilders enjoying the contemplation of the industries
so active there; and he had drunk deep in the philosophy of Lucretius which, permeated with the idea of
evolution, refused to see in the history of the arts and
crafts merely an expression of degrading vanity and
greed and not rather a proof of progressive development. We may, if we will, repeat the time-worn judgment that Rome scorned labor, but we must of course
remember that Cicero's circle was not all there was of
Rome.

[2] Vergil, *Georgics*, I, 121-146. The Corycian gardener, *ibid*.
IV,ʳ125; cf. *ibid*. II, 458. Horace also plies the hoe on the farm,
Epist. I, 14, 39.

In Cicero's time[3] most of the work in the household, in the shops and factories, and on the farm, at least in and near Rome, was performed by slaves and ex-slaves. All of Cicero's household servants are of this class, as are his secretaries, his business managers, and stewards, his readers, librarians, couriers, the tutors of his children and even the men who help him delve out historical and philosophical details for his essays. Atticus, his publisher, has a host of trained slaves who not only copy the manuscripts neatly but also read the proof with a view to correcting the substance. When Cicero needs repairs made or new buildings erected on his estates, he is apt to let the contract to his slave farm manager,[4] and slaves and freedmen are frequently mentioned as the renters of estates and gardens.[5]

The city house of the rich man swarmed with slaves assigned to petty jobs of caring for the jewel box, keeping the shoes, dancing at supper, guarding the linen chest, and whatnot. These were evidences of wealth and a household might run to hundreds and thousands of souls for the purpose of demonstrating a thing so all-important. The larger farms were generally under the supervision of a slave manager (vili-

---

[3] Park, *The Plebs in Cicero's day;* Kuehn, *De Opificum Romanorum condicione;* Blümner, *Privat-Altertümer,* p. 589; Brewster, *Roman Craftsmen and Tradesmen of the Early Empire;* Paul-Louis, *Le Travail dans le monde romain.*

[4] Cic. *Quint. Fr.* III, 1, 2; 1, 5 and 33; 9, 7.

[5] Cic. *Ad. Fam.* XVI, 18, 2; Labeo, in *Digest,* 14, 3, 5, 2.

cus) who had a swarm of slaves working for him.
Varro and Columella both assume that this troupe is
adequate for all the general work, and on a large farm
even for such special work as carpentry, masonry, and
smithing. The earlier jurists also, like Alfenus and
Trebatius, mention weavers, smiths,[6] barbers, bakers,
and other skilled artizans as being found on individual
farms.

It is true, however, that the independent small farm
never quite disappeared from Italy, persisting especially in the inexhaustible districts of the Po Valley,
in the mountain valleys[7] where at times only small
plots were available, and on the southern coast where
Greek tenacity still clung to old methods. A tendency
was also noticeable, which in the Empire increased rapidly, of renting lands to freedmen and slaves[8] on
shares, the slaves presumably gaining their freedom
in most cases where they had proved themselves trustworthy enough for such contracts.

In factories slaves were generally employed in
Cicero's day. In the Arretine potteries, and in the
brickyards, we note that freedmen are managers, which
implies slave-labor for the heavy work. In the factories of Campania the evidence does not suffice for
a decision since Greek cognomina in that region are

[6] *Digest*, 33, 7, 12, 5, and 16, 2.

[7] On his Sabine farm Horace cultivated a part under the charge
of a *vilicus*, but also had five renters upon parts of it, *Epist.* I,
14, 1-3.

[8] *Digest*, 14, 3 and 4 passim.

not significant. The situation at Pompeii implies a
very large number of free citizen laborers, a thing we
may assume probable wherever Greeks worked.

Some instructive membership rolls of laborers' gild
at Ostia, reveal a remarkable scarcity of free native
labor there in the second century of the Empire. A
list[9] of ship carpenters contains 320 names of skilled
workmen. Slaves to be sure do not figure in the list;
probably they were not eligible for membership in the
gild. But we cannot conclude that they were not at
work in the yards. Only four men are free immigrants; such in fact are rarely found at Rome. However, few names on the list bear the good old stamp
of the true Latins. Greek cognomina are very numerous; perhaps some that bore these names were
Neapolitan and South Italian ship-yard men, but
other indications rather favor the view that the Greek
cognomina here also indicate servile parentage. The
most striking fact is the great abundance of the imperial family names, borne of course by freedmen of the
imperial household and their descendants. When we add
to these the other names that belong to the servile class,
names like Verna, Restitutus, Mansuetus, Successus,
Hilarus, Fortunatus, Vitalio, Publicius, we discover
that at least three-fourths of these ship-wrights were
freedmen, or, at most, a generation or two from that
stage. The same conclusion is reached by examining
the membership lists[10] of the transport-helpers gild

[9] *C. I. L.* XIV, 256.

[10] *C. I. L.* XIV, 250 and 251. This gild consisted of men who

containing nearly four hundred names: among these are found a large number of Ostia's former public slaves designated by the name Publicius or Ostiensis.

In the great number of small shops where producing and retailing were not yet divorced,[11] we have already had occasion to notice the following several types of shop keepers: (1) The handicraftsman is often a free citizen who rents the shop and conducts the business on his own capital, himself working at the bench with perhaps one or more slaves. The plumbers of Rome often illustrate this type. (2) A second type is found in shops where a freedman or slave by way of reward for faithful service is lent some capital at interest or on shares which together with his own peculium suffices for the conduct of such a business. Many cases discussed by the Jurists under *De Tributoria actione,* fall into this class (Digest 14, 4). This system was

---

owned and ran the barges and lighters that helped load and unload large ships outside the harbor and transport the produce from the harbor to Rome. It is worthy of note that former slaves of Ostia and their sons had gained the means to engage in this business.

[11] It is evident that in a few peculiar trades, "custom work" continued by the side of ordinary handicrafts shops. Gaius, for instance, cites a case where a man brings his own gold to the jeweler to have it made into specified articles (III, 147). Of course work in jewelry has always lent itself to this system, since when broken or out of fashion the material will usually be worth reworking. There is no reason to suppose, however, that there was much customwork in other lines during the Republic, though Diocletian's edict proves that in the third century when capital was disappearing the custom system reasserted itself everywhere.

very extensive and doubtless many of the Pompeian shops directly connected with dwelling houses were thus conducted. (3) Again, men of some means also owned shops of various kinds which they supervised but conducted through slaves or freedmen acting as their agents, such agents generally receiving a percentage of the profits as an incentive to industry. Cases of this kind, which seem also to have been very numerous, are discussed under the title *de Institoria Actione* (Dig. 14, 3), where phrases frequently occur like: "if your slave acts as institor in a taberna or at a money-changer's table."

A study[12] of all the inscriptions in which the subject is explicitly designated as a workman shows clearly that slaves and freedmen dominated in the industries in the Empire. Of 1854 occurrences of the names of workmen, 67 are slaves, 344 are designated outright as ex-slaves, 459, though free, have Greek cognomina and therefore are largely ex-slaves, 919 give an indefinite form of name from which no conclusion can be drawn. Only 65 are demonstrably free-born citizens. From this list it would seem to be a fair inference that about 15-20 per cent. were free born and 80-85 per cent. slaves and ex-slaves. Of course this does not give a wholly accurate picture of the situation in the industrial world, for the slaves naturally are less fully represented in such records than citizens. Furthermore a large part of the *liberti* did not acquire

[12] Kuehn's careful and very useful dissertation, *De Opificum Romanorum Condicione*, Halle, 1910.

their freedom till quite old, many receiving it on the death-bed as an act of kindness from their masters. If our records gave a census of the men *while at their work* instead of inscriptions upon their tombs the list of slaves might well exceed that of the freedmen.

These conditions are so surprising that one is almost at a loss to explain what became of the poor free stock of Rome, and hazards at a solution must be offered with some diffidence. In the first place Caesar and the triumvirs who had by large promises attracted much of the proletariat group into the armies of the civil wars, scattered them over the world in colonies. Those who were settled on farms in Italy, in places like Cremona, Luceria, and Beneventum, were doubtless saved for Italian society, though not for urban industry. Those sent westward to Cordova, Hispalis, Tarraco, Arles, Orange, Lyons, and other colonies of Spain and Gaul, created centers of Roman civilization from which the Empire long drew heavily for sturdy citizens. But the large numbers colonized in Greece and the East, in Philippi, Corinth, Dyme, Buthrotum, Beirut in Syria, Sinope and Heraclea on the Black Sea, and elsewhere, seem to have been quickly Hellenized. At any rate they were all drawn from the channels of commerce and industry to agriculture and a large part of them was lost to Roman culture.

It must also be pointed out that the inscriptional evidence may in part misrepresent the facts. For instance, it is possible that the easterners at Rome regarded industry more highly than the native Italian and were therefore more apt to record a lowly metier on their tombstones. Perhaps the native often preferred an honorable life of ease on the corn-doles to mingling with slaves at the work-bench. Such considerations would explain a part of the striking percentages furnished by the inscriptions. And yet the freedmen too were very quick to catch the spirit prevalent at Rome. Trimalchio after making a fortune in trade says: "manum de tabula, I retired from active business, and began to lend my money through freedmen, then I bought estates, and built this palace." We may also assume that many of the Roman proletariat disappeared into the silent wilderness and rough mountain regions as did so many of the "poor white trash" of our South when driven out of the race for a decent livelihood by slavery. In our civil war it was this class that terrorized several states with brigandage and petty pilfering. The inquiry still leaves many questions unanswered but on one point it seems to lead back to a definite conclusion that most of Rome's industry was in servile hands.

The conditions of the slave-laborer varied widely. On large farms where a fellow-slave was manager, much depended upon his temper, but since the landlord seldom met his slaves, all the harshness of unsympathetic profit-seeking might find expression in such managers. The same was of course true in mines to which the lowest class generally drifted, and in factories we may presume that a hard régime of driving found entrance through managers bent on gaining their owner's gratitude by means of large profits. In such places there were no minimum hours of work, and the lash and chain were frequently used. Yet we must beware of filling in the picture from modern conditions of slavery where a difference of race and state of culture has aggravated the evils inherent in the system. Apart from a national pride in his race, which the Roman like any modern possessed, there is at Rome no evidence that any slave was not considered a potential citizen and thought gifted with as good blood and keen intellect as his master. The Romans had too many business managers of superior wit, literary men, artists, doctors, architects, teachers, and secretaries, in their households to draw any false conclusions on that score. Indeed the Plautine intrigue is generally based on the assumption that when a young man is at his wit's end through a reckless faux pas he can rely upon his slave to find a way out. Cicero's solicitous and generous letters to Tiro, which if unaddressed might be mistaken for missives to some highly favored young relative, showed how unrestrained the friendship might grow between master and man in the daily intercourse over books and business. The trust that men showed in their procurators, who travelled at leisure over the provinces conducting the large and confidential affairs of their masters, could not but preclude the emergence of any general scorn for the subject class; and the custom of placing and equipping slaves and freedmen in mercantile shops on a partnership basis which was so general under the ancient system of small-shop

production, gave unlimited opportunities for free development to slaves and freedmen.   Indeed modern
slavery has nowhere offered such opportunities; they
were not even found in the society of the rigid class
system of modern European states where slavery was
unknown.

Measured merely in economic terms, the position of
the free-born laborer was more precarious than that of
slaves and freedmen.   He had less opportunity to
reach the sympathy and support of a rich patron.   He
had no access to positions of trust since these fell to
trusted slaves, well trained, and long known.   The
sinecures of well-mannered attendance fell to those
who knew the routine.   The free laborer had no master
from whom to get funds for shopkeeping, he did not
fit in well with a troop of slaves either on the farm
or in the household where discipline must be uniform.
In factories, in mines, or at the docks he might find
work if he asked no more than the daily cost of a slave,
which seldom exceeded fifteen cents a day.   A slave
drudge could usually be bought for two hundred dollars[13] that is, about twenty dollars per year, capitalized
and insured.   His annual keep would come to twenty
or thirty more, including the price of two tunics, a pair
of shoes, some twelve or fifteen bushels of wheat, i. e.,
a soldier's ration, some table remnants in the form of

[13] On prices of slaves, see Wallon, *Histoire de l'esclavage*, II,
159.   See Cato's list of allowances, *R. R.* 56-9; Cato, however,
was considered a hard master.   In Cato's day the ration of oil
was very small.   As oil later was much cheaper the ration
increased.

oil, wine, and vegetables, and a straw cot in the slave barracks. On the assumption that his job was temporary and therefore did not incur any waste in idle seasons, the free man might ask for a trifle more than this, but only a trifle.

Unfortunately we have not many notes on actual wages. In Delos[14] during the third century B.C. the temple records indicate that unskilled workmen generally received from twenty to thirty cents per day, whether free or slaves hired out by their owners. Strange to say the best artistic work, that, for example, of architects, was not much better paid. Municipal clerks in Caesar's colony at Urso[15] in Spain received twenty cents per day; probably Horace received little more than that as a *scriba* in the quaestor's office at Rome. For Egypt during the Augustan age we have considerable information but this unfortunately is not quite applicable to the rest of the Empire, since the whole province was practically a vast governmental institution where free competition was not yet permitted. Under the circumstances of course wages were abnormally low, ranging generally from about three to eight

---

[14] Glotz, *Les Salaires a Délos*, Jour. des Savants, 1913, 206; cf. Guiraud, *La Main d'oeuvre industrielle dans l'ancienne Grèce;* Francotte, *L'industrie*, I, 327.

[15] Dessau, I. L. S. 6087, LXII. The lictors received only half that amount, viatores a third, and heralds a fourth, but these were likely to be shopkeepers who were only occasionally called upon for service.

cents per day.[16]　Cicero[17] once speaks of a somewhat
puny slave as not worth twelve cents a day, presumably
a sum quite below the normal wage of an average
laborer.　The soldier's pay was 225 denarii (about 15
cents per day, without food) under Caesar, but soldiers at that time expected a part of the booty or a
share in some colony after the war.　Diocletian's edict[18]
issued when the Empire was a wreck tried to force
down the price of labor as well as of all other commodities.　Such was the Emperor's idea of controlling
the high cost of living.　The wages there given are in
addition to "keep," such as it was.　The more important items are the follows:

Unskilled workman	10.8	cents.
Bricklayer	21.6	"
Carpenter	"	"
Stone Mason	"	"
Blacksmith	"	"
Shipbuilder	21-26	"
Painter	32.4	"

[16] West, *The Cost of Living in Roman Egypt, Class. Phil.* 1916,
304; Westermann, *An Egyptian Farmer*, Univ. Wisc. Studies,
1919, 178.

[17] *Pro Roscio Com.* 28.　It is impossible to take this as the
normal wage in Cicero's day, though handbooks generally do.
Cicero in fact is emphatically insisting on this slave's low value
as a workman.　In the parable of Our Lord, Math. 20, 2, workers
in the vineyard are assumed to earn one denarius per day.

[18] For Diocletian's edict, See Ch. XXII.　An interesting discussion of its bearing upon the question of the cost of living may
be found in Abbott, *The Common People of Ancient Rome*, p. 145.
See Pauly-Wissowa, *Art. Diocl. Edict.* for bibliography.　An item
on the wages of a miner is found in the Dacian wax tablets of

These wages are in addition to "food and lodging" for
the workman, and although in modern estimates of a
"living wage" in America these two items make up
only about 35 per cent. of the "budget," in Cicero's day
the bare necessities constituted at least 80 per cent. of
the daily expense if the laborer was married. Diocletian's list of wages therefore seems generous in comparison with Republican prices. For the end of the
Republic I think we may safely conclude that the
wages found at Delos probably still held, and that ordinary unskilled labor might expect about one denarius
per day or about 17-20 cents measured simply in gold.
This was approximately the wage generally paid Italian
farm labor at the harvest season in 1870 before the
entry of Victor Emmanuel.[19]

Obviously the ancient free laborer did not rear a
large family and send his children to college. Could
he live at all? Certainly not as well as the urban
slave, for the slave was not only kept fed and clothed
up to the point of efficiency in a position to acquire a
peculium, but so too were his wife and children.
Furthermore the children born in the household were
apt to be trained in some skilled occupation if only with
a view to more profitable service, an advantage which

---

the second century A.D. The workman contracts to work for
half a year for $6.30. This salary was doubtless in addition to
board and lodging, *C. I. L.* III, 948.

[19] *Monographia della cittá di Roma*, III, p. cxxii. If a man hired
out for a full year to ensure himself board and lodging through
the winter he received only half a lira per day.

frequently placed them in a position in which they could profit from contact with the master. The free-born laborer must find his own lodging and if he had a family he must feed his children; his wife of course generally earned her own living. But is it likely that laboring men reared families upon such wages? If we compare the wages with the laboring man's budget of necessities, forget present-day conditions and think rather of the conditions of the English laboring man before the repeal of the corn laws, the Italian work-man before 1870, or the Japanese poor before the Great War, we shall find that somehow it could be done.

In reckoning the cost of living, we soon realize that "living" is a term of innumerable meanings especially in a society dominated by slavery. Cicero felt that his son while a student at Athens could not live on less than four thousand dollars a year, since as the son of an ex-consul he must keep up appearances and asso-ciate with young aristocrats like Messala and Bibulus. Cicero himself felt that the dignity of his position de-manded a town house in the most aristocratic quar-ters—it cost about $200,000—a suburban villa, and at least one seaside retreat for vacations; sometimes he had three. Cicero of course was far from wealthy; he merely tried to live as he thought an ex-consul should. But, the workingman was not expected to include the cost of appearances and respectability in his budget. He was only expected to keep body and soul together, and the state even aided him in this. As for the rest the

sun kept him warm and reduced his bill for clothing
to the items demanded by a scant sense of modesty;
government officials and charitable citizens gave him
free baths and amused him gratis on all the holidays.

His menu called for no meat.[20] The invincible legionaries of Rome had conquered the world on a fare
of wheat porridge, and the state in Cicero's day gave
every citizen applicant at Rome a soldier's ration of a
bushel of wheat per month at about one-third the market price; under the Empire, this ration became a free
gift. In cities which had no corn doles, this staple cost
about seventy-five cents per bushel or two and a half
cents per day per person.[21] To this he generally added
a bit of cheese and some vegetables, olive oil, and wine.
In Diocletian's list which is higher than Republican
prices, cheese costs seven cents per pound; three cab-

[20] The Sicilians drafted for the army in 1915 were so unac-
customed to eating the meat of the army rations that compulsion
had in many cases to be applied. In 1906 I found that the regular noonday meal at an osteria for workmen near a Roman factory
cost five cents. It consisted of a half pound of bread, a slice of
cheese and a glass of wine. The daily wage was then two lire.
In 1916 the wage had risen threefold and the price of the meal
also.

[21] For prices of wheat see Rostowzew, Pauly-Wissowa, art. *Frumentum*. The prices varied normally from 40 cents to about $1.20
per bushel, fluctuating considerably because the poor farmers
generally had to market their grain as soon as it was ripe. The
lack of transportation in winter tended to make prices high in
February and March. Polybius, II, 15, and XXXIV, 8, cites
some very low prices from Spain and the Po valley before these
regions had been opened up to regular commerce. Such prices
should not be reckoned in making a normal average.

bage-heads[22] or six turnips could be got for a cent, vegetables which can be raised almost every month of the year on sunny slopes near Rome. A pint of *ordinaire*[23] cost about one cent, and that, generously mixed with water, might suffice for a day. The oil, of which a small quantity was used, sold at a trifle more. That is practically the entire bill for food. It would in fact be wholly misleading to draw up a complex schedule of prices to compare with the many items that go into making the monthly index of prices now issued by the Department of Labor. Eight cents per day, or six cents with a ticket of admittance to the corn doles, paid the grocer's bill.

As for clothing, one pair of shoes,[24] frequently dispensed with, cost at most half a dollar. Five pounds of wool at ten cents a pound, or less, sufficed for two tunics, which his wife wove by lamplight. To naked limbs Italy tempered the winds.

Rents at Rome in the Republic we should consider low. Caelius[25] was considered very extravagant when he was thought to have paid $1,500 per year for a house in the fashionable quarters. Cicero insisted that this rental was only $500, and that a false rumor had

[22] See Diocletian's Edict, V and VI.

[23] Columella, III, 3, 10, gives 300 ses. per culleus (120 gals.) as a fair price. Martial, XII, 76, implies that an amphora (6 gal.) costs about 20 asses.

[24] See Diocletian's Edict, IX, 5 a.

[25] Cic. *Pro Caelio*, 17; Plutarch, *Sulla*, 1, implies that 2000-3000 sesterces was the price of cheap apartments barely available for respectable Romans in Sulla's day.

been spread by the owner for advertising purposes. If a man like Caelius paid $500 on the Palatine what did a basement or an attic room in the Subura bring? We have no prices for Rome, but in the heyday of prosperity at Delos[26] many shops and houses, presumably of a fair type meant for occupancy by the shopkeeping class rented at one or two dollars the month. With labor and building material as cheap as they were at Rome we have no reason to think rentals there much higher than at Delos. Till recently farm laborers of the Campagna have reckoned house-rent as practically nothing. They raised up *capanne* with their own hands, making them out of a few poles and some waste straw; and these suffice in that climate. Ancient workmen could do as much, or they rented a room or two in the cheaply built tenement houses, or slept in their shops or in the narrow rooms behind the shops. House-rent was a small item to men who need not consider questions of station.

The Roman workingman must also have his bath and a post-balneal chat with his friends. For this the cities or public spirited citizens usually provided numerous public houses where admission was free, more commonly one-fourth of a cent or at most a cent. This was the workingman's club house.

It appears then that the laborer, thanks to state

[26] See Roussel, *Délos*, p. 149. At Pompeii a residence of fair size that had been converted into a fullery rented at seven dollars per month, *C. I. L.* IV, 1, p. 392. Later Martial and Juvenal frequently complain of the high rental of their attic apartments.

charity and the genial climate of Italy, need not starve
or freeze to death.   If he kept good health and could
find work, his wage would permit of marriage, for his
wife could perhaps support herself by spinning, weaving, or shopkeeping; and if there were children, they
too were put to work at a very early age.   Nothing
was left over for pleasure to be sure, but the Roman
government knew the dangers of an unamused rabble,
and on all the numerous holidays supplied games and
amusements gratis: chariot races, theatrical perform-
ances, wild beast hunts, gladiatorial shows, processions
and naval battles.   The Emperors had discovered a
very simple narcotic with which to sooth the crowd
infected with the diseases induced by slavery and a
non-productive economic system, and they administered
it with constant and certain success: panem et circenses.

There was but one deep concern not provided for.
Where were the surviving relatives to find as much as
ten dollars with which to pay for the cremation of the
body at death, the niche for the burial crock and the
jug of wine for a respectable wake?   To allay this
terror the workmen formed burial societies which collected small monthly dues with which to meet the necessary expenses.   The society also provided a respectable funeral procession from among its members.

During the Empire there were neither slave uprisings nor labor-revolutions in Italy.   Apparently the
laboring man was fairly happy; whether he could in
such conditions also be a good citizen is quite another
question.

The laborers of every craft had their collegia,[27] or labor gilds, but in the face of slave competition these could in no sense be unions organized for the purpose of bettering wages and conditions by collective bargaining. We never hear of labor strikes in Italy.[28]

Obviously if a laborer refused to work on the terms offered him a slave would be put in his place. It may be that the early gilds, assigned by tradition to the regal period, had grown out of direct economic needs. Industry probably had a healthier life at that time when commerce was more active and slavery had not yet permeated the city. The political strikes of the early Republic, the secessions to the Sacred Mount, may then have copied labor methods or may have found their strength in such labor gilds. But of such things traditions say nothing. In the late Empire again when the state was organizing the gilds for public purposes, granting certain immunities in return for services in grain transportation, fire protection, and other quasi-public duties, the gilds often exerted pressure upon the state through their patrons in order to obtain further privileges and exemptions. So, for instance the bargemen[29] of the Tiber secured some kind of monopoly

[27] Waltzing, *Les Corporations;* Ruggiero, Diz. Epig. *Art. Collegium,* by Waltzing; Kornemann, *Art. Collegium* in Pauly-Wissowa; Abbott, *The Common People of Ancient Rome,* p. 209.

[28] Strikes sometimes occurred in Eastern cities where free labor was not entirely at the mercy of slave economy; see Ruggiero, *loc. cit.* p. 358; Buckler, in Anatolian Studies pres. to Sir Wm. Ramsay, p. 27.

[29] Ruggiero, *loc. cit.*

with the help of a powerful friend, and the fullers of Rome brought suit to have their former water rights restored them. But such instances are proofs of new tendencies and do not indicate the purposes of earlier gilds. During the Republic the chief object of these many organizations seems to have been social, to use a very broad term. As is usual where shops are small and carry a very limited stock, shoppers go from one to the other to bargain. Consequently makers of the same article aggregate to the same section of the city.[30] The result is that the community of interest naturally arising from practicing the same metier is strengthened by personal acquaintance and an interest in the same locality. Thus a natural social group already exists for the formation of a burial-aid society, for some community of worship, and for social gatherings over wine and "shop-talk." By inscribing on stone their membership list together with all the dignified titles of petty offices they created a world of seeming importance where for a while they could forget the low esteem in which the outside world seemed to view them.[31] The

[30] Besides the many special fora we know numerous streets called by some special craft at Rome, e.g. vicus frumentarius, v. lorarius, v. materiarius, v. pulverarius, v. sandaliarius, v. unguentarius, porticus margaritaria. Jewellers usually gathered on the Via Sacra, potters on the Esquiline, tanners in the Trastevere, etc.

[31] Some of the gilds seem like the medieval gilds to have made a permanent place for themselves in annual religious festivals. (The *Shipwrites* at York gave "Building of the Ark," the *Goldsmyths* gave the "Magi" and the *Fysshers and Marynars* produced "Noah and the Flood.") So the Roman carpenters were apparently called upon to furnish the pine used in the celebra-

real binding cord that held them together was of course the very practical service of the society in collecting the petty dues and procuring the columbarium for the burial urns. The division of costs thus reduced the dread expense of dying and the fear of roaming as unburied ghosts, and the poor man could then contemplate the inevitable with some complacence. Nor were the social gatherings wholly for purposes of pleasure: the libations provided for the cult of the spirit of departed members and patrons in reason of which the members often called each other *comestores* and *convictores*. The following lines taken from the "regulations and by-laws" of such an organization will afford some insight into their little world.[32]

"It is unanimously voted that whoever wishes to enter this society shall pay an initiation fee of one hundred sesterces (about three dollars at this time) and an amphora of wine, and shall pay a monthly due of five asses (three cents)."

"If a member in full standing dies there shall be drawn for his account three hundred sesterces, one-

---

tion of Magna Mater and to carry it in the procession. They accordingly assumed from that time on the name of *dendrophori*. Shipwrights and sailors had regular parts to perform in the festival of Isis. In Cicero's day the officers of the gilds displaced the local officers in the direction of the street celebrations of the Compitalia. Indeed evidence may some day come to light proving a direct connection between the medieval "mystery plays" performed by gilds and the ancient "mysteries" in which labor gilds also had a share.

[32] The *leges* of the *Collegium Dianae et Antinoi, C. I. L.* XIV, 2112, Dessau, *I. L. S.* 7212.

sixth of which shall be divided among the attendants of the funeral. The funeral procession shall go on foot."

"Any member who commits suicide shall not be buried by the society."

"If any member who is a slave shall become free he shall provide the society with an amphora of good wine."

"If an officer elected in due order does not give a dinner to the members he shall be fined one dollar."

"The officers are each to furnish an amphora of good wine, two cents' worth of bread for each member, four sardines, and provide for the service."

"If any member causes a disturbance by changing his seat he shall be fined twelve cents; if anyone insults another member the fine shall be 36 cents; if he abuses the presiding officer the fine shall be 60 cents."

CHAPTER XVIII

The First Decades of the Empire

JULIUS CAESAR's program was apparently not thought out in economic terms, and yet Caesar more than any other Roman statesman seems to have considered the economic aspects of his political measures. It would be hazardous to attribute a definite policy to him, though it may be safe to say that his admiration for the Gracchi had led him to comprehend the needs of industry and commerce while his own aristocratic associations gave him a conservative respect for property rights. It is quite clear that his struggle with Pompey cannot be interpreted simply in economic formulae. To be sure, the Senate raised the cry that Caesar if victorious would disregard property rights and would confiscate lands far and wide for distribution to the rabble. Pompey pretended to believe that landowners throughout Italy would at once through fear of Caesar enlist in his own legions; but they did not. It is true that most of the senators—who were usually large land-owners—supported Pompey, but not, it would seem, because they thought their properties in danger, but rather because they had learned during Caesar's consulship that the Senate's power and prestige would vanish if Caesar were victorious. The men of property who did not belong to the Senate trusted Caesar as much as Pompey, and their attitude was justified when after his victory he disregarded the demands of his radical followers for confiscations, the cancellation of debts, moratoria and land distribution.

Caesar's term as dictator lasted only five years and most of this time was spent in warfare, but the plans which he laid for the empire during his few months of administrative work reveal an unusually clear insight into its material needs as well as a striking capacity to shape a lasting program of economic reforms. Had Caesar lived long the hoary traditions of political laissezfaire imposed by native individualism would doubtless have been ended. He clearly intended to give some state aid to commerce throughout the empire. He rebuilt Corinth, sending there a colony of urban freedmen, that is to say, men who were accustomed to trade and who spoke Greek. The real purpose of this colony became apparent when he drew up plans to cut a canal through the Corinthian isthmus that would afford a short and safe passage from Asia to Italy.[1] The plan for the canal was dropped at Caesar's death, but Corinth throve nevertheless, and a generation later was mentioned as the most prosperous city in Greece. Several of Caesar's other colonies were chosen with the same sure insight into commercial needs. Pompey had given administrative centers to Pontus and Bithynia, but it was Caesar who saw that the inclusion of these

---

[1] Suet. *Jul.*, 44. An inscription soon to be published by Taylor and West, *Am. Jour. Arch.* 1927, commemorates the transportation of a Roman fleet across the Isthmus.

provinces in the empire implied an obligation to give them commercial connections with Mediterranean shipping. Hence he sent freedmen colonies to the Black Sea harbors of Sinope and Heraclea. This was not an effort to Romanize the region, for the colonists were men who spoke Greek and soon forgot the little Latin they had ever acquired at Rome. The colonies therefore not only benefited Pontus and Bithynia, but removed from Rome a foreign element that refused to be assimilated.

For another colony of the same kind Carthage was chosen with equal wisdom. Suffering from its usual myopia the Senate had refused to rebuild Carthage lest it should attract a Punic population and become dangerous to Rome. Utica, an "allied" city had been allowed to become the governor's residence and the commercial port of the province and of the large agrarian colonies of Gracchus and Marius—an anomaly difficult to match. Caesar corrected this error by ordering a colony to Carthage, and the city was rebuilt to become one of the most important harbors of the empire. In Spain, Hispalis (Seville) was planted in the center of Andalusia, at the point of the Guadalquivir reached by sea tides and still accessible to seagoing vessels.[2] Arelate was also planned as a port of Gaul on the Rhone to supplant Marseilles, the Greek city which had hitherto dominated the trade of all the Gallic country. And finally the port of Rome was not to be neglected.

[2] One of Caesar's colonial charters, drawn up for Urso in Spain, has been preserved; see Dessau, *Insc. Lat. Sel.* 6087.

The harbor at Ostia was unsatisfactory because the mouth of the Tiber quickly clogged up with silt and the roadstead of the river was unsafe because of the swift current. Besides, the harbor at Puteoli attracted much more shipping than Ostia, as we have noticed. Caesar projected a barge canal[3] from Rome along the valley of the Tiber down to Ostia, then on south along the low coast to Puteoli. The whole scheme, which envisioned the commercial needs of the Empire from the Black Sea to beyond the Straits of Gibraltar, was the first of its kind in history. When we consider that Caesar had but a few months for its consideration and that much of it was actually carried out we may well believe that with a few years of peace Caesar would have advanced a large paternalistic program in favor of state aid to commerce and perhaps to the industries that fed and required the trade. Had such a plan been projected with the wisdom which Caesar displayed and been adopted as a permanent policy of his successors, the course of Rome's development, it is needless to say, would have been materially changed.

Caesar also revealed a keen interest in the development of agriculture. It was he who projected the tunnel which Claudius later attempted to make in order to drain the Fucine Lake and reclaim a few thousand acres of rich arable land in central Italy. He also set his engineers at work to devise a plan for the draining of the Pontine Marshes,[4] partly to reclaim flooded

[3] Plut. *Caes.* 58; Suet. *Claud.* 20.

[4] Suet. *Jul.* 44, Cic. *Phil.* V. 7.

land, partly to make the surrounding region healthier. These two projects have had to await the enterprise of modern engineers, since the emperors that followed Caesar lacked his vision and energy. But his mind penetrated beyond the immediate view of reclaimed acres and increased produce. He understood that Italy's free stock must be saved if the heart of the Empire was to be sound. With this in view he decreed that at least a third of the laborers employed on the ranches of Italy must be free citizens. This is the first effort at Rome to check the spread of slavery, and taken in conjunction with the extra-Italian colonization of many thousands of freedmen it reveals a readiness to undertake the social reconstruction of Italy.

The Gracchi had long ago pointed out that a large citizen-body of small land-owners would be preferable to a few plantation owners exploiting slave labor, but even when citizenship was extended throughout Italy in 89 B.C. all parties at Rome had combined to exclude the new citizens from an effective system of voting. In a municipal law which Caesar left incomplete at his death, we find a clause which for the first time incorporated the local citizen-census lists of the Italian municipalities in that of the national list made at Rome. It is probable that this was a preliminary step toward holding national elections by local balloting. At any rate the fragment that we have shows clearly that Caesar had broken with the aristocratic tradition which accorded the city of Rome a pre-eminent position over the other municipalities of Italy.

Similarly Caesar's interest in the provinces and the provincials marks a new departure. In Gaul and Spain he had extended Roman citizenship freely, and many provincials—Suetonius says eighty—were actually admitted into the Senate to the mortification of the old nobles. Caesar's behavior in Gaul even before he became dictator must have surprised his contemporaries. By directing his campaign of conquest along the Rhine and confining his warfare as far as possible against the German tribes in the north until Gaul was enclosed, he was able to take the province with little damage to its people and property. Most of the slaves and booty were taken in the north. Caesar confiscated no lands except from a few rebellious individuals. He planted no colonies, and he left the tribes autonomous while granting Roman citizenship to large numbers of the natives. It was apparently his belief that Gaul would in time become an integral part of Rome, and he intended to leave it prosperous and well-disposed. Caesar in fact had accepted the logical consequences of the democratic theories of the Gracchi, of which however they had themselves not seen the full meaning. There is apparent in all of Caesar's work a remarkable insight into the needs of all classes, a breadth of sympathy, a consistency and consecutiveness of principle which tempt us to believe that in time he would have been led to the fashioning of a large economic program. His death removed a man who had revealed the capacity to use political power in laying a new structure for a great Empire. After his death the vision was lost and

Rome reverted to its old tradition that the government should confine its activities to political administration.

The death of Caesar threw the world into turmoil again, when Antony, Lepidus and Octavian, who commanded armies, overawed the forces of the government and compelled the Senate to vote them absolute powers. In order to get money with which to pay their troops, they proscribed three hundred senators and two thousand knights, confiscating and selling their properties for cash.[5] No uglier deed is recorded in Roman history, and yet except for the annihilation of many families that had given distinction to political history, and the dread precedent which was to hang as a deterrent to initiative and independence, the changes wrought in the economic life were not great. Many large estates changed hands throughout Italy, for men of property in the far corners of the peninsula were struck down as well as those near Rome, but they were usually sold off in units, and the slaves and tenants continued to work under the new masters as under the old. We are not aware that industrial capitalists suffered to such an extent as to hamper production or trade, for the ensuing period seems to be more prosperous in this respect than the preceding. If industry was largely in the hands of freedmen, as it apparently was, its escape could be attributed to the political obscurity of this class.

More profound were the effects of the war in 42 when the triumvirs had defeated Brutus and Cassius

[5] Appian, *Bell. Civ.* 4, 8, ff.

at Philippi, and were obliged to provide the promised bonus in land to the one hundred thousand soldiers who were now to be demobilized.[6] This time the triumvirs simply selected some twenty cities of Italy which had most strongly favored their opponents and confiscated the arable lands of their inhabitants. The immediate havoc was heartrending. Since the allotment to each soldier must have been at least fifteen jugera, about a million acres of good arable land changed hands. Here great and small suffered equally because most of the lands in the richer municipalities were owned in large tracts, and farmed by renters or slaves, and all had to move on, for the dispossessed owner sold off his slaves as best he might, and the recipients who were now to be working peasants could make use of no tenants and but here and there a slave. If 100,000 unmarried soldiers received lots, fully as many tenants and slaves, a large part of them possessed of families, had to go. When Vergil, who was fortunate enough to have his property returned through the intercession of powerful friends, thanked Octavian in his first eclogue for the favor, he did not fail to express his sorrow for the homeless evicts who were compelled to migrate to far-off provinces. What was Italy's loss here was gain to provinces like Africa and Spain, and it was not so long before these very migrants were producing rich crops in the provinces to compete on the Roman market with the products of those who had displaced them.

[6] Kornemann, Art. *Colonia*, Pauly-Wissowa; Kromayer's comments in *Neue Jahrbücher*, 1914, p. 161.

There was, however, a favorable aspect in the disaster. Many large estates farmed by unfree labor had been divided into a great number of small holdings to be farmed by working peasants. These were soldiers, to be sure, and some were barbarians or adventurers, but many were the poor of rural districts recently recruited—like the legions of Ventidius from Picenum—who had not been in the army long enough to be wholly unfitted for work. Despite the great injustices done in such land distributions by Sulla, Caesar, and especially by the triumvirs, the fact remains that when half a million farm lots had been distributed to working farmers by this method, we must assume that for a while at least the evils of concentration were checked.[7] Varro a few years later happens to express the opinion—somewhat rhetorically perhaps—that no land was so well cultivated as Italy; and in the middle years of Augustus' rule it is likely enough that there were as many contented peasants in Italy as there had been since the Punic wars. However, this situation did not last very long. The trend to Junkerdom was very strong in Italy,[8] where the aristocracy for centuries had

[7] After Actium when Augustus had the resources of Egypt at his disposal he bought land for the soldiers. According to his Res Gestae, 16, he spent about thirty million dollars in Italy and thirteen million in the provinces for such lands. We may well believe that the price of land responded to such a market.

[8] A few years earlier Cicero had said that the allotments of Sulla made at Praeneste twenty years before (with a prohibition of alienation) had already fallen into the hands of a few owners, Leg Agr. II, 79.

been compelled by law to place their material investments in respectable estates, where there were no
stocks and bonds in corporations to employ capital, and
where landowning alone gave the proper caste to re-
tiring industry. And after all it was but twenty of a
hundred municipalities that had suffered transforma-
tion under the triumvirs. A fear of slave power,
apparent since the servile war of 75, which induced
land-owners to seek free tenants who would lease
parcels of their farms, seems to have exerted a whole-
some influence during this period. The fact that the
word *colonus*[9] had come regularly to designate tenants
in Augustus' day would indicate that leasing was then
usual. This system required less of an initial outlay,
less supervision and assured a more interested attention to the land. But it must not be supposed that the
system brought back Italy's vanishing native stock,
since farm slaves were often set free to become freedmen tenants.

After Actium came a long period of peace for Italy
and the provinces, forty-five years under the steady
hand of Augustus. Life was safe again, private property unmolested, pirating and brigandage suppressed,
the frontiers safeguarded, crimes quickly punished,

---

[9] Coloni (renters) are mentioned as very numerous on some
estates in Caes. *B. C.* 1, 34, 1; II, 56. The word occurs freely in
Cicero, *Caec.* 94; *Cluent.* 175; *ad Fam.* 13, 11; etc.; in Varro
R. R. 1, 4, 3; 1, 40, 2, etc., in the Jurists of Augustus' day:
Alfenus, *Dig.* 19, 2, 30; Labeo, *Dig.* 19, 2, 60, etc. The imperial
jurists have this use of the word over two hundred times. Leasing of land was therefore customary.

commerce and industry given a free range if not directly encouraged. It was an era of much material prosperity, of the accumulation of large fortunes especially in provincial investments, but also in the growth of industries. It is the period when the larger factories mentioned in previous chapters extended their trade farthest.

Of the provinces Africa probably underwent the most rapid changes during this period. Julius Caesar before his death had made Numidia a province and had given its capital Cirta (Constantine) to the adventurer Sittius to distribute to his motley army of Romans, Spaniards, and Berbers. Here was a vast colony extending from the very heart of Numidia down to the sea, ruled under the forms of Roman law, where good agricultural land was to be had cheap. What was even more important, Caesar ordered the rebuilding of Carthage as a convenient Roman port for the old Gracchan and Marian settlements, and since he had exacted a fine of some five million dollars from the three hundred Romans who had aided the senatorial cause in Africa[10] (an average of $12,000 for each individual, which betokens surprisingly large holdings), there must have been much good land thrown on the market in the neighborhood. When now in lieu of failing texts we examine the African inscriptions of the Augustan period, we find that at the very time that proscriptions and land distributions in Italy were driving Italians to emigrate, there was a decided influx of

[10] *Bell. Afric.* 90; 97.

Roman citizens into Africa, especially into the old
province.[11] For instance, several towns of the old
province, especially coast towns like Hippo (Bizerta),
Curubis, Neapolis, and Carpis, and we must add Simi-
thu, whence Roman buildings got so much of their
pleasing "Numidian" marble, attributed their rehabilitation to Julian (Augustan) colonization, though we
know that no official colonies were settled in these
places. It seems that in these towns, as well as in
many others, Roman citizens emigrating from Italy
settled down and were permitted by Augustus to form
independent local organs of self-government by the
side of the native governments.

Actual settlements of veterans were also made at
several places like Uthina, Thuburbo and Sicca, as
their inscriptions prove. It is interesting to note that
when these old half-abandoned towns got new life
from Roman immigration the descendants of the old
Punic inhabitants, who had escaped into Numidia when
Carthage fell, now returned in large numbers. The old
Carthaginian towns came to be half Semitic again, as
we can see from the great number of shrines and tomb
symbols sacred to Baal Ammon (Saturnus) and Tanit
(Juno Caelestis). At Carthage and Hippo in fact the
Punic people were permitted local self-government, as
we know from the Punic coins they struck. So the
African province prospered by the influx of both Ro-
man and Punic peoples, villages grew to cities, and this
created markets for the farm produce, which in turn

[11] See *Classical Rev.* 1925, p. 15; *Am. Jour. Phil.* 1926, p. 53 ff.

fed industry and commerce. Except for the settlement of some of the veterans and the permission of local self-government to ethnic groups, whether Punic or Roman, Augustus did not interfere in the process. Africa had resources which would be developed in time if the province was left to herself. As we shall see, progress was steady—even in the inevitable concentration of estates—and during the Augustan period Africa became, after Egypt, the foremost producer of wheat in the Empire.

Spain[12] continued to be a land of riddles and inconsistencies. The south, semi-tropical, luxuriantly fertile, and well-dotted with old cities; the vast central plateau, high, semi-arid, scantily populated with rough and free village folk; the north and northwest mountains with their independent shepherd and hunting tribes; the Mediterranean coast with old trading cities long under the influence of Greek and Punic commerce: each differed from the other in every essential of culture. The people were chiefly Iberian in all parts. They had originally come from North Africa and belonged to the Berber stock. The center was called Celt-Iberic, to be sure, but that only means that the Celts had pushed down into the center during the fifth century. Later they had largely been driven back

[12] Strabo's third book is very illuminating; Schulten, art. *Hispania* in Pauly-Wissowa is full and accurate, and his *Numantia* is useful. See also Van Nostrand. *Reorganization of Spain by Augustus, Univ. Calif.* 1916; Charlesworth, *Trade routes*, 150 ff.; Albertini, *Les divisions administratives de l'Espagne*, 1923; McElderry, *Jour. Rom. Stud.* 1918, p. 53.

to Gaul by the Iberians,[13] and in Augustus' day Iberians predominated here as elsewhere. In the south and east the natives had come into contact with Aegean culture for a thousand years because Spain was the most productive mining country of the ancient world. The gold, silver, and copper mines of the Sierra Morena range were reached by way of Gades and the towns of the eastern coast. The famous tin mines of the northwest were accessible directly by boat or by overland caravans. The traders of Mycenean Crete had resorted here, then the Phoenicians, the Etruscans, the Greeks, the Carthaginians, and the Romans in turn. The Iberians of the coast were exploited by each and learned the arts of each in turn.

The mining operations were as scientifically carried on as anywhere and the steel blades of Spain were as much sought after in ancient times as they have been ever since. The linen and woolen textiles of Spain made from home-grown flax and wool by well-trained weavers on intricate looms were likewise highly prized in Rome. The sheep and cattle breeding from pedigreed stock had awakened the comment of Greek travellers. Vines, olives and African fruits were introduced early and covered the gardens of Andalusia before ever the Romans came. In the south, particularly under the tutelage of the Phoenicians of Gades and Malaca, the Turditani had risen to great prosperity, living in self-governing cities. On the eastern coast, where Greek contacts were numerous, there was awak-

[13] Schulten, *Numantia.*

ened for a while some skill in art,[14] but this disappeared when the Greeks were driven off by the Carthaginians.   Apparently the Iberians were adepts at as-
similating the arts and crafts of their tutors, but there
is little evidence of any independent development after
the stimulus of example had left.   The cultural history
of ancient Spain—as of mediaeval and renaissance
Spain—is largely a story of external influences.

The Greeks and Phoenicians, interested in trade
rather than in territory, had only planted trading posts.
Even the wealthy Punic city of Gades had taken very
little territory.   Conquest was not attempted till the
father of Hannibal set out to create an empire as a
substitute for Sicily, lost in the First Punic War.   To
win territory quickly, he exacted a very small stipend of half a tithe, but he apparently confiscated
the mines of the Sierra Morena.   By the treaty that
ended the Second Punic War, Rome took Spain from
Carthage, that is she assumed sovereignty over the
south and east and took over full ownership of the
mines.   When Polybius visited Spain, the national
mines of Rome were employing 40,000 miners and extracting silver to the amount of twenty-five thousand
drachmas per day or about two million dollars per
year.   In Strabo's day these mines had been let to
private (probably equestrian) contractors.

The management of the province as a whole was
quite typical of Roman methods.   Property rights were
as usual respected.   The only Roman settlement made

[14] Carpenter, *The Greeks in Spain.*

at the time was a colony at Italica of old and sick soldiers who could not be brought home. The lucrative commerce which Carthage had monopolized was simply allowed to take its own course, and the rich Punic and Phoenician merchants of Gades fell heir to it. In fact they received all the advantages of Rome's backing because Gades was inscribed as an ally of Rome and thereby gained free entry into every port within the Roman federation of allies. In Augustus' day the merchants of Gades controlled a large part of the commerce of Spain. According to Strabo, "they built and sent out the largest merchant vessels of the Mediterranean and the Atlantic trade,"[15] and few of their citizens were to be seen at home "because those who were not engaged in traffic on the seas were enjoying life at Rome." There was only one city of the Empire outside of Rome which had as many citizens of the knight's census as Gades, and that was Padua, the home of wealthy landlords. Strabo's statement is a startling reminder of how the Roman people of the Republic neglected the commercial opportunities of their provinces. Meanwhile Rome was doggedly forcing the poor and semi-barbaric tribes of the centre to acknowledge submission. Through a hundred years of spasmodic outbreaks of guerilla warfare this useless task continued—induced partly by a legalistic instinct for properly signed treaties, partly by a desire for military glory and booty on the part of governors. Nowhere did the senatorial government more clearly

[15] Strabo, 3, 5, 3; 3, 2, 5-6.

demonstrate a blindness to commercial advantages while meticulously following up traditions of "political duty."

By the time of Augustus, Baetica (Andalusia) was quite completely Romanized. That fact is due largely to Caesar's colonization and grants of privileges in 45-44, very little to any efforts of the Republican régime. The only colony of Romans planted here during the Republic was at Cordova, a colony established by Marcellus to serve as the governor's residence in 152. The town itself remained half Iberic, but the garrison and recruiting station placed there doubtless did much to bring Roman speech and manners to this imitative people. In point of fact, southern Spain had so long been under foreign influence that nationalistic sentiment and the native language were on the wane; and since the foremost men of Gades were themselves trading chiefly with Rome and aping Roman customs, even this Punic city had become a centre of Romanization. Of Roman settlers investing in land there were a certain number, but we seldom hear of them.[16] However, it was Caesar who hastened the process, though not by any intentional policy. When he came to Spain to quell the last opposition in 45, he found that a large number of the Baetican cities had thrown in their lot with the sons of Pompey, partly because the elder Pompey had in his youth made a reputation

[16] Caesar, *Bell. Civ.* II, 18-22, mentions a *conventus* at Hispalis and the colony at Cordova. They had provided Varro with two cohorts. *Bell. Alex.* 53 mentions a *vernacula legio*, probably of mixed troops.

in quelling the Sertorian revolt, partly because Caesar's
governor had treated the natives brutally. Caesar
needed land at the time for veterans and urban freedmen. He therefore expropriated the lands of several
cities which he captured in this campaign, and several
of these cities lay in the heart of the rich valley of the
Baetis (Guadalquivir). Hispalis (Seville), to which
seagoing vessels could sail at high tide, he settled with
veterans. It has been a rich farming and trading
center ever since. To Urso he sent a charity colony
from Rome consisting largely of freedmen. Ucubi,
Itacci, and Hasta were other colonies of his in southern
Spain. To several communities he gave Latin rights
in return for aid. These settlements will largely account for the Romanization of which Strabo speaks.

The case of the nearer province of Spain was somewhat different. Here only the coast towns and a few
of the tribes along the Iberus river had to any extent
become Romanized. But when Caesar first advanced
into Spain in 49 and met the forces of Pompey at
Ilerda, the tribes nearby had to decide which party to
favor. The fact that a large number of them—still
far from ready for municipal life—received Latin
or citizen rights soon after shows that they chose
shrewdly and that Caesar paid for services in the usual
fashion. In Pliny's list of Spanish cities taken from
Augustus' time we find the Iberus valley as far as
Burgos enjoying special privileges.

Augustus spent three years in Spain in subjugating
the last remnants of independent tribes in the west

and northwest. Upon the completion of this task he founded some military colonies, the most important being at Saragossa (Caesaraugusta), Bracara Augusta, and Emerita (Merida)[17] which Agrippa beautified, and he connected these places with good military roads. Some friendly municipalities were also given Roman citizenship, but except for Baetica, the eastern coast, and the military colonies, the Spanish tribes lived on as before.

In reviewing the conditions of Spain we find that Caesar and Augustus did not depart from the principles of the preceding government. The Senate had set out to pacify Spain and to get its tribute of half a tithe. It had not interfered with social conditions or with economic institutions. The generals had granted citizenship to influential individuals who had been friendly. Caesar and Augustus followed the same principle, but, having full power to punish and reward, they could act more quickly and effectively, especially since the exigencies of their wars offered large opportunities. Gifts of land, of franchise, and of immunity from taxes were reminders that loyalty was profitable. The colonies planted in hostile country were chiefly military posts placed where military roads joined. They would serve perhaps as Romanizing centers, but

[17] The ruins of Merida are imposing in their present drab setting, but the archaeologist should keep in mind that state funds supplied the resources with which to beautify this veteran colony, and that other Spanish towns which did not have such funds show very few traces of Roman architecture on a grand scale.

there is nothing to indicate that rewards were offered for learning Rome's language, or for dwelling in cities according to Roman ways. And the long roads which Augustus mapped out, along the coast from Gaul to Gades, the northern one through Saragossa to Cantabria, and the inland one from Hispalis through Emerita to Salamanca, were primarily for military purposes, as their stations prove. They also served trade, and Romanized towns sprang up along their course, but that was not their chief purpose.

One has only to read Strabo's interesting account to see that Spain, especially southern Spain, was materially prospering under Roman rule,[18] that Spanish (chiefly Punic) ships were bringing goodly cargoes of wines, oil, grain, linen, wool, metals, wrought and unwrought, salted meat and fish to Italian ports, and that the people were rapidly assuming Roman ways; but except for a few places like Italica, Hispalis, Corduba, Emerita, and Tarraco, the Iberians were assuming merely a surface culture such as they had acquired from the Greeks and the Phoenicians before—a fact that modern excavations have recently brought to light. And it is not likely that either Caesar or Augustus concerned themselves about the matter. Noninterference in domestic matters had long been a cardinal principle with Roman governments.

[18] Rome accorded free trade and free agriculture to Spain as to the other provinces. Oil and wine were produced and exported freely all through the republican period: Polyb. 34, 9; Varro, *R. R.* 1, 8, 1; 1, 31, 1; Strabo, 3, 2, 6; 3, 4, 16; *Bell. Hisp.* 27, (for Africa, see *Bell. Afr.* 43; 50, 67, 97.)

In Gaul, the Narbonese province was now considered practically an annex to Italy. The tribes, Iberians near the Pyrenees, Celts in the center, Ligurians nearer the Alps, were so diverse that foreign penetration had been easy. Besides, the great commercial Greek colony, Marseilles,—which never tried to dominate except through trade—had accustomed the peoples to foreign ways and wares. Rome had at times helped Marseilles against inroads of the mountain folk in return for a road to Spain across her territory and for naval aid in various wars; and in 118 (as an aftermath of Gracchan efforts at commercial colonization, a colony was placed at Narbo where Roman traders and money lenders settled in large numbers.[19] It is apparent also that Italian settlers began to drift into this region as Cisalpine Gaul filled up. Many of the natives went to school in Marseilles to study literature, oratory, and philosophy, and some of these students were later attracted to Rome, for instance, the poet, Cornelius Gallus, and Pompeius Trogus, who for a while was Caesar's chief secretary. In the civil war, Caesar punished Marseilles for lending support tô Pompey, and took part of her territory to found a colony of veterans of the sixth legion at Arelate on the Rhone,[20] another of veterans of the seventh legion at Baeterrae and still another of the tenth legion at Nimes. He left Marseilles her ancient rights and autonomy, but the new Rome colony at Arles, because

[19] Cic. *Pro Font.* 13; Diod. V, 26.

[20] Constans, *Arles Antiques*.

of its advantageous position, captured much of Marseilles' trade in Gaul. As a consequence of these movements almost all of the Narbonese provincials who were not citizens had attained the Latin rights, only nations of the remoter rural villages were excepted, and these were "attributed" to larger cities to help pay the expense of orderly government. Nimes, for instance, had supervision over twenty-four such villages. When Caesar took the rest of Gaul the new provinces became a large field of exploitation for the business men of the Narbonese province which accordingly became very prosperous.

The three provinces of further Gaul[21] also enjoyed peace and honest administration under the policy of non-interference. Adopting certain hints from Caesar, Augustus simply drew the provincial boundaries of the newly conquered tribes, sent responsible and honest officers to govern them, and assigned fixed taxes which were generally gathered with honesty and without quibbling. In laying out these provinces he included fourteen Celtic tribes with the Iberian Aquitanians, and a few others with the Belgae, perhaps in order to avoid having one very large nationalistic group, though his purpose may only have been to make the three provinces uniform in size. Their social and political institutions were not disturbed. The tribal rule in the sixty-four tribes (civitates) continued as before under

[21] Hirschfeld, *Kleine Schriften*, p. 42; Rostovtzeff, *Social and Econ. Hist.* 202 ff. (referring generally to a later period); Jullian, *Histoire de la Gaule*, vol. III, IV.

the direction of a meeting of the nobles, called *ordo*, for, as Caesar says, the landlords were the only ones that counted, the common folk being almost serfs. These councils of nobles elected the chieftain or *vergobret* (later sometimes called *praetor*). Such a system of government did not especially attract Roman immigrants. Poor citizens would not care to enter the class of semi-servile peasants, and rich Romans, if they chose to buy out or displace Celtic landlords in that vast cityless region, would find the surroundings uncongenial and the problem of adaptation to a Celtic tenantry and economy discouraging. Hence, since neither Caesar nor Augustus expropriated territory for Roman centers (except for a capital at Lyons), central Gaul showed but few signs of Romanization for a century at least. When in the French museums one studies the collections of household articles from ancient cemeteries one is impressed by the lateness and poverty of the Roman ware. It is, in fact, inferior in workmanship to the splendid collections of bronze ware that have survived from the pre-Roman La Tène period.

The Romanizing process began slowly from the boundaries, from the Narbonese province and Lyons in the South, and from the camps in the north where the armies kept watch on the Rhine. Trade[22] there

[22] Wool and *sagi*, Strabo, 4, 4, 3; Hor. *Odes* III, 16, 35. Wine and oil: Strabo, 4, 1, 2: "The grape does not easily ripen" (near the Cevennes); Diod. V, 26: The climate in Gaul is too cold for the vine, hence the Gauls make a drink from barley. During the empire the vine was introduced as far as the Moselle.

was of course.   Gaul raised an immense amount of wool and had some to spare for dealers who supplied the Roman armies; wine and oil went up the Rhone in large quantities, especially from the Narbonese province, for olives did not thrive in central Gaul, and vineyards made but slow progress northward.   The food and clothing for the Roman armies of the Rhine were bought in part in the province, in part transported through it.   There was grain enough raised for home use and for sale to the armies, but we seldom hear of the exportation of wheat to Rome.   The only food products of importance which Rome received from here were salt-pork—from the oak forests—and several kinds of cheese.   Iron mines were worked in Aquitania and the south in Caesar's time, and centers of iron manufacture to supply the needs of the province are mentioned.   The luxurious villas, however, which excavators have found in the region belong to a later day.   On the whole, Celtic Gaul remained under Augustus, and long after, primarily a region of drinking, hunting, and jousting barbarian lords and their hard-working farm folk.   There is no sign that Augustus cared to change the situation so long as the provincials paid their tribute and kept peace; but the feudal system, such as it was, naturally gave way when wars came to an end.   Augustus deprecated the fact that Caesar had bestowed citizenship on many

---

On the export of wheat to Rome, Pliny, *N. H.* 18, 66; pork, Strabo, 4, 2, 2; metals, Caes. *B. G.* 3, 21 and 7, 22. The famous pottery and glassware of Gaul developed later.

chieftains and had even introduced some of them into the Roman Senate. He did not follow this example, whether because he wished to please the Roman aristocracy or whether his three years' sojourn in Gaul convinced him that the Celts were unprepared for citizenship. There is no evidence that he preferred to see the village communities grow into cities. When he moved down Bibracte from the hill-top and founded Augustodunum in the valley to take its place, his purpose was, doubtless, to destroy a dangerous stronghold rather than to inaugurate a policy of urbanization. Augustus has been charged with negligence and shortness of vision because of his laissez-faire policy in Gaul, but Gaul was attracted all the more speedily by a generous course. Had succeeding emperors emulated his honest administration and respect for native institutions, the Romanized Gaul of a later day would have been a stronger bulwark of defence at critical times than it ultimately proved to be.

In the province of Asia Caesar had instituted a much needed reform when he declared an end of the contract system of tithe-gathering, and placed the stipends of the several communities at two-thirds of the average tithe. But the civil war which followed proved disastrous. First, the Senate, in 43, authorized Brutus and Cassius[23] to impose a forced loan on the province for the provisioning of the army which they were then

[23] Brutus and Cassius, Cic. *Phil.* X, 26. The Greek letters of Brutus, (Hercher, *Epist. Graec.* 177 f.) containing requisitions for funds are in my opinion genuine (not however the answers). Antony, App. *B. C.* V, 1, 4.

gathering.   The amount decided upon was ten times the annual stipend—that is, a full year's crop—to be supplied within two years.   The Senate had promised to repay the "loan" with interest after the war; but what if the Senate did not win?   The cities demurred in vain; they had to borrow and give, for Brutus and Cassius were at hand with their armies and would not listen to excuses.   Their worst fears were realized. The Senate lost, and Antony, who took the east as his portion, was so far from inclined to alleviate the suffering of the province that by way of punishment for the aid given the liberators, he imposed an equivalent charge, not as a loan, but as a penalty.   The results of this appalling treatment are nowhere described to us. We may be sure, however, that there were many bankruptcies and much transferring of properties because of them.   However, it is not likely that Roman investors increased their holdings here at this time, for Romans living in Asia suffered as severely as the natives in both exactions, and wealthy men in Italy had in part been struck by the proscription of 43 while those not so abused had opportunities to buy land at home if they wished to invest.

Inscriptions, however, indicate that some of the imperial estates of Asia originated at this time, and it has been generally held[24] that the Attalid stipendiary land had become ager publicus during the republic, and that Augustus seized it as imperial property.   This is

[24] Since the appearance of Rostovtzeff, *Röm. Kolonat*, see esp. p. 283 ff.

not plausible in view of Augustus' procedure else-where. Firstly, there is no proof that the Senate had turned stipendiary land into ager publicus; secondly, though Augustus, like Caesar and the triumvirs, at first disposed of state revenues at pleasure and without accounting, he kept his accounts in good order, and when the division of provinces was made between the Senate and the imperial fiscus in 23, we find no shuf-fling of accounts. So far as we know, ager publicus and stipendiary land with the possible exception of the Chersonese,[25] regularly went to the account of the aerarium. The imperial estates found in Asia, cer-tainly not large in Augustus' day, if we exclude those of "Galatia," may have come from the properties of proscribed senators and knights which Antony—less meticulous than Octavian—may have drawn into his personal accounts during his ten years' control of the east.

Property rights of the natives remained as they were before, in so far as they had not been lost through debts. The natives had of course suffered severely by being practically stripped of two complete crops by Antony and Brutus. However, a long peace followed with fairly honest tax-gathering on a reduced scale,

[25] The Chersonese had once been Attalicus ager (Cic. *Leg. Agr.* II 50) and had apparently become ager publicus by 63. It probably was a private estate of the king, not "crown land." Since the republican armies had found easy transit here we may suppose that Augustus for military reasons placed it in Agrippa's possession for the time being. I know of no other instance of the kind.

and the province seems soon to have reached moderate prosperity again.

We must conceive of Asia during the Augustan period as a country of home industry, without centers of great wealth, with few slaves and little factory production. The free villages throughout the interior raised enough food for themselves and for the cities of the coast, but no more. The men farmed their small plots or pastured sheep, while the women and children wove and spun clothing, tapestries, and rugs. They had much skill in reproducing old and artistic patterns and knew the secrets of good dyeing. The rugs and embroideries of Anatolia have a long ancestry. Ephesus[26] and the cities of the southern route, Tralles and Apamea, were flourishing, the latter two much engaged in the trade of the road, the former also in sea commerce. The central road from Smyrna running through Sardes tapped good shepherd country as well as the quarries of Phrygian marble at Synnada which Augustus used at Rome. The ships of the coast-towns brought much gain, for Anatolian traders were found on all the seas. But the great prosperity which had come when Alexander first opened the east and which lasted while Rome took slaves from the warring

[26] On prosperous cities of Asia see Strabo: Ephesus largest, 14, 1, 24 (Cf. Reisch, *Ephesus*, 1923, vol. III); Apamea next, 12, 8, 15; Cyzicus, 12, 8, 12; Quarries at Synnada, 12, 8, 14; Laodicea growing, 12, 8, 16; Colossae, ibid.; Pergamum, 13, 41; Sardis and Philadelphia shattered by earthquake but in rich country (cf. Butler, *Sardis*, 1921, p. 31), 13, 4, 9-10, Hieropolis, 10, 4, 14; Tralles, 14, 1, 42.

tribes of the interior, had passed with the establishment of peace and the rise of the west.

East of the province of Asia lies Galatia, which became an imperial province in 25 B.C. when King
Amyntas was killed in battle and left his whole kingdom to Augustus.[27] The region contained vast imperial domains besides temple-estates and Roman colonies, all of which give it a peculiar aspect in economic
history. Since much confusion has resulted from assigning to Asia certain peculiar institutions that belonged to Galatia, it may be well to make some distinctions. The Galatians were Celts who had broken
in and settled about Ancyra (the present capital of
Turkey) in the third century B.C. Since Amyntas,
the captain of the Galatian horse, had deserted to the
triumvirs at the battle of Philippi, the victors made
him king of his tribesmen, and also ceded Lycaonia,
Pisidia, southern Phrygia and Isauria to him, extending his kingdom southward to the Taurus plateau.
The Galatian tetrarchs had presumably owned vast
ranches throughout their hill country, all of which
Amyntas seems to have taken as his own. Strabo
speaks of 300 herds belonging to Amyntas on the plains
of Lycaonia alone. The half-barbaric Anatolian folk
who lived between old Galatia and the Taurus belonged
to a large number of temple or priest states and these

[27] Ramsay, *Studies in the Province of Galatia*: *Jour. Rom. Stud.*
VII, VIII and XII; *The Tekmoreian Guest-Friends;* also in *Ann.
Brit. Sch. Ath.* 1912, 65; Meyer, *Die Grenzen der hell. Staaten.*
On Amyntas see Dio 47, 48; 49, 32; Strabo, 12, 6, 4; App.
B. C. 5, 75.

Augustus seems to have claimed as having been royal property.[28] At any rate, when Augustus inherited the kingdom in 25, he became more than sovereign in these theocratic communities, he became lord of the temples and of the temple-tenants as well. The only way to explain this fact is to assume that Amyntas had considered these properties his own, for Augustus did not usually seize temple properties. And this assumption will also explain why large imperial domains, originating in royal and temple estates, came into existence early in south Phrygia and Pisidia, whereas the old province of Asia reveals but few fiscal properties before the widespread confiscations of the Severi.

The colonies which Augustus sent into this new property are also peculiar. Augustus planted a colony at "Pisidian" Antioch in 25, drawing the settlers from

[28] Temple lands had a checkered experience. The Attalids were wont to interfere, cf. Strabo, 14, 1, 26 and *Am. Jour. Arch.* 1913, 368; probably Amyntas had taken possession of those of Pisidia. In the Republic the senate was apt to recognize the status quo, see Strabo, 14, 1, 26; 12, 3, 34, and Ditt. *Or. Gr. Ins.* 440. The colonial land and domains of lower Phrygia and Pisidia came to Rome under various categories, and historians must not simplify the problem. Servilius when he defeated the pirates confiscated some land (Ormerod, *J. R. S.* 1922, 49); Murena, who followed him, organized the country around Cibyra and Milya (Strabo, 13, 4, 17); Amyntas cleared the country from Cremna to Lystra and probably took it for his herds (Strabo, 12, 6, 1 and 4), Quirinius in 11-6 B.C. removed the Homonadeis to suitable colonies (Str. 12, 6, 5). Probably the six colonies between Olbasa and Lystra consisted of a few veterans, some of the transported 4,000 barbarians, and perhaps some of the six alae Phrygum that have vanished from our records. The lower Pisidian colonies show very few Roman inscriptions.

the veterans of the fifth Gallic legion—presumably
thinking that they might find congenial company near
the Galatian country. He seems to have made free use
of temple-lands in the allotments. The purpose of the
colony was military, for Amyntas had been killed in
an attempt to check the raid of the wild Taurian tribe
of Homonadensis. A few years later Augustus decided to finish that war and had his general attack the
mountaineers from both north and south. This war,
conducted by Quirinius, the Syrian governor of Bib-
lical story, was brought to a successful end by 6 B.C.
and then a line of new colonies skirting the base of the
Taurus from Olbasa to Lystra was planted to protect
the plains for all time. Presumably veterans and some
of the captive barbarians were used, and the land allotted was partly territory then taken from the enemy,
and partly territory previously taken by Murena and
by Amyntas.

Henceforth there was peace in this region. But it
would be a mistake to assume that the strange con-
glomeration of peoples in the so-called Galatian provinces ever became a cultural or economic force. How
little Augustus cared whether or not they were Romanized may be judged from the fact that he settled Gauls
instead of Italians at Pisidia. Inscriptions show the
inevitable results of this procedure. The six colonies
planted in 6 B.C. were swallowed up in the Anatolian
confusion so soon that Latin inscriptions from them
are very rare, while in Antioch Greek soon began to
predominate. In Galatia proper no attempt was made

to Romanize except to build a temple to "Rome and Augustus" and to institute a community worship, which, however, soon broke down. The last meeting of the *koinon* seems to have been in 101 A.D. In the later Empire, though Celtic was tenacious, the Greek language finally conquered.

CHAPTER XIX

EGYPT AS IMPERIAL PROVINCE

EGYPT is the best known of Rome's provinces. Its peculiar economy revealed by thousands of papyri has been so much discussed,[1] and its influence over the rest of the Empire so frequently affirmed that it calls for a special description. Yet Egypt, the least Roman of all the provinces, must be studied quite apart, lest we be enticed by the abundance of the evidence to represent it as typical. It is well to remember that wages in Egypt were for a long time only a third of the standard wage elsewhere, that food prices were unusually low, that Egypt had its own debased currency, and furthermore, that no other province reveals the peculiar social conditions that obtained there. Augustus, who took Cleopatra's kingdom at her death and established it as a Roman province, virtually severed it from the rest of the world, not only because he wished to control a rich source of revenue, but because its institutions were so incompatible with those of Italy that he desired it to be closed to Roman contacts.

[1] A few of the more convenient compendia are Milne, *A History of Egypt under Roman Rule*, 3rd ed., 1924; Schubart, *Aegypten*, 1922; Schnebel, *Landwirtschaft in Aegypten;* Mitteis-Wilcken, *Chrestomathie*, Vol. I, 1912 and *Griech. Ostraken*, Vol. I; Rostovtzeff, *A Large Estate in Egypt*, Madison, 1922; *Social and Econ. Hist.*, Bibliography, pp. 570 ff.

To comprehend the peculiarities of Egyptian institutions we are compelled to glance at their origins. Nature long ago eliminated normal society in Egypt. Until the Nile was put under control during the nineteenth century, the river imposed autocracy and servility as the price of existence. Individualism was out of place, and had been ever since the valley had been fully settled several thousand years before Augustus. The Nile flood of every September provided the chief source of livelihood, and as the population grew, extensive canals and barriers had to be built to direct the flood and carry cultivation as far as possible toward the desert wastes. Private individuals and feeble communities could not direct such extensive work. Since a strip of land a thousand miles long had to be kept under a uniform system, the undertaking must be national in scope, and only a king who was at the same time recognized as a deity possessed the authority and resources to carry it through. Thus even before our records begin a deified king was owner of Egypt and his subjects were his tenants and obedient worshippers.

During the period of Persian dominance, before Alexander the Great and Ptolemy Soter succeeded to its ownership, temple-estates and private individuals had secured possession of much land, and many other arable portions had gone to waste through neglect of the canals. Soter and his great successor, Philadelphus, recognized the status quo at first, but soon began the arduous task of reclamation, and introduced business-like methods in their administration. For form's

sake, since the peasants must be kept in obedience, they
became Egyptian deities like the Pharaohs before them,
but they did not intend to become Egyptians. For their
residence they built up Alexandria as a free Greek city
on the edge of Egypt and invited large numbers of
Greeks to enter their service to help manage their great
estate. They systematized the tax collecting, repaired
and extended the canals, thereby opening up for cultivation much new land where they could plant their
Greek and Asiatic soldiers to earn their own livelihood
when not engaged in wars. They especially improved
the great lake-basin of the Fayum by draining out a
large water-logged area[2] and by running deep canals
at a higher level than before, nearer the edge of the
escarpment, thus greatly increasing the arable acreage
of this very fertile basin. They also nationalized much
of the land that had fallen under the control of temple-
estates and some of the taxes that had been collected
by the temples. They furthermore devised methods of
distributing the produce which they received in rents
and taxes so as to exclude competition in their markets ,and in this way they were able to make additional
profits. Thus they not only created monopolies for the
sale of their produce, but they gradually extended such
monopolies to wares made from the collected goods.

[2] The nature of this work is especially revealed by the Zenon
correspondence, discussed by Rostovtzeff, op. cit. Cf. Westermann, *Jour. Eg. Arch.* 1923, p. 85, (the "bitter soil"), *Pap. Soc.
It.* 422: "The soil had not been plowed before" having recently
been drained. For the canals in the Fayum, see Boak, in the
Geogr. Rev. 1926, 353.

For instance, they controlled the manufacture and sale
of oil made from their sesame and other plants, of beer
made from their barley, of the manufactured papyrus,
and in some instances they even built state factories.[3]
The nationalization of industry was then carried further till even banking and, to some extent, shipping fell
under state control. Thus Egypt became, for a while,
not only a royal landed estate, but a royal business
enterprise as well. It is doubtful whether history can
point to any other captains of industry with so large
a dependency of human beings as the early Ptolemies
and their business managers controlled.

The policy of the Augustan management will be
more readily understood if we give some definite details of the preceding Ptolemaic system which are
revealed by the Revenue Laws[4] of Philadelphus and
the correspondence of the king's stewards. The king,
as has been said, owned large domains; in one village[5]
where much land had been given to his soldiers at
least half of the land nevertheless still belonged to him.
The peasants who worked this land paid, besides the
regular taxes, a rental of about one-third of the crop.

[3] For the state control of the temple-production of fine linens,
see Persson, *Staat und Manufaktur*, Lund, 1923.

[4] Grenfell and Mahaffy, *The Revenue Laws;* the Zenon papyri
discussed in Rostovtzeff, op. cit. Important additions have been
made especially by Edgar, *Annales du Service*, Cairo, vol. 22-4;
Westermann, *Jour. Eg. Arch.* 1923, p. 81, and 1926, p. 45; Vitelli,
P. Soc. Ital. nos. 854-69; Edgar, *Zenon Pap.* vol. I.

[5] Kerkeosiris (in 118 B.C. after much land had been given
away), *Tebt. Pap.* 60, 61. For "exempted land" see *Tebt. Pap.*
5, pp. 37 and 90.

The land which he did not own outright he suggestively called "exempted land," implying that he might claim it if he chose.   Such land comprised temple properties, various tracts that had somehow escaped the hands of the Pharaohs, and also lands which the kings had given in small lots to soldiers, or in large farms to officers, or in extensive estates or fiefs of 10,000 arouras (about 6,800 acres) to great officials like his chief steward and the president of the Museum.   The income from such lots and estates served in lieu of salaries.   The smaller lots were doubtless meant to remain as heritable gifts if the recipient had sons who could take their father's place in the army.   The fiefs were apparently given only for the period of service.   All such land, however, paid to the king a produce tax which in the case of grain-land, averaged about one and one-half bushels to the acre.   This is less than a tithe, since in Egypt wheat usually produced about twenty-five bushels to the acre.   The tax was apparently considered equivalent to the seed.   On grain and oil land this tax was collected in kind, but on vineyards, fruitlands, and gardens the tax was collected in money.   As wine-land is far more productive than grain-land this tax brought very good returns; the records seem to imply an average of fifty drachmas per aroura (fifteen dollars per acre), to which was added the sacred tax of one-tenth or one-sixth (according to the position of the holder), and in addition a ground tax.   All land-owners were also required to devote some five days—or give an equivalent in money—to labor on the canals.

But the farmers did not have to bear the whole burden of the state budget. There was a poll-tax for all natives, a house-tax—which brought little since the Egyptian adobe huts were not costly—and for village folk engaged in trade and crafts an occupation tax, running from small sums up to fifty dollars a year, according to occupation. The latter was, in some instances, levied in the form of a purchase price for a monopolistic trade-concession in a village, a privilege that went to the highest bidder. In fact, such monopolies—resembling the salt and tobacco monopolies in Italy today—played a large role in production and distribution. We happen to have that part of the Revenue Law which gives full details regarding the oil monopoly.[6] We find that the government bureau decided how much oil would be needed for the year, ordered each farmer to sow a prescribed acreage and provided the requisite seed. The state took its portion due it in taxes (and in rents if the land was domainland) and bought the rest at a fixed price. In 258 B.C., for instance, the price at which the farmer must sell to the state was five cents a quart for sesame seed and half as much for castor seed, etc. The cultivator could not even retain a portion for his own use; he must sell all of it to the state. Every village had to provide a house for the manufacture of the oil from the seed. State contractors, who bought the concession, made the oil, paying a specified salary to the

[6] See especially paragraphs 39 ff.

laborers, who in their turn were compelled to produce
a specified amount of oil each day, and then distributed
the oil to the local merchants who had bought the
retailing concession for the respective villages. But
these retail merchants were also compelled to sell the
oil to the villagers at a fixed price—twenty-five cents
per quart in 258. Competition was prevented by a
fifty per cent. import duty on foreign oil. It is estimated that the shrewd king made, over and above the
tax, a profit of twenty-five per cent. on this monopoly.
And we know that to a certain extent similar monopolies existed for the production and sale of salt,
papyrus, beer, linen, jewelry, perfumes, bricks and
other articles.

From the correspondence of Zenon, the agent of
Philadelphus' steward, we have recently learned something of the king's methods of promoting agriculture.
Instead of giving his masterly steward, Apollonius, a
salary, the king allowed him to develop and gather the
revenues of a fief of 10,000 arourae (about 6,800
acres) on the new land being opened up in the Fayum.
He sent an engineer to extend the irrigation canal further northward so as to water more land and to drain
off a part of the lake which then existed in the low
area northwest of Philadelphia. The fief of Apollonius lay near this great canal and was to receive
water from it; we have, in fact, the engineer's map of
the ditches which were to be made.

On a part of this land Apollonius had to set aside
for the king's benefit certain soldiers' allotments from

which he would derive no benefit; on a part he tried
to colonize peasants whom he was allowed to invite
from the Delta.   Another portion of his land he leased
out to a group of peasants who engaged after much
bickering to take the leases at a rental of one-third of
the crop.   Several large farms he rented out to skilled
Egyptian farmers who imported laborers, among them
some Arabian shepherds.   On much of the land he
planted vines, olives and various fruit-trees, doubtless
at the king's request. One day the king sent an order
that Apollonius must attempt to grow two crops per
year.   Apparently a quick crop was to be sown in
August or September—as soon as the water had risen
high enough in the canals for artificial irrigation—and
this crop was to be harvested in time to catch water
for a second crop in the winter before the Nile had
fallen.   It has been surmised[7] that a quickly maturing
wheat (called "three-months" wheat) was introduced
to serve for the second crop.   Then when the estate
was well under cultivation the king came to inspect it.
From all this personal interest in the tract we may
infer that the king considered it an experimental station and a temporary concession which might possibly
revert to the crown.   In point of fact Apollonius lost
his fief when he was discharged from his stewardship
on the death of the king, and the tract, except for the
soldiers' allotments, probably became a royal domain.
When we survey the vast activities of the king, we are
not surprised to discover that he had an annual revenue

[7] Schnebel, *Landwirtschaft in Aegypten*, p. 145.

of over 15,000 talents—more than the entire revenue
of the Roman Empire in Cicero's day. Egypt's budget
to-day is about 35,000,000 pounds sterling, which is
more than ten times as much; but wheat, from which
Philadelphus derived most of his revenue, was then
worth in Egypt only a fifth of what it is to-day.

Such was the province that Augustus found when
he succeeded Cleopatra as lord of Egypt—such in
theory, but half-ruined by the mismanagement of a
century. The later Ptolemies had not been skillful
rulers. Cleopatra's father was noted chiefly for his
ability to heap up debts, and she for various striking
qualities not conducive to success in administration.
To keep themselves in favor with their subjects they
had had to be lenient rulers, to grant allotments and
concede privileges[8] with a free hand. Hence the
temple properties and private estates had increased at
the expense of the royal domain, and many allotments
originally given as temporary concessions to soldiers
and officers had become private property. When the
neglected canals[9] clogged up with silt much land had
to be abandoned, and most of the monopolies had disintegrated into licensed privileges,[10] inviting graft on
the part of the state officials. The old schedules of
taxes remained in theory, without, however, a justi-
fiable basis, since numerous properties had been trans-

[8] *Tebtunis Pap.* no. 5 is illuminating in showing what allowances and concessions had to be made as early as 118 B.C.

[9] Suetonius, *Aug.* 18.

[10] Persson, *Staat und Manufaktur*, p. 18.

ferred to a different class of holders. Thus in some
instances free lands had passed into the hands of
natives when the descendants of the original holders
had inter-married with Egyptians.

Augustus followed the usual Roman course when he
confirmed property rights and tax impositions where
he found them without removing inconsistencies or
examining the source of established privilege. It is in
general true that where he found crown land—now
much reduced in area—he accepted it as a Roman possession and charged full rental (about one-third of the
crop) ; where he found private property he recognized
it as such, collecting the established taxes whether or
not the classification was justified by present circumstances. He might have reasoned that the cleruch
lands originally given to Greek and Oriental soldiers
for service in the army no longer deserved a privileged
classification, since the Ptolemaic army was now disbanded; but he apparently did not. Nor did he ask
how certain Egyptians had acquired such privileged
properties, though he strictly observed the traditional
social distinction between Egyptians and Hellenes.[11]
To a certain extent his course was justified since these
lands had long been bought and sold at market prices
which had adjusted themselves to the established en-
cumbrances and exemptions. He merely instituted a
thoroughgoing census to be taken every fourteen years

[11] See *Der Gnomon des Idios Logos*, Schubert, Berlin, 1919,
which penalizes marriage between Egyptians, Greeks and Romans.

so that the established taxes might be carefully exacted with reference to the amount and quality of the land. To be sure he transferred ownership in some properties but only when new circumstances compelled the opening of the question. For instance, he had occasion to take possession of considerable royal property in the name of the state. Cleopatra's palaces and gardens must have been confiscated, and probably some of those that Antony had acquired in Egypt—though many of them seem to have been transferred to such of Antony's relatives[12] as were loyal to the government. A large number of Cleopatra's officers and soldiers who had held "gift lands" had fallen at Actium in the war against Rome, and their lands were doubtless taken as well; Augustus would, in any case, have felt privileged to transfer such land under the caption of war-booty to the officers and ministers of the victorious Roman army. This is probably why we later find parcels of land here and there, especially in the Fayum (the center of cleruch-land) in the possession of men like Maecenas[13] and Agrippa, not to mention Livia and her

[12] The *Antoniane ousia* in Egypt is frequently mentioned in the papyri. Antony's son Jullus was protected by Octavia and was probably allowed to inherit. Of Antony's two daughters, nieces of Augustus, one married Domitius (grandfather of Nero), the other married Drusus, Augustus' stepson. Both must have received properties from Antony's estate. However Antony's house on the Palatine at Rome was confiscated and assigned to Agrippa and Messala: Dio, 53, 27.

[13] Rostovtzeff, *Social and Econ. Hist.* p. 573, has a very useful list made partly from unpublished papyri of Roman properties in Egypt. Many of these properties concentrated by inheritance

two sons. A Roman general had a customary right to a generous share of the spoils of war for himself, his officers, and his soldiers. Since after this victory Augustus gave his soldiers colonial allotments and all citizens of Rome a bounty of 400 sesterces,[14] it would be strange if he had not given his officers a generous share as well. But we need not suppose that Augustus permitted himself the irregularity of disposing in this manner of old rent-producing domain lands. He probably followed tradition and inscribed that as Roman property, its produce to be shipped to Rome.

There is one other change which is somewhat more irregular, though quite in accord with Roman custom. He secularized most of the temple fields,[15] providing in the place of their produce moderate pensions from the state for the upkeep of the Egyptian cults. The reason for this change was partly political, partly social. The temple-estates had, in their growth, gained control over large groups of semi-free peasants. Rome's custom—not always put into practice—was to subordinate religious cults to the state and not to encourage priestly dominance over the population through economic control. At any rate a levelling was desirable since some temples had acquired more than

in the hands of Nero, when he alone survived of the Julio-Claudian house, but he also confiscated with great brutality. When he died, such properties, both patrimonial and confiscated, passed to Vespasian, and because of the change of dynasty became crown property.

[14] *Res Gestae Divi Aug.* 15.

[15] *Tebt. Pap.* II, 302 ff.

they needed while others had less.   Henceforth, a
reasonable annual stipend was secured to all.   Secular
privileges, however, were not entirely abolished.   The
manufacture of fine linens[16] for priestly robes, and of
papyrus (of which the priests used much) was permitted.

The taxes, which had become quite unscientific, were
allowed to remain with few alterations, but were
exacted with rigor, and the method of collecting them
was simplified.   The Ptolemaic grain tax,[17] averaging
about one and one-half bushels to the acre out of a
yield of about twenty-five bushels to the acre, seems
not to have been altered.   Vineyards[18] continued to
pay about fifty drachmas (now debased) per aroura,
and in addition the old temple tax (secularized by
Philadelphus), and the unexplained Ptolemaic eparoura of about six more.   This makes in all about
sixty-six drachmas the auroura on wine lands.   But
the drachma had fallen so low in silver content during
the later Ptolemies that the tax was now lighter than
before even though the price of wine had also fallen.
Since vineyards yield about 500 gallons per acre on
good land in Egypt and wine then sold at about three-
fourths of a drachma per gallon, this tax is nearer a
sixth than a tithe—which accords with ancient custom

[16] Otto, *Priester und Temple*, I, 302; Reil, *Beiträge zur Kenntnis
des Gewerbes*, 5 and 97; Persson *op. cit.* 27.

[17] The usual tax, one artaba per aroura, *B. G. U.* 563, cf. *Oxyr.
Pap.* 1044; Wilcken. *Chrest.* 225; 226; 227; 235; 238.

[18] *Pap. Rylands*, 192, b and comment.

for stipendiary wine-land in the Mediterranean. Other fruitland paid the sacred tax and the eparoura but only a half of the primary tax, and this also was collected in a depreciated currency. The forced labor[19] of a few days per year on the canals—an absolute necessity still recognized in Egypt—was of course continued.

For the gathering of taxes in kind and in money Augustus, true to the ancient Roman practice and the reforms of Caesar in Asia, gradually did away with the contract system in vogue in Egypt, and consequently with most of the monopolistic machinery invented by the Ptolemies. The usual Roman substitute was to hold the communities responsible for the stipends. In Egypt, however, fixed stipends were not feasible, since no one could foretell in what year the Nile might fail, nor had the Egyptian villages ever had the machinery of self-government. However, a compromise was devised. Each community was asked to submit to the prefect a list of responsible and trustworthy property owners and from these he chose for each a board of collectors to serve for three years.[20] The office—as in the case of Roman municipal magistrates—was to be considered an honor and without remuneration. To Egyptians, accustomed to being

[19] *Tebt. Pap.* II, Appendix, I. There is no connection between this canal work and forced labor under serfdom. The peasants appreciated the necessity of it as our farmers in the western states know the need of contributing three days per year to the repair of roads. When serfdom arose it sprang from other beginnings, not from the corvée on canals.

[20] Oertel, *Die Liturgie*, p. 162 ff.

exploited in forced duties, the office doubtless bore a less favorable aspect, and in time it came to be a grievous burden. But so long as the government ruled with a fair sense of responsibility we hear of little complaint.

As in the Ptolemaic régime the non-agricultural folk also had their burdens. The poll-tax[21] upon adult males, from which Romans and citizens of the three Greek cities were exempt, amounted to about 16 drachmas of the reduced currency during the first century. The occupation taxes[22] which had usually been collected in the form of a purchase price for a village concession were now generally paid for licenses to conduct shops. So, for instance, we have documents from the Fayum which specify that oil sellers and bakers paid 96 drachmas per year for their license, while fullers and beer sellers paid twice as much. This seems to have been a fixed tariff and not, as before, a varying price dependent upon the highest bid. In the late Empire we shall also hear much of the old Ptolemaic "crown-gold" tax—an irregular exaction of gifts. Philadelphus, on the occasion of a festival, had succeeded in extracting over two million dollars in gifts to pay the expenses of his celebration. How insistent the king was in demanding presents we may see from

[21] *Tebt. Pap.* II, 306 and comment; *Oxyr. Pap.* 1436, 8; Wilcken, *Gr. Ostraka*, I, p. 230.

[22] Persson, op. cit. p. 20; Wilcken, *Chrest.* 315, 316, 137, 318, 251.

a letter recently found:[23] "The king has repeatedly issued orders for crown gifts; do all you can and in haste . . . The gifts must reach Alexandria within three days . . . Also send what is due from us for the king's birthday." Needless to say Augustus and Tiberius did not make such demands, but Caligula reinstituted the custom and in the third century, with the constant change of bankrupt emperors, this royal robbery became one of the most burdensome of taxes in Egypt as elsewhere. As for customs duties[24] these were reduced since Rome had no interest in protecting monopolies in Egypt, and had, in fact, never favored protective tariffs. Moreover, Egypt was so productive and prices were so abnormally low, unless propped up by monopolistic control, that foreign goods were not naturally attracted there. With free trade established (for the Roman 2-4 per cent transit duties did not hamper trade) Egypt could serve as a route of transit for goods bound from lower Arabia and India for Rome.

Of political and social changes that affected conditions there were but few. Having disbanded the Ptolemaic army, Augustus stationed a small Roman army, now of two, now of three legions in a camp near Alexandria and placed the province in the charge of a

[23] *Pap. Soc. Ital.* 514; Gifts to Philadelphus, Athenaeus, V, 203.

[24] Wilcken, *Archiv. Pap. Forsch.* III p. 185; Edgar, *Ann. du Service*, 23, nos. 73-5. A part of the tax on commerce in Egypt went to pay the police who protected the goods from nomad raids, see Fiesel, *Geleitzölle*, in *Gött. Nach.* 1926, 57. Such was the famous tariff of Koptos.

knight. Indeed he issued a decree that no Roman senator could enter the province without his permission. He seems to have recognized from the first that Egypt was a problem in business administration rather than in political control—for the population was too servile to cause serious revolts. The exclusion of senators was considered necessary because Egypt, with its great resources, might readily be made the basis of a revolutionary clique; furthermore, the governor, who was a mere knight, would suffer much in prestige if he would have to pay court to senators in the presence of the natives.

Cornelius Gallus, the first prefect,[25] suppressed an incipient revolt in central Egypt, and established the southern boundary against the inroads of the Nubians. The second, Aelius Gallus,[26] attempted, with insufficient knowledge of the problem, to add the Arabian coast of the Red Sea, the region of Mecca, to the province. It was supposed to be a prosperous country, known to the Romans chiefly because of the caravans of spices, perfumes, pearls, and precious stones that had come thence—partly from India—to the coast towns of Palestine. Aelius made no permanent conquest of value, but through his expedition the Romans at least learned a valuable lesson in commercial geography, and because of the knowledge they gained the old trade-route for such wares was wisely reopened

[25] Strabo 17, 1, 53; *C. I. L.* III, 14147.

[26] Strabo 16, 4, 22; Lesquier, *L'armée Romaine d'Egypte*, p. 9; Dessau, *Gesch. Röm. Kais.* I, 380.

through Egypt. The road from the middle Red Sea, at Myos Hormos to Koptos on the Nile, was made safe and inviting by the building of cisterns[27] at the caravan-stations in the desert, and the placing of guards along the route to protect traders. A special duty was levied at Koptos for the upkeep of the stations and the police. The Greek traders soon saw the advantages of this route, and presently the Arabian and Indian trade began to put in at Myos Hormos, cross to the Nile, and proceed thence to Alexandria and Rome. Strabo makes this interesting comment (II, 5, 12): "Since the Romans have recently invaded Arabia Felix with an army, of which Aelius Gallus, my friend and companion, was the commander, and since the *merchants of Alexandria* are already sailing by way of the Nile and the Arabian Gulf as far as India, these regions have become far better known to us than to our predecessors. When I accompanied Gallus up the Nile as far as Syene I learned that as many as a hundred and twenty vessels were sailing from Myos Hormos to India whereas formerly, under the Ptolemies only a very few ventured to undertake the voyage and to carry on traffic in Indian wares."

The third prefect, Petronius, carried out a task even more essential to the welfare of the province. The early Ptolemies had extended the canal system with great wisdom and had instituted a two-crop culture on much dry land so that in fact unflooded land could be made more profitable than the flooded portion, provided

[27] Strabo, 17, 1, 45. Philadelphus had first made this route.

the canals were kept clean. Augustus found that the canals had been badly neglected, and Petronius set the army to work clearing them out, after which the peasants were ordered to keep them in condition. As a result much land that had gone to waste was reclaimed, and Strabo[28] relates that a rise of twelve cubits in the Nile at Memphis now counted for as much as fourteen cubits had before, which is equivalent to saying that thousands of acres on the edge of the valley were restored to cultivation. The recent excavations of the peasant villages of Karanis and Philadelphia on the edges of the Fayum have shown that these places recovered during the Augustan period the air of prosperity and the abundance of dwellings which they had possessed two centuries before, but which they had temporarily lost during the reigns of the last Ptolemies. Such accomplishments indicate that Augustus was discovering that the government might well perform other functions than the political ones to which the old republican régime had confined itself.

However, it must not be supposed that Augustus had any intention of carrying social paternalism beyond the point where the treasury was somehow involved. An abstract of the regulations of the Idios Logos,[29] the bureau of special taxes, recently found, reveals how old social customs were generally accepted outright by him and how little the Roman government

[28] Strabo, 17, 1, 3; Cf. Suet. *Aug.* 18.

[29] Schubert, *Berl. Gr. Urk.* vol. V, 1919; cf. paragraphs 38-40, 44, 48, 49, 54, etc.

cared to alter the stereotyped caste system imposed by
the Greeks. There is not a hint that the native Egyptian might ever earn the right to Roman or even
Alexandrian citizenship, or establish a claim to community self-government which the Spanish and Gallic
tribes possessed. Such regulations as the requirement
to register in the native town at the census taken every
fourteen years, and the necessity of producing a pass[30]
when leaving Egypt, imply that freedom of movement
was not completely established in the case of natives.
This may have mattered little since free labor had
hardly any market outside of Egypt, but it is significant
of Rome's policy not to alter social conditions.

It would be interesting to know whether the partial
liberation of Egypt from the monopolistic system
affected any betterment in economic conditions. We
have abundant proof of a rise in wages, but until we
know more about the purchasing power of these wages
a final answer is not possible. Even though we can
now weigh and estimate the silver contents of the deteriorating coins in Egypt we do not know to what
extent an artificial exchange rate with the Roman
denarii kept some fiat value in them. However, since
few denarii reached Egypt it is safest to assume that
these coins generally passed for very little more than
the market value of the metal. Furthermore, in comparing wages with the price of wheat, we are not
absolutely certain that we have a right to reckon the
Egyptian artaba as invariably equal to 29.1 liters
(eight-tenths of the imperial bushel) as is usually done.

[30] Gnomon, *ibid*. 64.

The Ptolemaic silver drachma of the third century had about 3.6 grammes of silver (about the same as the Neronian denarius, which exchanged for about twenty cents' worth of gold). Before Cleopatra's day the drachma had been debased and lightened so that it was usually worth less than a half of its face; and when Tiberius gave a stable currency to Egypt, he took as the standard the four-drachma pieces then current which had only about twenty-five per cent. silver. This tetradrachma was probably recognized as equivalent to the Roman denarius, making one drachma exchangeable with the sestertius, but we must add that very little was thus exchanged: Egypt still went her own course. However, when we find wages in Roman Egypt four times as high as in the early Ptolemaic day, we do not forget that the coins used in payment were worth only about one-fourth as much as before, and that the actual weight of silver received had not increased. These tetradrachmas continued to be issued on the Tiberian standard till about the time of Septimius Severus, in that respect faring somewhat better than the Roman denarius. After Septimius there was a further debasement though it was not as rapid as at Rome. The tetradrachma now lost about half of its value but remained at this value till Aurelian's day. During the last years of anarchy at Rome it was debased like the Roman denarius into a bronze coin with merely a silver wash. Diocletian then, in reforming the currency of Rome, also abolished the separate coinage of Egypt and introduced the Roman aureus and denarius.

It must be apparent, therefore, that the Egyptian coin can hardly be taken as a useful standard of values for wages and prices, and that it serves us only as a common denominator for comparing labor and wheat when we happen to have contemporaneous prices for both. But we must keep in mind the fact that wheat itself probably had an increasing purchasing price in terms of the other commodities, since so much of the Roman tribute was carried off in the form of wheat that no surplus can be assumed. The following, apparently representative items, are taken from the lists drawn up by West and Segré[31] The artaba of wheat is supposed to be eight-tenths of the English bushel, or 29.11 liters. Wages are for unskilled labor.

In comparing these items it is fair to question the validity of the wheat prices for 79 A.D., and 190 A.D., both of which rise above the normal curve. There were frequently years of scarcity in Egypt when the price would rise sharply while wages would hardly respond to such rises if they lasted only a year. Furthermore, some of our wheat prices happen to be given for spring and

---

[31] Segré, *Circolazione Monetaria*, 1922; West, *The Cost of Living in Roman Egypt;* Class, Phil. 1916, 293; Milne, *Ann; Arch. Anth.* 7, 51. It is very doubtful whether Segré is correct in speaking of the imperial Egyptian currency as a fiat coinage; its intrinsic value was probably recognized. He certainly is mistaken in supposing that the issue of the tetradrachma by Tiberius at one-fourth the original value involved an act of confiscation. The late Ptolemies had debased the coin and Tiberius simply stabilized it at the value current in his day. To revalorize the money would have been an economic crime; to start a new currency would simply have been confusing.

	Wheat	Wages	Daily wage in terms of artaba
	Ptolemaic		
270 B.C.	2 drachmas per artaba	270-220 B.C., 1–1½ obols	average $\frac{1}{10}$
c. 100 B.C.	1600 copper drachmas	c. 100, 200 copper drachmas	$\frac{1}{8}$
	Roman		
18 B. C.	3½ drachmas (at least 50% alloy)	c. 1 A.D., 1 sestertius	$\frac{1}{8}$?
79 A.D.	10 drachmas (scarcity price?)	78 A.D., 5 obols	$\frac{1}{12}$
125–180 A.D.	c. 8 drachmas	125–180, 6–8 obols	$\frac{1}{8}$–$\frac{1}{6}$
190	18 dr. (high price)	215, 12 obols	$\frac{1}{9}$
255	18 dr.	255, 24–36 obols	$\frac{1}{6}$–$\frac{1}{3}$
Diocletian's edict c. 301	166 *den.* per artaba (100 *den.* for 2 modii. 100 *denarii* = 43.5 cents)	301, 25 den. and food (about 33 den.?)	$\frac{1}{5}$?

summer when prices were naturally higher than at

harvest time. Nevertheless the items suffice to justify the statement that wages rose gradually though very slowly if measured in terms of wheat. In fact, they seem to have doubled in Egypt during this period of 500 years. When we compare the prices of wine and oil[32] we are justified in believing that wheat itself had risen not a little in the scale of commodity prices, and that therefore the Egyptians received even higher wages in terms of other articles. To be sure we are less certain of the Egyptian liquid measure than of the dry, and furthermore, wines and oils varied much in prices according to quality so that a fair average is not easy to establish. In the Revenue Laws of the third century B.C., when Ptolemaic viticulture was new, the price of wine was high. A measure of forty liters then bought four artabas of wheat. During the later Ptolemies the same measure bought only two artabas, and in the first century of the Empire only one, and this low price continued into the third century when it rose again to two. The forty-liter measure of oil bought about 24 artabas of wheat in the middle of the third century B.C.;[33] during the later Ptolemies about 10, during the first century of the Empire about 8,

[32] See Segré, pp. 134-145.

[33] Oil was abnormally high in Ptolemaic Egypt because of the royal monopoly and a prohibitive import duty. The peasants, however, did not get any of the advantage of this price because they were compelled to sell all the sesame and castor beans to the state at a fixed low price. The price of oil was far lower during the Roman régime but the market was free and it is likely that the peasants made a better profit than before.

rising slightly to about 10 before 255 A.D. We are, of course, not sure that wine and oil were fair indices of commodities in general, but so far as the evidence goes we may believe for the present that Rome's use of much Egyptian wheat practically removed the surplus and thus kept its price at a somewhat higher level than that of other articles. If, then, we find that the labor wage steadily improved in terms of wheat, we shall probably find, when more evidence is in, that it had far more than doubled during the Roman régime if measured in terms of a more complete list of commodities.

There had, of course, been a very serious need of adjustment. During the early Ptolemaic days labor wages were only about one-third as high as in Greece[34] while wheat stood at about one-half the price current at Delos. Under such conditions the royal monopolies had been able to make very large profits, both upon natural products and upon the manufactured wares that were exported. We know very little about wages in Italy since slaves were so generally used, but we know that during the Ciceronian[35] period and again in

[34] Beloch, *Griech. Gesch.*[2] vol. 4, 321 ff.

[35] Cic. *In Verr.* III, 163-181, seems to place the normal price at 3–3½ sestertii the *modius;* Tac. *Ann.* XV. 39, implies that 3 sest. is a very low price in the year 64 A.D. In the early part of the second century when the denarius is worth about twenty per cent. less, four sestertii per modius is considered a low price in Umbria: C. I. L. XI, 6117; that is however about the maximum price fixed by Diocletian in 301. In the wheat country of Pisidia the normal price seems to have been a little over two sestertii per modius in Domitian's day; see Robinson, in *Am. Phil. Ass.* 1924, p. 7.

Nero's day wheat brought nearly twice as much in Italy as in Egypt. The fact that Diocletian could, in 301, impose the same scale of prices and wages in Egypt as in the rest of the Empire, shows that Egypt had by that time nearly adjusted itself to the economic system that prevailed throughout the Roman world. Had Augustus adopted the monopolistic régime of the early Ptolemies, that would hardly have been possible. We may infer that one factor in this gradual rise of wages was the gradual release of the natives from the Ptolemaic restriction of movement. We learn from Strabo[36] that Alexandrian merchants captured most of the Oriental trade opened up by the efforts of Aelius Gallus and that this trade expanded rapidly. We know also that Alexandrian glassware, papyrus, jewelry, and linen enjoyed a world-wide market. All of this free industrial and commercial activity must have drawn many natives from the interior and created a healthier labor market than before. And finally, Rome, after a period of hesitation recruited the two Egyptian legions from the province, thus providing occupation for at least a few thousand natives.

However, we must not suppose that the adobe villages of the fellahin were transformed into cities of marble. Excavations have revealed little change in their appearance except that they were not falling into decay as during the preceding century. The rather pleasing tomb-portraits of seemingly prosperous folk of the Roman period which have been found at

[36] Strabo, 17, 1, 13.

Hawara are of Greeks, not of Egyptians, and a fragment of a census of Theadelphia (second century A.D.), while listing numerous small properties in the possession of natives, also shows that over half the land was owned by outsiders (Alexandrians and Romans) though these constituted only one-tenth of the list of possessors.   Another census of the same time lists 6,475 Hellenes in the Fayum.   These were, of course, the prosperous as well as the socially recognized class. There were, of course, many complaints of oppression. The taxes were high and, since the canal system had already been built before the Romans came, and the populace kept it in order, there was no excuse for their continuance at the former high rate except the invalid one that they were customary and could be had. The Alexandrian Greeks were offended chiefly because the rulers were no longer countrymen of theirs.   The Egyptians had, at first, no plausible grievance except that a greater rigor and more firmness lay behind the Roman administration of taxes.   Their complaints should not be taken at full value in estimating the success of the Roman rule.   One would hardly draw serious conclusions from the car-loads of protests that are sent to the tax commissioner's office in New York City at every new assessment.   With such qualifications it may be said that Augustus' rule was beneficial. But his reforms were very restricted and conservative, and reveal no thorough-going plan of amelioration. On the whole, he seems merely to have followed the ideals of the best of the old republican administrations,

which were to preserve law and order, avoid paternalism, recognize established customs so long as the
natives remained peaceful, and collect the customary
taxes as honestly as possible and to the full.

After this brief review of the typical provinces during the Augustan period, a few generalizations may be
in place. With economic questions Augustus concerned himself far less than had Julius Caesar. The
work of governmental organization and administration—a subject which we could not review—was vast
enough for one man's lifetime. Augustus had found
a dictatorship wrecking republican institutions, and he
had to shape a government which would recognize old
customs enough to be acceptable to the conservative
Romans, and which would at the same time be strong
enough to hold together a heterogenous group of provinces. Every spare moment was occupied in the task.
Only where political administration directly involved
questions of economic and social well-being did the
latter receive consideration. Nowhere, except in
Egypt, do we find a tendency under Augustus to make
drastic changes for the benefit of industry or commerce, and there, in lowering tariffs, and loosening the
bonds of monopolies, only to introduce Roman customs
of unhampered trade. Commercial colonization and
agrarian reforms in which Caesar showed an interest
did not in themselves concern Augustus. Furthermore,
he avoided interfering with established property rights.
During the triumvirate he had shared in the blame for
confiscations, but after he became princeps he refused

to countenance such procedure. His victorious army, after Actium, received a bonus in lands bought by state funds. His colonies were wisely planted, but military and political considerations usually governed the choice of their location. Nor did he greatly concern himself about social conditions in the provinces. There is not an act clearly traceable to a desire to Romanize or, as has so insistently been claimed, to "urbanize" and thereby to civilize the natives of the provinces. He insisted, wherever possible, that there should be some community or orderly tribe responsible for the preservation of peace—and the tax gathering—in every nook and corner of the Empire, and when this was not possible, as in Egypt, he tried to find a substitute. But after that was secured, each community was permitted to go its own way. Economic and social laissez-faire has never been more consistently practised. After all it was probably the quickest road to success if he really cared for Romanization. Peace through the Empire gave the opportunity for material development to those who desired it, and prosperity brought satisfaction and goodwill towards the government, which in turn invited closer relations and a natural assimilation of Roman customs. Prosperity also provided the means for acquiring the amenities of urban life, so that those who craved them drifted to villages and cities. It is true that many cities throughout the rural regions of the Empire dated their beginnings from the Augustan period, but this development was a concomitant, not a purposed goal of the Augustan peace.

There was some growth in industry and commerce. The preceding summary chapters on large-scale production and trade drew their illustrations from this period of peace and safe communications. The period, however, does not reveal any revolutionary inventions or new forms of organization. The increase was noticeable but it was also limited by the obstacles of slavery and the disrespect for gainful trade which still hindered the best of the Romans from sharing in it. Provincials seem to have profited more than Italy, but no one section of the Empire gained predominance, and the provincials on the whole continued to occupy themselves with the industries in which they had been brought up.

CHAPTER XX

Italy During the Early Empire

The economic history of the century between Augustus and Hadrian runs into ravelled strands. The Empire is world-wide and at peace. The seas are safe for commerce, and military roads, well-built and policed, run through all the provinces. There are no prohibitive tariffs or restrictive laws limiting the scope of industrial enterprise, and the state has no economic policy either helping or hindering business: men are at liberty everywhere to develop their resources and prove their capacity. The end of the century shows favorable balance sheets almost everywhere, and the demonstration of wealth in stately public buildings and luxurious private houses becomes especially conspicuous in the reign of Hadrian.

Italy prospered also, though unevenly, and we must therefore particularize before attempting a generalization. In 33 A.D. there was a peculiar panic in the real estate market of Italy which historians are wont to interpret as proving unhealthy conditions. Tacitus (*Ann.* 6, 22) says that money lenders were found to be charging illegal rates and were ordered to adjust their loans at legal rates within eighteen months, and furthermore, to invest two-thirds of their capital in Italian real estate. Usurious rates are usually a symptom of hard times, when mortgages are being fore-closed, and the order to invest in farms indicates quite definitely that a large number of owners must have been surrendering their properties at low values. But of course such a situation might have arisen from temporary causes such as two or three years of unseasonable weather. The remedy prescribed by the Senate naturally led to disaster. Creditors began to draw in their loans at once, and in the stringency that ensued, properties were thrown upon the market everywhere, with a consequent drop in prices. As a result the emperor established land-banks for the purpose of lending state-funds without interest to farmers for a term of three years. Since five million dollars sufficed to check the panic and stabilize values, the basic trouble could not have been very serious. It would be hazardous to generalize from this incident as to the agrarian conditions throughout Italy. Apparently, the stringency was temporary and had become serious only because it had been unwisely handled by the Senate.

A brief survey of conditions in the several parts of Italy will prove that the land was on the whole prosperous. In the south, to be sure, the old Greek cities remained inert.[1] The commerce which had brought them some degree of prosperity under Roman protec-

---

[1] Strabo in his account of this region, bk. VI, finds little to say about the cities of his own day except that Brundisium produced much wool and had a good harbor. The abundance of wool is an indication of much pasturage.

tion during the Gracchan days had not increased after
the Roman peace assured the same privileges to all
Mediterranean ports.   Their agriculture sufficed for
domestic needs, and Pliny[2] records the production of
some wine for export.   The mountain country in the
rear, in Calabria and Apulia, continued to be pasture
land for wealthy ranchers, who were chiefly Romans
employing slave labor.   In fact, there was a threat of
a serious slave uprising[3] among the rough herdsmen in
24 A.D., and later Domitia, who had excited the
jealousy of Agrippina, lost her life on the charge that
through her negligence, the slaves on her southern
ranches had become a menace to public safety.

In Campania there were a number of changes.
Puteoli[4] which had been the best commercial port cf
Italy during the republic and had therefore developed
a vigorous industry for itself and Capua, was now
feeling the competition of Ostia, where Claudius, at
great cost, had built a splendid harbor.   Fewer ships
now put in at Puteoli. The letter of the manager of the
Tyrian docks at this harbor who, in the second century,
complained of a serious decline in revenues, gives
explicit information on the point.   The trouble was
not solely due to Ostia's rivalry.   The fact is that the
industries of Puteoli and Capua were dwindling so that
shippers no longer were sure of return cargoes.   For-

[2] Pliny, *N. H.* 14, 69, especially at Tarentum, Consentia,
Tempsa, Thurii and Grumentum.

[3] Tac. *Ann.* 4, 27; On Domitia Lepida, *Ann.* 12, 65.

[4] See chapter XVI.

merly soldiers had been obliged to equip themselves at
home for each campaign, and this had given work to
the Italian makers of armor; now the armies were
fixed on the frontiers and were equipped with arms
and armor in military factories or at nearby provincial
towns; the pottery that Campania formerly produced
for wide distribution was meeting the obstacle of
Gallic production; Capua's bronze utensils were being
sent to the north in diminishing quantities, and her
lucrative perfume trade had given way to the Arabian
and eastern products handled by Alexandria. It must
not be supposed, however, that the rest of Campania
was suffering seriously. Factory production had
doubtless been lucrative to the owners, but the workmen had been largely slaves, so that the prosperity
had not spread as widely among the free population as
might be supposed. The sound economic welfare of
the region depended, after all, upon the inexhaustibly
rich volcanic soil, the equable climate and the supply
of water which made irrigation possible during the
summer. The famous brands of Campanian wine were
as popular as ever at Rome[5], and found a good market
also in the ever-growing population of rich villa-folk
who had retired to this bay. Campania then, as now,
was covered with vineyards and fruit trees, between
the rows of which an intensive cultivation of garden

---

[5] Pliny, 14, 69-71. Several new brands; Pompeian wines somewhat strong and do not keep well; 14, 62, Falernian less used,
but the Faustinian brand from the Falernian region has excellent
reputation.

crops continued all through the year. On the slopes of Vesuvius the system was slightly different. Here water was not available for irrigation, and closely packed vineyards and orchards were more profitable than cereals. Many villas have recently been excavated in this vicinity.[6] Some of these villas were splendidly furnished and evidently served the landlord for his own residence as in the case of the Bosco Reale villa described above, whereas others were obviously farmsteads designed only to house a steward and his slaves, but with no provision for the owner's residence. In practically all of those that were situated inland we find evidences of capitalistic specialization chiefly in wine-production under slave labor. The owners were probably in most cases the petty aristocracy of Pompeii, Herculaneum and Naples, though we also find a large imperial estate of Agrippa Postumus there.

The town of Pompeii we have discussed above. During the Empire—till the destruction in 79—it prospered moderately without any significant changes in its economic system. The houses of the well-to-do, probably mostly landlords—though when the harbor has been excavated we may find evidence of wealthy merchants also—constantly give proof in the interior decoration of an increase in a certain middle-class luxury. The wine trade, the woolen business, the fish-packing are also somewhat in evidence, but industrial

[6] Della Corte, in *Not. Scavi*, 1921, 415 ff.; 1922, 459 f.; 1923, 271 f., and Rostovtzeff, *Econ. and Soc. Hist.*, p. 496, note 26, and p. 503, note 21.

production continues on the whole along the lines of the small-shop system already described. The Via Abondanza, now being excavated, shows that many of the old residences of this famous street were being turned into shops. That, however, has no special significance, since this street was a main thoroughfare leading from an important gate to the Forum. Naturally, the inhabitants would be driven out by the increasing amount of traffic and would seek residence on quieter streets. Many were also moving to their country villas outside the walls, since the assurance of peace had removed the premium upon residence within the protection of the fortifications.[7] In so far as Pompeii can be taken as an index, this region was prosperous to the end. To assume, as has been done, that the region was on the point of decay simply because Pompeii was not rebuilt after its destruction is naïvely to forget that the soil was destroyed beyond any hope of immediate recovery. One cannot raise vineyards on top of thirty feet of loose, dry cinders.

In west-central Italy we have little news of important changes. Rome grew as the residence of the

[7] Rostovtzeff, *loc. cit.*, p. 514, in an interesting note has perhaps over-emphasized the importance of changes on this street; see Engelmann, *Fuehrer d. Pompeii*. I should also hesitate to use the evidence of the pretty Amorini frescoes of the house of the Vettii as recording the industries in which the Vettii were engaged. We should have to assume that besides producing and selling wines, oils and flowers, they were also producers and sellers of clothing, jewelry, perfumes and other things. Presumably the pictures were intended to illustrate the industries of the town.

court, the ruling aristocracy, and the exploiters of the empire must grow, but its prosperity was of small importance to the region in which it was placed. In fact, the importation of the tribute in grain by the emperors, who had to sell at low prices what they did not distribute free of charge to the poor, made Rome a useless grain market for the neighborhood.

However, Rome still had to buy such farm products as wine, oil, meat, vegetables, poultry and the like, and doubtless took all that the dry Campagna could produce. As a residential town Rome developed no factories, but inscriptions prove that the small shops were numerous and did a thriving business. The economic life of the city was, however, abnormal, feverish, and unhealthy. The luxurious households, each with its scores or hundreds of slaves, the frequent games, and the distribution of free food by cowardly emperors to buy smiles from the rabble drew an undesirable population. The unbelievably cruel murders of old members of the aristocracy by the tyrants that followed Augustus constantly transferred properties from the hands of the traditional owners to those of flatterers and freedmen, a process that spread havoc far beyond the families immediately struck.

The country about Rome had taken on a new aspect. Suburban villas grew up thickly along the coast from Civita Vecchia to near Antium and on the Alban and Sabine hills. Many of these had gardens and orchards, but such properties were pretentious rather than productive. The level land of the Campagna was largely given over for nine months of each year to herds that grazed in the mountains through the dry season. When Pliny rode to his country villa at Prattica he saw nothing but herds of sheep till he came to the woods near the coast.[8] When Nero planted a veteran colony at the depleted town of Antium he soon found that the colonists sold out and drifted on to the provinces where during their service they had noticed better land. Yet Seneca had a very productive vineyard at Nomentum, and Columella had raised wine successfully at Albano, Ardea, and Cervetri.[9] On the whole we must picture the Campagna of Nero's day much as it is to-day, though with more pleasure villas on the coast and in the hills.

Tuscany had long before this time fallen into decay and it made no apparent progress during the Empire. The early prosperity had depended upon the capacity of the Etruscans to exploit the virgin soil and its tillers, the mines of iron and copper, and the commerce protected by friendly alliances with the Carthaginians. Now the soil was tired and the erosion of the hillsides quickly wasted the benefits of manuring; commerce

----

[8] *Epist.* 2, 17; Antium, Tac. *Ann.* 14, 27. The temporary increase in land values near Rome in Augustus' day, due to the lavish coinage of gold brought by Augustus from Egypt, probably had no permanent effects, see Suet. *Aug.* 41; Dio Cass. 51, 21. The recent spread of wheat culture in the Roman Campagna was induced by war-prices and patriotic appeals. It will hardly be lasting.

[9] Seneca's farm, Pliny, *N. H.*, 14, 48-51; Columella, 3, 3, 3; On Columella's experience as vintner, 3, 9, 2, *et passim.*

had taken other routes, and the metal industry had died when the Romans opened the Spanish trade to the world. Strabo saw little but mounds of cold slag at the old iron town of Populonia.[10] Even Arretine pottery, which in the Augustan day went to all parts of the Mediterranean, was now losing its vogue in competition with the cheaper imitations of the Auvergne factories.[11] Perugia had not recovered from the ravages of the civil war, and even Florence, though recolonized with veterans, made no progress despite its fertile valley. In fact, we hear very little about Tuscany throughout the Empire. Only Luna, at the edge of Tuscany, with its quarries that supplied so many shiploads of Carrara marble to Rome, showed a vigorous life.[12] Columella and Pliny[13] mention Tuscan wine and wheat as products, but with no great enthusiasm. It is likely that grain fields and pastures—though not very profitable ones—spread over most of the region, and that the Romans who owned large estates here let them out to tenants, as was usual in the case of distant wheat-lands.

Of central Italy with its mountains we have but little information. We know that large areas were

[10] Strabo, 5, 2, 6.

[11] See chapter XVI.

[12] Strabo, 5, 2, 5. This marble began to be used at Rome when Caesar was proconsul of Cisalpine Gaul, and perhaps its importance was first appreciated by him and his chief engineer Mamurra.

[13] Pliny, *N. H.* 14, 34 and 17, 21; Columella, 2, 6.

used for summer pasture for flocks that came down to the coast the rest of the year. We also know that large proprietors accumulated estates in the richer valleys and used them especially for horticulture. But here, more than elsewhere, the old small-farm system with proprietor-peasants continued in vogue. We have a mortgage record from the hills behind Beneventum,[14] and another from the foothills of the Apennines south of Piacenza, both dating from the beginning of the second century, which yield some significant facts. Both of these records give the names of the owners with the names of the farms which they owned. The names of the farms belong apparently to the Augustan census, and as they are listed separately we are able to discover that the eighty-nine original properties of Beneventum had fallen into the hands of fifty proprietors by Trajan's day. However, the owners fared very diversely. One proprietor had secured possession of eleven of the old farms, but on the other hand, thirty-two of the proprietors still owned only single farms. And in no case can the property be considered a very large estate. The largest is valued at about $25,000 (500,000 sesterces); twelve fall between $24,000 and $5,000; seventeen between $5,000 and $2,500; twenty between $2,500 and $700. Probably there were smaller lots not listed because the interest on the mortgage would hardly repay collecting. Even after the period of accumulation, therefore, we do not find what might be called large estates here. Of course

[14] Beneventum, *C. I. L.* IX, 1455; Veleia, *C. I. L.* XI, 1147.

we cannot determine the acreage because the land would vary greatly in value. Productive vineyards on the best valley-land might be worth $200 per jugerum, while in the high mountains behind Beneventum, too rocky even for grazing, values would descend to almost nothing. If we dared assume that all was average improved arable land, worth about $100 the jugerum, the farms would range from five to 166 acres, but we may be sure that extensive mountain pastures were included as they certainly were in the second document.

The situation at Veleia, south of Piacenza, is somewhat similar. Here, too, after a first parcelling of the hilly land there had been some expansion of holdings, though exact figures are not available. In studying this inscription De Pachtere[15] was able, in some measure, to locate the farms mentioned and thereby to discover the interesting fact that it was in the mountains devoted to pasturage and timbering that the costlier properties grew up, whereas the garden plots of the fertile valley were largely in the hands of small peasants. If, by the discovery of similar tablets, this were proved to be typical of the Apennine regions, we should have to assume that at least the rougher part of Italy had not come under the plantation system by Trajan's day. That wealthy proprietors came into possession of the timber and pasture lands is natural enough. They alone could profitably exploit such

[15] De Pachtere, *La Table Hypoth. de Veleia*, Paris, 1920, corrects the observations of Mommsen, *Hist. Schr.* II, p. 588, and Kromayer in *Neue Jahrb.* 1914, p. 145 ff.

property. De Pachtere has, however, pointed out another fact of importance. His study of the names in the inscription shows that the original mountain folk of the Veleian tract were now to be found only here and there in the rougher country, that citizen proprietors at first displaced them, probably citizens of Placentia, and that by Trajan's day several of the largest properties had fallen into the hands of freedmen with un-Roman names. We may well believe that these freedmen were business-folk of Placentia who had gone into farming and cattle-raising. Many of the landed estates of Italy must have been the properties of the municipal landlords, belonging in part to the local aristocracy, in part to successful trades-people and bankers who were eager for a more respectable station in the society of the town.

The Po valley was, during the first century, as it still is, the most flourishing part of Italy.[16] The black alluvial soil was very deep and far from being exhausted. Two centuries before, the Boii, Senones, and Lingones, below the river, had been driven off and Aemilius Scaurus had opened up large areas south of Padua by draining out the marshes which till then had covered that region. Rome had systematically sent colonies there. North of the Po the native peoples, the Insubres, Cenomani and Veneti, though very much reduced in number, had remained and become Roman

---

[16] See the interesting chapter by Strabo, book V, especially 5, 1, 12, with notes on the Alpine region in 4, 6. Occasionally however Strabo depends upon old sources.

citizens. Without planting official colonies in their midst, Romans and Italians had, nevertheless, settled among them in their search for land. Here the settlers accumulated large properties, became the leading men of the Romanized towns, and found cheap labor for their estates among the poorer natives of the foot-hills.[17] In Augustus' day Padua had the largest number of knights (500 with a census of $20,000) of any city in Italy outside of Rome.[18] We may assume that these men were local landlords, and that a dozen other cities of this region listed a goodly number of the same class.

The products of the valley were wheat—mostly for use in the growing cities—a great deal of wine,[19] which brought good prices in the cold mountain regions of Dalmatia and Noricum, hogs grown in the oak forests of the foot-hills and shipped in great quantities to Rome, lumber and pitch from the lower Alps and Apennines, and wool from extensive herds about the foot-hills, some of which was spun and woven by the townswomen and exported as finished products. Trade was active in that growing country where large amounts of raw products were available in exchange for luxuries. Ships went up the Po as far as Cremona and Placentia. Cities like Milan, Comum, Verona,

[17] Strabo, 3, 4, 17, a Massilian anecdote regarding Ligurian laborers; Diodorus, V. 39.

[18] Strabo, 5, 1, 7.

[19] Strabo, 5, 1, 12, hogs, grain, pitch, wine, wool; iron works at Comum, Pliny, *N. H.* 34, 144; timber, ibid. 16, 66 and 90.

and especially Aquileia[20] carried on a vigorous trade
over the passes cleared of brigandage by Augustus,
getting cattle, hides, slaves, ore and timber in return
for wine, finished metal-ware, pottery, and cheap jewelry. As the country had relatively few slaves and
freedmen and had been settled by the Italians before
the day when trade and industry had been bemeaned
by servile contacts, the economic development continued
in a healthy manner. The cities that stood out as the
most important during the first century were Padua,
Mediolanum (Milan), Verona, Cremona (until it was
destroyed in the civil war of 69), Aquileia, Placentia,
Bologna (till it was devastated by a fire in 53), Mantua, Parma, Brixia, Comum, Vicetia, Ravenna, Vercellae and Tergeste (Trieste). It is not surprising
that the seat of government was eventually moved to
this populous region.

It would be interesting, in view of the later developments of the colonate on the farms and of the gild-
system in the cities, to know in detail exactly what
changes the century witnessed in economic conditions.
As far as industry is concerned, we can only say that
capitalistic production made little progress except in
the brick factories at Rome where it was due wholly
to a change in building methods. In the production of
copper-ware, iron-ware, pottery and glass-ware[21] on

[20] For Augustus' roads into the Alps, Cartellieri, *Die Röm.
Alpenstrassen, Philologus, Supp.* 18, 1926; Strabo, 4, 6, 6-9; The
amber route explored, Pliny, *N. H.* 37, 45; Aquileia, Strabo 5,
1, 8; Majonica, *Museo dello stato, Aquileia.*

[21] See chapter XIV.

the other hand there was a loss of export trade, probably because of the self-sufficiency of the provinces that had formerly imported from Italy, and perhaps, too, because of the increase in the cost of slaves at home. The small shops, manned largely by independent *liberti*, could take care of the demands of each town. This change did not involve a serious economic dislocation at the time. Capitalistic production, based upon slavery, had actually benefited but few citizens, and the slaves who lost employment by the change could be transferred to the fields where there was a scarcity of labor. Nor did production greatly decrease, for the growing cities of Italy required more wares than before. There were doubtless more free men at work, perhaps with a slave or two, in independent shops at the end of the century than at the beginning. We get an impression from the inscriptions that the gilds of free craftsmen grew in number as was to be expected from the change in the form of the industry just noted. And it is also clear that the free industry of the provinces also benefited from the change. We must add, however, that the shift from capitalistic to small-shop production scattered accumulated funds. And this fact proved to be of some importance when at critical moments for the state the emperors did not find large accumulated funds to borrow from and had therefore to resort to debasing currency or making forced requisitions when they needed ready money.

As for the forms of production on the farms, large and small, the evidence is unsatisfactory, and very diversely interpreted. Perhaps historians have been too prone to simplify the problem in an attempt to read the origins of third century conditions into those of the first century. Italy is large and the different regions vary much in natural resources. We do not get far when we insist on the basis of some incidental complaint of a Roman writer that Italy—all of Italy—was drifting away from garden culture to wheat raising[22]— or the converse; or that slavery was giving away to the tenant system, or the contrary.

When we examine the references to the products of the soil the evidence seems to indicate that cereal culture and perhaps olive growing were slightly decreasing through the century, that cattle raising held its own, that wine culture, horticulture and gardening slightly increased. Our safest authority is Columella's book on farming, written about the middle of the century, though in reading him we must remember that on the estates which he had managed he had given special attention to, and therefore had a lively interest in, viticulture. In fact those estates—at Albano, Cervetri, Ardea, and Carseoli—happened to lie in regions largely given over to wine and fruit raising. However, he knew every form of agriculture and his book was meant to be a "Complete Farmer," though he doubtless wrote it for those most apt to buy such a book—

[22] Rostovtzeff, *Econ. and Soc. Hist.*, p. 95, says of Nero's period: "Italy was therefore gradually becoming a corn-land again." The statement seems to rest on his hypothesis that Italy had exported much wine during the Republic but could no longer do so because of successful viticulture in the provinces.

the rich gentleman farmer. In Columella we get no hint that viticulture was suffering for lack of a market.[23] Very likely there was no suffering. The Italians were more numerous, wealthier, and were buying more of the homegrown brands than in the previous century. There never had been much exportation from Italy. Practically the only market that had formerly called for Italian wines was Gaul, and thither Marseilles had carried the old brands of Greek wine besides her own. There is every reason for supposing that the Italian wine-grower had a better market in Nero's day[24] than before the Italian wine-god was dignified by the song of a great poet. Columella (3, 3, 9) gives an interesting calculation of what the wine-grower not too far from the Roman market might expect to make. For convenience he bases his reckoning upon a seven-jugera plot, but of course he means that this is but a fragment of a large estate. (I shall call his sestertius, five cents, and his amphora, six and one-half gallons.)

Cost of 7 jugera (4⅔ acres) of undeveloped land	$350
Purchase price of a skilled vintner (slave)	400
Cost of cuttings, props, and implements	700
Interest (6%) on above, till vines produced (2 years)	105
Total cost	$1,555

Therefore the annual interest (at 6%) on the investment would be $93.30. In reckoning the returns,

[23] Col., especially third book, and Pliny, *N. H.*, 14, 59-72.

[24] See chapter XIII.

Columella believed that vineyards ought to produce 1,500 quarts per jugerum (560 gallons per acre; he adds that Seneca's estate at Nomentum yielded 4,000 quarts per jugerum). Average wine when the price was low at Rome was three cents per quart. The annual production of each jugerum was, therefore, $45, or $315 for the seven-jugera plot—a profit of over $31 per jugerum. If Columella's items are correct we can only conclude that wine culture must have been very attractive, even though he does not allow properly for a sinking fund. He adds that there might be a further profit from selling cuttings from the vineyard—which seems to indicate that in his day viticulture was healthily extending its range. Now neither he nor Pliny speaks directly of the conditions of viticulture. Both of them mention the better brands of Italy,[25] however, and from these references we find that wine was apparently grown in all the regions that are still considered good producers. Pliny explicitly names several new brands that had recently gained popularity, and cites only the Falernian as less in vogue than formerly, but it seems that the Falernian had lost its popularity only because the Faustinian estate of the same region had built up a rival reputation. The impression one gains from both these authors is that viticulture was spreading at this time.

[25] Some Italian wines are mentioned in the Periplus 6 and 49 as going to the far east. Slopes of Vesuvius and Sorrento, Columella, 3, 2, 10; Nomentum, *ibid.*, 14; Albano, 14; Pompeii, Fregellae, North Italy, 27; Picenum, Faenze, 3, 3, 3; Massic, Sorrentine, Albanian, and Caecuban among the foremost, 3, 8, 5; Ardea, Carseoli, 3, 9, 2; Cervetri, 6; Pliny, *N. H.*, 14, 59-72.

This impression is strengthened by reference to Domitian's famous edict of the end of the century in which he forbade the planting of new vineyards in Italy, and ordered the cutting down of half the vines in the provinces[26]—an order which was presently revoked when delegations from the provinces protested. Domitian was not a good economist and his edicts were issued impulsively, but his reasons for proposing an effective restriction were probably pressing.   To the Italians he stated that an insufficient amount of wheat was being produced because of the constant increase in the number of vineyards, which was probably true. Vineyards require a large outlay in plants, presses, vats, jars and skilled slaves, and for this reason they attract permanent investments and are seldom cut. Viticulture does not balk at one or two poor years as do annual crops.   It is apt to over-expand, as Italy has recently found to be true.   To the provincials on the other hand Domitian asserted that excessive wine drinking led to rioting.   In any case his command to destroy the vineyards was over-drastic, as he had to confess presently, but there are no reasons for assuming that he was dishonest in his explanations or that his chief purpose was to protect Italian viticulture.   There is no evidence that Italian exports could or did increase

[26] Suet., *Dom.* 7, 2; 14, 2; Philostr., *Vita Soph.* VI, 222, *Vita Apoll.* VI, 42; Stat. *Silv.* 3, 3, 11.   That this decree had any connection with the famine mentioned in Revelations or with the temporary distress due to a severe winter in Pisidia in 93 A.D. is wholly unlikely.   The climatic variations throughout the Mediterranean basin are very great.

afterwards.   We do know from the inscriptions of the African domains that on the imperial estates in Africa viticulture was restricted by Trajan and Hadrian.

Concerning the status of cereal culture, Domitian's edict is proof that in his day Italian grain did not suffice for the needs of the population.   Whether, however, this insufficiency reflects conditions due to a year of poor crops—Italian wheat crops have a range of variation of about thirty per cent. due to climatic conditions—or whether the deficiency was constant we hardly know.   The latter is probable.   If we approach the question from Columella's references we may perhaps find some clues, though we must note at once that this author is not as good an authority on cereals as on wine.   We first notice that he usually assumes that grain is grown between the rows of vines or fruit trees[27]—in what he sometimes calls an *arbustum*.   This practice is still in vogue in a large part of the Po Valley, in Campania, and elsewhere.   The roots of the trees and vines are compelled to strike deep because those near the surface are deliberately severed; then the surface soil is used for garden products, grain, and hay.   One's first impression in riding from Milan to Bologna today is of traversing a vast orchard, but census statistics show that this very area now produces large quantities of wheat, maize and garden stuffs as well as fruit.   The present system—which was also the ancient one—will explain Columella's surprising

[27] Col. II, 2, 24 and 9, 6; V. 6, 11; V. 7, 3; V. 9, 7; V. 9, 12; V. 10, 5-6; etc.

statement that he had not seen wheat in Italy producing over fourfold[28] (about seven and one-half bushels per acre), that is, less than half a respectable crop. Columella prided himself chiefly upon his vineyards and orchards, and most of his manure was used to fertilize these. Grain was to him a subsidiary crop and was allowed intervening space to bring what it might. We can therefore hardly draw the conclusion that his statement represents a normal yield where wheat was given adequate consideration. To be sure the Italian soil had long been over-cropped with wheat and was tired of it, but Italian farmers were skilled in the use of manures and especially in the practice of rotation with nitrogenous plants like alfalfa, clover, and several kinds of beans. Columella's enthusiasm for alfalfa[29] as a very productive plant which enriched the soil reads like the seed catalogues of our west a generation ago.

We may be sure that in cereal country like Tuscany and parts of the Po Valley wheat was still brought up to standard production, even if it yielded but half a crop in the vineyards of Latium. Nor had cereal culture been driven out of Italy by foreign competition. The Roman writers who lived in the city were much concerned about the city's grain supply, but that is no reason why we should fail to note how small an item it was in the total of Italy's production. In Nero's day

[28] Col. III, 3, 4.

[29] Col. II, 2, 7; 10, 24. *Medica* (lucerne) was also recommended by Vergil (*Georg*. I, 215). Servius says in his commentary on Vergil that Venetia was quite covered with it.

Egypt sent about five million bushels of wheat to Rome annually while Africa sent about twice as much.[30] That would suffice for the capital alone, and reveals why cereal-culture could be neglected in the vicinity of the city. But the rest of Italy had a population of about fifteen million souls[31] and they would require more than 150 million bushels a year. It is doubtful whether one per cent. of this amount was supplied by Sicily and Sardinia. Gaul, Spain and the eastern provinces probably raised only enough for their own large populations. Now 150,000,000 bushels is as much as modern Italy raises when harvests are good. At present[32] Italy includes Sicily and Sardinia, but on the other hand vineyards and olive groves are now probably taking more space than in ancient times, and much land is today used in new crops like maize, tobacco, and oranges. We must conclude therefore that wheat was

[30] *Epit. de Caes.* 1, 6; 5,000,000 bushels in Augustus' day. Later Josephus says that Egypt contributed a third and Africa two-thirds of Rome's supply, *Bell. Jud.* II, 386. The Romans usually reckoned twelve bushels per man per annum for the food supply.

[31] The citizen census of Claudius in 47 yielded nearly six million, of which perhaps one-fourth lived outside of Italy. The census recorded adult males (*Roman Census Statistics, Class. Phil.* 1924, p. 339) so that the whole population was probably 15-18 million. Of this number about 1,000,000 lived in Rome.

[32] *Statesmen's Yearbook*, 1925: in 1922 the acreage in wheat was 11,403,665, the production 145,000,000 bushels. Other cereals 6,000,000 acres, wine 12,000,000, olives 7,000,000. The wheat acreage could readily be raised fifty per cent. if viticulture were reduced to reasonable proportions.

very extensively and successfully raised during the first century, but also that the soil had to be very carefully cultivated in order to produce the amount needed. The Romans must have observed that if social conditions should alter so as to result in a niggardly or wasteful use of the soil it would go hard with Italy's needs.

We come now to the knotty question of agrarian labor and the leasing systems. There were various systems in vogue adapted to varying circumstances. There were certainly in every section of Italy large estates farmed by slaves directed by a slave-steward under the landlord's supervision,[33] and at the other end of the scale there were, especially in the interior, small peasant-proprietors who worked their own farms. So far all authorities agree. To these types may be added the following though without great certainty as to the extent of their distribution. Columella[34] suggests that when the estate is too far away for an owner's personal inspection and the crop is a simple one like cereals, it is best to rent it out. Since, however, he warns against renting it to a middleman who places slaves on the farm he apparently means that free working renters should be found for it. Pliny, the younger, speaks

[33] This is the system usually assumed by Columella on the vineyards of central Italy, though at the beginning, I, 7, 1, in speaking of farm labor, he discusses the rental system first.

[34] 1, 7, 3-7. Volusius liked renters born on the farm, inheriting the lease, as it were; Saserna advocated long term leases; free lease holders were better for the land than slaves; on distant estates one must lease (in this case he probably means a middleman).

repeatedly of having to find new *coloni,* and in one
instance of the difficulty of finding a good *conductor.*[35]
Now *coloni* may be small peasant farmers placed by the
owner, or they may be large contractors (mercanti di
campagna) who according to convenience place either
peasant farmers or slaves on the land; but a *conductor*
does not labor with his hands: he is a middleman contractor. Pliny therefore leases his farms but we cannot
be sure of the nature of the labor. Heitland,[36] in his
excellent survey of agrarian conditions, holds that the
colonus of this period is generally to be considered as a
middleman who works the estate with slave labor supplied as a part of his equipment by the owner. There
is proof that such a system existed, and furthermore
it is well vouched for as common by the jurists of the
next century. That it was the prevailing system when
the owner was absent is not so certain. We remember
that in the previous century Domitius had hundreds,
probably thousands, of working *coloni;* that Horace
while employing eight slaves about his house, also
rented out five individual plots; we notice that Colu-

[35] Pliny, *Epist.* 7, 30, 7, *conductor* (It is often asserted that
conductor is used only of imperial estates). Pliny, *Epist.* 10, 8,
speaks of five-year leases; in this case he seems to refer to a
distant farm let to a colonus (mercante di campagna, conductor)
and in 3, 19 there is a question of providing slaves for such a
colonus. In 9, 31 where he speaks of several coloni, he may be
referring to the peasants. In 9, 37, he is about to introduce
rental in kind on shares because his renters fall in arrears when
they engage to pay cash.

[36] *Agricola,* p. 256.

mella speaks of the possibility of the middleman using his own slaves (not the owner's) ; we hear of Vespasian placing peasant *coloni* on the imperial estates; finally both Columella and Pliny, the elder, insist that a free tenant is preferable to slave labor.[37]   All of this militates against Mr. Heitland's view.   But apart from casual references, the agrarian situation in various parts of Italy does not favor the assumption of any uniform type throughout the peninsula.   In Cisalpine Gaul, for instance, where inscriptions indicate that slaves were less numerous than elsewhere in Italy, and where the local aristocracy of landlords could find numerous Celts and Ligurians willing to rent small plots (we must assume small individual plots because of the farm tools used), slave farm-labor is not probable, and the wide extension of the system of small leases in the previous and following centuries would indicate that such leases were common throughout the first century also.

On the Veleian and Beneventan tracts mentioned above, we can be sure that many owners farmed their plots, the family seems to be doing the work in the old-fashioned way with the aid of a slave or two; and even on the larger estates the owner, not his agent, usually placed the mortgage, and in such cases he

[37] Domitius in Caes. *Bell. Civ.* I, 17.   He promises 15,000 soldiers four jugera each out of *his own estates;* later (*ibid.* I, 34) he manned seven ships with his own slaves, freedmen and tenants. Horace, *Epist.* I, 14; Vespasian, Pais, *Storia della Col.* p. 344 and *Lib. Colon.* 230, 236; Columella 1, 7, 5; Pliny, *N. H.* 18, 36.

would seem to be living on the estate. Presumably like Horace, he had working tenants as well as slaves. What system would be chosen would depend somewhat upon the crop. Wherever a large investment was involved, as in vineyards, the master would wish to keep the responsibility, and was apt to do so by choosing his *vilicus* and his slaves; on grain-lands, however, renters might well be trusted. But, as we learn from Pliny's letters, the choice would also depend on whether the buildings of the place were provided with slave quarters or tenants' houses, whether the estate was already stocked, and if it was not, what the neighborhood could best provide. In general then we must assume an abundance of slave labor,[38] especially on large estates, whether the owner or an agent or a middleman had charge; we may also assume peasant proprietors, and to a considerable extent the working peasant renter, who is so frequently mentioned in third century writers. There is very little evidence for the existence of free hired labor, or for the employment of contractors to take over a part of the work, though we are told that Seneca sold his grape crop on the vine to a contractor.

The growth of the imperial estates must be considered because of their peculiar treatment later. Augustus had inherited large landed estates in Italy[39] and

[38] By advocating marriage among the slaves and offering freedom to a mother of four children Columella (1, 7, 19) at the same time indicates that slaves had risen in price, and that care was taken to preserve the supply.

[39] Hirschfeld, *Kleine Schriften*, p. 544. Few imperial estates existed till later in Tiberius' reign. Tac. *Ann.* 4, 7. For Claudius, see Tac. *Ann.* 12, 65; Nero's estates in Africa, Pliny, *N. H.* 18, 35.

the provinces from men like Maecenas and Agrippa, and he had appointed procurators to exploit them. Tiberius added to this inheritance (now called *patrimonium*) not only from his personal inheritance but also from the confiscated estates of Sejanus and the wealthy mine-owner Marius—though up to his day confiscated estates were usually sold and the funds turned into the state treasury. Caligula seems to have added the properties of Sextus Pompey to the patrimonium, and Claudius certainly increased it somewhat. Under Nero, who murdered so many of the aristocracy, the patrimonial estates grew rapidly.

We have already mentioned the rich Marian tract of Africa which had by this time apparently accumulated in the hands of Roman nobles. And it is chiefly to this region that Pliny refers when he says that Nero seized half of Africa. The confiscations were doubtless even more extensive in Italy. Definite information comes to us only in later inscriptions, as, for example, when we notice that imperial estates are mentioned as adjacent farms seven times in the Beneventan mortgage tablet and four times in the Veleian one.[40] Since Nero was the last of his line these properties could no longer reasonably be called "patrimonial" by Vespasian; but Vespasian did not sell them or turn them over to the senatorial treasury. He took charge of them in the name of the fiscus, the imperial treasury, and appointed fiscal procurators to exploit them. Being

[40] Some of these tracts may be due to Vespasian's reclamation of *subseciva* in the mountains.

not only a business man, however, but also a ruler responsible for the welfare of Italy, he adopted, apparently as his regular policy, the system of placing working life-tenants on these domains. The details of his system are not revealed but since the *coloni* needed more supervision than could be given by the occasional visits of the procurator, and since these Italian estates confiscated from senators frequently had stately villas and gardens, we may well believe that the procurator found it convenient to place some middleman *conductor* in the villa to supervise the *coloni* and collect the rent. Very likely he was asked to exploit the "home-field" as pay for his services. This is merely a conjecture based upon the assumed needs and the fact that we find such a system on the African estates later. In Africa the conductor got his labor free from the coloni. We hear of nothing of the kind in Italy as yet, and we may feel sure that several of the confiscated estates of Italy had slaves so that labor-service was not desired. But we may also be sure that when the old slaves died the system in vogue in Africa would readily be adopted as feasible. The old theory therefore that the servile colonate of the third century had some connection with the imperial estates is wholly reasonable.

It must also be noted that the growth of imperial estates could hardly have resulted in greater productiveness. Ordinarily the substitution of free peasant renters for slave labor seemed to Pliny and Columella desirable, provided the owner watched his property. To speak of capitalistic farming with slave labor as "scientific agriculture" is a modern nuance not excused by our sources. But imperial ownership entailed a serious difficulty in that the owner could not possibly watch his property. He must employ a procurator who in turn must find contractors (*conductores*) for the various estates, and both of these were apt to look to their own profits. In fact it was very easy for them to enter into collusion to their mutual advantage and thus to betray the interests of the estates as well as of the *coloni*. But this was not all. The procurator did not have the funds to rehabilitate wasted estates, he probably did not have full liberty to exploit them with slave labor when that course might have been advisable, and he did not have the owner's keen interest in devising new methods for improving them. Dio of Prusa[41] gives a vivid account, fictitious perhaps, but fairly representative, of what happened to such a confiscated estate in Euboea when the emperor, possibly Nero, destroyed the owner. The estate consisted for the most part of a ranch in the rough hill country, and the arable soil was worth little because there was no adequate market near at hand. The shepherds of the estate were the simple rustics of the vicinity. When the owner had been struck down and his properties confiscated, the imperial procurator came out to Euboea in due season to take possession. Finding what seemed an unprofitable ranch, he swept off the herds and whatever else proved salable, and departed without even paying the wages of the shepherds. When some years

[41] The seventh oration.

later Dio travelled through the region he found that a few of the rustics were squatting in fear and trembling on the abandoned land, and that the town, whose meager sustenance had depended upon the thrift of the country population, lay in utter neglect. This may not be a fair picture of what ordinarily resulted, since Greece had long suffered from economic distress, but we may well believe that such things could and did occur in the poorer mountain districts of Italy when the imperial procurator took charge of confiscated estates.

Various imperial acts demonstrate some concern for the population of the arable parts of Italy. This appears first when Nero settled some of the veterans in Italy whereas preceding emperors seem to have chosen provincial colonies for the purpose. We have spoken of the failure of his settlements at Antium; at Tarentum more of his colonists seem to have remained, to judge from the mention of several of them in inscriptions. Among those who received an officer's allotment in Tarentum in the year 60 was Columella, whom we have repeatedly cited. Tacitus mentions Capua and Nuceria as also receiving veterans. It is not unlikely therefore that Nero used up some of the confiscated properties for this purpose, though it is not probable that he gave away highly developed vineyards or orchards to soldiers. Vespasian, who was an intelligent observer of Italian conditions, rarely colonized veterans in Italy, preferring rather to send them to the provinces. The veterans of his day had served twenty years and were obviously not material with which to increase the rural stock of Italy. There is, however, an inscription of Nola and a line in the Liber Coloniarum which indicate that some colonists were placed in Campania. Vespasian's favorite method was apparently to settle long-term peasants as *coloni*[42] on the domain land. That at this time the state was cognizant of a scarcity of a sound body of freemen in Italy is apparent from the fact that recruiting for the legions was henceforth carried on almost wholly in the provinces. If Vespasian set out to substitute free *coloni* for slaves on the imperial domains it was probably because he had learned what the conditions at home actually were. It has been conjectured with some plausibility that his generosity in granting citizenship and Latin rights extensively in Spain was in part due to the need he felt for a new recruiting ground outside of Italy. We may also note for future reference that in two of the places settled by *coloni*, Vespasian also leased to members of his *familia*. Apparently good slaves of his household were given their freedom and placed among the *coloni*. If this was a general practice, as it certainly was later, it will help to explain the humble conditions in which we presently find the colonate.

Nerva's reign was brief, but two significant acts of his have been recorded. It is said that he introduced a bill to the comitium to buy land in Italy for 60,000,000 sesterces for allotment to the poor. This would suffice for only about 10,000 small lots, but the fact that

[42] *Liber Col.* Lachm. 230, 234, 236, 261.

purchasing was necessary would seem to indicate that his predecessors had assigned practically all of the suitable lands of the imperial domains to *coloni;* for it is not likely that the poorer people of Rome would look with complaisance upon slave cultivation of domain lands while they were asking for allotments. The second measure is the famous institution of free alimentation[43] of which we have spoken above. Of its details we hear nothing till Trajan's day, but Nerva's bureau doubtless worked them out. The plan was to lend money in perpetuity on farms throughout Italy, the interest on which would be gathered by committees of each community and distributed to parents of free-born children for their nurture. It would seem that about a hundred million dollars were thus placed. To judge from ancient comment the chief purpose was to aid the poor in rearing their children—in fact to encourage a more abundant offspring. That much was expected of the institution we may infer from the popularity of the theme on official monuments. And this in turn implies that the birthrate was widely felt to be insufficient. Statistics and explanations we do not possess. The emperor, however, had a second purpose as well, if we may believe Dio (68, 2, 1). It was to aid the farmers with rural credits at a fair interest rate; and since sums were lent only to about ten per cent of the valuation of the mortgaged estates the

[43] *Alimenta*, Hirschfeld, *Kais. Verwaltungsbeamten*, 212-224; De Pachtere, *La Table Hypoth. de Veleia;* Carcopino, in *Rev. étud. anc.* 1921, 287; Ashley, in *Eng. Hist. Rev.*, 1921.

distribution was very wide.   The outpouring of so large a sum must have cheapened money, relieved debtors to some extent, and accordingly raised prices on products and land for a while.   Unfortunately the loans seem to have been perpetual so that they rested as a servitude on the land, and after the first relief had spread its effects the farmers were doubtless less able than before to face lean harvests.   The plan may have been more successful as a charitable institution than as a relief to agriculture.   But even its charitable purposes failed before the end of the century, for when the coinage was debased, the returns from the loans sufficed only for the payment of the salaries of the personnel connected with the combined bureau of "roads and alimentation," and very little then reached the children of the poor.

CHAPTER XXI

THE PROVINCES IN HADRIAN'S DAY

WHEN Hadrian made his long tour through the Roman provinces a little more than a century after Augustus' death he found the Mediterranean world in a state of material prosperity and contentment that it has never again as a whole attained. Here we can only note the trend of economic development in a few typical provinces under a century of Roman rule. The province of Africa, as we have seen, was at first a mere strip; under Caesar and Augustus, Numidia and the fertile ribbon of coast-land now called Tripolis were added to it, and presently Caligula annexed Mauritania. The African tribute of grain in Caesar's day had been exceedingly small even after the addition of Numidia: 300,000 bushels[1] of wheat compared with about 10,000,000 bushels[2] a century later. The increase in cereals is astonishing, even if we note that a part of it was due to the addition of Mauritania and of imperial estates that were formerly non-tribute paying. It means not only that the Roman immigrants were putting stipendiary land under careful cultivation

---

[1] Caes. *Bell. Afr.* 97; Plut. *Caes.* 55, Caesar also secured a tribute of olive oil in Tripolis; Gsell, *Rivista Tripol.* I, p. 41.

[2] Josephus *Bell. Jud.* II, 386 (64 A.D.).

442

but that many Numidians had stopped wandering about
with their herds and taken to agriculture.

Progress was, however, not uniform throughout the
province. In the regions of Carthage and of Dougga
the best lands had been taken long before the Augustan
day so that few of the new settlers went there. They
had to go further up the valley, or into the plateau that
lay between Sicca and Mactaris south of Thugga, or
else into the Punic harbor towns. For a while it
seemed that these districts would be thoroughly Romanized. But presently immigration almost ceased,
when confiscations ended at home and when the emperors began to send their discharged veterans to Asia,
Syria, and the Balkan valleys. Henceforth each section of Africa developed in its own peculiar way.
Carthage, supported by a productive plain, winning the
trade of the Bagradas and Theveste roads, and enjoying the favors of the governor's staff, grew rapidly, at-
tracting large numbers of Punic peoples who had gone
inland, and of Numidians who had learned to like
urban ways. Carthage became populous, rich and un-
Italian. Handsome residential palaces sprang up in
the suburbs as they had near Rome; on the farm lands
outside, however, few traces of large villas have been
discovered. Presumably the landlords preferred to
live in the city. Farther off, near the hills of Uthina,[3]
where there were natives to employ as tenants and
laborers, many large villas have been found.

The region about Dougga proves to have had a curi-

[3] *Inventaire des mosaiques.*

ous history.   Here, though the land was fair and had long been settled, the villages developed into cities more slowly than in the less fertile regions south of it.   The reason was simply that a few Roman nobles acquired this untaxed property early and farmed it through contractors who used the native village-folk as renters.[4] Under Claudius and Nero several of these owners fell victims to imperial tyranny and the estates were confiscated.   The emperor's procurators organized the vast estates into convenient complexes and put a *conductor* in charge of each.   Such conductores held contracts for five years, supervised the work of the small tenants, collected the rents, and made their own profits by exploiting a "home-field" free of rent.   In order to draw appropriate profits out of their "home-fields" they were allowed to stipulate in their contracts with the tenants that each must work for them six days per year at busy seasons.   Thus their own labor costs were reduced to a minimum.   This system, which had apparently been evolved by private landlords even before the emperors seized the land, was well adapted to the interests of absentee owners; but it obstructed the development of the tenantry and of the land.   The procurators appointed by the emperors, and the conductores, hired for brief terms, concerned themselves little about the conditions of the tenants; and they did not risk their profits in agricultural experiments or in manuring and rotating crops.   Besides, imperial owner-

[4] Frank, *Inscriptions of the Imperial Domains*, Am. Jour. Phil., 1926, pp. 55 and 153.

ship was final; the tenants had no hope of being able ultimately to buy the plots they were cultivating, nor could outsiders with new methods come into the community. Finally, the thirds that belonged to the Emperor did not enter the regular trade channels of the communities but were sent off directly to Rome. The economic life of the region accordingly was largely stifled and several of the villages deteriorated.[5] Thugga, to be sure, grew as the center of the region and acquired several handsome buildings, chiefly through owners of private estates, it would seem; but when one remembers the wealth of the soil in this neighborhood and the long period of its exploitation, Thugga can hardly be considered a great honor to imperial cultivation. If the picture we get of this region is typical we must conclude that imperial ownership of land played but a small part in the great development of Africa.

The inscriptions[6] that have been found in this region have evoked much discussion. They are interesting for

[5] The tenants of the Saltus Burunitanus call themselves *rustici tui vernulae et alumnae* C. I. L. VIII, 14464. At Thignica, a village of the Saltus region, only two citizens are recorded on the nearly three hundred dedications to Saturn. See Toutain, *Cultes paiens*, vol. III.

[6] C. I. L. VIII, 14464, 25902, 25943, 26416. The most careful study of them is in Rostovtzeff's *Röm. Kol.*, but this is somewhat marred by a mistaken tendency to derive African customs from Ptolemaic rules. Carcopino's article in *Mél. de Rome*, 1906 is valuable. Van Nostrand, *The Imperial Domains of Africa*, has a convenient but not wholly reliable translation of the inscriptions.

what they tell of imperial methods in Africa, even though we may not employ them to explain economic changes elsewhere. They mention several peculiar practices, as for instance the subjection of citizens to procuratorial rule instead of to the jurisdiction of some self-governing municipality. This may be a natural consequence of extensive imperial land-holding; but it is also possible that several of the local town meetings of the early Roman settlers had dribbled to the vanishing point when private landlords bought in whole townships.[7] Here also is the first appearance under Roman institutions of the *corvée,* the exaction of personal service from tenants as part of the rental. There is no reason for connecting this practice with compulsory canal labor in Egypt. It is more likely that when great lords acquired the lands of whole townships they personally took charge of such road and temple repairs as were needed and in return transferred to their own account the five or six days of work that the tenants had formerly owed to public service.[8] But quite apart from old practices there would be nothing strange in taking out a part of the rental in service in a country where slaves were scarce and native tenants plentiful.

These inscriptions also reveal the presence of the peculiar institution of *emphyteusis.* Some wise landlords, even before the Emperor came into possession,

[7] In Italy the imperial *coloni* long remained under municipal jurisdiction, Front. *Contr. agr.* II, 53.

[8] Caesar's charter for the *coloni* at Urso shows that inhabitants of towns were required to give a few days of their time to road and fort building; cf. *Am. Jour. Phil.* 1926, 167.

had invited better service by promising to give heritable leaseholds on rough land to tenants who would
plant them in orchards. These plots were to be rent-
free until the orchards became productive and there
was to be no tax on such small crops as would grow
between the rows of the immature trees. When the
Emperors first took possession this practice was discouraged by the procurators and conductores who concerned themselves only with immediate profits. However, when Hadrian visited Africa on his tour of the
provinces he learned that much of the land which was
too rough for plowing or which had been worn out by
constant cropping in wheat might well bear olives or
vines with profit. He did not wish to encourage viticulture because he appreciated the point of view of
Domitian's prohibition. He accordingly issued a decree, applicable apparently to the whole of the province, legalizing the cultivation of unused or abandoned
ground, practically on the conditions referred to above.
This decree, if it was indeed applied to the whole province, must have had a very extensive effect, not so
much on the imperial estates where we know that the
conductores discouraged tenants from taking advantage of it, as on the wide tracts still held as pasture
land by roving nomads. The very fear of losing such
land would induce these tribes to cultivate what was
arable. We may also suspect that landlords acquired
tracts from the nomads by using the decree as a threat.
The landlords were of course not particularly eager to
apply the decree directly and plant orchards for which

they would eventually have to pay the state a full rental of one-third of the fruit; but they might tell the nomads that they intended to do so and thus frighten them into selling their stipendiary lands. This would account for the wide extension of private plantations in the midst of Numidian tribes during the second century.[9] State revenues would of course largely profit by the arrangement since the lords would be aware that if they neglected to cultivate any tract for more than two years they would in turn forfeit claim to it. We may well believe then that Hadrian's decree *de rudibus agris* was responsible for a wide extension of agriculture and of material prosperity.

The old free Phoenician coast towns south of Carthage seem on the whole to have been stationary. Some of the trade which they had possessed during the late republic now went to Carthage, and their hinterland was narrow and not very productive. Yet their trade continued to such an extent that several of them had offices at the shipping bureau of Ostia.[10] Most of this coast will bear olives (and some wheat when the climate is favorable) for a distance of fifteen or twenty miles from the water's edge. From there on westward for fifty to seventy miles there is little but useless waste

[9] There are many extensive private estates even in the midst of native tribes; cf. the Saltus Beguensis (C. I. L. VIII, 25946) owned by a Roman senator in the midst of the Musulamii.

[10] Calza, *Bull. Com.* 1915, 75 and *Guida di Ostia*, p. 106. Here there were among the few whose names have survived, *stationes* of the shippers of Carthage, Sabrata, Syllecte, Curubis, Gummi, Missua and Hippo.

except during the winter rains when the nomads from the mountains and the oases drive in their flocks to graze for three or four months.[11] West of that there is a plateau extending from Sicca down to Thelepte which gets a trifle more rain. More important still, the subsoil strata of the valleys in this district carry enough moisture to insure good crops of olives if the trees are carefully watered through the first few summers. This region was dominated by nomads when the Romans came,[12] whereas in the second century of Roman occupation a vast orchard of olives spread from Mactaris down past Sufes, Cillium, Sufetula and Thelepte. These towns grew rapidly with clusters of villages and large villas along all the roads. In the region between Sufetula and Cillium the remains of a thousand olive presses have been found.

And yet today Sufetula has less than a hundred inhabitants and the vicinity is inexpressibly bare. To discover the causes of Rome's agrarian success here is

[11] Wheat will mature here in good years. At Sfax the olive has now been carried fifty miles inland under special methods of cultivation. The rainfall is: 20 cm. at Sfax; 30 cm. at Sousse; 40 cm. at Tunis. The climate has not changed since Roman days.

[12] Marius marched through unplowed country for nine days from Lares to Capsa (Sall. *Jug.* 91). Banditry in this region necessitated the storage of provisions in hidden cellars in Caesar's day, *Bell. Afr.* 65. Even Thysdrus was then a very small town, *Bell. Afr.* 97. Toutain, *Cultes paiens* III, shows that the old cults extended as far as Mactaris; south of that town along the plateau the cults belong to the Roman period. Augustus' survey of the region (Bartel, *Bonn. Jb.* 1911) was not for purposes of colonization, any more than the surveys in Gaul or Egypt.

not easy, but the story was something like this. It seems that accident rather than foresight on the part of the government deserves the credit, for no one then knew that the soil of this southern plateau was worth cultivating. The Romans at first attempted only to stop the migrations which led to banditry. Not having dealt with such arid regions before they did not comprehend the reason for these migrations, and being Romans they considered that civilization implied settled abodes and the cultivation of the land. In the year 14 A.D. Tiberius' army built a military road for the legion which was to establish order. It ran from Tacape at the southern bend of the sea, where the winter camp was to be, westward to the oasis of Capsa, then north over the plateau to Ammaedara, the site of the summer camp near the edge of the lands then cultivated. This road cut off the migrations from the mountains on the west and from the desert on the south. The Gaetuli and the nomad part of the Musulamii were enraged, and under the leadership of Tacfarinas[13] broke out into a general revolt in the year 17. The war continued with guerilla raids over the deserts for seven years, when Tacfarinas fell. Some of the nomads then moved westward to live in the traditional manner of their ancestors, while others accepted apportioned lands and promised to live in peace. Since permanent abodes require new resources, and but little grain could be raised in this region, it is not unlikely

[13] Wars with Tacfarinas, Cagnat, *L'Arme Romaine*[2] I, On the road of 14 A.D. see De Pachtere, *C. R. Acad. Inscr.* 1916, 273.

that the natives introduced olive culture. About the summer camp at Ammaedara a settlement grew up to supply the soldiers, and the traffic on the direct road from Hadrumetum created villages wherever there were springs of water. Roman veterans from the camp settled where the land seemed to promise returns, and Phoenicians came in from the coast towns, Numidians supplying them both with labor.[14] In time Romans from Carthage as well as Italy heard of the new settlements, invested in land, and hired skilled *conductores* from the neighboring towns to exploit their plantations. In a century the whole region was flourishing. The same story is about to be repeated today with the French in the role of the Romans, Arabs replacing Phoenicians, and Berbers replacing Numidians.

This would seem to be a typical example of Rome's procedure in Africa before Hadrian's day. It shows little concern for social or economic conditions among the natives; it follows the old policy of establishing order in the customary way and bringing in the taxes. To be sure, some historians have surmised that Tiberius' army was sent down to clear off the natives and make room for Roman colonists. The question whether

[14] Flavius Jucundus, a veteran granted citizenship apparently by one of the Flavians, was among the first settlers at Cillium. He came in time to seize the one small stream of water and hence could raise wine by irrigation. Other inscriptions of the place show names of citizens of Numidian parentage. Phoenician cults also appear early. This will illustrate the average type of settlers on this plateau region. Many colonists, whatever their origin, married native women.

the government during the first century A.D. thought in economic or political terms is of some importance. Since, however, the land was barren, since there was little migration from Italy at the time, and since the region about Sufetula and Cillium shows no evidence of colonization before the Flavian period, it is hardly wise to assume an economic purpose in the campaigns of Tiberius' day. We reach a similar conclusion when we test the equally hazardous opinion that the government of the first century attempted to civilize the natives by trying to transform them into city-dwellers. Proof for such a hypothesis is completely wanting. Veterans were here and there given lands and a municipal nucleus; at other places native villages grew to cities because Roman military roads polarized trade or because, when migrations were stopped, cultivation became necessary and cultivation in time aggregated the tribes. Finally, where Romans took up land they needed native renters and laborers and these therefore naturally drifted toward the cities. But in all this, natural economic and social forces rather than governmental politics were at work. How little the government really concerned itself about the question is shown by some recent inscriptions which prove that even in the third century the tribal organization of the natives existed by the side of the new settlements between Cillium and Thelepte.[15]

[15] Cagnat-Merlin, *Ins. Lat. Proc.* 102, 103, C. I. L. VIII, 23195: Musunii in the third century between Thelepte and Cillium; Mesnage, *Romanisation de L'Africa*, p. 176.

In the region west of the plateau just spoken of, it was chiefly the army moving westward that gave rise to new settlements.[16]   In the Flavian days when it was found that the land south of Ammaedara was well enough settled to be secure, a veteran colony—veterans were then largely Italians—was planted, and the camp moved westward to the Numido-Punic town of Theveste which commanded a fairly productive plateau plain.   In the early days of Trajan it moved on westward once more, again leaving a colony of veterans. This group to judge from Flavian recruiting lists consisted largely of Asiatics who had won citizenship.   The city grew in time to be one of the most prosperous of the province.   The legion itself may have camped at Mascula for some years but not for long.   By 123 it had taken up its permanent abode at Lambaesis, where it could protect the central Numidian plains from the raids of the wild tribes that hid in the lofty Aures and that came up the pass from the region of Biskra. Here, not far from the camp, the legion was set to work to build a model town at Timgad with forum, temples, theatres, a library, and a splendid bath at each gate.[17] The city was to serve as a self-supporting garrison colony to help protect the valley, and though the rainfall there was scanty, it lay near the lofty and well-forested Aures mountains that supplied spring water

[16] Cagnat, *L'Arme Romaine*.   For Theveste see Gsell, *Ins. Lat. Alg.* p. 286.   The bricks made by the army at Theveste bear dates between 81 and 96, but the occupation probably lasted longer.

[17] Ballu, *Guide de Timgad.*

for personal use and some even for irrigation—a blessing rare enough anywhere in Africa.[18]   The colonists
here were largely African Romans or Romanized Afri-
cans, at least at first.   From Marcus' day on the veterans of Africa were more and more of mixed stock,
for the soldiers of Lambaesis married the native wom-
en of the place and their sons entered the legion.   Thus
cultivation spread westward with the advance of the
legion; soldiers from all parts of the world, the Romans of Africa, and the Numidians attracted to a fixed
habitation by the opportunities for profit, all mingled in
making up the rapidly growing population.

We need not continue the survey, for the four regions discussed will illustrate the silent but effective
work accomplished under the *pax Romana*.   We are
not to suppose, however, that Roman civilization
spread thus everywhere or that the natives were compelled to share in it where they chose not to do so.
The mountains that lie between the Bagradas and the
sea were hardly touched.   The shepherding natives
lived on there in their old customs.   So, too, did the
clans of the Aures, and a part of the proud old tribe
of Musulamii who lived in the mountains between
Sicca and Madauros.   Even near flourishing cities
whole tribes of natives who gladly took leases or work
from Romans and mingled peacefully with them kept
their ancient organization under their sheiks and clung

[18] For irrigation in this region see the third century inscription
of Lambasba (C. I. L. VIII, 18587) stating the hours during
which each person may use water.

to their customs and religion even as they now do at the side of French colonies. The Berber has a strange capacity for resisting the ways of European culture while profiting from them, and a change of garb does not imply a change in his nomad blood.

Rome's penetration and "development" of Africa was, as elsewhere, slow, and it was firm only in demanding that some semblance of responsible government must exist everywhere. But considering that she had no colonizers to spare from Italy and that the Numidians were as they were, her methods were strikingly successful. The ruins of the splendid public buildings of cities like Thugga, Sufetula, Thysdrus, Thamugadi, Cillium, Madauros, and the rest, which now rise out of juniper brush and alfa grass, testify that Rome's occupation had been very different from that of Carthage. And those cities were clean, well drained and abundantly supplied with cisterns. The Romans had the capacity to find what the soil could yield in every peculiar valley and the enterprise to make the yield full. The fact that, though no direct efforts at Romanizing were made, and though the Romans in this vast area were relatively few in number, Africa in the third century produced the most vigorous portion of Rome's literature, suggests that Rome had not pursued the wrong course. In one respect, however, Rome failed. The Numidians were a religious people and the exacting Punic religion had met their needs. The Roman imperial cult, on the other hand, did not take root, and although the Romans generously erected temples to Punic gods—though under Roman names—merely forbidding human sacrifice, this syncretism left the Numidians cold. Later Christianity fully satisfied their needs and swept Africa more rapidly and more thoroughly than any province. It might have completed the work of Romanization but unfortunately two forms of faith divided the province and it was the heretical form that gained the adherance of the less civilized Numidians who stood most in need of the unifying influence of the state religion. We shall revert to Africa and its fall later, and shall then see that the final catastrophy was not due to Rome's policy of laissez-faire, which after all accomplished more than compulsion could have done.

Africa continued to produce chiefly raw materials, and most of these were consumed at home. Neither the natives nor their masters—Carthaginians and Romans—developed any crafts or arts here worthy of mention. The ubiquitous floor mosaics of which they were very proud, and which later provided some "arabesque" patterns to the Moors who developed a new school of designing in Spain, are generally childish in conception and execution. The products of the soil were limited by the vagaries of African climate. Vines do well here and there in the north, but south of Zaghouan only if irrigated, and there are very few springs in that region that do not run dry in summer. Wheat is also a precarious crop south of Zaghouan, and even where, as in the plains of Carthage, it is brought to maturity by winter rains, the parched summers pro-

hibit the rotation of crops essential to long continued
wheat culture.   Further west the land is so uneven
that it suffers much from erosion when exposed by the
plow.   Hence the time was sure to come when the
province would yield less wheat than it had in the
prosperous days of Hadrian.   The olive, on the other
hand, which is capable of enduring long droughts, was
certain to increase in favor.   In the north it was introduced on hillsides where wheat gave up the contest;
in the high valleys about Sufetula it was able to tap
moist strata which annual plants could not reach, and
about Hadrumetum it was watered by the accumulations of the last spring rain carefully directed to the
roots so that it could endure the summer.[19]   At Sfax
though the annual precipitation is but 20 cm. the Arabs
who have learned the secrets of the climate readily
produce fifteen gallons of oil per tree.   The Carthaginians had learned some of these methods but it was
under the Romans that olive culture was first introduced on the inland steppes.   Other products[20] of the

[19] For adaptation of crops to climate in various parts of the
African province see *Am. Jour. Phil.* 1926, p. 55.

[20] Charlesworth, *Trade Routes*, for export. Figs, Pliny, *N. H.*
15, 69, a new kind then recently introduced into Africa and much
sought after in Rome; also lex Manciana, C. I. L. VIII, 25902;
Pliny describes a garden at the oasis of Gabes, *N. H.* 18, 188;
vegetables and grain grow between *vines*, these under pome-
granates, above which rise in turn *figs*, *olive trees*, and *date palms;*
there is but slight exaggeration. Dyes, *N. H.* 30, 45 and 5, 12;
fish, Strabo 17, 3, 17, Pliny, *N. H.* 31, 94; marble, the inscriptions
of Simitthu. A Roman inscription records an association of
merchants who import African grain and oils C. I. L.VI, 1620.

province were figs, dates from the oases, wool, dyes, fish, some valuable wood for cabinet-makers, ivory, and the excellent Numidian marble of Simitthu. But exports were not very important. The growing population of the cities absorbed most of the produce. Rome drew ten million bushels of wheat from the province for her own use in Nero's day, and this amount probably continued to be supplied into the third century. Since north Africa to-day produces about fifteen times that amount of cereals with agriculture less well developed, the drain on the province could not have been heavy, and it must be remembered that a considerable portion of the wheat came not from the tribute but from the rental of imperial estates.

Roman Spain is still an enigma, for relatively few of the ancient sites have been excavated. For some reason the Spanish cities, with the exception of a few built by Rome, did not take on the display that one finds in Roman Africa, nor on the other hand did splendid country villas spring up as in Gaul. Yet we know that in the south and east there were very productive centers of cultivation, many populous cities and a vigorous commerce, and that even the less productive central plateau prospered. Baetica was Romanized as quickly as Narbonese Gaul and before Africa, and seems to have suffered less from imperial confiscations than either of these; in fact, like these two provinces, Baetica was, for several reigns, spared the imperial cult, being considered too civilized for its imposition; and even throughout the rest of Spain

Latin rights were granted by Vespasian at a time when Africa and central Gaul were far from ready for them. The mystery deepens when we consider that while Spain had an honorable share in Rome's literature long before Gaul and Africa, she ceased contributing to it by the time that the two latter became the centers of literary production.

As to Spain's prosperity, especially in the South, there can be no question. No province is so highly praised on this count as Spain is by Pliny, Mela, and Martial, who knew the province well. Monte Testaccio,[21] near Rome's ancient docks is a mound of fragments of the amphorae in which Spanish products, chiefly wine, oil, and packed fish, had been carried to Rome. The heap is 150 feet high and half a mile in circumference. It is an effective proof of Spain's productivity, and when we note that all through the western provinces fragments have been found bearing identical markings we know that these same products went in large quantities as far as England, Holland and Germany. Vast herds[22] on the central plains sup-

[21] C. I. L. XV, pt. 2 with Dressel's introduction. The dated inscriptions come from about 140-225 A.D. but the center of the mound is doubtless a century older. Inscriptions from the imperial domains do not occur till the third century. Rostovtzeff's hypothesis (*Staatspacht*, p. 425; *Soc. Econ. Hist.* p. 533) that these jars brought goods chiefly from imperial lands has not been proved. On Spanish oil, Pl. 15, 1 and 17, 17, 31. Reid, *Rom. Munic.* has called attention to Cicero's reference to Cordovan oil in *Pro Arch.* 26.

[22] Production and commerce, McElderry in *Jour. Rom. Stud.* 1918, 94 ff.; Schulten, *Hispania* in Pauly-Wissowa. Wool,

plied wool which was spun for export in towns like
Cordova and Saguntum; the linen of the northern
regions—an old industry—was prepared in Saetabis,
Emporia, and Tarraco to please the connoisseurs of
Rome; the Spanish steel blades of Bilbilis and Toledo,
were prized as the best; the esparto grass from the
dry wastes was exported widely for ropes and mats;
Spanish horses and sheep were of thoroughbred stock;
the corporations of fisheries of the southern waters of
Spain, which bought their concession from the state,
produced the choicest "garum" that the Romans could
find.   Finally the mines[23] of iron, lead, copper, tin
silver, quicksilver and gold were still among the most
productive known to the ancient world.   The state still
owned the mines, but if we may judge from the regulations of the copper mines of Aljustral and from other
inscriptions, they were largely worked by Spanish contractors on a fifty per cent. basis and fed Spanish

---

Strabo, 3, 2, 6, Col. 7, 2; flax, Pliny, 19, 10 cf.   Catullus 12;
steel, Pliny, 24, 144-149; Hor. *Odes*, 1, 29; esparto (alfa) Pliny,
19, 30; horses, Pliny, 8, 166; fish and garum, Strabo, 3, 1, 8;
3, 2, 6; 7; 3, 4, 2; 3, 4, 6; Pliny, 31, 94 (a corporation of fish
packers).

[23] Lead, Besnier, in *Rev. Arch.* 1920, 211 ff., largely a by-product
of silver mines; much used for water pipes in the first century
in Italy; British lead, more easily mined, captured the market
in the second century; copper, Vipasco (Aljustral), see lex
metalli C. I. L. II, 5181, Pliny, 34, 4; tin, Strabo, 3, 2, 9; 3,
5, 11; Pliny, 34, 156; Spanish tin shipped as far as India, Pliny,
34, 163; *Periplus*, 7; silver, Strabo, 3, 2, 3; 3, 2, 10; Pliny, 33,
96; 34, 165; quicksilver, Pliny, 33, 118; Vitruv. 7, 9, 4; gold,
Tac. *Ann.* 6, 19, Pliny, 33, 66, 78 and 80.

industry. Such prosperity should have left more evidence of itself in art than we have as yet found. Possibly the remains that have come to light are not representative, but it may also be that we have over-estimated Spain's civilization because of the early appearance of Cordovan literature and because of the fact that Vespasian dared give Latin rights to the whole province.

It is a plausible conjecture that Vespasian's act was not so much a recognition of an advanced civilization as a necessary step toward creating a recruiting ground for legions after he had decided that Italy must be spared. Where was one to draw recruits for thirty legions outside of Italy? To be sure, it had not been customary heretofore to enroll *Latini* in legions, but one might begin, and we know that henceforth Spain supplied more legionaries than auxiliaries.[24] It seems very strange that Vespasian did not at the same time raise the old Latin colonies of Caesar's day to full citizenship. The grant of Latinitas implied that urban self-governing communities were formed with town charters like those of Italian cities, and fragments of two of these new charters have been found so that we know the usual custom was followed.[25] Whether the

[24] Most of the Spanish auxiliary cohorts seem to be of the first century, Cheesman, *The Auxilia*, p. 62; the lack of *tabulae* of dismissal granting citizenship to Spanish auxiliaries seems to indicate that citizenship was given to these *Latini* on enrollment, as McElderry suggests, *op. cit.* p. 82.

[25] Hardy, *Three Spanish Charters*.

process could have been logicaly carried out among
the mountain tribes of the northwest is very doubtful.
The custom of "attributing" rural and pastoral districts to urban centers must have been resorted to lib-
erally, and if some of the "towns" later vanished
perhaps no awkward questions were asked, provided
the chieftain of the tribe saw to it that the taxes were
paid. The fact that the Basque language is still spoken
in a wide area of northern Spain warns us not to be
oversure of Vespasian's conventionality.

We have said that there is little evidence of imperial
landed property in Spain. Julius Caesar during his
two campaigns in 49 and 45 B.C. had confiscated territories of communities that had aided his enemies, but
he had apparently used these in rewarding friendly
communities and in colonizing veterans and urban
freedmen; Augustus took territories from the Lusi-
tanians after his war with them, but used them for the
planting of colonies, chiefly of veterans; Tiberius confiscated the mines of Marius in the Sierra Morena, and
these mines, like those that Scipio had taken from Carthage, remained state property. Nero's confiscations
involved some Romans who had lands in Spain, but
Galba seems to have sold[26] these properties. It is probable that the imperial procurators had few agricultural

[26] Cicero in his list of Ager Publicus (*Lex. Agr.* II, 49-51)
mentions only the old Carthaginian property near Carthago
Nova; Galba's sale of Nero's property, Plut. *Galba*, 5. The
procurators mentioned in Baetica before the third century
(Hirschfeld, *Kl. Schr.* 570) were probably engaged on the state
mines. *Vita Severi* 12, 3 cum magnam partem agri per Gallias,
per Hispanias, per Italiam, imperatoriam fecisset.

estates to manage in this province before the time of
the Severi. These vengeful emperors, however, spread
havoc here as they did in Italy and Gaul; and from
their time we may count the beginning of the decadence
of Spain.

To sum up the little we know of conditions in Spain
during the period before the Severi we seem to find
that the south was so well civilized and so well exploited by the natives before Roman colonization began
that fewer Romans gained a foothold here than in
Africa or Asia. Presently, however, the civil wars
entailed some colonization, and Augustus settled many
of his veterans in Spain. For a while Roman influence
was strong and the descendants of early settlers entered into the political and artistic traditions of Rome
itself.[27] Then, to our surprise, this influence begins to
wane. Apparently the freedmen and the veterans
merged into the native stock instead of making cultural centers, and during the Empire new immigrants
from Rome were too few to stay the decline. To be
sure, the Latin language spread; self-interest in trade,
and the speech of returning Spanish veterans carried
it through; but even of the Spaniards who learned
Latin few delved beneath the surface; no classical
manuscripts except ecclesiastical ones survived in
Spain, and except for old cities like Emerita, Tarraco

[27] E. g. The Senecas, Lucan, Columella, Quintilian, the ancestors of Trajan and Hadrian. We cannot with certainty point
to a single person of Spanish stock that attained distinction at
Rome.

and Italica, which were partly built by Romans, few have any traces of distinguished public buildings, temples, and theatres. In this respect Spain is far inferior to Africa where more Romans had settled. Rome, though she unified the peoples and established peace which guaranteed great prosperity, penetrated no deeper beneath the surface of the Iberian civilization than had the Phoenicians, Greeks, and Carthaginians in their day. From each of these foreign peoples the Iberians borrowed crafts conducive to comfort and to material prosperity, but for the rest they passed on unscathed.

Narbonese Gaul became a land of abundance. The barbaric Celts beyond were learning to live in houses, to use southern table-ware, to drink wine, to spend money and to borrow more on mortgages. The old province soon learned that it was a profitable business to produce and purvey for this large market and to exploit its credits. Orchards and vineyards made good profits, for central Gaul was still supposed to be too cold for fruit culture. Large farmsteads sprang up all through Provence and the valleys of Savoy where these fruits would grow.[28] Potteries and foundries abounded in Auvergne supplying the new markets, and large trading cities like Narbo and Arelate grew rapidly. Narbo carried Mediterranean goods to Aquitania and the

[28] Lafaye, *Inventaire des Mosaiques de la Gaule;* Pottery: Gummerus, in Pauly-Wissowa, IX, 1488. Hermet, *Les Graffites de la Graufesenque*, 1923; for potters near Metz, *C. R. Acad. Inscr.* 1924, 67.

western coast and Arelate took the place of Marseilles
as the harbor of the Rhone river traffic.[29] Narbo, being an older town and having a well-established clien-
tele, grew to be the larger city at first, but Arles soon
profited by its superior advantages and leaped ahead.
Arles in fact attracted many clever freedmen traders
and bankers, used Celtic workmen on the river traffic,
and also drew upon Marseilles' business men who were
experienced in the Celtic trade. It became a busy, rich,
ugly, polyglot harbor town, the distinguishing building
of which was then, as it is to-day, an enormous amphi-
theatre.   Agrarian towns like Nemausus (Nimes),
Arausio (Orange) and Vienna prospered also but they
advanced with more dignity and took time to build for
the future. The Maison Carrée of Nimes is one of
the most pleasing temples of the Roman world, the
Pont du Gard which carried Nimes' aqueduct is splendidly impressive still, and the theatre at Orange remains one of the largest of the west.

The history of Celtic Gaul[30] makes strange reading
for those who are seeking paternalism and the mis-
sionary spirit in Rome's government. In Gaul, at any
rate, one can hardly speak of "civilizing, urbanizing,
and Romanizing policies." It is probable that more
Gauls lived in urban or village groups before Caesar's

[29] Constans, *Arles Antique*, 1921: the canal which Marius had
dug along the lower course of the Rhone was apparently widened
so that large vessels could go up as far as Arles.

[30] Jullian, *Histoire de la Gaule*, IV-VI; Cumont, *Comment la
Belgique fut Romanisée;* Rostovtzeff, *Econ. and Soc. Hist.* Ch.
VI; Reid, *Municipalities*, p. 177 ff.

conquest than a century and a half later, for the Celts were naturally clannish and liked community life. But Caesar stormed and destroyed many of the larger *oppida,* and the few market towns which he organized in their place did not by any means restore old conditions, nor did the emperors urge the building of cities in Gaul. The Romans still believed that landlords did well to live on their farms as they had in the days of Cincinnatus. Augustus recognized the cantonal organizations for purposes of government and did not require an urban machinery. So far as he was concerned, the elders of the tribe could, if they chose, meet and pass their ordinances in any grove or roadside provided they saw to it that the tribal assessments were paid. And later, when Latin or citizen rights were bestowed upon the members of a tribe, no effort was made to fix an urban center for the "municipality." Nevertheless, one is surprised to find that the Gauls were so tardy in aggregating. The reason may be that the Gallic landlords who, as a ruling aristocracy had needed communal life in the days of political importance, now centered all their interests on their estates and their favorite sport of hunting, and hence preferred to live on their farms with their stables and their tenants.

Fustel de Coulanges[31] long ago pointed out that Gaul

[31] *L'Alleu et le Domaine rural* (1899), p. 42; Grenier, Art, *Villa* in Darem.-Saglio; *Habitations Gauloises*, 1906; Koepp, *Die Römer in Deutschland* for the Rhinelands. Since Galba punished the Treveri by taking some of their lands (Tac. *Hist.* 1, 8 and 53) and a hundred of their elders soon after escaped to Germany

in the Roman Empire became a land of manor houses, not of cities, and he held with some exaggeration that nine-tenths of the modern towns of Gaul bear the names of Gallo-Roman farms, not of early villages. The fact is significant, and excavations of villa sites since his day have proved him not far from correct. Grenier, who has described many of those ruins of manor-houses, reports fifty-three near Metz in an area of ten km. square, some so large as to cover two acres of ground. They are equally numerous near Rouen and in the country of the Allobroges. North of Metz near the Rhine they occur with a peculiar regularity about two miles apart, signifying perhaps a bestowal of confiscated lands upon friendly nobles along the frontier. In no part are they wholly lacking, while in certain prosperous portions they reach a very striking magnificence. One at Chiragan above Toulouse covers an area of six acres with its stables, store rooms, work shops, baths, and pavilions. Such villas grew, like those we know from medieval times, to be self-suf-ficing communities with houses for the tenants as well as the slaves, even providing at times a temple, a school and a theatre for the community. They became cen-ters of culture, and the fact that classical literature had a more vigorous life in Gaul than elsewhere in the west during the fourth century was due to the interest which these grandees took in their libraries. We hear not a

---

(*ibid.* 5, 19) it is likely that Roman public lands must be assumed in this region. Such lands would probably be treated like the *Decumates* of the right bank (see Klio, 1924, 253).

little about large debts in Gaul through the first century. It has been suggested that the lords probably expanded beyond their immediate income in the early days of building and improving their farmsteads. Apparently they caught up later; the soil was rich and new, and contact with the south taught them to raise wine and fruits successfully, and commerce brought their grain, wool and stock to profitable markets. The incidental references[32] to enormous properties in the works of writers like Ausonius, Sidonius and Ammianus must have read like fairy tales to their contemporaries in Italy.

But agriculture, though the mainstay of Gaul, was not the only source of profit. Lugdunum (Lyons) became a distributing center for the goods that came up the Rhone and a depot for the produce which was to be exported, and its merchants soon gained control of the trade which passed in and out. By Hadrian's day Lyons had easily surpassed the cities of Provence. As the residence of the united governments it also became the home and resort of first importance in Gaul. The frontier posts, also with their camps of seven or eight legions and numerous auxiliaries, started a lively current of trade along and to the Rhine. Gaul was allowed to supply the arms and armor, the horses, the food, and the clothing for these camps. That these items were not small we can infer from the fact that when the state later took the armories in hand we find factories at Amiens, Soissons, Rheims, Treves, Mâcon

[32] Dill, *Roman Society in the Last Century.*

and Strasbourg. And it was not only the soldiers who needed supplies. By the second century the legions had become more and more stationary, the soldiers frequently married and towns grew up outside the camps to house their families as well as the traders and camp followers. The new commerce that arose in this way along the frontier is well reflected in the inscriptions and ruins of Treves[33] which became the chief distributing center when Lyons was burned. Here and in nearby towns like Noviomagus we find a strange group of pretentious tombstones belonging to parvenu tradespeople, Germans, eastern freedmen, Celts, Romans, and provincials who had found such success in their commerce that they needs must display on their tombstones the evidence of their prosperity: river barges full of wine-barrels, shelves loaded with bolts of cloth, wagons of fruit, money bags, account books and counters heaped with coins. Verily Gaul was prosperous.

In the East we find a great diversity of conditions during the early Empire. Greece had long been a waste land. Polybius[34] speaks feelingly of the rapid decrease in the population there during the second century B.C. The land was exhausted from long intensive cultivation

---

[33] C. I. L. XIII, 3633 ff.; Espérandieu, *Recueil de la Gaule*, vol. VI, Drexel, *Röm. Mitt.* 1920, 83 ff. (not accepted by Rostovtzeff, *Soc. and Econ. Hist.* p. 534, n. 26). The persons commemorated on the famous monument at Igel seem to be eastern freedmen to judge by the Ganymede symbolism so popular in Syria (Cumont, *After Life*, p. 159).

[34] Polybius, 37, 9.

and from the erosion of the steep hillsides, trade had gone eastward with Alexander's conquests and westward with Rome's rise to power, the richer lands had bought the slaves that Greeks had used in industry and agriculture, and with the increase of poverty, celibacy and the exposure of children became prevalent. The decline continued steadily, as Strabo indicates.[35] Arcadia had reverted to pasturage in his day, and most of the cities of the Peloponnese were in ruins; only Corinth, colonized by freedmen as a commercial city, was in a flourishing condition. Incidental references in the works of Dio of Prusa, Plutarch, Pausanias and Apuleius show that conditions did not improve during the Empire. Athens kept a fairly prosperous look because of the charitable gifts of emperors and courtiers, who received ugly commemorative statues in return for public buildings, and also to some extent because of tourist and student expenditures, but the old trade and industries of Athens were gone. A few shrewd men throughout Greece had taken advantage of the decay of agriculture and had accumulated deserted land for pasturage and for olive groves. Some of these gained wealth. But the dwindling of the public benefactions, which had so frequently been mentioned in the inscriptions of the third century B.C., and the relative scarcity of imperial estates, which so often grew up where there was prosperity, show that Greece was not recovering. Plutarch was doubtless exaggerating when he reported that the whole of Greece could

[35] Strabo, 8, 8, 1-2 and 8, 6, 23.

not have mustered a regiment of 3,000 hoplites in his day, but even after large deductions have been made the statement is still significant.

Asia was somewhat more fortunate. During the first two centuries of the Empire Rome gradually brought the principalities as far as Armenia under her direct government, and as the boundaries moved eastward the military roads were extended with them. The northern road[36] from Nicodemia to Ancyra was pushed on to Melitene with a branch to Nicopolis, and branch roads were sent off into central Cappadocia and north to the Black Sea. Similarly several branches were built from the Ephesus-Syria road both southward into Cilicia and northward into Cappadocia. The Flavian emperors, Trajan and Severus, are most frequently mentioned on the milestones of these routes. All this activity resulted in not a few economic changes. Internal trade benefited, and since the climate of the various villages and highlands varies greatly crop failures were usually limited in area and their disastrous effects could be obviated by good communications; furthermore, industries in several of the cities could draw raw material from a larger area. From various inscriptions[37] we learn that the garment, tapestry, and dyeing industries mentioned by Strabo as prosperous in old Asiatic cities like Laodicea, Philadelphia, and Thyatira continued to do well. The popu-

[36] Charlesworth, *Trade Routes*, 82; Anderson, *Jour. Hell. Stud.* 19, 52 ff.

[37] C. I. L. III under these cities.

lation shifted somewhat with the road building. Some of the old cities fell into decay, not because Anatolia was suffering economically, but because the new routes attracted folk to more favorable situations. Many villages gained a large enough population to win municipal privileges. This was not due to the fact that the Roman government especially favored the growth of large cities (indeed the emperors seem to have preferred the auxiliary soldiers of the rural villages to the urban folk of Hellenized cities) but to the fact that the opening of easy communications naturally resulted in aggregation. However, even this readjustment must not be overemphasized. The village folk of central Anatolia seem to have liked the freedom of their old open-air life, and leisurely agriculture and grazing continued as before. Foreign commerce did not greatly expand. The ports of Ephesus, Tarsus, Cyzicus, Nicomedia, and Sinope all benefited by the extension of Roman territory, and traders from these towns are mentioned on inscriptions found far and wide, but such traders had to deal with moderate quantities. Nowhere in Asia do we hear of capitalistic production on a large scale. The excavations[38] have revealed rather magnificent Roman public buildings at Ephesus. Some evidence of prosperity at Sardis, even after the disastrous earthquake of 17 A.D., and in many cities baths, porticoes and aqueducts date from this period. Pliny's letters,[39] however, reveal the fact that an unwholesome

[38] Reisch, *Ephesus*, vols. II and III; Butler, *Sardis*, I, p. 31.
[39] Pliny, *Letters*, Bk. X.

rivalry between the cities led them to build quite beyond their means upon borrowed money, and one must
not gauge their prosperity by the extent of foundations
that sometimes received no adequate superstructure.

The economic conditions of the various strata of
society in Asia Minor cannot as yet be clearly defined.
Here and there we hear of very wealthy landowners
and these were not only Romans but Greeks and
natives.   It is wholly probable that throughout the
country the old Attalid fiefs had devolved into large
latifundia upon which the rural village folk served as
free tenants for wealthy stipend-paying landlords.
Many of the cities certainly had villages attached to
them as before, a system which Rome could well countenance since she employed the custom in the Alps, in
Gaul, and in Spain of "attributing" villages to cities
in order to ease the work of the central government.
But it is also apparent from Dio of Prusa that the inhabitants of such villages clamored for full rights as
citizens of their respective cities.   It did not greatly
concern Rome whether or not these rights were
granted.   On the imperial estates the old villagers were
treated according to the customs of the country and
considered life tenants, if as they seem to be, the inscriptions found near Philadelphia are typical.[40]   There
in the days of Septimius several groups, in remonstrat-
ing against the lawlessness of soldiers, not only speak
of themselves as born on the estate, but say that their
ancestors had also been tenants there.   At that time

[40] Keil und Premerstein, *Dritte Reise*, 1914, Nos 9, 28, 55.

there is no evidence of anything resembling serfdom on those estates, but our evidence is scanty.

There is another group of natives, or rather several diverse groups, that present a peculiar problem. Very many of the temples had had large fields attached to them which had been worked by *hieroduli;* i. e., sacred slaves or serfs. The temple of Comana[41] in Cappadocia, and of Comana in Pontus, for instance, each had about 6,000 hieroduli in Strabo's time. Some of these people were temple slaves and some were temple courtesans who were also probably slaves. But the men who worked the lands are doubtless to be considered serfs. When Rome set up her own government over such estates in Pontus and Cappadocia and appointed the priest, the Roman governor had to decide the status of these serfs, and Roman law had no place for serfs. What happened in such instances we do not know, but probably not the same thing in all instances. If the custom of the country was accepted Rome would recognize a quasi-serfdom, as we know she did everywhere in the fourth century. In Pontican Comana, however, the hieroduli may have been classified as free tenants, for a municipality later appears here. In other instances the hieroduli were probably classified as slaves. In Amyntas' temple-estates near Antioch of Pisidia Strabo[42] says that the governor abolished the old order, and since we know that the people of this

[41] Strabo 12, 23, 16 and 3, 34.

[42] Strabo, 12, 8, 14; Cf. Ramsay, *Studies in Galatia* J. R. S. 1918.

region later attained to citizenship in Antioch, it is likely that he disregarded the servile condition of the hieroduli (Strabo so calls them) and classed them as free tenants of the temple-farm which was converted— apparently at once—into an imperial estate. But our knowledge of how far, or rather how soon, Rome adopted serfdom in Anatolia cannot as yet be decided. And the problem is not settled by generalizing from one or two vague instances.[43]   It is not impossible, however, that Asiatic custom had something to do with establishing a precedent for the later widespread custom of adscribing tenants to the soil.

[43] There is a brilliant discussion of the problem in Rostovtzeff, *Röm. Kol.* 300 ff. but his conclusions seem to go far beyond what the evidence justifies.

For commerce in the neighboring province of Syria see West, *Commercial Syria under the Roman Empire*, Am. Phil. Ass. 1924, 159-189; and Charlesworth, *Traderoutes*, 2nd ed.

CHAPTER XXII

Beginnings of Serfdom

The student of the political history of Rome who surveys the reigns of the five "good" emperors will probably gain the impression that conditions under them were satisfactory. If, however, he penetrates deeply into the cultural history of the time he learns that this impression is incorrect. Roman literature, for instance, came to an end with Tacitus and Juvenal. There is not one Latin poem or essay of even fifth rate quality in the century that follows, not one penetrating work of criticism or philosophy, not one good original narrative in prose or verse. There is not even any learned work of value. Mental vitality and the creative faculty seem to have disappeared. This is a fact of first rate significance, for we cannot point to any period of history where such mental torpor continued through a long period of sound social and economic conditions. Hypotheses which blame the disasters of the later Empire entirely upon the political anarchy of the third century and the inability to stem the foreign invasions that followed are, therefore, inadequate. It would seem more likely that these disasters were the effects of an incapacity which was already betraying grave symptoms in the second century, and that these symptoms rose out of a growing disease which has

perhaps been insufficiently diagnosed. Not only literature was in decadence, all the arts were rapidly declin-
ing. The Marcus column and the triumphal arch of
Septimius are decorated by sculptors who failed in
composition as well as in technique; the later decorative paintings of Ostia are puerile in subject and
execution, and when we come to the middle of the
third century the sculpture is not even fair stone-
cutter's work. Rome's religious life also was bankrupt. Oriental cults flourished everywhere and the
Roman gods remained in evidence only in some official
inscriptions or where their names merely served to
cover non-Roman connotations.

In political administration, self-government was
failing everywhere. Trajan had to send out personal
representatives to the provinces to check the accounts,
to correct abuses, and to give advice to the local governments, while Hadrian extended the system of "cor-
rectors" to the cities of Italy itself. In jurisprudence
there still seems to have been some vitality left, for
the task of adapting and interpreting the old legal
principles to an evergrowing citizenry in the provinces
called for able minds. But it is noteworthy that the
very jurists who attempted this task were the ones
who began to lay the basis in the Roman code for
imperial despotism. Evidently they no longer had any
faith in the capacity of the people to think soundly or
govern wisely.

In surveying the third century we shall have to speak
of failing agriculture, of a breakdown of the machinery

of production and distribution, of debasement of the currency, of oppressive taxation, and of all the economic evils that accompanied civil and external wars, but in doing so it is well to bear in mind that the Romans entered upon this period of distress already incapacitated. In the third century there was little evidence in the people of the old-time vigor, the spirit of independence and self-reliance, the capacity to meet new situations, the mental alertness, the refusal to accept defeat that once had characterized the Romans. The barbaric invaders that the emperors had to meet were no stronger than those defeated by Curius, Scipio, and Marius; the legitimate drain upon Rome's resources was less than that willingly sustained in the wars with Hamilcar and Hannibal; and it is hardly probable that the agrarian troubles of this period would have baffled farmers like Cato. The conditions in fact were no worse, but the Empire did not have the same men with whom to work out its salvation.

Without repeating at length what has been said before,[1] we may suggest again, however, that the economic decline of the Empire can hardly be understood without reference to the fact that the old stock that had made Rome what it was no longer existed. The extended wars of the republic had cost heavily in men; the new opportunities offered in Africa, Spain, Gaul,

---

[1] See Chapter XII; *American Hist. Rev.* 1916, 689 (criticized by Miss Gordon, in *Jour. Rom. St.* 1924); Park, *The Plebs in Cicero's Day;* Nilsson, *Imperial Rome,* pp. 339 ff.; Seeck, *Gesch. d. Untergangs.* vol. I.

and Asia had scattered many Italians to the four
winds; tyranny had struck down many of the leading
men, forced others to migrate, and discouraged the
rearing of families. Into the center to take the place
of all these had been brought slaves in great hordes,
and the children of these strangers were now the
dominant element in and about the ruling city. It is
possible that these new citizens might in time have
proved the equals of the stock they had displaced, for
mixed races have more than once developed strong
nations. However, a long time was needed for an
effective amalgamation of such diverse elements, especially of a slave stock which entered the citizen-body
under a burden of antipathies and social disadvantages.
It would have required more centuries than were available to breed through wide areas the community of
interests, the national pride, the social sympathies that
make for national solidarity. When the emperor himself wrote out his egalitarian doctrine for this confused
population he wrote in Greek. The substance and the
language of his book are the best commentary on the
utter wreck of Roman culture. Rome still seemed
prosperous to the casual observer but it was a thin
prosperity lasting on through peaceful times without
creating surplus resources for future contingencies.

As we have seen, however, conditions were not the
same throughout the Empire. In Italy there are signs
that the agrarian communities were not prospering.
Vespasian's decision to cease recruiting in Italy, Domitian's effort to encourage cereal culture, Trajan's rural

credits, charities, and colonization in Italy,[2] Hadrian's
supervision of municipal administration in Italy may
only point to mistaken ideas of how to keep the center
of the Empire strong against future crises—a purpose
in itself wholly commendable. But they seem to indicate that decay was actually apparent to the eye.
Paternalism was seldom so common in Roman administration as to run ahead of needs. Italy's soil had been
intensively cultivated for a very long time, and though
many parts had had periods of rest and recuperation,
various areas must have been sadly over-cropped and
were doubtless demanding ever longer periods of rest.
The tenant system also was spreading in the second
century, as the casual remarks of the jurists prove,
and the tenants of absent landlords are notoriously
merciless with land.

Industry had drifted away from capitalistic enterprise with the decrease of slaves and the advance of
provincial production. Socially this was not a disadvantage to Italy, for the class of free (or rather freedmen) shopkeepers and producers increased in Italy as
elsewhere. We must recognize the fact, however, that
serviceable accumulations of capital which might have
proved of value to the government at critical moments
were thus dispersed.

We must also note that the government was expanding its obligations far more widely than before and
raising its tax assessments accordingly. Under Nerva
and Trajan a very large sum (perhaps a hundred

[2] Pais, *Storia d. Colon.* pp. 36; 181; 234; 242.

million dollars) went to Italian charities. From Vespasian's day to Hadrian's very much road building was undertaken[3] in Spain, Africa, Gaul, the Danube country, Anatolia and Syria, and the government was also aiding cities with public buildings as never before. Lavish sums were of course expended in capitals like Rome, Athens, and Carthage, but this was not enough. Hadrian's biographer states that there was hardly a city of the Empire which was not beautified by the great traveller, and excavations throughout all the provinces have proved this statement true. The civil service bureaus were also becoming very costly. Whereas in Augustus' day, senators and knights served in the provinces without salaries and the emperors' own freedmen kept the fiscal offices, now an increasingly large group of knights, drawing salaries of from 100,000 to 300,000 sesterces, were on the government payroll. All this made for efficiency, but the budget grew enormously and the taxes were heavy. There was as yet little complaint, but when the invasions and civil wars of the next century came there was no surplus and no margin for the new taxes that were necessary. And surpluses were especially needed in that day when a government could not acquire funds at critical moments by the issue of bonds, and there were no very wealthy individuals from whom the state could borrow.

[3] Besnier and Chapot, art. *Via* in Darem.-Saglio; brief summary of Hadrian's building activities in Gregorovius, *The Emp. Hadrian*, Ch. 22-5; Weber, *Untersuchungen, passim.*

In the provinces the situation was diverse. Gaul fared well, though it objected now and then to the burden of taxes. Spain, on the whole, had found a dead level of contentment: the center and north built few cities, quite satisfied with their old, semi-barbaric life of shepherding and meager farming, though complaining at times of too frequent army levies; the south sent large supplies to Rome in tribute. Africa was prosperous, building cities and rapidly enlarging its area of cultivated land, but we must admit that the generosity of Severus to his native country accounts for much of the apparent prosperity. Asia was entering into her inheritance of a widened Empire, and Syria was profiting from commerce with the ports of Mesopotamia and Arabia that had been annexed. Egypt, however, was apparently less flourishing than before. It is true that the Nile flood constantly fertilized a large part of Egypt so that the soil continued to bear well, but this by no means brought prosperity to the whole province. The Ptolemies and Augustus had opened for agriculture a wide strip of land beyond the flooded area by extending the canals into them and keeping these canals cleared. Such land could bear two crops per year if it was well irrigated by hand at the beginning of the Nile's rise and again before the flood fell; since such land bore two crops annually the state was apt to levy a heavier tax upon it[4] despite the

[4] Westermann, *The Uninundated Lands*, Class. Phil. 1921, 169. At present the dams preserve a rather constant level in the canals which ensures three crops per year over a large area with the result that the fields get even less silt while producing more than ever. An agrarian crisis is inevitable.

extra labor required for its cultivation. This was quite reasonable, for the owner had time between crops to work at irrigation. But there were natural limits to such intensive cultivation: the canals, for instance, needed constant cleaning and repairs—which they did not always get—and the water which stood in the canals for some time before being lifted retained but little of its fertilizing silt. Hence, eventually, the lands which were exploited for double crops were precisely the lands that were receiving least fertilization and were constantly deteriorating. It is primarily for this reason, I think, that we hear so many complaints about unusable land and exorbitant taxes in Egypt in the second and third centuries.[5]

After Marcus Aurelius begins the period of misrule and civil wars that shattered the whole economic structure of the Empire. The despotic spendthrift, Commodus (180-192), wasted the resources and undermined the morale of the nation. After his death and a few months of civil war Septimius Severus (193-211), the African, usurped the power, spending more than half of his reign in destroying his rivals and

[5] Rostovtzeff, *Soc. and Econ. History*, Ch. XI, with notes, has collected most of the references in the papyri to the distressing conditions in Egypt. The complaints naturally became the more numerous when local magistrates become responsible for the gathering of the taxes; but we also hear of relief measures like those of Hadrian, *Rev. Ét. Grec.* 1920, 375; Westermann, in *Jour. Eg. Arch.* 1925; and the vigorous bidding for the lease of public lands which is in evidence in almost all the collections that have come out (e. g. Van Hoesen and Johnson in *Am. Phil. Ass.* 1925, 213) indicates that conditions were not utterly unendurable.

opponents. The confiscations in Italy, Spain, Gaul, and Asia brought vast areas into the imperial domain. In these expropriations the leading men of many of the provincial cities fell, and a large part of the resources which formerly supported the cities now went directly to Rome to pay for the tyrant's petted armies, courtiers, and spies. Only Africa, his native province, and Syria, that of his wife, Julia Domna, were to some degree spared, and in these provinces several friendly cities were granted the Jus Italicum with immunity from taxes, which, of course, laid a heavier burden upon the rest. Caracalla (211-17), their vicious son, and Elagabalus (218-222), a great-nephew of Julia, who had been a priest of Baal in Syria, continued to disgrace the government, which the weak rule of Alexander Severus who succeeded them could not restore to respectability.

There followed fifty years (235-285) of anarchy and successive usurpations, a period of almost constant civil wars, and consequently of foreign invasions, for the Persians and German tribes seized the opportunity to invade and plunder. Northern Gaul, the Balkans, and Syria were devastated.[6] During this period twenty-six men, mostly barbarians—Illyrians, Dalmatians, even the Arab sheik, Philip, and his son—reached the throne, while a larger number attempted to do so

[6] Rostovtzeff has brilliantly told the story of this period in his ninth and tenth chapters. His view however that a certain social policy directed the action of the armies seems to be unproved.

and failed. Each usurper in turn found the treasury empty and an army demanding bribes for support. To obtain the necessary funds they resorted to debasement of the currency, forced capital levies, proscriptions of the well-to-do with confiscations, and when these did not suffice they had to allow their troops to plunder. These internal contests were not by policy a warfare of poor against rich, of peasants against cities, of provincials against Italians, of despots against the cowardly and humiliated senate, or of barbarism against culture; but, as happens when authority has broken down, the unscrupulous appeared on the scene at once, and wealth, especially accessible wealth accumulated in cities, suffered first and most constantly. By the time that exhaustion came so that Diocletian was permitted to restore some semblance of order the economic structures of the Empire lay in fragments.

The severest drain upon the imperial resources was probably caused by the foreign invasions already mentioned. We may well doubt whether these would have taxed the capacities of a Caesar or a Trajan, and they certainly found unusual encouragement in the defenselessness of the frontiers at times when the Roman armies were engaged in fighting each other. Nevertheless eastern and central Europe were at this time feeling the stress of vast folk movements due to pressure in the rear and the Roman frontiers would, in any case, have felt the strain. It was in the third century that the Gothic tribes began to move westward from southern Russia, and the strong Frankish nation was being

formed out of various Germanic tribes north of the
Rhine. Caracalla had to defend the Raetic frontier
against the Germans 'n 213. Twenty-two years later
Maximin was compelled to defend the Rhine from the
same tribes. About 258 they permanently occupied
the Agri Decumates, and also the mountain passes of
northern Italy, thus exposing the peninsula to future
raiders. At the same time the Franks overran Gaul
and a part of Spain before they were driven back by
the Gallic forces of Postumus.

On the Danube and the Black Sea the Goths caused
fully as much disaster. They menaced the Balkan
provinces continually after their first successful raid
in 228, and the incursions of their Black Sea fleet into
Asia Minor or Greece in 256, 258, 263, 264, 265, 267
and again repeatedly between 270 and 284, entailed
not only much loss of property but necessitated a dangerous distribution of troops for guard duty. And
finally this was also the period when the ambitious
Sassanid dynasty of Persia mastered the Parthians
and began to menace the Empire. Fortunately Palmyra
had grown strong enough under Roman protection to
serve at times as a successful buffer state, but Palmyra
itself grew over-strong and had to be subdued at great
cost.

It is difficult to place these destructive wars in their
proper perspective in an economic history, especially
since we have no reliable statistics regarding the
forces involved or the methods used to pay the costs.
Property losses in the raids through Gaul, the Bal-

kans and in Asia Minor were serious enough to the provincials, but were eventually repaired when the Rhine and Danube frontiers were restored. The permanent loss of the Agri Decumates and of Dacia did not seriously impair the imperial treasury. The losses in soldiers were probably less severe than that entailed by the civil wars of the same time. But the incessant taxation required to pay for the mercenary troops enrolled and to feed, clothe, and arm the troops, must be reckoned as one of the chief factors in the destruction of imperial resources. Had it been possible to spread the costs of such sudden wars over a period of years, as is now done by means of national loans, the consequences need not have been so serious. Under the circumstances, however, the whole cost of each year's misfortune had to be drawn out of the taxpayer during that year, and in many cases the taxpayer's resources were drained beyond the limits of recovery. The historian who asserts that the invasions and civil wars of the third century ruined the Empire is not far from the truth. However, he must not insist that these were primary causes. The fact that Zenobia of Palmyra alone was capable of holding back the Persian hordes and that Postumus with the resources of Gaul at his command could successfully protect the Rhine shows that small forces efficiently used might have saved the Empire.

It will be necessary to illustrate in some detail what happened to the currency,[7] to taxation, and to agricul-

[7] Mattingly, *Coins of the Roman Empire;* Hammer, in *Zeit.*

ture during this period. Augustus had established a carefully planned currency system, issuing the gold *aureus* at one-fortieth of a Roman pound (worth about $5.40 in our gold), and the silver denarius at a ratio of $12\frac{1}{2}$:1. The aureus exchanged for twenty-five denarii. Nero reduced the aureus to one forty-fifth of a pound and alloyed the silver piece about one-tenth. This was the beginning of debasement, but we must hasten to add that the reduction probably represents an actual appreciation in the value of the precious metals due to an observed diminution of the supply. At any rate it was Pliny, a contemporary of Nero, who first mentions that much gold was being lost to the Empire in Indian trade. The denarii of Trajan (at least the later ones) and of his three successors show about twenty per cent. of copper alloy, while the aureus remained stable. However, this gradual reduction of a second ten per cent. in the value of the subsidiary coin probably caused no noticeable flurry in the market, though it is apparent that business was not ready to accept fiat money and that in the Forum the denarius sank in time to its actual value. The necessary readjustments were not difficult to make in the market since the aureus continued in circulation as a standard of values. Thereafter, as we learn from the jurists, the denarius constantly fell to its true value with refer-

---

Numis. 1908, 1 (on the amount of alloy); Cesano, in *Diz. Epig.* II, 1634 ff.; Segré, *Circolazione Monetaria;* Maurice, *Numismatique Constant.*, and Bernhart, *Münzkunde*, 1922 (for bibliography).

ence to gold as reduction continued. For instance, when Gaius,[8] about 175 A.D. (the denarius was then seven-tenths silver) had placed a certain fine at 10,000 sesterces, Ulpian, writing some fifty years later, reckoned the amount at fifty aurii; and conversely, when Gaius had mentioned a hundred aurii as the amount of a fine, Paulus, writing when the denarius had only about ten per cent. of silver, equated the sum with 100,000 sesterces. If the jurists thus recognized the actual copper content of these coins we must assume that the bankers also did. The market, therefore, had to adjust itself, but there is no reason to assume that up to the time of Caracalla there was any sudden shock comparable to that sustained by European exchanges after the great war.

Caracalla reduced the aureus from one forty-fifth to one fiftieth of a pound, and since the denarius was losing its standing he issued a new silver coin, which has variously been called the "Antonianus" and the "double denarius," but this also had fifty per cent. of copper alloy. When, soon after this, civil wars brought on a monetary stringency the process of debasement became more rapid, for each new usurper began his reign with an empty purse and baskets full of obligations. During the fifty years of anarchy the silver coin gradually dropped from a silver content of fifty per cent. to one of under five per cent. Thus the coin after fifty years fell to less than a tenth of the value it had had in Caracalla's mintage. But even thus

[8] See *Vocab. jurisp.*, s. v. *aureus*.

the depreciation was but slightly more than that in some European countries after the great war, where business has, nevertheless, succeeded in weathering the storm. Rome had an advantage over modern nations in that there were then no national or corporation bonds subject to constant depreciation, and the gold aureus, though seldom seen, was legally in circulation as a standard to which contracts could be adjusted. Even Diocletian in his famous edict recognized the actual value of the debased silver (or pretended to), so that he quotes its price in terms of a pound of gold. We may assume, therefore, that every new issue of washed denarii gradually found its true place in the market without serious consequences, even though the state sometimes had to resort to compulsion to stop speculation in the exchange.[9]

Diocletian and Constantine were able to stabilize the currency temporarily by issuing a gold aureus (solidus) of one seventy-second of a pound, bringing out also the old Neronian denarius in silver (ninetenths pure) and legalizing the circulation of small coppers in sealed bags (folles) worth about nine solidi. Since the ratios of the three metals now stood about 1:18: about 1,800 (i. e., copper: silver, about 1:100), we find that gold had appreciated somewhat, but Diocletian's list of market prices proves that it was still useful as a standard of values. However, there is little evidence at this time of capitalistic enterprise,

[9] Dittenberger, *Or. Gr. Ins.* 515 (reign of Septimius); *Ox. Pap.* 1411 (about 260 A.D.).

and as taxes were being gathered largely in kind, and even salaries were being paid in kind, we must assume that "natural economy" had largely returned, and that relatively little gold and silver were in circulation or called for. Our conclusion is that neither the lack of metals nor the debasement of the currency was a serious factor in the economic debacle before 250, but rather that the imperial currencies followed the road to degradation at about the same rate as the government and society in general, and that debasement was an effect rather than a cause of the wreckage. It is clear, however, that all permanent trust-funds of the earlier charitable institutions, such as the imperial *alimenta,* were practically valueless by the time of Constantine.

Taxes under Augustus had been reasonable and fairly well distributed, though Italy was free from direct taxation. The government of that day still received much unpaid service and spent little except for the task of keeping peace. During the Empire road building and the erection of public buildings increased; an expensive civil service bureau grew ever more costly, the army was augmented to about 400,000 men by the time of Severus, the pay of the men had been doubled, and the custom of giving lavish donations to the soldiers had become fixed. Taxes had increased accordingly. To be sure, the taxes on farm produce remained in most provinces at the ratios placed at the time of conquest. In this matter complaints from the provinces are largely to be attributed to the fact that the Romans instituted more meticulous collections, more careful surveys and more complete assessments than their predecessors, and also to the fact that reductions were difficult to secure when, because of over-cropping or erosion a piece of land became less productive than it formerly had been. It was in the cities that increases in taxation were more noticeable, because property, poll, occupation and sales taxes were constantly being devised and insistently imposed whenever the government needed more funds. In addition, there were irregular impositions. The so-called crown-gold[10] which was at first supposed to be a free gift from the citizens to the emperor at his inaugural, came to be regularly demanded in large fixed sums, and in the period of anarchy, when almost every year brought a new inauguration, this burden became distressing. No less distressing, especially in the border provinces, were the old customary demands of the government that passing officers and moving armies be housed and fed. It is probable that during the peaceful second century, this evil was no more noticeable than during the republic—for even Gaius Gracchus had called attention to the wrongs inherent in the system. But when the crises came during the reign of Septimius and after, when the regular commissary departments of impecunious emperors broke down, and soldiers were literally hungry on the march and took the law into their own hands, these *collationes* often amounted

[10] See *Oxyr. Pap.* nos. 1433, 1441, 1659, for instances of such exactions.

simply to pillaging and looting. The documents of Asia and Egypt[11] are particularly numerous on this point, and had the Danube region and Gaul been equally verbose at the time we should surely possess as many petitions for relief from these quarters also.

The subject of *munera*,[12] compulsory unpaid civil service, deserves some elaboration. The Greek and Roman governments, which began before the days of coinage and budgets, made much use of unpaid municipal service. The fiction that civil service was an honor which more than amply paid for the time and effort expended upon it was carried to such a point that upon election to a magistracy a man was happy to contribute a considerable sum out of his pocket for games or a public building. But during the Empire there were many tasks in any growing city which were onerous without bestowing any particular distinction. In the national civil service the emperors instituted salaries for such tasks but the municipal budgets had no allowances for them. The city councils (the one hundred *decuriones*) simply designated men to undertake at their own expense such commissions as supervising the city police, the water bureau, the record office, the

[11] See Gradenwitz, *Index zum Theodosianus*, s. v. *collatio* and *angaria*. The practical effects are well seen in Keil-Premerstein, *Denk. Akad. Wien.* 1914, Inscr. 9, 28, 55; *Pap. Soc. It.* 446, 683; Ditt. *Or. Gr. Ins.* 519; 527; 609; 665; Cass. Dio. 78, 3; Gromatici (Lach), p. 165.

[12] On *Munera* see *Digest* 50, 4-10 especially for the practices of the 2nd and 3rd centuries, and Gradenwitz *op. cit.* s. v. *munus;* Oertel, *Die Liturgie*, on Egypt; Liebenam, *Städteverwaltung*.

road building, the heating of the baths, and even required them to defray the expenses of the necessary repairs within the city. The emperors recognized the procedure and legalized it. Furthermore, since upon the removal of the contract tax system, the cities had willingly assumed responsibility for the local quota of imperial taxes, the city councils now designated commissions to allocate and collect these taxes. Even in the second century it had happened at times, if the land was exhausted or the city dwindling, that the taxes fell short. In such cases the decuriones, or the board of ten (decaproti) appointed for the task, failed to secure the fixed amount. The emperor, however, pressed for payment, and when such instances became numerous during the third century he decreed that the decuriones were responsible for the full amount. They frequently had to make up the sum due out of their own purses. The same situation arose with reference to the other *munera* and especially with reference to dues imposed for the housing and feeding of officers and soldiers. The final burden imposed upon the decuriones was the decree compelling them to take up abandoned farms and cultivate them so that their revenues might be paid. As we have said, the decuriones could, at first, designate suitable men to undertake the munera, but since these could plead for a substitute the government finally cut off delay by laying the responsibility directly upon the decuriones, or rather the *curiales,* from whom the decuriones were chosen. The municipal honors came to be so burdensome that, as the famous fiftieth book of the Digest shows, every device had to be invented to compel men of some substance to accept office. The position of magistrates became a heritable burden, and in some places where victims could not be found the office was imposed upon criminals, Jews and Christians.

This extension of compulsory service affected not only the well-to-do but in time the labor gilds[12] and merchants' associations also, at first at Rome, and later throughout the Empire. Shipowners were early offered immunities in return for the compulsory but paid service of bringing the state grain to Rome from the provinces and of providing military transports. Then when Septimius undertook to grant free oil at Rome, and Aurelian added wine distributions and substituted bread for grain in the dole, the oil and wine merchants and the bakers of the city were placed under government control. Severus Alexander organized all the gilds of the city under governmental supervision in order to have them at public call when necessary. In the municipalities this process was not so rapid as at Rome, but even there the fabri, dendrophori, and centonarii (smiths and carpenters, lumbermen, and makers of felt and blankets) were organized as local fire brigades and released from the obligation of providing other munera in return for this service. The steps in

[13] The earlier jurists are chiefly concerned with the suppression of illegal gilds (Digest, Bk. 47, 22) but Theodosian's code gives a broad picture of labor in bondage; see Gradenwitz, s. v. *collegium;* Kornemann, art. *Collegium* in Pauly-Wissowa.

the further development of compulsory service are lost to us, but we may infer from the legislation of the fourth century that when the state increased the burdens of the gilds which had been organized for the civil service, the members attempted to change their occupations, with the result that the state made membership compulsory and finally hereditary. By the middle of the fourth century laborers throughout the Empire were bound to their occupations in a caste system from which there was hardly any way of escape and in which every member was at the command of the government for specified service.

Tenants (*coloni*) somehow became bound to the soil during the same period. Libraries have been written on the origin of serfdom in the Roman Empire, but the details of the process still elude us. As yet we are only sure of the fact that in the responses of Ulpian and Papinian the *colonus* is a free tenant, whereas a decree of Constantine of the year 332 A.D.[14] assumes

[14] Codex Theod. V. 17, 1. The principle theories regarding the origin of the Roman colonate are the following: Zumpt, *Rhein. Mus.* 1845, and Savigny, *Vers. Schr.* II, referred it to the settlement of barbarian captives in bondage; Wallon, *Hist. de l'Escl.* 1847, believed that tenants were bound to the soil for fiscal reasons as laborers to gilds and curiales to the curia; Rodbertus, *Jahrb. Nationalök.* 1864, thought that bound coloni were ex-slaves given tenancies but kept in subjection; Heisterbergk, *Entst. d. Colonats*, 1876, suggested that native tenants in the provinces were adscribed to the soil to ensure the grain supply; Fustel de Coulanges, *Le Colonat romain*, 1884 (after the Burunitan inscr. was found) proposed that perpetual tenants of the African type who had no written contracts sank to the status of serfs by natural economic processes; Pelham, *The Imp. Domains* 1890,

that he is bound to the soil. The momentous change had certainly taken place before 332, for that decree simply comments on the duty of citizens to restore fugitive *coloni* to their masters, and on the right of masters to bind and employ as slaves such *coloni* as attempted to escape. Serfdom of various kinds had been known here and there within the Empire. Varro speaks of the practice in Egypt, Asia and Illyricum, but implies that Roman custom did not recognize the status. Since the emperors were constantly in need of free soldiers in the provinces it is not likely that the practice was encouraged, but of this we cannot be sure. We have seen that the Romans found a mild form of serfdom in vogue in Asia, but we have not as yet found definite evidence proving that it continued long beyond Strabo's day, and there is some evidence for assuming that the emperors were wont to count the tenants of

---

supposed that paternalistic emperors to protect tenants permitted heritable tenancies and that in later times of stress imperial agents made these customary leases compulsory; Seeck, *art. colonatus* in Pauly-Wissowa, points to several factors: the economic weakness of coloni in Italy, the native non-citizen coloni of the provinces, and the barbarian captives settled on land; Rostovtzeff, Klio, 1901, referred to Asiatic models; later in *Stud. Röm. Kol.* 1911, he preferred to emphasize Ptolemaic precedents, and recently, *Jour. Land and Publ. Utilities*, 1926, he has concluded that the Roman colonate was "a legitimate child of the social revolution of the third century."

Whatever may have been the precise occasion for the decree which first legalized adscription to the soil it must be admitted that most of the hypotheses mentioned above call attention to factors which probably contributed to the declension of the colonate and created customs which made the decree acceptable.

temple-states as free. The fixed requirement of dike-labor in Egypt and the *operae* of tenants upon domain lands in Africa, which have so frequently been referred to as entering-wedges for the institution of serfdom, have nothing in common with adscription to the soil, and may be dismissed from consideration.

The change of status in the case of the *coloni* was revolutionary and assumes firstly, a very humble station on the part of these tenants, which in turn presupposes a long devolution from early imperial conditions, and secondly, a governmental crisis that induced some emperor to resort to a drastic measure. To comprehend the submission of the *coloni* to serfdom it is well to remember that many of them were sons and grandsons of slaves who had been freed and given tenancies because of the increasing scarcity of free labor, that in many places barbarian captives were being used as semi-free tenants, that the emperors sometimes assigned their humbler freedmen to allotments on the imperial estates, that many of the *saltus* were tenanted by lowly provincials who probably had never reached the status of citizens, that on the extensive imperial estates the *coloni* could seldom reach the ear of the owner, being forced to submit to the imperious commands of master-farmers who acted in collusion with the procurators, and lastly, that short-term contracts had become increasingly rare, having been supplanted, especially upon the imperial estates, by life-long tenancies based simply upon custom and unprotected by written mutual agreements. Under such conditions the tenants naturally fell more and more into dependence upon the whims of the owners and their agents.

But a slow decline in the social status cannot account for the loss of freedom. This must, after all, have rested upon some imperial decree which has been lost to us, and the occasion for such a decree must have been easy to find at the end of the third century. The constant cry during the anarchy of 235-285 was for taxes and food supplies, and the surest source of both was the land. In Aurelian's day, when tenants were leaving their holdings because of heavy taxes or poor yields, the decuriones of each city were made responsible for the legal quota of taxes, and land-owners were compelled to take up tracts that had been deserted. Their answer to such decrees must have been that they could do so only if they were given power to hold their tenants. The emperor must have had the same difficulty in holding his own tenants on the vast state domains when those lands were deteriorating under long tenant culture and prices were being imperilled by piracy that cut off good markets. It is not an improbable conjecture that the compulsion originated on the emperor's own estates. At any rate, when Diocletian found the currency system so clogged that he had to accept taxes in produce we may well believe that his large body of agents scrutinized the returns of all lands with special care and reported tenants who left their plots. As we have noticed, the *coloni* were bondsmen before 332. The decrees that made them so were probably occasioned by the economic crises and the fiscal straits of the late years of anarchy or during the reign of Diocletian, and serfdom, as was long ago observed, is part and parcel of the legislation which forced the *decuriones* to life-service in the burdens of the curia and the craftsmen to bound service within their gilds. In the case of the colonus serfdom developed to a logical conclusion more speedily than in that of the others because he was the most important cog in the machine that produced taxes and food supplies.

The institution of serfdom may possibly have helped to stabilize agriculture for a while, since the *coloni* now knew that an attempt to escape would probably entail slavery. But as Westermann[15] has well pointed out, the Empire was now at the mercy of unwilling and inefficient *coloni* who could hardly take any interest in the one most important task of producing food. The evils of the system grew since the number of potential landed proprietors was now limited by the disqualification of all tenants, and as some of these proprietors went into bankruptcy because of high taxes and unwilling labor, others who knew how to escape taxation through bribes or personal influence purchased lands on forced sale, acquired more by "patronage" and entered the train of the emperor's nobility.[16] The direct result of the colonate was therefore a rapid extension of latifundia.

[15] Im *Am. Hist. Rev.*, 1915, p. 724.

[16] Zulueta, *De patrociniis vicorum*, Oxford.

Diocletian completely reorganized[17] the military, financial, and administrative systems, creating a machinery of government which, as long as he lived, was as efficient as it was vast and oppressive. The basis of it was the army which was increased so as to provide a mobile striking force as well as a frontier guard. The administrative districts were narrowed down and packed with paid officials who were to spy, report and especially to see that the taxes were gathered. The taxes, increased once more to keep abreast of the increased cost of government, were now for the first time levied on a uniform plan throughout the Empire, not, however, at a fixed rate, as before, but at a rate annually announced (the indictio) and theoretically reckoned on the needs of the year. In view of the economic debacle which had brought back "natural economy" the fact was recognized that taxes in kind would be easier to pay and collect than those in money. Hence a new plan of assessing had to be devised and it was put into operation at heavy expense. All lands were reclassified according to yield. The *jugum* was made the unit and this was reckoned as twenty jugera of normal arable land, or forty jugera of the second class, or sixty of the third. Vineyards and olive yards, which were worth more than grainland, were assessed according to the number of plants (225 olive trees or 450 vines); pasture land was taxed according to the

[17] Bury, *Hist. of Later Roman Emp.*, ch. II; Vinogradoff, in *Cambridge Med. Hist.* I, p. 543. The *jugum* has been discussed again by Lot, in *Rev. Hist. Droit*, 1925, but without conclusive results.

number of cattle grazing upon it, and each laborer on the farm was also taxed against the landowner at the value of a *jugum*. Since the cities brought in the taxes the emperor did not have to increase his staff for the purposes of collection, but he was compelled to build granaries everywhere and appoint officials to supervise the distribution of the grain; and having this produce, he had it doled out to the soldiers and civil servants in lieu of salary-money. This again entailed great expense. The whole system evidences the complete disorganization of Rome's business. The land-tax was, of course, the mainstay of the government, but the occupation tax on trades and crafts was no less meticulously exacted; the "crown-gold" was now regularly demanded every five years from the decuriones, while state senators had to submit to a special levy called the *aurum oblaticium*.

Diocletian's attempt at reforming the currency led to speculation and price fluctuations, since experience had taught men that such reforms usually did not last long. Therefore, in 301 the emperor drew up a list of maximum prices,[18] copies of which were to be posted especially in his own province in the East where Roman coins were now for the first time used to displace local

[18] Blümner, *Der Maximaltarif der Diocletian;* also *Edict. Diocl.* in Pauly-Wissowa V. 1948; Abbott, *The Common People of Anc. Rome*, p. 145. The lists have been found only in Greece, Egypt and the East. It has been suggested that the Caesars of the west may have had them posted in perishable material. There is, however, no proof that they were posted throughout the Empire.

issues. Since his chief purpose was to ensure low prices—of labor as well as of goods—we may suspect that the current "denarius" was somewhat overrated in terms of gold (a pound of gold was valued at 50,000 "denarii"). However, the list, with this evaluation, affords at least an opportunity to compare prices of various articles and in that respect it has value as an historical document. Using gold as a standard we arrive at the following list of prices for some of the standard articles:

Wheat	bushel	75	cents
Rye	"	45	"
Beans	"	45	"
Lentils	"	75	"
Italian wine	quart	22½	"
Olive oil	"	18–30	"
Honey	"	15–30	"
Pork	pound	7.3	"
Ham	"	12	"
Beef	"	5	"
Lamb	"	7.3	"
Butter	"	10	"
Cheese	"	7.3	"
Eggs	dozen	5	"
Peasants' shoes	pair	52	"
Soldiers' shoes	"	33	"
Women's shoes	"	26	"
"Patrician" shoes	"	65	"
Wool	pound	22	"
Laodicean wool	"	65	"
Purple wool	"	$217.40	
Best linen thread	"	3.13	
Manual labor, per day		11	cents + food
Bricklayers, masons, carpenters, smiths, bakers, ship builders		22	" " "

Marble cutters, mosaic workers_____	26	cents + food
Painters_____	32	" "
Decorative painters_____	65	" "
Teachers, per pupil, per month_____	22	" "
Teachers in arithmetic_____	33	" "
Teachers in Greek or geometry_____	87	" "

Coppersmiths, scribes, tailors, etc., are paid by the piece.

It would, of course, be instructive to compare these prices with those obtaining earlier, but unfortunately we have no data for a comprehensive list outside of Egypt. We know, however, that the average price of wheat reckoned in gold was about the same in Cicero's day as in Diocletian's, and since wheat was the most important item in the poor man's budget and in the general market, it would seem that prices had not changed much. Certainly the Diocletian price list does not support a hypothesis that the world was suffering from a scarcity of wheat, that is, from a disastrous deterioration of the soil. Commerce on the seas was now safe and could be depended upon to supply grain in places suffering from scarcity. We must also add that when it was possible for this emperor to reinstate the Neronian silver denarius, and to issue enough gold aurei to serve as a basis for his coinage at practically the old ratios, we are not justified in believing that the lack of precious metals was a serious factor in Rome's decline.

It is more difficult to compare wages with previous ones, for Diocletian's list includes food in the daily wage. This inclusion, however, is itself significant.

If, for instance, large building operations were being undertaken at this time we should expect a money wage for masons and carpenters. Only when smiths and masons were confined to such petty work as landlords might need in repairing old houses would it seem reasonable that this system would become prevalent. In point of fact there was but little new construction except on public work done by soldiers or public slaves. So few buildings were indeed raised during the period of anarchy that all the decorative arts fell into desuetude and the craftsmanship on the buildings of the period reveals astonishing crudity and puerility. The inclusion of food in the wage is therefore only another indication of how industry had disintegrated. The wage itself had, however, remained about stationary, since eleven cents and food would be about the equivalent of the old time wage of a denarius per day. This may seem surprising since one expects to find wages falling with the decline in enterprise. However, the decline in the demand for labor had been balanced by. the decided decrease in the number of slaves and the increased adscription of labor to gilds and farms.

This is not the place to describe the final debacle that resulted from Rome's inability to repel the advancing barbarians. We may indicate briefly, however, the situation in various parts of the Empire just before the end. Egypt, which suffered less from invasions than any other province, was not a serious source of concern, though its large and futile population was of little use in the defense of the Empire. The Nile continued its age-long duty of fertilizing a large part of the valley so that grain was available for the new capital of Constantinople at least. And the government was still able to protect the fleet which carried that grain. Furthermore, Probus had set the army at work to clear and repair the canals once more so that production, which had diminished through the third century, was again fairly good during the fourth. The excavations of the University of Michigan at Karanis[19] have demonstrated that the effects of Probus' work were immediate and that the Fayum, at least, continued to be productive for two centuries after that. Yet conditions in general were not good. It is probable that Diocletian's edict, which compelled Egypt to accept Roman money and the imperial scale of prices and wages, came as a shock and upset the accepted economic customs adapted to this peculiar region. At any rate it is remarkable how many private and local coinages sprang up in the later period in Egypt, devised apparently in order to readjust business to local conditions.[20] The failure of efficient government on the part of the state, and the gruesome burden of taxes imposed upon a servile people caused discontent and destructive divisions. Men of some capacity acquired vast estates here and there, built up local fiefs, secured control of the populace and defied the tax gatherers and recruiting officers. Serious religious differences

[19] See Boak, in *The Geogr. Review*, 1926, 353.

[20] Milne, *History of Egypt*, ch. XI and *Numis. Chron.* 1926, 43 ff; Bell, in *Jour, Egypt. Arch.* 1924, 207.

also arose because of the intensity with which the people gave support to the various Christian sects and monastic organizations. Egypt, therefore, despite her enduring resources, was breaking up into futile segments, ready to fall an easy prey to the invading Arabs.

The cities of Asia and Syria suffered severely during the Persian wars, not only from the raiding enemy but also from the lawlessness of the Roman troops constantly marching through them. Yet the majority of these Asiatics had never adapted themselves to a life that depended upon security. Large cities had not grown up except along the coast where Greeks were numerous, and even in these cities the remains show that expansion stopped with the second century. The simple folk of the villages who were content to live from hand to mouth made up the majority of the population and their properties were hardly worth the effort of raiding. Here a very primitive economy was the rule as it always had been. The Syrians of the coast towns were enough interested in trade—in the fifth century they still carried on commerce with Gaul—and consequently in safe seas to favor an efficient government. Those of the interior realized the importance of protecting the border. Both did their share in keeping the eastern Empire semi-effective. There is apparent, also, a certain natural force in the people. They had kept only what they needed of Hellenism, and the wholly extraneous Roman culture they had simply sloughed off. Christianity they had accepted as kindred to their own religions, and had infused it with some of their ancestral beliefs. It had united them as nothing had before; their bishops and their priests became a powerful influence throughout the Asiatic churches, and even far to the west. Asia still had much native vigor, but it had become apparent that her capacities were not adapted to a western program under Rome's supremacy.

Africa was also far from exhausted. Her surplus of grain was, in fact, a necessity for the city of Rome to the last. Her misfortunes are almost wholly due to the mistakes of the Roman government. Failure to keep one legion there—which would have sufficed in a province so well protected by nature—made it necessary to arm and trust barbaric tribes in Numidia and Mauritania before they were adequately Romanized. They grew confident of their strength and became a danger instead of an aid on the far distant border of the Empire. Oppressive taxation and the spread of serfdom among the natives, who were held down to heavy labor on vast estates, did not conduce to love of Rome. During the third century there was apparent a revulsion against Roman customs among the natives, and though Christianity appealed strongly to them the natives gradually accepted the heterodox Donatism rather than the orthodox cult, largely because the latter had secured the support of Rome, their oppressor. The crusades which the Donatist fanatics undertook in the name of their faith were at times merely plundering expeditions against rich villas and

Romanized cities. To many of these tribes the Vandal invasion seemed a deliverance. Belisarius had the wisdom to see that the native population must be won over by friendly deeds, but the Byzantine emperors often forgot this doctrine. The magnificent ruins of Byzantine times that are so numerous in North Africa do not bear witness to any renewed prosperity there but rather to Rome's failure to win the good will of the natives, for they are to a large extent the remains of forts. When the Arabs came, parts of Africa were still very productive; but the natives did little to protect their country and its wealth. Most of them accepted the conquerors as friends, quit their hated tenancies and drifted back to nomadry.

From Gaul[21] we get a charming picture of the aristocratic villa life of the fourth and fifth centuries in the pages of Ausonius and Sidonius. We find great Celtic nobleman, owners of splendid villas, sometimes of several, discussing their libraries, writing poems and long epistles to their friends, inspecting their estates, hunting, playing tennis, entertaining their spiritual advisers, discussing their schools of which they are very proud, and riding to Ravenna on affairs of state. Numerous villas that have been excavated demonstrate that these pages are not imaginary. Gallic agriculture was still relatively new, and the land was far from exhausted. To be sure these nobles with their vast estates throve on the servile system. Their laborers

[21] See Dill, *Roman Society in the Last Century;* Ausonius, *Ordo Urbium* and *Mosella.*

whom they seldom mention were doubtless bondsmen and exceedingly poor, but they were at least of the same race as the lords, and apparently more contented than the natives of Africa working for wealthy Romans whom they seldom saw. Gaul remained on the whole a land of villas, but there were thriving cities also. In Ausonius' day Treves had grown to be the first city in Gaul (the sixth in size in the Empire) because it "fed, clothed, and armed" a large part of the Rhine forces. The numerous villas that Ausonius mentions on the banks of the Moselle may well have been built from the profits of that industry. Arles, Toulouse and Narbonne come respectively tenth, eighteenth, and nineteenth in his list of imperial cities and they seem to have profited from the trade which the landlords fostered. Even far-distant Bordeaux, which comes twentieth in the list, is praised for its wide boulevards, marble palaces and excellent schools. Gaul, in fact, was rich in resources. Properly organized it might well have saved itself from the invasions as Postumus had demonstrated and brought on a speedy renaissance of culture. But the province was of course not allowed to act for itself; it had to await the commands and obey the orders of the Roman government. Moreover, a part of its dependable manhood of the middle classes had been reduced to serfdom and made unfit for army service, and its wealth was being used to pay for the defense of the weaker parts of the Empire.

As we review the economic conditions in the prov-

inces before the fall of the Roman government, therefore, we do not find that either the population or the
natural resources of the Empire were exhausted, but
we do find a lack of intelligence and spirit in the
effective employment of those resources that inevitably
resulted in confusion, disharmony and illwill. The
disease apparent in the spiritual life as early as the era
of Marcus Aurelius had spread everywhere. Rome's
unifying and civilizing power had failed even then and
the provinces, no longer feeling the magnetic force
that earlier had drawn them toward the center, drifted
off listlessly, intent only upon their own concerns. The
failure of the old native vigor in Italy gave an opportunity to various rude officers in the army to seize the
supreme power. We cannot be certain that after Commodus any Roman of the old stock reached the throne.
For over a century the emperors usually came from
the Balkan region with occasionally a Gaul, an African,
or an Arab; from the time of Valentinian the emperors
are usually Germans. Seldom did one of them comprehend even the elementary social and economic needs of
the Empire and none was remotely aware of the traditions that had made Rome powerful. Their simple
task was to hold the Empire together by force so as to
keep intact the taxing machinery which enabled them
to pay for that force. When this system wasted the
resources, weakened the machinery of production and
distribution, and, by the institution of serfdom, incapacitated the citizenry of the Empire for army service,
the dull emperors hired German mercenaries to protect
the frontier until those mercenaries took over as their
own the Empire which they were paid to guard.

INDEX